Comparative, European and International Criminal Justice

Volume 2

D1807360

Editor-in-Chief
Roberto E. Kostoris, University of Padua, Padua, Italy

Series Editors
Mirjan Damaška, Yale University, New Haven, USA
Juan Luis Gómez Colomer, Jaume I University, Castellón de la Plana, Spain
Giulio Illuminati, University of Bologna, Bologna, Italy
John Jackson, University of Nottingham, Nottingham, UK
Bruce Smith, University of Denver, Denver, USA
Mark A. Zöller, University of Trier, Trier, Germany

Advisory Editors
Lorena Bachmaier Winter, Complutense University of Madrid, Madrid, Spain
Marta Bargis, University of Eastern Piedmont Amedeo Avogadro, Vercelli, Italy
Silvia Barona Vilar, University of Valencia, Valencia, Spain
Mireille Delmas-Marty, Collège de France, Paris, France
Emilio Dolcini, University of Milan, Milan, Italy
Piotr Hofmański, International Criminal Court, The Hague, The Netherlands
Maria Kaiafa-Gbandi, Aristotle University of Thessaloniki, Thessaloniki, Greece
André Klip, Maastricht University, Maastricht, The Netherlands
Raimo Lahti, University of Helsinki, Helsinki, Finland
Renzo Orlandi, University of Bologna, Bologna, Italy
Francesco Palazzo, University of Florence, Florence, Italy
Viorel Paşca, West University of Timişoara, Timişoara, Romania
Paulo Pinto de Albuquerque, European Court of Human Rights, Strasbourg, France
Ulrich Sieber, Max Planck Institute for Foreign and International Criminal Law,
Freiburg, Germany
John A. E. Vervaele, Utrecht University, Utrecht, The Netherlands
Anne Weyembergh, Université Libre de Bruxelles, Brussels, Belgium
James Q. Whitman, Yale University, New Haven, USA
Raúl Zaffaroni, Inter-American Court of Human Rights, San José, Costa Rica

Associate Editors
Michele Caianiello, University of Bologna, Bologna, Italy
Marcello Daniele, University of Padua, Padua, Italy
Michele Papa, University of Florence, Florence, Italy
Pier Paolo Paulesu, University of Padua, Padua, Italy

This book series focuses on criminal justice from multiple perspectives. In particular, it addresses three main areas:

– Comparative issues, including historical ones, in order to highlight the common roots of criminal justice in common and civil law systems, both past and present.
– European issues, in order to raise awareness of the link between national and transnational levels, in the perspective of the European Union law and the European Convention on Human Rights law, in the area of criminal justice, namely focusing on the protection of fundamental rights and on judicial and police cooperation.
– International issues, namely those related to the functioning of the International Criminal Court and of the other international criminal tribunals, but also in regard to international human rights courts.

The book series addresses the phenomenon of criminal justice with a particular, but not exclusive, focus on procedural aspects, from a multidisciplinary perspective – an essential approach in today's globalized world.

It provides academic readers with authoritative and timely debates on the emerging issues of criminal justice, and also offers judges and lawyers useful indications and suggestions.

More information about this series at http://www.springer.com/series/16095

Merita Kettunen

Legitimizing European Criminal Law

Justification and Restrictions

 G. Giappichelli Editore

Merita Kettunen
Helsinki, Finland

ISSN 2524-4558   ISSN 2524-4566   (electronic)
Comparative, European and International Criminal Justice
ISBN 978-3-030-16176-7 ·   ISBN 978-3-030-16174-3   (eBook)
https://doi.org/10.1007/978-3-030-16174-3

This Springer imprint is published by the registered company Springer Nature Switzerland AG.
The registered company address is: Gewerbestrasse 11, 6330 Cham, Switzerland

Preface

European criminal law consists of EU criminal law and influences stemming from the ECHR regime. The legitimacy of this European criminal law has not really been theoretically examined by criminal law researchers. Many of the previous studies on European criminal law start from the dynamic rationale of general EU law rather than from the thinking which reflects the discipline of criminal law. This work aims to fill this space. The work provides a criminal law-oriented normative view on how the use of European criminal law, and in particular the use of EU criminal law, could be legitimized from the perspective of criminal law doctrine. In other words, the work aims to show how, under which criteria, the use of criminal law as it stands, and the enactment of criminal legislation in particular, can be seen as legitimate. Thus, the aim of this work is not to argue for the legitimacy of criminal law in general. This research suggests that European criminal legislation ought to respect and follow certain European criminalization principles. The research adopts a constitutional approach since the limits for the use of European criminal law, the European criminalization principles, are derived from European constitutional norms. Constitutional elements are also increasingly important to criminal law, especially in its European transnational context.

The main research question is how the use of European criminal law can be justified. The research starts by illustrating the differences of traditional and European criminal law. It then reflects on differences between general EU law and EU criminal law to illustrate the special character of European criminal law. The research claims that even though the European states have lessened their autonomy by engaging in cooperation in the field of criminal law, this cooperation actually increases their sovereignty because it enables the Member States to react better to cross-border crime which affects their interests.

The use of European criminal law needs to respect the normative paradigm which it was designed to follow. In the EU context, this normative paradigm is expressed in the safeguard mechanisms included in the substantive criminal competence provision enshrined in the Treaty on the Functioning of the European Union (Article 83 TFEU) and in the European principles of criminalization that can be derived from this Article. The European Convention on Human Rights regime also provides a value basis for criminal law enacted at both EU and national levels. This research focuses on the use of substantive criminal law as it stands at the level of criminalization (enactment of criminal legislation). It is also possible to draw some general conclusions on the acceptability of European criminal law.

The legal basis for the legislative act and its *ratio legis* affect the teleological interpretation of the Union's substantive criminal legislation. For this reason, the choice of legal basis is not merely a technical legal issue. The question of legal basis is in fact a normative issue and an issue of criminal policy. The choice of legal basis determines the type of instruments that can be used to enact EU criminal legislation, namely whether the legislation is given in the form of a regulation or a directive. This determines how EU criminal law affects national law and its application. The legal basis affects how much flexibility there is for the Member States in the implementation of that instrument into the national criminal justice system.

The research shows that the European criminalization principles ought to guide the choice of legal basis when legislative proposals include criminal law content. Recent changes in how the Court of Justice of the European Union interprets the Treaties support this argument. The Court has changed its doctrine to allow the *travaux préparatoires* to the EU Treaties as evidence. In these cases, the *travaux* are used in order to establish the *ratio legis* of the Treaty provisions. The Court refers to the *travaux* only when textual interpretation is not sufficient and when the *travaux* can add value to the interpretation by establishing the *ratio legis*. The Court has only made static references to the *travaux*, meaning that the Court has relied on them only when the reference does not entail constitution-building through dynamic Treaty interpretation.

Criminal law measures are highly intrusive for those individuals on whom they are imposed. In this individual rights-sensitive sense, criminal law is a highly political field of law, which needs to be enacted in a democratic process. Since criminal law is also a highly sovereignty-sensitive area of law, criminal legislative mechanisms at the transnational level should be fundamental rights sensitive and respect the core contents of national criminal justice systems and thus also state sovereignty. The principle of legality demands that criminal legislation is interpreted strictly. The principle of *ultima ratio* requires that criminal legislation is used sparsely. From this criminal law perspective, the *travaux préparatoires* of the Treaties ought not to be utilized to support dynamic interpretations of the Union's substantive criminal law competence if this would increase the scope of the Union's substantive criminal law competence or change its nature. The *travaux préparatoires* of the Union's substantive criminal law competence in addition to the Court's new interpretation method support this kind of restrictive interpretation.

The writing process of this book has been multilayered. This book is based on my doctoral dissertation (titled 'Legitimizing the use of transnational criminal law—The European framework') that I defended in 2015 in the Faculty of Law, University of Helsinki. I want to thank professor Neil Walker and professor Thomas Elholm for their comments on the doctoral thesis during its pre-examination. I would also like to thank my thesis supervisor Sakari Melander, professor Kimmo Nuotio and professor Dan Frände for their support and comments; professor emeritus Raimo Lahti for his continuing encouragement; and my colleagues at the University of Helsinki for their support. Most of all I want to remember and thank my family and friends for their support during this process.

Helsinki, Finland   Merita Kettunen

Contents

1 Introduction 1
  1.1 Objective and Structure of the Book 1
  1.2 Preview of the Book 5
  1.3 Theoretical Framework and Methodology 8
    1.3.1 Constitutional Pluralism 8
    1.3.2 A Normative Study 14
    1.3.3 Rules of Interpretation 16
  References 42

2 The Nature of Traditional Criminal Law 47
  2.1 Criminal Law as an Expression of State Power and
    Sovereignty 47
  2.2 Justifying the Use of Criminal Law as an Institution:
    The General Justifying Aim 53
    2.2.1 Looking Ahead 53
    2.2.2 More than Words 59
  2.3 Justifying the Use of Punishment in Individual Cases 62
  References 64

3 Features of European Criminal Law 67
  3.1 Dimensions of European Criminal Law 67
  3.2 History of European Criminal Law 69
  3.3 Basic Values of European Criminal Law 75
    3.3.1 Protection of Human Dignity as a Precondition
      for European Criminal Law 75
    3.3.2 Pluralistic Democracy as a Precondition for European
      Criminal Law 99
    3.3.3 ECHR Regime and Criminal Policy 104
  3.4 Difference Between National Criminal Law and European
    Criminal Law 111
  3.5 Difference Between General EU Law and EU Criminal Law 117

        3.5.1   Vertical Direct Effect   117
        3.5.2   Primacy of EU Law   119
        3.5.3   Indirect Effect/Conforming Interpretation   119
    3.6   Criminal Law Decision-Making in the EU   121
    3.7   Legal Basis Determines the Union's Competence to Enact
          Substantive Criminal Legislation   127
        3.7.1   Rules on the Choice of Legal Basis   129
        3.7.2   Implicit Substantive Criminal Law Competence
                Pre-Lisbon and Its Meaning Today   131
        3.7.3   *Travaux Préparatoires* Advocate That Article 83 TFEU
                Was Intended to Exhaust Union's Substantive Criminal
                Law Competence   135
        3.7.4   Nature of the Substantive Criminal Law Competence
                of Article 83 TFEU   139
    References   146

**4   Theoretical Ideals for European Constitutional Structures
    and Criminal Legislation**   151
    4.1   Heterarchical Constitutional Structures of the ECHR Regime   151
        4.1.1   Heterarchical Constitutional Structures Pertaining Between
                National Legal Orders and the ECHR Regime   151
        4.1.2   Heterarchical Constitutional Structures Pertaining Between
                the ECHR Regime and the EU Legal Order   155
    4.2   Heterarchical Constitutional Structures of the EU Law   159
        4.2.1   Primacy of EU Law, Member States as the Masters of the
                Treaties, Principle of Sincere Cooperation   159
        4.2.2   Criminal Law Specific Heterarchical Constitutional
                Structures   165
    4.3   Heterarchical Constitutional Pluralism in the European
          Legal Space   167
    4.4   European Criminalization Principles   168
        4.4.1   Subsidiarity and Proportionality: The Transnational
                Dimension of *Ultima Ratio* Principle   169
        4.4.2   Respect for Fundamental Aspects of National Criminal
                Justice Systems   173
        4.4.3   The Principle of Legality: Transnational Dimension   176
        4.4.4   Respect of Fundamental Rights: Transnational Dimension . . .   182
        4.4.5   Protected Interests: Transnational Dimension   188
        4.4.6   European Criminalization Principles Can Be Derived from
                Article 83 TFEU   190
    References   194

5 Ideals Shaken by Realities 197
   5.1 Opinion 2/13 on the Union's Accession to the ECHR........... 197
        5.1.1 Inter-Party Cases 198
        5.1.2 Conflict of Jurisdictional Competence................. 200
        5.1.3 Conclusions 203
   5.2 Choice of Legal Basis-Doctrine Versus European Criminalization
       Principles: Normative Problems Arising 205
        5.2.1 Possible Implicit Legal Bases for Substantive Criminal
               Law Competence 205
        5.2.2 Possibility of Directly Applicable EU Criminal
               Legislation 229
        5.2.3 Full Harmonisation of Penalty Scales 237
        5.2.4 Nature of Criminal Law as the Reflector of Sovereignty
               Forgotten? 240
   References.. 242

**6 Conclusions: European Criminal Law—Justification
and Restrictions.**... 245

Sources 253

Abbreviations

CDDH	Steering Committee for Human Rights
Charter	Charter of Fundamental Rights of the European Union
CJEU	Court of Justice of the European Union
CLS	Council's Legal Service
EA	EURATOM Treaty
EAW	European Arrest Warrant
EC	European Community
ECHR	Convention for the Protection of Human Rights and Fundamental Freedoms
ECtHR	European Court of Human Rights
EEC	European Economic Community
EP	European Parliament
EPPO	European Public Prosecutor's Office
ESCB	European System of Central Banks
ESM	European Stability Mechanism
EU	European Union
EURATOM	European Atomic Energy Community
FD	Framework Decision
GCC	The German Constitutional Court
ICCPR	International Covenant on Civil and Political Rights
ICTY	International Criminal Tribunal for the former Yugoslavia
OLAF	European Anti-Fraud Office
PIF Convention	Convention on the protection of the European Communities' financial interests
TCE	Treaty establishing a Constitution for Europe
TEU	Treaty on European Union
TFEU	Treaty on the Functioning of the European Union
TRNC	Turkish Republic of Northern Cyprus
UK	The United Kingdom of Great Britain and Northern Ireland
VCLT	Vienna Convention on the Law of the Treaties

Chapter 1
Introduction

1.1 Objective and Structure of the Book

The scope and legitimacy of European criminal law[1] is, and has been, a topical issue in the constitutional development of the European Union (later, EU or the Union) and in academic discourse concerning EU criminal law.[2] This work examines *how the use of European criminal law can be justified.* In other words, the work aims to show how, under which criteria and principles, the enactment of European criminal legislation can be seen as legitimate.[3] The application of these European criminalization principles legitimates the use of criminal law in the European transnational context. The purpose of this research is not so much to argue for some changes to the law, but instead to justify the law as it stands. This is achieved by identifying the appropriate legal basis for the approximation of criminal law. This legal basis contains European criminalization principles that ought to be applied when new EU criminal legislation is enacted. This study shows how and why criminal law is special by its nature,[4] and why it should not be equated with other fields of EU law.

The idea of separating between autonomy (decision-making power) and sovereignty (the impact a state has outside its borders and *vis-à-vis* other states in the sense of external sovereignty, and the power and responsibilities the state has

---

[1] European criminal law consists of EU criminal law and of influences stemming from the ECHR regime. More on the concept, see Chap. 3.1.

[2] See, for example, Asp (2012); Herlin-Karnell (2012); Klip (2016); Melander (2011); Nuotio (2011); Melander (2013); Miettinen (2013b), p. 194; Huomo-Kettunen (2014a), p. 301; Huomo-Kettunen (2014b), p. 23; Öberg (2014); Miettinen (2015); Galli and Weyembergh (2013).

[3] Thus, the aim of this work is not to argue for the legitimacy of criminal law in general.

[4] For an opposing view, Miettinen (2015), p. 508. Miettinen does not see a reason why criminal law should be regarded any differently from other fields of EU law by stating that 'criminal law is not, from the perspective of EU institutional practice, special.'

© Springer International Publishing Switzerland and G. Giappichelli Editore 2020
M. Kettunen, *Legitimizing European Criminal Law*, Comparative, European and International Criminal Justice 2, https://doi.org/10.1007/978-3-030-16174-3_1

towards individuals in the sense of internal sovereignty) has influenced my thinking process. The conferral of powers from the EU Member States is seen as a limitation of autonomy within certain limits determined in the EU Treaties, and not as a limitation of sovereignty. The decrease of autonomy is a result of sovereign states limiting their decision-making options in order to gain greater sovereignty. In this sense, a high value is given to the constitutional norms that enshrine this limitation of autonomy and to their object and purpose. The *travaux préparatoires* of the EU Treaties are also given great value since they can clarify the purpose and intent behind those constitutional provisions. Today, the *travaux* of the EU Treaties clearly are acknowledged as acceptable source of the EU law and they can be used to interpret the EU primary law as will be shown in Sect. 1.3.3.3.2.

The idea of separating between autonomy and sovereignty relates to the shifts of competences from European states to the EU and the ECHR regime. The sovereign states choose to participate in these types of cooperation under terms determined in the treaties. Their participation takes place under a certain *ratio*, or logic and purpose. This work emphasises the *ratio* behind these forms of cooperation, and, in the EU context, utilises the *travaux préparatoires* of the EU Treaties to show the conditions and *ratio* behind the Union's competence to approximate substantive criminal law. The purpose and *ratio* of the substantive criminal law legal basis illustrates under which terms the Member States have chosen to limit their autonomy in the field of substantive criminal law. It follows from this, that the use of transnational criminal law in the European framework that takes place under those same terms is legitimate.

I argue that even though the European states have lessened their autonomy by engaging in cooperation in the field of criminal law, this cooperation actually increases their sovereignty because it enables the Member States to react better to the cross-border crime affecting their interests, as long as that criminal law cooperation respects the normative paradigm it was designed to follow. In the EU context, this normative paradigm is expressed in the safeguard mechanisms included in the substantive criminal competence provisions enshrined in the Treaty on the Functioning of the European Union (Article 83 TFEU), and in the so-called European criminalization principles that can be derived from it. The European Convention on Human Rights regime (later ECHR regime) functions as a value set for criminal law enacted at the EU and national level.

Thus, this work builds theory on the justification of the use of transnational criminal law at the European framework. This work articulates the preconditions for the acceptable use of transnational criminal law by telling in which circumstances and under which limiting criteria criminal law can be enacted at the European level. The research focuses on the level of criminalization (the enactment of criminal legislation), which also enables conclusions to be drawn on the acceptability of European criminal law in general. Normative legitimation of European criminal law and legislation is argued to stem from the fact that it fulfils the preconditions for acceptable European criminal law.[5] The research studies the limits and justifications of the use

---

[5] On the different functions of theory of crime and punishment, see, Lappi-Seppälä (1994), p. 29.

of substantive criminal law, but at times draws examples also from criminal procedural norms. Substantive criminal law is nevertheless the focus of this work.

The research is not only about the special features of European criminal law, but rather about the justification for enacting European criminal law. Theoretical ideals for European constitutional structures and criminal legislation are presented in Chap. 4. These ideals describe *how the different legal orders—the national legal orders, the EU legal order and the ECHR regime—could ideally function and co-exist together* (heterarchical constitutional structures). They also describe *what features should be taken into consideration when transnational European criminal legislation is enacted* (European criminalization principles). Chapter 5 illustrates *how these ideals are not necessarily realized in practice*. In this context, European criminal law shows itself to be as much a political as it is a legal phenomenon. The last chapter draws conclusions on the general justification for the existence of European criminal law as well as justifications for EU-level criminal legislation.

The *approach* adopted in this work is the *constitutionalization of criminal law*. The concept of constitutionalization means that a polity is provided with a constitution, made constitutional or brought into line with a constitution.[6] It expresses a movement towards attaining features that constitutions and constitutional legal systems usually have.[7] It is also described as an attempt to subject the exercise of power to the discipline of constitutional procedures and norms.[8]

In the transnational context, constitutionalization is a dynamic process-oriented concept that refers to governance outside the state structures and to the transfer of governmental decision-making to non-state actors.[9] The concept of transnational law refers to legal phenomena that affect behaviour beyond the borders of a single state. These legal phenomena include law-making processes, norms, and legal institutions, such as courts. Transnational law can affect both public and private actors. Thus, transnational law can refer, for example, to rules that are used to solve norm conflicts, to determine the competent jurisdiction, or to norms that simply apply in a geographical area that is wider than a single state. The concept is often used to describe or study phenomena of the current legal society that is affected by numerous different legal sources. Both the EU and the ECHR regime can be described as transnational legal regimes.[10] Both of them affect more than one state. Even rulings of the ECtHR, which are strictly binding only in relation to the respondent state party, affect the other contracting states in a substantive sense, in the sense that the same principles apply to all contracting parties.

---

[6] *A dictionary of modern legal usage* (1995).

[7] Craig (2001), p. 127.

[8] Loughlin (2010), p. 47.

[9] Tuori (2010), p. 14; Loughlin (2010), p. 47.

[10] Menkel-Meadow (2011), pp. 100–104; Thus transnational law is a broader concept than public international law (law affecting state actors) or private international law (law affecting private actors concerning contracts or family law, for example, or choices of law). See also, Anna Margherita Russo (2012).

Just as the term transnational law is used to attenuate the difference between national and international law, the concept of transnational criminal law refers to a type of criminal law that is neither national criminal law nor international criminal law.[11] Previously, transnational criminal law has been described to form out of international treaty law, that does not fall under the core of international criminal law, the crimes against humanity such as genocide that are also norms of *jus cogens*. Following this description, transnational criminal law is more regulatory, concerning such crimes as drug crimes for example. The core of international criminal law is highly morally entrenched, whereas transnational criminal law is more regulatory.[12] European criminal law is a form of transnational criminal law. It includes the transnational regulation concerning criminal law stemming from the EU and the Council of Europe, but also that national regulation that implements the European level norms and principles. European criminal law can also implement international treaty obligations by European level regulation or by respecting the international treaty obligations in the European courts (the CJEU and the ECtHR), for example relative to crimes of terrorism.[13]

In today's world non-state actors—such as the ECHR regime and the EU for example—have great influence on national government and policy-making. The interdependence between states has increased. Public interests are regulated increasingly beyond the constitutional frameworks of the states.[14]

In this book, the concept of constitutionalization describes the development whereby European law, particularly the EU law, acquires features associated with constitutionalism. Constitutionalization is seen as an umbrella concept to describe the constitutional development of the EU and the multi-level governance[15] within Europe, focusing on the interrelationship between the EU legal order, the ECHR regime and the national legal orders. Constitutionalization in the transnational context is a broader concept than governance. In addition to governing actions at the transnational level, constitutionalization also refers to shifts of state power. Constitutionalization is seen as an evolutionary counterpart to revolutionary constitutionalism where constitutionalization is seen as dynamic and on-going process of speech acts,[16] which aim at constitution-building process beyond the state.[17]

---

[11] Boister (2003), pp. 953–976.

[12] Ibid. (2003), p. 953; Nuotio (2007), pp. 692–696; Nuotio (2014), p. 1136.

[13] Nuotio (2014), pp. 1128–1136.

[14] Peters (2005), pp. 39, 41.

[15] *Multi-level governance* describes the shift of power from states to other levels of government and to non-governmental actors. This also entails the dispersion of power to multiple centers. Multi-level governance suggests non-hierarchical relationships between the actors and indicates uncertainty concerning sovereignty, since the center of power varies from situation to situation. Cairney (2012), pp. 154–155, 161–163. On governance, see Hill (2013), pp. 19–20. On governance in EU context, see de Búrca and Scott (2006), p. 2; Christiansen (2016), pp. 98–104.

[16] Tuori (2010), p. 14.

[17] Grimm (2010), pp. 16–17.

The concept of *constitutionalization of criminal law* is used to refer to the growing importance of constitutional elements (this work focuses on the constitutional elements of the EU legal order and the ECHR regime) within criminal law. To be more precise, the constitutionalization of European criminal law means that the exercise of transnational (and national) criminal power is subjected to the constitutional norms of EU primary law and of the ECHR regime. In this sense the legitimation of the use of transnational criminal law is an issue of constitutional law. The concept of constitutionalization of European criminal law is used to refer to a normative demand where European criminal law is expected to follow the EU Treaties and the ECHR that are seen as constitutional by their nature. From the perspective of European legislator the concept of constitutionalization refers to the normative demand that the European criminal law legislator ought to exercise its power in line with the abovementioned European constitutional norms and in the line with the methods of interpretation used by the Court of Justice of the European Union (CJEU) and the European Court of Human Rights (ECtHR). The normative legitimacy of using European criminal law is drawn from its conformity with constitutional norms, in particular with the fundamental and human rights norms and with those norms which support the logic of fundamental rights protection, such as Article 83 TFEU.

1.2 Preview of the Book

The introductory chapter explains the basic research questions and methodologies. As explained above, this work examines *how the use of European criminal law can be justified*, or in other words, how and under which principles the enactment of European criminal legislation is legitimate. This work is founded on a premise that enactment of European criminal legislation does not limit state sovereignty but only limits decision-making autonomy. The EU Treaties, and in particular Article 83 TFEU concerning the approximation of substantive criminal law, enshrine the conditions for limiting the decision-making autonomy. The *travaux préparatoires* of the Treaties can clarify the purpose and *ratio* of the limitations of the decision-making autonomy. This is why the preparatory works of EU primary law are strongly emphasized in the argumentation. The introductory chapter also explains how the CJEU has started to utilize the *travaux préparatoires* of the Treaties to support its interpretations of the Treaties. Section 1.3.3.3.2 on the *travaux préparatoires* of the EU Treaties contains theory building concerning the methods of interpretation of EU law. In parts, it is a result of research cooperation with LLD Samuli Miettinen.[18] As explained above, this work approaches the research task from the perspective of constitutionalization of criminal law. The requirements of the legitimate use of European criminal law, the enactment of European criminal legislation, are drawn from European constitutional norms. These norms include the

---

[18] See, Miettinen and Kettunen (2015).

ECHR and the EU primary law. The introductory chapter also explains the fundamental rules and principles for interpretation of the ECHR and the EU law. The argumentation follows this logic of interpretation throughout the work.

Chapter 2 describes the nature of criminal law at the level of national law. Since this study adopts the approach of constitutionalization, it is only natural that the nature of criminal law as a reflection of state sovereignty is explained. Chapter 2 also explains the different levels of justification for criminal law. The level of justifying the existence of the criminal justice system in general and the level of criminalization, the enactment of criminal legislation, can be justified by forward-looking consequentialist reasons and by the communicative function of criminal law. Differently, the justification of the use of punishment cannot rely solely on consequentialist or utilitarian reasons, but also needs to adopt a deontological and backward-looking approach in order to respect the individual to whom the punishment is being imposed. A description of the nature of national criminal law in the abstract is necessary in order to establish the differences between criminal law at the domestic level and criminal law at the transnational European level. Chapter 2 is therefore necessary so that conclusions can be drawn in Chap. 3, which examines the features of European criminal law, on the differences between these two levels of criminal law.

Chapter 3 examines the features of European criminal law. The basic difference between criminal law at the domestic and the European level is drawn: even though the European level is active in norm-creation, it is the domestic level that implements and applies criminal law whether it is purely national law or influenced by European norms. The history of European criminal law is briefly described to remind the reader of the evolutionary process of the cooperation in the field of criminal law that has been characterized by a strong emphasis on intergovernmentalism. Criminal legislative work is still consensus-seeking by its nature. This is shown when the decision-making process of EU criminal law is explained and analyzed. The basic values of European criminal law, the principles of democracy, rule of law and respect of human dignity, are sedimented in the ECHR as the core of the human rights protection. These principles are examined from the perspective of substantive criminal law. The study shows how these principles affect substantive criminal law in the concrete. Chapter 3.3 concerning the ECHR regime as a value foundation for European criminal law contains also some new theory concerning the kind of influence that regime has on national and EU criminal law and what it tells about its nature from the perspective of punishment theories. Chapter 3 also examines the difference between general EU law and EU criminal law to demonstrate the special nature of criminal law within EU law itself. It is demonstrated that some principles and doctrines of general EU law, the principle of primacy and indirect effect for example, do not apply normally in the field of EU criminal law. This shows that criminal law is a special field of law amongst other fields of EU law. Lastly, Chap. 3 explains the rules on choosing the legal basis for EU secondary legislation. The Union's pre-Lisbon implicit criminal law competence is also described. It is concluded that based on the *travaux préparatoires* of the Treaties, it is clear that Article 83 TFEU is meant to exhaust the Union's substantive criminal law competence and that the pre-Lisbon case law that established the Community's implicit criminal law competence is no longer relevant in the current Treaty framework.

Chapter 4 examines the theoretical ideals for European constitutional structures and criminal law. Firstly, European constitutional pluralism is described. The chapter shows, that through certain constitutional principles of the ECHR regime and the EU it seems evident that the constitutional structures pertaining between the national legal systems, the ECHR regime and the EU are meant to be flexible and accommodating by their nature. This also means that the constitutional structures do not suggest a hierarchical relationship amongst the legal systems. Instead, the interrelationship amongst the systems can be better described as heterarchical, meaning that the constitutional structures do not follow a hierarchical model that is usually associated with constitutionalism. Instead, the constitutional structures are meant to accommodate each other without hierarchical structuring between them. Chapters 4.1 to 4.3 form a theory of constitutional structures between the ECHR regime, the EU and the national legal orders. This flexible constitutional model is later assessed in the light of recent case law of the CJEU. Secondly, Chap. 4 identifies those European criminalization principles that ought to guide the criminal legislative work in the EU. These principles are derived from the EU constitution and more precisely, from Article 83 TFEU. Here, it is argued that EU criminal legislation that follows the normative content of these principles is legitimate. Chapter 4.4 takes inspiration from the academic Manifesto on European Criminal Policy[19] and further develops the transnational dimension of these so-called European criminalization principles.

Chapter 5 demonstrates how the law in action might not always be in line with the normative ideals that are identified in Chap. 4. Firstly, the CJEU's Opinion 2/13 on the Union's accession to the ECHR is analyzed and it is argued that the Opinion does not really seem to accommodate the ECHR or the Member States' sovereign choice on the level of human rights protection. Secondly, Chap. 5 examines other possible legal bases for EU criminal legislation. It is argued that due to the sovereignty-sensitive nature of criminal law, EU level criminal legislation ought to be enacted on the basis of Article 83 TFEU. This embodies power-restricting principles similar to those generally acknowledged at the level of national criminal law, and the emergency brake procedure that ultimately can be used to protect national sovereignty. EU criminal legislation could also be based on Article 352 TFEU (the so-called flexibility clause) but only exceptionally and under the criteria established in the said article. Chapter 6 provides a summary of conclusions.

---

[19] The Manifesto on European Criminal Policy (First published in internet in the Online-Journal 'Zeitschrift für Internationale Strafrechtsdogmatik' https://sites.google.com/site/eucrimpol/manifestmanifesto; published also in (2011) 1(1) European Criminal Law Review).

1.3   Theoretical Framework and Methodology

1.3.1   Constitutional Pluralism

Constitutional pluralism is used as a theoretical framework to describe the constitutional reality of European criminal law. Constitutional pluralism is one aspect of a broader concept of legal pluralism, which is not an attribute of law, but instead an attribute of a social field or societal space,[20] meaning that there are more than one functioning legal order in one social space. For example, in Europe, the ECHR regime and the EU legal order overlap with national legal orders.[21] Constitutional pluralism recognizes that there are also different post-state entities in addition to states that have constitutional authority.[22]

Pluralism manifests itself in the plurality of claims made over authority. The different overlapping constitutional legal systems can have claims over authority and these claims may vary from situation to situation.[23] Pluralism does not seek to settle the claims in one order or to suggest hierarchical structures between the orders. Instead, it embraces the plurality of constitutions and seeks to accommodate the different institutions and systems in the absence of settled hierarchical structures.[24] The interaction of the different orders is not necessarily subject to common legal rules but rather takes a more open, political form.[25]

Legal systems gain their constitutional nature through mechanisms that are established for the assessment of the legality of all other norms in comparison with the constitution. The EU legal order and the ECHR regime both have courts which interpret the treaties in reference to the other norms. Each constitutional system has its own highest authority to interpret that constitution or treaty system. Both the EU's and the ECHR's court regimes have compulsory jurisdiction over the member states.[26] Both, the existence of the court regimes of the EU and the ECHR and their compulsory nature develop the constitutional nature of the legal systems in question.

The European Court of Human Rights (later ECtHR) has clearly stated its position on the nature of the ECHR regime. It has stated that the European Convention for the Protection of Human Rights and Fundamental Freedoms[27] (later, the ECHR

---

[20] Griffiths (1986), pp. 1, 12; Teubner (1991–1992), pp. 1443, 1451.

[21] Also unofficial legal systems, such as religious belief systems, can be regarded as one aspect of legal pluralism (Griffiths 1986, pp. 1, 8). Also different kinds of instruments of soft law, such as the ethical standards for doctors, could be regarded as an aspect of legal pluralism.

[22] Walker (2003), p. 4; Walker (2002), p. 17.

[23] See also Walker (2002), pp. 317, 346–350.

[24] Halberstam (2012), pp. 160–164, 175; Schiff Berman (2007), p. 1166.

[25] Krisch (2012), pp. 203–204.

[26] Stone Sweet (2009), pp. 639–640.

[27] European Treaty Series No. 5, Rome 4 November 1950.

or the Convention) is a constitutional instrument of European public order.[28] Whether all of the member states to the Convention agree is another issue.[29] The manner of incorporation of the ECHR varies: some countries represent monist systems, some have dualist systems. Regardless of the manner of incorporation, the Convention has the status of a binding international treaty. When a state accedes to it, it becomes a part of the national legal systems.[30]

Some contracting parties, for example Austria[31] and the Netherlands,[32] recognize the ECHR to have a constitutional status in their legal system. In France, the ECHR is superior to the national Acts of Parliament,[33] but the ECHR does not impose supremacy over the French constitution. In Finland, the ECHR is seen to have constitutional status indirectly, because the Convention had great influence on the Finnish fundamental rights reform of 1995.[34] Similarly Norway and Sweden enacted new statutes in order to fill the gaps of their constitutions in the light of the ECHR.[35] In the Spanish constitution, the ECHR is ranked below the national constitution but above conflicting national statutes. However, the Spanish constitution stipulates that the national provisions concerning fundamental rights and liberties will be interpreted in conformity with the international treaties, especially the ECHR.[36] In Italy, the ECHR has a status of ordinary law.[37]

The manner of incorporation, the formal hierarchical status which the Convention is given within national legal orders, or the Convention's nature as a kind of surrogate

---

[28] *Loizidou v. Turkey (Preliminary Objections)* App. no 15318/89 (ECtHR, 23 March 1995), para 75.

[29] Keller and Stone Sweet (2008).

[30] Pellonpää (2012), pp. 47–50; Keller and Stone Sweet (2008), p. 683.

[31] Thurnherr (2008), p. 325. The Austrian Constitutional Court has stated directly that the ECHR has been elevated to the constitutional status. However, the Austrian Constitutional Court has set limits to the authority of the ECHR by stating that the state authorities are bound to the constitutional principle of state organization even if there would be discrepancy between them and the Convention (An die verfassungsrechtlichen Grundsätze der Staatsorganisation ist der Gerichtshof aber auch im Falle eines Widerspruches zur Konvention gebunden.), see Austrian Constitutional Court, Judgement of 14 October 1987, collection number 11500 http://www.ris.bka.gv.at/Dokumente/Vfgh/JFR_10128986_86B00267_01/JFR_10128986_86B00267_01.pdf, accessed 25.6.2018, 3–5. Look also, Krisch (2007), p. 15.

[32] Often the Dutch courts do not find the provisions to be in violation of the ECHR but instead solve the conflict by interpreting the national provisions in conformity with the ECHR. See, de Wet (2008), pp. 236–237, 240–241.

[33] The Constitution of France 1958, Article 55 http://www.constitutionnet.org/sites/default/files/constitution_of_france_1958.pdf accessed 25 June 2018; Lambert Abdelgawad and Weber (2008), p. 115.

[34] Pellonpää (2012), p. 79.

[35] Wiklund (2008), pp. 182–184; Article 110 c of the Constitution of Norway refers to the Act relating to the strengthening of the status of human rights in Norwegian law (The Human Rights Act); Stone Sweet (2012), p. 1865.

[36] Spanish Constitution http://www.senado.es/constitu_i/indices/consti_ing.pdf, accessed 25.6.2018, Articles 95, 96 and 10; Soriano (2008), pp. 403–404; Krisch (2007), p. 6.

[37] Soriano (2008), pp. 403–406.

Bill of Rights do not define the constitutional status of the ECHR. What really defines the constitutional status of the ECHR is the judicial practice of the state parties.[38] The way in which the ECHR regime operates after its transformation through Protocol no. 11, which established the mandatory individual application procedure, supports the view that the ECHR regime is constitutional by its nature.[39]

Also the Court of Justice of the European Union (later CJEU) has evaluated the constitutional nature of the EU and stated that the European Union is a system of its own.[40] In the case of *Costa v ENEL* the Court distinguished the EEC Treaty (the Treaty establishing the European Economic Community) from international treaties.[41] The EU is said to have evolved from an international to a constitutional legal order.[42]

The CJEU has described the Treaties as constitutional by their nature and as a basic constitutional charter of the Union (the then Community).[43] Similarly, after the Lisbon Treaty entered into force, the Charter of Fundamental Rights of the European Union (later the Charter)[44] should also be given a constitutional status since it has the same legal value as the Treaties.[45] The Member States' accession treaties and general principles of EU law should also be regarded as constitutional. The EU constitution is a collection of the norms that create a foundation for the European Union's legal order. These are the norms concerning the EU's institutions and their functions, the Union's competences as well as the fundamental rights provisions and fundamental principles of EU legal order. As some principles of EU law are enshrined in the Treaties, they, as such, have a constitutional nature.[46] Also those principles that the CJEU has recognized through teleological interpretation of the Treaties, such as the principle of primacy, have the same hierarchical value as the Treaties, because they derive from the Treaties.[47] The CJEU has explicitly stated

---

[38] Keller and Stone Sweet (2008), pp. 682–686.

[39] Stone Sweet (2012), pp. 1859, 1860.

[40] Case C-6/64 *Flaminio Costa v E.N.E.L.* [1964] ECR p. 1195; Case C-294/83 *Parti écologiste "Les Verts" v European Parliament* [1986] ECR p. 1339.

[41] Case C-6/64 *Flaminio Costa v E.N.E.L.* [1964] ECR p. 1195. The Court stated that 'by contrast with ordinary international treaties, the EEC Treaty has created its own legal system'.

[42] Craig (2001), pp. 125, 130, 150.

[43] Case C-294/83 *Parti écologiste "Les Verts" v European Parliament* [1986] ECR p. 1339, para 23; Joined cases C-402/05 P and C-415/05 P *Yassin Abdullah Kadi and Al Barakaat International Foundation v Council of the European Union and Commission of the European Communities* [2008] ECR p. I-6351, para 281; Opinion 1/91 Opinion of the Court of 14 December 1991. Opinion delivered pursuant to the second subparagraph of Article 228 (1) of the Treaty—Draft agreement between the Community, on the one hand, and the countries of the European Free Trade Association, on the other, relating to the creation of the European Economic Area; Craig (2001), p. 130.

[44] Charter of Fundamental Rights of the European Union, OJEU 26 October 2012, C 326/396.

[45] Article 6 Treaty of European Union (later TEU).

[46] Joined cases C-402/05 P and C-415/05 P *Yassin Abdullah Kadi and Al Barakaat International Foundation v Council of the European Union and Commission of the European Communities* [2008] ECR p. I-6351, para 285.

[47] Jääskinen (2007), p. 349.

that 'the general principles of Community law have constitutional status'.[48] The CJEU's case law has played a key role in the process of constitutionalization by strengthening the effectiveness and autonomy of EU law.[49]

Even though the CJEU has described the Union's primary law as constitutional, whether or not the EU is a constitutional entity is a much-debated issue in the academic literature. The EU has been described as an unresolved constitutional entity,[50] and as a constitutional legal order that has not been figured out by constitutional theory.[51] Some say that the EU does not have a constitution or that EU is not a constitutional legal order.[52] Naturally it is clear that the EU does not have a written document that is called a constitution. The Member States' right to withdraw from the Union also seems to contradict the idea of constitutionalism in the EU context at least from a state centric perspective. As the United Kingdom's exit from the EU (Brexit) shows, a state's own volition and capacity to enter into relations with other states or exit them illustrates ultimate sovereignty.[53]

The use of the term *constitution* might seem misleading in EU context because the European Union is not a state,[54] but a distinctive *sui generis* legal entity. Hence constitutionalism ought to have a somewhat different meaning in the transnational context than in the national context.[55] It has been questioned whether the constitutional tradition formed in the state context could be used successfully in the EU context and that a constitutional theory of the EU should be constructed by keeping the state constitutional tradition merely as a reference point.[56]

It is feasible to understand the Union's constitutional legal system as an integral part of the Member States' legal systems even though it seems to be separate from the Member States' constitutions. EU law is implemented and enforced by the Member States, which means that without the actions and voluntary acceptance of the Member States the EU law would be toothless; it could not function. In this

---

[48] Case C-101/08 *Audiolux SA and Others v Groupe Bruxelles Lambert SA (GBL) and Others and Bertelsmann AG and Others* [2009] ECR I-09823, para 63. See also Rosas and Armati (2010), p. 3.

[49] von Bogdandy (2009), p. 30.

[50] Neil Walker (2001), p. 15.

[51] Weiler (1999), p. 8.

[52] For example, Dieter Grimm has stated that because the EU's powers are not derived from the people but from the Member States and because the power to amend the Treaties is left for the Member States, the EU does not have a constitution. Grimm (2010), p. 18.

[53] Michaels (2016), p. 53.

[54] The CJEU has stated for the first time expressly that the EU is not a state in Opinion 2/13 Opinion of the Court (Full Court) of 18 December 2014. Opinion pursuant to Article 218(11) TFEU—Draft international agreement—Accession of the European Union to the European Convention for the Protection of Human Rights and Fundamental Freedoms—Compatibility of the draft agreement with the EU and FEU Treaties. See also Steve Peers, 'The CJEU and the EU's accession to the ECHR: a clear and present danger to human rights protection' (EU Law Analysis, available in internet at http://eulawanalysis.blogspot.fi/2014/12/the-cjeu-and-eus-accession-to-echr.html, accessed 25 June 2018).

[55] Walker (2008), p. 519.

[56] Neil Walker (2006), pp. 3–6.

sense the Union's powers do not seem sovereign. Since the constitutional picture is overlapping and heterarchical[57] rather than hierarchical,[58] the Union and the individual Member States could be seen to create a new kind of hybrid constitutional jurisdiction where the ultimate sovereignty remains with the Member States because they have the option to withdraw themselves from the Union. However, as members of the Union, the Member States have to grant the EU primary law primacy over their national laws. Exception to this is naturally the Member States' option to withdraw from the Union and the minimum level of human rights protection that they have to guarantee as a party to the ECHR.

The interrelationship between the two transnational European legal systems[59]—the EU and the ECHR regime—is essential particularly from the Member States' perspective since they are enforcing norms stemming from both of these systems. The Member States of these two European regimes ought to accommodate the requirements stemming from both of these systems when implementing and applying them.

The CJEU has stated that the Union must respect international law, but that any international agreement cannot be primary to Union primary law and that it 'cannot have the effect of prejudicing the constitutional principles of the EC Treaty' in particular the respect of fundamental rights.[60] This means that the EU primary law and

---

[57] The concept of heterarchy is used to describe the new challenges of constitutionalism in European area, but the contents and the meaning of the concept of heterarchy in this context is still somewhat ambiguous. Hierarchical constitutional structures implies to vertical and pyramid-like power structures and to the existence of one absolute highest authority in one area, the sovereign in traditional sense. The etymological definition for heterarchy comes from the Greek words heteros (the other, different) and archē (meaning sovereignty). The concept of heterarchy could be used to imply a different kind of sovereignty or reign.

[58] Walker and Tierney (2011), p. 9; Walker (2002), p. 317; Avbelj (2011).

[59] Both of the systems ascertain that the rights and obligations of other international agreements prior to the accession to either of the systems are not affected by the accession to the EU or to the ECHR.

Article 351 TFEU regulates the status of agreements that are concluded before 1 January 1958 or for acceding States, before the date of their accession to the Union stating that the rights and obligations arising from those agreements are not affected by the provisions of the Treaties. This means, for example, that if an EU Member State has ratified the ECHR before its accession to the EU, the obligations deriving from the ECHR regime remain the same. However, the EU Member States ought to "take all appropriate steps to eliminate the incompatibilities established" (Article 351(2) TFEU). The second paragraph represents the general obligation of the EU Member States to respect their obligations to the Union as the principle of sincere cooperation requires while simultaneously fulfilling their obligations deriving from their international commitments.

In *Bosphorus*, the ECtHR has stated that "—a Contracting Party is responsible under Article 1 of the Convention for all acts and omissions of its organs regardless of whether the act or omission in question was a consequence of domestic law or of the necessity to comply with international legal obligations.—The state is considered to retain Convention liability in respect of treaty commitments subsequent to the entry into force of the Convention" (App no 45036/98, ECHR, 30 June 2005, paras 153–154).

[60] Joined cases C-402/05 P and C-415/05 P *Yassin Abdullah Kadi and Al Barakaat International Foundation v Council of the European Union and Commission of the European Communities* [2008] ECR p. I-6351, paras 291, 285, 305, 308, 309.

constitutional principles of the Union law ought to be given primacy over international law obligations. However, international agreements concluded by the Union have primacy over secondary Union legislation.[61]

It follows that from the CJEU's perspective, the ECHR should be understood as taking precedence only relative to EU secondary law. However, the effects of the CJEU's rulings are effective only within the Union's municipal legal order.[62] The EU Member States need to ensure that they comply with their obligations deriving from both the EU law and international law. In fulfilling this task, rules of public international law apply. For example, the Vienna Convention on the Law of Treaties[63] (later VCLT) applies to treaties made between states.[64] According to Article 27 VCLT 'a party may not invoke the provisions of its internal law as justification for its failure to perform a treaty'. Since Union law is an integral part of the Member States' legal orders, the EU Member States cannot invoke regional EU law provisions as a justification for their failure to fulfil their other obligations based on international treaties.

The ECtHR has evaluated whether an EU Member State may violate the provisions of the Convention simply by implementing the Union law.[65] As a general rule, even though the EU Member States have obligations arising from the Treaties, they still have responsibility to execute their obligations arising from the ECHR.[66] The ECtHR has developed a *doctrine of equivalent protection* that applies relative to the Union. According to the doctrine, state actions that are taken in compliance with legal obligations such as those deriving from the Union membership are justified as long as the relevant organization, here the EU, is considered to protect fundamental rights by ensuring their substantive guarantees and mechanisms controlling their observance. The level of the protection ought to be considered at least equivalent to that for which the Convention provides. According to the doctrine, if the fundamental rights protection in the organization in question is seen to be equivalent with the Convention in the abstract, the presumption will be that a state has not departed

---

[61] Case C-308/06 *The Queen, on the application of International Association of Independent Tanker Owners (Intertanko) and Others v Secretary of State for Transport* [2008] ECR p. I-4057, para 42; Joined cases C-402/05 P and C-415/05 P *Yassin Abdullah Kadi and Al Barakaat International Foundation v Council of the European Union and Commission of the European Communities* [2008] ECR p. I-6351, para 307.

[62] Joined cases C-402/05 P and C-415/05 P *Yassin Abdullah Kadi and Al Barakaat International Foundation v Council of the European Union and Commission of the European Communities* [2008] ECR p. I-6351; Opinion of AG Poiares Maduro, para 39.

[63] Vienna Convention on the Law of Treaties (adopted 23 May 1969, entered into force 27 January 1980) 1155 UNTS 331.

[64] Article 1. The Convention applies only to those treaties that are concluded after the entry into force on the VCLT (Article 4) 27 January 1980.

[65] *Matthews v. UK* App no 24833/94 (ECtHR, 18 February 1999); *Bosphorus Hava Yollari Turizm ve Ticaret Anonim Sirket v. Ireland* App no 45036/98 (ECtHR, 30 June 2005); Licková (2008), pp. 463, 479–482.

[66] *Matthews v. UK* App no 24833/94 (ECtHR, 18 February 1999), paras 32–35; Licková (2008), pp. 463, 480.

from the requirements of the Convention when it does no more than implement legal obligations deriving from its membership in the organization.[67]

In 2005, the ECtHR has found that the protection of fundamental rights in the Union law can be considered equivalent to that of the Convention system,[68] at that time reasoning its view by the fact that the Charter might become part of the Union's primary law.[69] Because the current Charter has the same legal value as the Treaties and since the EU might accede to the ECHR, the presumption of equivalence seems rather strong. Moreover, several articles of the Charter make reference to the Convention. For example, Article 52(3) states that in so far as the Charter contains rights which correspond to rights guaranteed by the ECHR, the meaning and scope of those rights is the same as those enshrined in the ECHR. In this sense, the Charter should be interpreted in the light of the text of the ECHR and the case law of the ECtHR.[70] ECtHR case law is not binding on the CJEU but merely an interpretative aid.[71] Even though both European courts, the CJEU and the ECtHR, refer to each other's case law, their interpretations in fundamental rights matters do not always correspond.

The presumption of equivalence is not unconditional. Any finding of equivalence can be reviewed if there are relevant changes in the protection of fundamental rights. The presumption of equivalence can be rebutted if the protection of Convention rights is seen manifestly deficient when considered in the light of the circumstances of a particular case.[72] Nevertheless, the doctrine expresses the ECtHR's openness towards the EU legal order. It is certain that since the EU and the Council of Europe have not yet made an agreement concerning the interrelationship between the Convention and the EU, neither of the European courts can rule on the matter with binding effects on the other system. At this time, their rulings can only affect their member states.

1.3.2   A Normative Study

This is a legal dogmatic study that interprets and systematizes valid European norms in order to develop the theoretical fundamentals of European criminal law.[73] This is a normative work because it does not simply describe and systematize norms. It also makes normative arguments that state which interpretative outcome ought to be

---

[67] *Bosphorus Hava Yollari Turizm ve Ticaret Anonim Sirket v. Ireland* App no 45036/98 (ECtHR, 30 June 2005), paras 155–156.

[68] Ibid., p. 165.

[69] Ibid., p. 159.

[70] OJEU C 14.12.2007/303, 33. See also Tobias Lock (2009), p. 384.

[71] Tobias Lock (2009), pp. 386–387; Scheeck (2006), pp. 837, 853.

[72] *Bosphorus Hava Yollari Turizm ve Ticaret Anonim Sirket v. Ireland* App no 45036/98, (ECtHR, 30 June 2005) paras 155–156.

[73] On legal dogmatics, see, for example, Peczenik (2005), p. 1; Tuori (2002), p. 284.

preferred over alternative ones.[74] This work studies European legal norms and takes a normative position on how the use of European criminal law can be justified and normatively evaluated.

This work locates itself in the fields of constitutional and criminal law, the main focus being on criminal law. It describes the constitutional status of the European legal space and also introduces a fresh way of understanding the European constitutional picture (in Chap. 4). Constitutions are not formally superior simply because of the process they have been created: they are also superior due their normative content.[75] Criminal law, having a close interrelationship to constitutional law, is a normative institution. In order to be able to analyse how European criminal can be justified,[76] the study explains key features and special characteristics of European criminal law (Chap. 3), presents ideals on which European criminal law should be based (Chap. 4.4) and evaluates if these ideals are fulfilled in reality (Chap. 5).

Constitutionalism, the theoretical framework of this study, can be understood as a methodological perspective or a research subject in itself. This research combines these two aspects. On one hand, the research tries to explain how the European constitutionalization process could be perceived (Chap. 4). On the other hand, the study examines European criminal law from the premises of constitutional law by explaining the key elements of European criminal law stemming from constitutional law (in particular Chaps. 3.3, 3.4, 3.5, 3.7) and builds the justification criteria for European criminal law from European constitutional law (main Chaps. 4 to 6).

Even though the research starts off from the premises of legal positivism,[77] law and morals are inevitably seen to be connected to each other. The immanent connection between law and morality manifests itself in legal principles, such as human dignity, the rule of law, or the democracy principle, for example. The contents of these principles are morally charged; either morally permitted or morally required.[78] The post-positivist take on the validity of law recognizes that in addition to the formal validity of law, there is the substantive validity of law. This gets its content for example from human and fundamental rights provisions.[79] According to Tuori the validity of legal norms has two aspects: a formal and a substantive aspect. Substantive validity entails legitimacy, or in other words ethical and moral justifiability, and the purpose of the norms.[80] Similarly Robert Alexy finds that the validity of norms has three dimensions; legal, social, and moral validity. Authoritative issuance, social efficacy, and the correctness of content are all elements of validity, but not in equal relation.[81]

---

[74] Van Hoecke (2011), p. 10.

[75] Tuori (2015), p. 14.

[76] On normative study of criminal law, see, Duff and Green (2011), pp. 3–5.

[77] On legal positivism, see Hart (1958), p. 593; Fuller (1958), p. 630; Hirvonen (2012), p. 35; Cryer et al. (2011), pp. 37–38.

[78] Alexy (2002), p. 77.

[79] Hirvonen (2012), p. 41.

[80] Tuori (2008), p. 183.

[81] Alexy (2002), pp. 89–94.

Even though this study understands law as a set of norms that are created by democratic legislative processes or customs, or recognized by Courts in adjudication, it also recognizes that law contains some non-positivistic moral elements that stem from fundamental rights and other constitutional principles such as proportionality. For example, criminal law is used to protect and realize the value foundation of fundamental rights. From a legalistic perspective, because constitutional norms are at a higher hierarchical level than secondary legislation, criminal law must be in harmony with constitutional law. Fundamental and human rights provisions have two different roles in which they affect criminal law. In their so-called offensive role they require the use of criminal legislative measures. Simultaneously, fundamental rights restrict the use of criminal law through the principle of proportionality. For example when a criminal provision is protecting one fundamental right it can be restricting another. Human and fundamental rights function in their defensive role in situations where they restrict the use of criminal legislative measures or the application of criminal laws.[82] The two roles of human and fundamental rights are present in the ECtHR's case law[83] as well as in different official documents.[84] This study also recognizes a close interrelationship between law and politics. When law is accepted as an outcome of human behaviour, it is easy to see law as a means to fulfil political agendas. Law is not considered as separate from the context in which it exists (social, political, moral). Thus the research does not hold to a strictly positivist approach on law.

1.3.3 Rules of Interpretation

1.3.3.1 Interpreting the ECHR

The ECHR imposes obligations on its Contracting Parties. The Convention contains negative obligations directed to the contracting parties not to violate the Convention rights and positive obligations for the contracting parties to actively protect the rights, for example through legislative measures. The principle of positive obligations can be derived from Article 1 ECHR according to which the contracting parties must secure the rights and freedoms of the Convention to everyone within their jurisdiction.[85] The Court has explicitly noticed that even though the Convention rights are essentially protecting individuals from interference by public authorities

---

[82] Tulkens (2011), p. 577.

[83] On the offensive role of human rights, see, for example, *M.C. v Bulgaria* App no 39272/98 (ECtHR, 4 December 2003).

[84] See for example, Recommendation No R (96) 8 of the Committee of Ministers on crime policy in Europe in a time of change, 5 September 1996; COM(2011) 573 final, Towards an EU Criminal Policy: Ensuring the effective implementation of EU policies through criminal law, Brussels 20 September 2011; Statement of the Constitutional Law Committee of the Finnish Parliament, PeVL 23/1997 vp.

[85] Greer (2006), p. 215.

(negative obligation), the contracting parties also have positive obligations stemming from the principle of effective protection of Convention rights. However, the contracting parties have a choice of means in fulfilling the positive obligations.[86] Another element of the ECHR regime that needs to be kept in mind is the principle of subsidiarity,[87] which means that the contracting parties are those who need to fulfil the Convention obligations. The ECtHR's task is simply to review whether the contracting parties comply with the Convention.[88]

The doctrine of margin of appreciation has been developed in order to strike a balance between national views on human rights and the uniform application of the Convention.[89] According to the doctrine the contracting parties have some room for manoeuvre when they are implementing their Convention obligations.[90] The state parties are free to choose the measures to fulfil the obligations deriving from the ECHR.[91] The doctrine enables flexible cooperation between national legal systems and the ECHR regime. While protecting some rights, other rights are often simultaneously restricted. The margin of appreciation enables the State Parties to balance the common good of society and the rights of individuals.[92] The more there is consensus on particular issue, the narrower the margin of appreciation is on that issue.[93] However, the limitations to the individual freedoms need to be proportional. Also, it is good to remember that some Convention rights, such as those enshrined in Articles 3 or 7 ECHR, cannot be limited based on Article 15(2) ECHR.

Because the articles of the ECHR are abstract and sparse, the interpretation of the provisions is particularly important.[94] There are two main principles of interpretation; teleological interpretation (which seeks the object and purpose of the Convention) and evolutive interpretation (the practical and effective interpretation of the ECHR as a living instrument).[95]

The ECtHR has stated that the interpretation of the Convention should be guided mainly by the rules of interpretation provided for in Articles 31 to 33 of the VCLT.[96] Article 33 VCLT concerns the authentic languages of the treaties and establishes that all languages used to authenticate a treaty are equally authoritative and the text

---

[86] *Marckx v. Belgium* App no 6833/74 (ECtHR, 13 June 1979), para 31; Pitkänen (2013), p. 55.

[87] Not to be mixed with the EU law principle of subsidiarity.

[88] Greer (2006), p. 216.

[89] Arai-Takahashi (2002), pp. 2–3.

[90] Greer (2006), pp. 216, 222.

[91] *"Relating to certain aspects of the laws on the use of languages in education in Belgium" v. Belgium* (Merits) App no 1474/62, 1677/62, 1769/63, 1994/63, 2126/64 (ECtHR, 23 July 1968), para 10; Arai-Takahashi (2002), pp. 2–3.

[92] Tümay (2008), p. 201.

[93] Brauch (2005), pp. 113, 128; de la Rasilla del Moral (2006), pp. 611, 617.

[94] Greer (2006), p. 193.

[95] Jacobs et al. (2010), pp. 65, 81.

[96] *Demir and Baykara v. Turkey* App no 34503/97 (ECtHR, 12 November 2008), para 65. See also *Golder v. the United Kingdom* App no 4451/70 (ECtHR, 21 February 1975), para 29; *Saadi v. the United Kingdom* App no 13229/03 (ECtHR, 29 January 2008), paras 61–62.

is presumed to have the same meaning in all of the languages. If there is a difference in meaning in different language versions, 'the meaning which best reconciles the texts, having regard to the object and purpose of the treaty' should be adopted. The ECHR is authentic in English and French.[97]

According to Article 31 VCLT, the terms of the treaty should be given the ordinary meaning in their context and be interpreted in the light of the object and purpose of that treaty. The purpose of the treaty can be found from the text, the preamble, and the annexes. Article 31(3)c VCLT notes that together with the context any relevant rules of international law applicable in the relations between the parties should also be taken into account. Article 32 VCLT contends that the preparatory work of the treaty can be used as supplementary means of interpretation either to confirm the meaning resulting from the application of Article 31, or to determine its meaning when an interpretation according to Article 31 VCLT either leaves the meaning ambiguous or obscure or leads to a result which is manifestly absurd or unreasonable. This means that the *travaux* can be used to support interpretation in practically all situations.

The *ordinary meaning* of terms can be sought from dictionaries (ordinary and natural meaning),[98] from other international treaty systems, or from different branches of law.[99] Sometimes the ordinary meaning is not the same as in the national legal systems.[100] However, it should be noted that a right to an opposite right cannot be derived from the Convention rights based on the ordinary meaning of the rights. For example, the right to life does not constitute a right to die.[101] The ECtHR often uses comparative law methods. When common standards are found, that meaning will be applied.[102]

The ECtHR has stated that the ECHR 'is a treaty for the effective protection of individual human rights and that the Convention must be read as a whole, and interpreted in such a way as to promote internal consistency and harmony between its various provisions' and that '[t]he Court must also take into account any relevant rules and principles of international law applicable in relations between the Contracting Parties'.[103] The issue of context sometimes arises in situations where applicants seek protection under provisions of a Protocol which the respondent state

---

[97] The ECtHR has referred to Article 33 VCLT in its case law regarding differences in the two official language versions, see, *The Sunday Times v. The United Kingdom* App no 6538/74 (ECtHR, 26 April 1979), para 48.

[98] *Luedicke, Belkacem and Koç v. Germany* App no 6210/73, 6877/75, 7132/75 (ECtHR, 28 November 1978), para 40; Jacobs et al. (2010), p. 68.

[99] *Branković and Others v. Belgium and Others* App no 52207/99 (ECtHR, 12 December 2001), para 57; Jacobs et al. (2010), p. 68.

[100] For example, in *Engel and Others v. the Netherlands* App no 5100/71, 5101/71, 5102/71, 5354/72, 5370/72 (ECtHR, 8 June 1976), paras 85–87, the Court contemplated if the applicants were objects of criminal charges or military discipline.

[101] *Pretty v. The United Kingdom* App no 2346/02 (ECtHR, 29 April 2002); Jacobs et al. (2010), p. 68.

[102] Jacobs et al. (2010), p. 69.

[103] *Saadi v. the United Kingdom* App no 13229/03 (ECtHR, 29 January 2008), para 62.

has not ratified. It is possible that where a more detailed provision of a Protocol is applicable in the case, a more general provision of the Convention might still apply. But if the situation does not fall under a more specific provision it cannot fall under a more general provision either.[104]

The Convention ought to be interpreted in the light of its *object and purpose*. The object and purpose of the Convention obligations is 'rather to protect the fundamental rights of individual human beings from infringements by any of the High Contracting Parties than to create subjective and reciprocal rights for the High Contracting Parties themselves'.[105] The Court has also stated that 'it is necessary to seek the interpretation that is most appropriate in order to realize the aim and achieve the object of the treaty, not that which would restrict to the greatest possible degree the obligations undertaken by the Parties'.[106]

The interpretation of the ECHR ought to be evolutive and dynamic so that the interpretation would match the social and political attitudes of the present time.[107] However, new rights cannot be created (derived) by means of dynamic interpretation.[108] The principle of effectiveness is described as the *bedrock of evolutive interpretation*.[109] Its basic idea is that the Convention rights ought to provide practical and effective protection. They should not be just theoretical and illusory.[110]

The Court finds that in addition to the effective realization of the Convention rights, the interpretation ought to be consistent with ideals and values of democratic society.[111] The principle of democracy is expressed in the preamble of the Convention and is a part of the value foundation of the Convention. Article 3 of Protocol 1 of the ECHR also secures democratic rights (right to free elections). In addition to these, democracy is an element of express limitation clauses in Articles 6 and 8–11.[112] The Court has numerously stated that democracy is the only compatible political model

---

[104] *Leander v. Sweden* App no 9248/81 (ECtHR, 26 March 1987), para 78; Jacobs et al. (2010), p. 70.

[105] Decision of the Commission as to the admissibility of App no 788/60 *Austria v. Italy* (11 January 1961) 19.

[106] *Wemhoff v. Germany* App no 2122/64 (ECtHR, 27 June 1968), para 8.

[107] Jacobs et al. (2010), p. 72.

[108] For example right for divorce does not derive from right to marry, case of *Johnston and Others v. Ireland* App no 9697/82 (ECtHR, 18 December 1986), para 53. See also *Cruz Varas and Others v. Sweden* App no 15576/89 (ECtHR, 20 March 1991), para 100.

[109] Jacobs et al. (2010), p. 73.

[110] "The Convention is intended to guarantee not rights that are theoretical or illusory but rights that are practical and effective." *Airey v. Ireland* App no 6289/73 (ECtHR, 9 October 1979), para 24; Affaire *Peltier c. France* App no 32872/96 (ECtHR, 21 May 2002), para 36. See also *Soering v. The United Kingdom* App no 14038/88 (ECtHR, 7 July 1989), para 87; *Demir and Baykara v. Turkey* App no 34503/97 (ECtHR, 12 November 2008), para 66.

[111] *Soering v. The United Kingdom* App no 14038/88 (ECtHR, 7 July 1989), para 87. See also *Kjeldsen, Busk Madsen and Pedersen v. Denmark* App no 5095/71 5920/72 5926/72 (ECtHR, 7 December 1976), para 53.

[112] Greer (2006), p. 199.

with the Convention,[113] because it includes respect for pluralism, tolerance, and broadmindedness.[114]

Article 31 VCLT also states that relevant rules of international law applicable in the relations between the parties ought to be taken into account also in the interpretation. The importance of international legal sources is evident in the ECtHR's case law.[115] Relative to EU law, the ECtHR has used the Charter as point of reference even though the Charter was not binding EU law at that time.[116] It is noteworthy that not all of the respondent states need to have ratified the international instruments that the ECtHR applies. It is enough that the ECtHR can conclude that a certain approach is adopted by a clear majority of modern societies.[117] To the ECtHR, the process of interpretation is a single combined operation,[118] and it seems that the separate interpretation principles mentioned in Article 31 VCLT cannot be put in a hierarchical order.[119] The methods of interpretation described in this chapter are utilized particularly in Chap. 3.3 and its subchapters.

---

[113] *Gorzelik and Others v. Poland* App no 44158/98 (ECtHR, 17 February 2004), para 89; *Zdanoka v. Latvia* App no 58278/00 (ECtHR, 16 March 2006), para 98; *United Communist Party of Turkey and Others v. Turkey* App no 19392/92 (ECtHR, 30 January 1998), para 45.

[114] *Gorzelik and Others v. Poland* App no 44158/98 (ECtHR, 17 February 2004), para 90.

[115] The ECtHR has stated, for example, that "[t]he Court, in defining the meaning of terms and notions in the text of the Convention, can and must take into account elements of international law other than the Convention, the interpretation of such elements by competent organs, and the practice of European States reflecting their common values. The consensus emerging from specialized international instruments and from the practice of Contracting States may constitute a relevant consideration for the Court when it interprets the provisions of the Convention in specific cases." *Demir and Baykara v. Turkey* App no 34503/97 (ECtHR, 12 November 2008), para 65. See also *Golder v. the United Kingdom* App no 4451/70 (ECtHR, 21 February 1975), para 29; *Saadi v. the United Kingdom* App no 13229/03 (ECtHR, 29 January 2008), para 85.

[116] *Demir and Baykara v. Turkey* App no 34503/97 (ECtHR, 12 November 2008), para 80; *Christine Goodwin v. the united Kingdom* App no 28957/95 (ECtHR, 11 July 2002), para 58; *Vilho Eskelinen and Others v. Finland* App no 63235/00 (ECtHR, 19 April 2007), paras 29–30; *Sørensen and Rasmussen v. Denmark* App no 52562/99, 52620/99 (ECtHR, 11 January 2006), para 37.

The Court has also used the Oviedo Convention on Human Rights and Biomedicine as a point of reference even though it is not ratified by all of the Contracting Parties. *Demir and Baykara v. Turkey* App no 34503/97 (ECtHR, 12 November 2008), para 81. See also *Glass v. the United Kingdom* App no 61827/00 (ECtHR, 9 March 2004), paras 58, 75.

[117] *Demir and Baykara v. Turkey* App no 34503/97 (ECtHR, 12 November 2008), para 86. The Court has stated that "[i] *t is not necessary for the respondent State to have ratified the entire collection of instruments that are applicable in respect of the precise subject matter of the case concerned.* It will be sufficient for the Court that the relevant international instruments denote a continuous evolution in the norms and principles applied in international law or in the domestic law of the majority of member States of the Council of Europe and show, in a precise area, that there is common ground in modern societies" (emphasis added).

[118] *Golder v. the United Kingdom* App no 4451/70 (ECtHR, 21 February 1975), para 30.

[119] Greer (2006), pp. 194–195; Jacobs et al. (2010), p. 65.

1.3.3.2 The Principle of Legality in Criminal Cases

The principle of legality is a central principle in criminal law affecting both the legislator and the authorities applying the law. It has a strong position in the ECHR regime. The criminal law principle of legality is explicitly enshrined in Article 7 ECHR.[120] The principle of legality is essential also in EU law. Article 2 TEU recognises rule of law as one of the founding values of the Union. The CJEU finds the principle of legality in criminal cases as an element of the broader rule of law principle.[121] The principle of legality is also enshrined in Article 49 of the Charter.

The principles of rule of law and legality relate closely to the democracy principle, because they protect individuals against despotism. In the field of criminal law, predictability and equality are fulfilled through the principle of legality. Traditionally the principle of legality is seen to consist of four elements. First, the maxims of *nullum crimen sine lege* and *nulla poena sine lege* must be applied, meaning that both the essential elements of crime and the punishment must be defined by law. Second, criminal provisions ought to be written in a clear and precise manner so that the scope of conduct that constitutes criminal behaviour can be easily understood. Third, criminal legislation cannot be applied retroactively, meaning that crime provisions ought to have effects only after the provisions have entered into force. And fourth, according to the principle of strict construction, provisions in criminal legislation must be applied within the limits of their wording. This also means that analogous interpretation to the detriment of the accused is not allowed.[122]

The principle of legality is enshrined in Article 7 ECHR as follows:

1. No one shall be held guilty of any *criminal offence* on account of any act or omission which did not constitute a criminal offence under national or international *law* at the time when it was committed. Nor shall a heavier *penalty* be imposed than the one that was applicable at the time the criminal offence was committed. (emphasis added)
2. This Article shall not prejudice the trial and punishment of any person for any act or omission which, at the time when it was committed, was criminal according to the general principles of law recognized by civilized nations.

---

[120] Many other provisions of the Convention also mention law. The rule of law is mentioned as the common heritage of European counties in the preamble, the right to life must be protected by law (Article 2), right to liberty can be deprived only in certain circumstances and following a procedure prescribed by law (Article 5), the right to a fair trial requires that the tribunal is established by law (Article 6), everyone is presumed innocent until proved guilty according to law (Article 6), interferences to Articles 8–11 can be made if they are *inter alia* prescribed by law, and so on. Greer (2006), p. 201.

[121] Case C-135/11 P *IFAW Internationaler Tierschutz-Fonds gGmbH v European Commission*, Opinion of AG Cruz Villalón, para 67; Miettinen (2013a), p. 113.

[122] *C.R. v. the United Kingdom* App no 20190/92 (ECtHR, 22 November 1995), para 33; *Del Rio Prada v. Spain* App no 42750/09 (ECtHR, 10 July 2012), para 46; Ashworth (2009), pp. 57–70.

The ECtHR has stated that the concepts of criminal offence, penalty, and law have autonomous meaning under the ECHR regime.[123] There are three steps (the so-called *Engel* criteria) when assessing if the offence is criminal. First one needs to ask whether the offence belongs to criminal law, disciplinary law or both concurrently in the respondent state. If the offense belongs to the field of criminal law, it is always a criminal offence under the *Engel* criteria. If the offence falls under disciplinary law, one needs to ask if the offence is criminal by its nature, or what is the nature and degree of severity of the penalty.[124] This means that the domestic classification is not the sole decisive factor in determining whether a conduct is considered as criminal. The concept of 'criminal charge' (in Article 6 ECHR) is assessed using the same criteria. In *Deweer*, the ECtHR found that 'the 'charge' could, for the purposes of Article 6 paragraph 1, be defined as the official notification given to an individual by the competent authority of an allegation that he has committed a criminal offence'.[125] The classification of the offence in national law is not decisive. Instead greater importance is given to the nature of the offence.[126]

The Court has assessed the concept of 'a penalty' in the case of *Welch v the United Kingdom*. First, it needs to be assessed if the measure 'is imposed following conviction for a criminal offence'. Similarly when analysing whether conduct constitutes a criminal offence, when analysing if the imposed measure constitutes a penalty, '[o]ther factors that may be taken into account as relevant in this connection are the nature and purpose of the measure in question; its characterization under national law; the procedures involved in the making and implementation of the measure; and its severity.'[127] In *Jamil v France*, a sanction was considered as a penalty because it was ordered in a criminal-law context, was intended to be deterrent and to prevent drug trafficking, and it could have led to a punitive deprivation of liberty.[128]

As for the concept of *law*, the term has the same meaning in all of the articles of the Convention in which it is mentioned. The concept is understood in its substantive sense instead of its formal sense. The concept of law consists of statute law and case-law. It includes statutes, enactments of lower rank than statutes, and unwritten law. The ECtHR has simply stated that 'the law is the provision in force as the competent courts have interpreted it'. However, there are two qualitative requirements for law: accessibility and foreseeability. Both the definition of an offence and the penalty must meet these qualitative requirements.[129] What is required for the definition of the offence and the penalty to be foreseeable depends 'to a considerable degree on the content of the text in issue, the field it is designed to cover and the

---

[123] See for example Greer (2006), p. 240; Jacobs et al. (2010), p. 297.

[124] *Engel and Others v. the Netherlands* App no 5100/71, 5101/71, 5102/71, 5354/72, 5370/72 (ECtHR, 8 June 1976), para 82. See also Jacobs et al. (2010), p. 297.

[125] *Deweer v. Belgium* App no 6903/75 (ECtHR, 27 February 1980), para 46.

[126] *Demicoli v. Malta* App no 13057/87 (ECtHR, 27 August 1991), paras 31–33.

[127] *Welch v. the United Kingdom* App no 17440/90 (ECtHR, 9 February 1995), paras 27–28.

[128] *Jamil v. France* App no 15917/89 (ECtHR, 8 June 1995), para 32.

[129] *Kafkaris v. Cyprus* App no 21906/04 (ECtHR, 12 February 2008), paras 139–140.

number and status of those to whom it is addressed.'[130] The Court has further defined that

> [a]n individual must know from the wording of the relevant provision and, if need be, with the assistance of the courts' interpretation of it, what acts and omissions will make him criminally liable and what penalty will be imposed for the act committed and/or omission -- Furthermore, a law may still satisfy the requirement of "foreseeability" where the person concerned has to take appropriate legal advice to assess, to a degree that is reasonable in the circumstances, the consequences which a given action may entail.[131]

The Court has further defined that '[t]his is particularly true in relation to persons carrying on a professional activity, who are used to having to proceed with a high degree of caution when pursuing their occupation.'[132] The Court recognizes that however clear wording the law has, there is always an element and a need for judicial interpretation and adaptation to changing circumstances.[133]

There is relatively small amount of cases relating to Article 7 ECHR. The cases relating to the principle of legality can be categorized into at least three groups, in which the applicant has asked either:

1) is the act or omission defined as criminal by law /is it defined clearly enough,[134]
2) whether criminal provisions have been applied retrospectively,[135] or
3) if the imposed sanction has been harsher than prescribed by law.[136]

The principle of legality also has a strong tradition and standing in EU law. Article 67 TFEU explicitly stipulates that the area of freedom, security and justice shall be constituted with respect for fundamental rights and the different legal systems and traditions of the Member States.[137] The CJEU has referred to the case law of the ECtHR concerning the principle of legality. In the case of *Regina v Kirk*, the CJEU stated that 'the principle that penal provisions may not have retroactive effect is one which is common to all legal orders of the Member States and is enshrined in Article 7 of the ECHR; It takes place among the general principles of law whose

---

[130] *Cantoni v. France* App no 17862/91 (ECtHR, 15 November 1996), para 35.

[131] *Kafkaris v. Cyprus* App no 21906/04 (ECtHR, 12 February 2008), paras 139–141.

[132] *Cantoni v. France* App no 17862/91 (ECtHR, 15 November 1996), para 35.

[133] *Kafkaris v. Cyprus* App no 21906/04 (ECtHR, 12 February 2008), paras 139–141.

[134] *C.R. v. the United Kingdom* App no 20190/92 (ECtHR, 22 November 1995), paras 35, 41–42; *S.W. v. the United Kingdom* App no 20166/92 (ECtHR, 22 November 1995), paras 37, 43–44. These cases illustrate well a few points presented above. Because the legal system belonged to a common law tradition, the Court took into consideration both the written and unwritten law. Because the written legislation had not yet been amended, the evolution of judicial interpretation weighted more. Thus retrospective application of criminal law was not at hand either.

[135] See for example *K.-H. W. v. Germany* App no 37201/97 (ECtHR, 22 March 2001), paras 11, 41, 75–91; *Streletz, Kessler and Krenz v. Germany* App no 34044/96 35532/97 44801/98 (ECtHR, 22 March 2001), paras 13, 46.

[136] *Welch v. the United Kingdom* App no 17440/90 (ECtHR, 9 February 1995), paras 26, 35.

[137] The Maastricht Treaty explicitly stipulated inter alia that judicial cooperation in criminal matters shall be dealt with in compliance with the ECHR (Treaty on European Union, signed at Maastricht on 7 February 1992, OJEC No C 191 29 July 1992, Title VI, Article K.2).

observance is ensured by the Court of Justice.'[138] In the case of *Dansk Rørindustri v Commission*, even though the CJEU did not refer to any particular cases of the ECtHR it made a general reference to the jurisprudence of the ECtHR trying to define the meaning of concept of 'law' and the scope of the concept 'foreseeability' relative to the principle of legality in EU law. The CJEU stated that these principles, which are found in ECtHR's jurisprudence, are 'consistently reflected in the case law of the Court' and that 'national law is limited by the general principles of law which form part of Community law and in particular the principles of legal certainty and non-retroactivity'.[139] It seems that the CJEU takes the ECtHR's jurisprudence concerning the principle of legality, including the different features of the principle and the definitions of the relevant concepts, as its own starting point for interpretation.

However, EU criminal law has peculiar features relating to the effect the principle of legality has in relation to directives and framework decisions.[140] As is well known, directives and framework decisions are binding only as to the result to be achieved and thus they need to be implemented into national legal systems. The CJEU has explicitly stated that a directive '*cannot, of itself and independently* of a national law adopted by a Member State for its implementation, have the effect of *determining or aggravating the liability* in criminal law of persons who act in contravention of the provisions of that directive' (emphasis added).[141] The same applies to framework decisions.[142]

---

[138] Case C-63/83 *Regina v Kent Kirk* [1984] ECR p. 2689, para 22. See also Melander (2010), p. 130.

[139] Joined cases C-189/02 P, C-202/02 P, C-205/02 P to C-208/02 P and C-213/02 P *Dansk Rørindustri A/S (C-189/02 P), Isoplus Fernwärmetechnik Vertriebsgesellschaft mbH and Others (C-202/02 P), KE KELIT Kunststoffwerk GmbH (C-205/02 P), LR af 1998 A/S (C-206/02 P), Brugg Rohrsysteme GmbH (C-207/02 P), LR af 1998 (Deutschland) GmbH (C-208/02 P) and ABB Asea Brown Boveri Ltd (C-213/02 P) v Commission of the European Communities* [2005] ECR p. I-5425, paras 215–220. See also Melander (2010), p. 131.

[140] With the Lisbon Treaty, directives are the new judicial form of cooperation in criminal matters (Lisbon Treaty, OJEU C 83/80, 30 March 2010, Article 82(2) and Article 83(1) of TFEU); Framework decision was created as a form of cooperation in the criminal matters in the Treaty of Amsterdam (Maastricht Treaty, OJEC C 191, 29 July 1992, enabled joint actions as the form of legal instrument in the field of criminal law (Title VI Article K.3 2(b)). Framework decisions replaced joint actions as legal instruments in the Treaty of Amsterdam, OJEC C 340, 10 November 1997, Title VI Article K.6 2(b)): numbering of the Articles changed in the Treaty of Nice, OJEC C 325, 24 December 2002, Article 34(2)b was the new numbering concerning framework decision as the form of cooperation).

[141] Case C-14/86 *Pretore di Salò v Persons unknown* [1987] ECR p. 2545, para 20; Case C-80/86 *Criminal proceedings against Kolpinghuis Nijmegen BV* [1987] ECR p. 3969, para 14.

[142] Case C-105/03 *Criminal proceedings against Maria Pupino* [2005] ECR p. I-5285, paras 44–45. The CJEU stated that the obligation on the national court to refer to the content of a framework decision when interpreting the relevant rules of its national law is limited by general principles of law, particularly those of legal certainty and non-retroactivity. In particular, *those principles prevent that obligation from leading to the criminal liability of persons who contravene the provisions of a framework decision from being determined or aggravated on the basis of such a decision alone, independently of an implementing law*". (emphasis added).

The case of *Advocaten voor de Wereld* concerned the question whether Article 2(2) of the Framework Decision on the European Arrest Warrant was in accordance with the principle of legality. Article 2(2) FD EAW contains a list of types of offences for which the verification of the double criminality is not required when a Member State asks another Member State to surrender a person pursuant to a European arrest warrant. The preliminary ruling was asked *inter alia* to discover whether Article 2(2) was compatible with the principle of legality: was the list of types of offences clear and precise enough? According to Article 2(2) the verification of the double criminality of the act is not required, 'if they (the types of offences listed in the article) are punishable in the issuing Member State by a custodial sentence or a detention order for a maximum period of at least three years and as they are defined by the law of the issuing Member State'. The CJEU found that Article 2(2) does not infringe the principle of legality, because the FD EAW is based on the principle of mutual recognition and 'does not seek to harmonise the criminal offences in question in respect of their constituent elements or of the penalties which they attract'. The requirements of the principle of legality needed to be met at the level of national legislation.[143]

This interpretation is a natural result of the principle of mutual recognition, but also of the nature of framework decisions and directives. Since they are instruments that are used to approximate criminal legislation (and not fully harmonize it), they cannot be considered to fulfil the *nullum crimen et nulla poena sine lege* requirement of the principle of legality according to which the definition of crime and penalty must be established by law. The CJEU's stand on the matter is clear: criminal liability or aggravation of criminal liability cannot be based on directives or framework decisions independently without (implementing) national law. Also, following from the principle of legality, the scope of conforming interpretation (indirect effect) and primacy are limited in the field of criminal law, because the interpretation of penal provisions must fit within the wording of the penal provisions (this issue will be dealt in more detail in Chap. 3.5). *All this means that framework decisions and directives cannot be perceived as law as the principle of legality in criminal cases requires.*

The information presented in this chapter is used in particular in Chap. 3.1 to describe the dimensions of European criminal law and in Chap. 3.5 concerning the differences between general EU law and EU criminal law.

---

[143] Case C-303/05 *Advocaten voor de Wereld VZW v Leden van de Ministerraad* [2007] ECR p. I-3633, paras 52–54.

1.3.3.3 Interpreting EU (Criminal) Law

In the Footsteps of Van Gend en Loos

This chapter presents principles that are used to interpret EU law. Firstly, *teleological interpretation* is examined since it can be recognized as the prevailing principle of interpretation. Next, the challenges the plurality of official languages in the EU brings to the interpretation of EU law are studied. Last, the CJEU's reliance on the method of *comparative law* is explained. This is an important element in the CJEU's methodology of interpretation because through it the Court has used it when recognizing general principles of law common to the Member States or general principles deriving from the constitutional traditions common to the Member States. The Court has then used those general principles in the interpretation of EU law in situations where it has found gaps or ambiguity in EU legal texts.[144]

The CJEU's interpretation of EU law is based on text, context, and *telos* (purpose). The CJEU established this in *Van Gend en Loos* by stating that when interpreting EU law 'it is necessary to consider the spirit, the general scheme, and the wording'.[145] The CJEU has also stated more expressly that in interpreting concepts of EU law one should use 'the generally recognized principles of interpretation, beginning with the *ordinary meaning* to be attributed to those terms in their *context* and in the light of the *objectives* of the Treaty' (emphasis added).[146] It can be recognized that these elements of interpretation seem equivalent to those mentioned in the Article 31(1) VCLT; '[a] treaty shall be interpreted in good faith in accordance with the *ordinary meaning* to be given to the terms of the treaty *in their context* and in the light of *its object and purpose*' (emphasis added). The CJEU has even explicitly found that as a rule of customary international law the VCLT binds the EU institutions.[147] The method of teleological interpretation is used by both of the European courts, the ECtHR and the CJEU. Even though the context and purpose of the ECHR regime and EU legal order are different, the courts use the same basic method of interpretation only within their own contexts.

The EU context differs from that of international law. Provisions of EU law ought to be interpreted as part of a constitutional, autonomous, one of a kind *sui generis* legal order.[148] Teleological interpretation does not refer solely to the purpose of the relevant provision but also to a systemic and constitutional understanding of the EU legal order and to the interpretation of the relevant provision in this context.[149]

---

[144] Maduro (2007), p. 6.

[145] Case C-26/62 *NV Algemene Transport- en Expeditie Onderneming van Gend & Loos v Netherlands Inland Revenue Administration* [1963] ECR p. 1. See also Maduro (2007), pp. 1, 4; Arnull (2006), pp. 612–613; Paunio and Lindroos-Hovinheimo (2010), pp. 395, 396.

[146] Case C-53/81 *D.M. Levin v Staatssecretaris van Justitie* [1982] ECR p. 1035, para 9.

[147] Case C-466/11 *Gennaro Currà and Others v Bundesrepublik Deutschland* [2012], para 22.

[148] Maduro (2007), pp. 4–5; Case C-6/64 *Flaminio Costa v E.N.E.L.* [1964] ECR p. 1195; Case C-294/83 *Parti écologiste "Les Verts" v European Parliament* [1986] ECR p. 1339.

[149] Maduro (2007), p. 5.

The general principles and doctrines of EU law (such as primacy, direct effect etc.) are outcomes of teleological interpretation aiming to ensure the effectiveness of EU law. Rights *and obligations* are created for individuals in addition to state parties by these general principles and doctrines. Thus EU law differs from traditional treaties between states (public international law).[150] The purpose of the Union goes beyond achieving economic integration by aiming towards greater European unity,[151] to an 'ever closer union among the peoples of Europe' (Article 1 TEU), and to promote peace and well-being of its citizens (Article 3 TEU).

The comparative law method is useful in order to interpret EU law in the 'best' way possible. Here, national law is used as a source to find out where this 'best law' can be found. The 'best law' needs to be balanced and it needs to fit with the context of EU legal system.[152] In this way the comparative law method is a tool for teleological interpretation, which can be seen as the prevailing method of interpretation of EU law also because of the plurality of languages and legal traditions, and the conceptual problems arising from this plurality. Teleological interpretation in the context of EU law guarantees uniform application at the national level better than for example literal interpretation. Comparative law method, and the references to the general principles of law common to the Member States, increases the legitimacy of an interpretation, because the legitimacy of EU law 'ultimately rests on the peoples of Europe and their mutual legal orders'.[153] This dependency of legitimacy, meaning that in order for the EU law to function effectively the Member States need to accept it as legitimate, is expressed in the principle of the Member States as the Masters of the Treaties and in Article 50 TEU concerning voluntary withdrawal from the Union (more on this topic in Chap. 4.2.1).

The interrelationship between textual and teleological interpretation was at hand in *CILFIT*. The CJEU stated that the EU has several official languages and that each language version is equally authentic. Thus comparison between different language versions is essential while interpreting EU law. The Court also noted that EU law 'uses terminology which is peculiar to it' and thus the meaning of concepts might vary depending on whether they are used in EU law context or in national law context. The significance of teleological interpretation side-by-side textual interpretation is emphasized. The CJEU stated that 'every provision of Community law must be placed in its *context* and interpreted in the light of the provisions of *Community law as a whole*, regard being had to the *objectives* thereof and to its *state of evolution* at the date on which the provision in question is to be applied (emphasis added).'[154]

---

[150] See, for example, Opinion 1/91 Opinion of the Court of 14 December 1991. Opinion delivered pursuant to the second subparagraph of Article 228 (1) of the Treaty—Draft agreement between the Community, on the one hand, and the countries of the European Free Trade Association, on the other, relating to the creation of the European Economic Area, paras 16–20.

[151] Ibid.

[152] Maduro (2007), pp. 1, 6–9.

[153] Ibid., pp. 1, 6–9.

[154] Case C-283/81 *Srl CILFIT and Lanificio di Gavardo SpA v Ministry of Health* [1982] ECR p. 3415, paras 18–20.

When comparing different language versions the main rule is that all of them have equal weight. That weight of importance cannot vary depending on how many people use the language, for example. Provisions of EU law ought to be 'interpreted and applied in the light of the versions existing in the other official languages'.[155] If all other language versions are equivalent and only one differs from all the others, the Court has not given precedence to the one differing language version.[156] The CJEU has stated that 'the different language versions of a community text must be given a uniform interpretation and hence in the case of divergence between the versions the provision in question must be interpreted by reference to the purpose and general scheme of the rules of which it forms a part'.[157] The CJEU gives emphasis to the objective and purpose of the provision when the comparison of different language versions cannot give a clear answer, meaning that teleological interpretation is decisive in these kinds of situations.[158] Otherwise, there is no hierarchy between the methods of interpretation of EU law.[159] Teleological and contextual interpretation can be seen as necessary to attain substantive legal certainty and predictability because the literal interpretation has proved to be quite challenging within the multilingual EU, where in addition to the general vagueness of language the different language versions can turn out to be contradictory.[160]

In the field of criminal law, literal interpretation has a pronouncedly strong place among the different methods of interpretation because of the principle of legality. Nevertheless, language nearly always leaves room for interpretation. Teleological interpretation is possible in every circumstance as long as the interpretation is possible within the wording of the penal provision. Because criminal liability cannot be determined or aggravated solely based on directives or framework decisions, EU criminal law operates through national penal provisions. Thus, a contextual teleological interpretation of EU criminal law can be made within the wording of national penal provisions. This means that there is less room for contextual teleological interpretation in the field of criminal law, than in the other fields of EU-influenced law in which the principle of strict construction does not play such a strong role.

---

[155] Case C-296/95 *The Queen v Commissioners of Customs and Excise, ex parte EMU Tabac SARL, The Man in Black Ltd, John Cunningham* [1998] ECR p. I-1605, para 36. See also Arnull (2006), p. 609.

[156] Joined cases C-283/94, C-291/94 and C-292/94 *Denkavit International BV, VITIC Amsterdam BV and Voormeer BV v Bundesamt für Finanzen* [1996] ECR p. I-5063, para 25. See also Arnull (2006), p. 609.

[157] Case C-30/77 *Régina v Pierre Bouchereau* [1977] ECR p. 1999, para 14.

[158] Arnull (2006), p. 610.

[159] Ibid., pp. 614–617. For example, in the case of *RTL Television* the Court used several methods of interpretation (literal interpretation, comparative method, *travaux préparatoires,* and teleological interpretation) and is therefore good in pedagogical sense to illustrate the Court's use of different methods of interpretation. [Case C-245/01 *RTL Television GmbH v Niedersächsische Landesmedienanstalt für privaten Rundfunk* [2003] ECR p. I-12489, paras 97–99. See also Arnull (2006), p. 616].

[160] Paunio and Lindroos-Hovinheimo (2010), pp. 395, 397.

Travaux préparatoires of the Treaties[161]

According to the VCLT, *travaux préparatoires* can be used as a tool to confirm or to discover the purpose and meaning of a Treaty provision. However, the status of the *travaux préparatoires* of the EU Treaties has not been entirely clear. Recent case law of the CJEU provides some further detail. The literature has not said much about their status as a source of law, and only very recently has the CJEU commented on the issue. Earlier, it has only sometimes referred to the *travaux préparatoires* in relation to secondary Community/Union acts. Since the status of the *travaux préparatoires* of the EU Treaties affects to what kinds of conclusion can be drawn on the issues that are examined in this work (choice of legal basis of substantive criminal legislation, the Union's accession to the ECHR and the legitimation of the use of criminal law at the EU-level), it is necessary to establish how the *travaux préparatoires* of the Treaties can affect the interpretation of EU primary law.

Literature does not say much about the status of the *travaux préparatoires* of the Treaties as a legal source, other than that the CJEU has not really used them as source of interpretation.[162] As a main rule, the contextual and teleological interpretation methods set limits to textual interpretation, which can be explained at least partly by the problems arising from the multilingualism in the EU. Also the linguistic expressions in the treaties can be somewhat ambiguous due to the Member States' need to have been able to achieve a consensus on the wording and the content of the provisions.[163] Sometimes the contextual and teleological methods can even override the natural textual meaning of the treaty provisions.[164] The *travaux préparatoires* of the Treaties, at least those of the original treaties, are not entirely published, indicating, as presented in the literature, that legal reasoning could not be based upon them.[165] This has been argued to mean that the Court's teleological or purposive interpretation has not been particularly oriented in historical developments, but rather on the context of the treaty provisions as a whole in which the particular treaty provision works.[166]

The literature has made only a few references to the CJEU using the *travaux* of the Treaties in its case law. There are two cases[167] in which the Court is argued to

---

[161] This chapter draws on ideas first published in Miettinen and Kettunen (2015), pp. 145–167.

[162] Piris (2006), pp. 38–55; Arnull (2006), pp. 612–615.

[163] Arnull (2006), p. 612.

[164] Case C-314/85 *Foto-Frost v Hauptzollamt Lübeck-Ost* [1987] ECR p. 4199, paras 16–17; Arnull (2006), p. 613.

[165] Arnull (2006), p. 614; Lenaerts and Van Nuffel (2011), p. 815; Craig and de Búrca (2015), pp. 63–64.

[166] Craig and de Búrca (2015), p. 64.

[167] Case C-149/79 *Commission of the European Communities v Kingdom of Belgium* [1980] ECR p. 3881; Joined cases T-134/94, T-136/94, T-137/94, T-138/94, T-141/94, T-145/94, T-147/94, T-148/94, T-151/94, T-156/94 and T-157/94 *NMH Stahlwerke GmbH, Eurofer ASBL, Arbed SA, Cockerill-Sambre SA, Thyssen Stahl AG, Unimétal - Société française des aciers longs SA, Krupp Hoesch Stahl AG, Preussag Stahl AG, British Steel plc, Siderurgica Aristrain Madrid SL and Empresa Nacional Siderurgica SA v Commission of the European Communities* [1996] ECR p. II-537.

have used the *travaux* of the Treaties as a source of law in its historically-oriented teleological interpretation. However, the cases, are not relevant in assessing the question at hand. One of the cases simply does not refer to the *travaux* of the Treaties,[168] and in the other case the reference to the *travaux* is not made by the Court but instead by the applicant.[169] A search conducted in the CURIA database revealed that in several cases the parties of the cases have relied on the intention of the constitutional legislator that can be constructed from the *travaux* of the primary law.[170] In most of these cases the Court has not utilized the *travaux* in its reasoning, until recently.

The use the *travaux préparatoires* as a source of interpretation when interpreting EU primary law relates to the more general issue of constitutional interpretation. There are many institutions and organs that interpret the constitution. However, only certain organs exercise authoritative constitutional interpretation, meaning that their interpretation of the constitution prevails over the possibly diverging views of the other institutions. There are two kinds of organs for authoritative interpretation: those which exercise *abstract* constitutional review *ex ante* before the legislation is promulgated, and those which exercise *concrete* case-by-case constitutional review *ex post* after the legislation has come into force.

There are different kinds of organs and institutions exercising constitutional review; those which exercise it *ex ante* such as the French Conseil Constitutionnel or the Finnish Constitutional Law Committee of the Parliament, and those exercising it *ex post*, like supreme courts or constitutional courts. They are both juridical and political organs since constitutional law is highly political.[171] The authoritative organs exercising constitutional review exercise political power in the sense that they solve policy disputes through the interpretation of constitutional law. The question to be asked is therefore whether the authoritative organs exercising constitutional review ought to take the purpose of the constitutional provisions and the intent of the constitutional legislator into account in their interpretation.

This relates to the question whether the constitution ought to be interpreted from the perspective of originalism or from that of living constitutionalism. First these concepts need to be defined. Even though the concepts are found mostly in American constitutional theory they can be useful in conceptualizing European, particularly EU, constitutional theory. Several orientations of originalism can be identified, that

---

[168] Joined cases T-134/94, T-136/94, T-137/94, T-138/94, T-141/94, T-145/94, T-147/94, T-148/94, T-151/94, T-156/94 and T-157/94 *NMH Stahlwerke GmbH, Eurofer ASBL, Arbed SA, Cockerill-Sambre SA, Thyssen Stahl AG, Unimétal - Société française des aciers longs SA, Krupp Hoesch Stahl AG, Preussag Stahl AG, British Steel plc, Siderurgica Aristrain Madrid SL and Empresa Nacional Siderurgica SA v Commission of the European Communities* [1996] ECR p. II-537, para 40.

[169] Case C-149/79 *Commission of the European Communities v Kingdom of Belgium* [1980] ECR p. 3881.

[170] See for example, Case C-264/81 *SpA Savma v Commission of the European Communities* [1984] ECR p. 3915.

[171] Stone Sweet (2007), pp. 69, 72. On the status of the Finnish Constitutional Law Committee, see, Kolehmainen (2008), p. 165.

of the intention of the framers or ratifiers, original applications originalism and original meaning originalism to mention a few.[172] Original meaning originalism can be divided further into two categories. Skyscraper originalism sees the constitutions as a finished product that guides future legislation. Framework originalism views the constitutions as frameworks for governance that are then slowly over time complemented to fit the existing societal and political circumstances. According to the skyscraper originalism, amendments are the only way to change the constitution, whereas the framework originalism allows constitutional construction by the judiciaries. Even though also in framework originalism the judges need to take into account the constitution's original meaning, the judges have certain discretion relative to it.[173]

Living constitutionalism refers to interpretation as construction rather than as interpretation as ascertainment. This kind of construction through judiciaries or political institutions is needed when the Constitution is vague or silent on issues, or institution building is necessary in fulfilling the purposes the constitution sets.[174] Living constitutionalism is associated with framework originalism since framework originalism leaves room for future constitutional construction that could be developed through living constitutionalism.[175]

The EU has only one authoritative organ exercising constitutional review, the CJEU, which exercises mainly concrete *ex post* constitutional review. This means that the EU does not have any authoritative institution that could evaluate the constitutionality of Union legislative acts in abstract *ex ante*. Such an institution would be very useful in evaluating the appropriateness of the choice of legal basis of legislative acts for example. The CJEU can, however, give an opinion as to whether an agreement that the Union is making with third countries or an international organisation is compatible with the EU Treaties before the agreement is concluded.[176]

There are two ways of *ex ante* control in the EU legislative framework concerning criminal law: subsidiarity control by national parliaments and the emergency brake procedure. Both of these *ex ante* controls are exercised at national level by national authorities and they are *not* authoritative in interpreting *Union law*. Instead, they interpret national law vis-à-vis Union law. The subsidiarity control is not a very strong procedural hindrance to the legislative work. The emergency brake procedure on the other hand is strong*er* procedural hindrance, but it is not entirely clear if the CJEU can evaluate the appropriateness of the claims made under the emergency brake procedure (more on this in Chap. 5.2.4).

---

[172] Fleming (2012), pp. 1171, 1174–1175.

[173] Balkin (2009), pp. 549, 550–551. On the role of the original/framers' intent in interpretation, see e.g. Redish and Arnould (2012), p. 1485; Raz (1999).

[174] Balkin (2009), pp. 549, 559–560.

[175] Ibid. p. 560.

[176] Article 218(11) TFEU.

The VCLT,[177] particularly articles 31 and 32, set the rules of interpretation of international treaties. According to Article 31 VCLT,[178] the terms of the treaty should be given the ordinary meaning in their context and be interpreted in the light of its object and purpose. The purpose of the treaty can be found from the text, the preamble, and the annexes. Article 32 VCLT[179] contains that the preparatory work of the treaty can be used as *supplementary* means of interpretation *to confirm* or *determine* the meaning, or when the interpretation according to Article 31 VCLT either leaves the meaning ambiguous or obscure or leads to a result which is manifestly absurd or unreasonable. The *ratio legis*, or the object and purpose as it is put in the Article 31, is given a decisive role on how a treaty provision ought to be interpreted. The *travaux préparatoires* can be used to determine or to confirm the meaning of the provision.

The object of interpretation is the text of the treaties. The interpretation of the text starts from intuitively assuming the 'ordinary meaning' of the text. After this, supplementary means of interpretation can be used to confirm or revise this original assumption or hypothesis. Preparatory works can have influence in the interpretation through four routes: if the meaning of text is left ambiguous (article 32.a), if the interpretation would leave to manifestly absurd or unreasonable result (article 32.b), if the parties have intended to give a term a special meaning (article 31.4), or merely to confirm the meaning resulting from the application of article 31 (article 32). The last mentioned means, the confirmation of textual and contextual interpretation, is

---

[177] Vienna Convention on the Law of Treaties (adopted 23 May 1969, entered into force 27 January 1980) 1155 UNTS 331.

[178] Article 31. *General rule of interpretation*. 1. A treaty shall be interpreted in good faith in accordance with the ordinary meaning to be given to the terms of the treaty in their context and in the light of its object and purpose.

2. The context for the purpose of the interpretation of a treaty shall comprise, in addition to the text, including its preamble and annexes:

(a) Any agreement relating to the treaty which was made between all the parties in connexion with the conclusion of the treaty;

(b) Any instrument which was made by one or more parties in connexion with the conclusion of the treaty and accepted by the other parties as an instrument related to the treaty.

3. There shall be taken into account, together with the context:

(a) Any subsequent agreement between the parties regarding the interpretation of the treaty or the application of its provisions;

(b) Any subsequent practice in the application of the treaty which establishes the agreement of the parties regarding its interpretation;

(c) Any relevant rules of international law applicable in the relations between the parties.

4. A special meaning shall be given to a term if it is established that the parties so intended.

[179] Article 32. *Supplementary means of interpretation*. Recourse may be had to supplementary means of interpretation, including the preparatory work of the treaty and the circumstances of its conclusion, in order to confirm the meaning resulting from the application of article 31, or to determine the meaning when the interpretation according to article 31:

(a) Leaves the meaning ambiguous or obscure; or

(b) Leads to a result which is manifestly absurd or unreasonable.

interesting in the sense that it opens the possibility to rely on the *travaux prépara-toires* practically in every case of interpretation.[180]

The applicability of the VCLT has two dimensions in the EU context. The Court has found that some provisions of the VCLT bind the EU institutions and form a part of the EU legal order as rules of customary international law.[181] This means, *inter alia*, that the EU institutions need to respect the rules of interpretation stipulated in the VCLT when they *are interpreting international treaties*. However, the VCLT does not apply to the interpretation *of the EU law itself*. The CJEU has found that the EU law is not ordinary international law, but something else instead.[182] As explained above, even though the VCLT is not a legal source of interpretation of EU law, similar rules of interpretation as those of the VCLT are recognized by the CJEU in *Van Gend en Loos* judgment.[183]

Recently the CJEU has used the *travaux préparatoires* of the Treaties as a means of interpretation in its case law in trying to establish the *ratio legis* of the Treaty provisions.[184] A comprehensive search made in Curia database revealed how often the CJEU has referred to the *travaux préparatoires* of the Treaties in its case law.[185] The search was conducted in French to ensure that every relevant case was included in the list of results, and to make the search easier since then the search could be run through with the term of '*travaux préparatoires*', to which there are several English equivalents, such as preparatory work, works, *travaux préparatoires*, intent or objective pursued by the Treaties etc. The search covers the entire EU and EC law history.

---

[180] Mortenson (2013), pp. 780, 785–787.

[181] Case C-386/08 *Firma Brita GmbH v Hauptzollamt Hamburg-Hafen* [2010] ECR p. I-1289, para 42; Case C-466/11 *Gennaro Currà and Others v Bundesrepublik Deutschland* [2012], para 22.

[182] Opinion 1/91 Opinion of the Court of 14 December 1991. Opinion delivered pursuant to the second subparagraph of Article 228 (1) of the Treaty - Draft agreement between the Community, on the one hand, and the countries of the European Free Trade Association, on the other, relating to the creation of the European Economic Area.

[183] Case C-26/62 NV *Algemene Transport- en Expeditie Onderneming van Gend & Loos v Netherlands Inland Revenue Administration* [1963] ECR 00001. See also Maduro (2007), pp. 1, 4; Arnull (2006), pp. 612–613; Paunio and Lindroos-Hovinheimo (2010), pp. 395, 396.

[184] On the case law where the Court has used the *travaux préparatoires* of the Treaties in interpreting the Treaties, see Case C-61/03 *Commission of the European Communities v United Kingdom of Great Britain and Northern Ireland* [2005] ECR p. I-2477, para 25; Case C-370/12 *Thomas Pringle v Government of Ireland, Ireland and The Attorney General* [2012], paras 135–136; Case C-583/11 P *Inuit Tapiriit Kanatami and Others v European Parliament and Council of the European Union* [2013], paras 50, 59, 69; Case C-62/14 *Peter Gauweiler and Others v Deutscher Bundestag* [2015], paras. 98–100; Case C-286/14 *European Parliament v European Commission* [2016]. On the Court's use of *travaux préparatoires* of the secondary legislation, see Arnull (2006), pp. 614–615; Miettinen (2013c), pp. 99, 106.

[185] Curia search in French with the term "travaux préparatoires", no time limits, Documents = Documents publiés au Recueil : Arrêts - Ordonnances - Avis - Décisions (procédure de réexamen), Documents non publiés au Recueil : Arrêts - Ordonnances (Toutes) - Décisions (procédure de réexamen) and with terms "travaux préparatoires" or "traite", within 1 year, the same documents.

Five relevant cases were found in which the Court refers to the *travaux* of the Treaties. Even though the number is small, their appearance is recent and frequent, meaning that these cases reflect an entirely new line in the Court's jurisprudence. Even though the older preparatory works of the Treaties might not have been widely reported or published,[186] by contrast, the *travaux préparatoires* of the more recent Treaty amendments, such as the Constitutional Treaty (even though it did not come in force) and the Lisbon Treaty, are rather well documented and published. Perhaps the proper publication of the *travaux* gives the CJEU a proper mandate to use them as a source of law, as the *EURATOM, Pringle, Inuit Tapiriit Kanatami, Gauweiler, and European Parliament v European Commission* cases demonstrate.

Before going through the relevant cases in detail, it is worth mentioning that the search also showed that there is another type of group of cases where the Court has used the *travaux* of the primary law to interpret it: the acts concerning the conditions of accession to the Union.[187] Even though in these cases the Court interprets primary law by using its preparatory works, this group of cases differs from the relevant cases in that the Court does not interpret the TEU or TFEU or their predecessors. Nevertheless, this group of cases still demonstrates that the Court uses preparatory works to primary law in its interpretation of that primary law.[188] Also, Article 52(7) of the Charter explicitly states that the explanations of the Charter of Fundamental Rights ought to be taken into account in the interpretation of the Charter.

The five cases in which the Court refers to the *travaux préparatoires* are fairly recent. The first of this line of judgments was given in 2005 and was about whether the military uses of nuclear energy could fall within the scope of the EURATOM Treaty.[189] The Court first noted that articles 1 EA and 2 EA indicate that the Treaty objective is essentially civil and commercial, but that since the treaty provisions did not expressly exclude the military purposes it is essential to interpret the issue taking into account factors other than the text itself.[190] Then the Court stated that taking into account the historical background of the Treaty is not sufficient, but nevertheless the CJEU took into account the *travaux préparatoires* which indicated clearly that the Member States had differing views on the matter, and therefore the Treaty could not be seen to be intended to cover military uses of nuclear energy.[191] Then the Court used contextual and teleological methods to interpret the issue and concluded

---

[186] Miettinen and Kettunen (2015), pp. 145, 149–150.

[187] Search conducted in French with terms "travaux préparatoires, Acte d'adhésion", no time limit, documents include judgments, orders, opinion of the Court, decisions published in the ECR, and judgments, orders and decisions not published in the ECR.

[188] See for example Case T-493/93 *Hansa-Fisch GmbH v Commission of the European Communities* [1995] ECR p. II-575, paras 35–37; Case C-273/04 *Republic of Poland v Council of the European Union* [2007] ECR p. I-8925, para 57.

[189] Case C-61/03 *Commission of the European Communities v United Kingdom of Great Britain and Northern Ireland* [2005] ECR p. I-2477, para 25.

[190] Ibid. pp. 27–28.

[191] Ibid., para 29.

that 'the Treaty is not applicable to uses of nuclear energy for military purposes'.[192] In this case the Court began to build its argumentation starting from the historical interpretation concerning the intent of the Treaty's drafters. The reference to the *travaux* was not decisive factor in the argumentation; instead the traditional CJEU interpretation paradigm of contextual and teleological (purposive) interpretation of the text gained more impetus.

In the second case, the *Pringle* case, the CJEU referred to the *travaux* of the Maastricht Treaty, when it evaluated whether 'an agreement such as the ESM Treaty (the Treaty establishing the European stability mechanism) is in breach of the 'no bail-out clause' in Article 125 TFEU'.[193] First the Court used the textual method in interpreting the wording used in Article 125 TFEU, based on which the Court found that the article is not intended to prohibit granting of financial assistance to another Member State. Next the Court used contextual method, by referring to other articles concerning the economic policy, in particular Articles 122 TFEU and 123 TFEU, based on which it came to the same conclusion as that based on textual interpretation. Only third the Court examined the objective of Article 125 TFEU. In order to be able to state the objective, the Court looked into the preparatory works of the Maastricht Treaty, according to which 'it is apparent … that the aim of Article 125 TFEU is to ensure that the Member States follow a sound budgetary policy'. Thus the Court found that 'a stability mechanism such as the ESM is not compatible with Article 125 TFEU unless it is indispensable for the safeguarding of the financial stability of the euro area as a whole and subject to strict conditions' and that since 'the ESM and the Member States who participate in it are not liable for the commitments of a Member State which receives stability support and nor do they assume those commitments, within the meaning of Article 125 TFEU' it follows 'that Article 125 TFEU does not preclude either the conclusion by the Member States whose currency is the euro of an agreement such as the ESM Treaty or their ratification of it'.[194] In this case the *travaux préparatoires* had a decisive role in determining the question at hand, since the nature of the ESM mechanism was compared with the objective of the Article 125 TFEU, that was found from the *travaux*, to determine the appropriateness of the ESM mechanism.

In the third case, the *Inuit Tapiriit Kanatami* case, the CJEU refers to its previous judgment in the *Pringle* case, saying that the interpretation of EU law does not require only taking into account the wording and the objectives of EU law provisions, but also their context and EU law as a whole. In addition, the CJEU considered the origins of a provision 'may also provide information relevant to its interpretation'.[195] In evaluating whether 'the General Court committed errors in law in its examination of whether the contested regulation was of direct and individual

---

[192] Ibid., para 44.

[193] Case C-370/12 *Thomas Pringle v Government of Ireland, Ireland and The Attorney General* [2012], para 129.

[194] Ibid., paras 130–136, 146–147.

[195] Case C-583/11 P *Inuit Tapiriit Kanatami and Others v European Parliament and Council of the European Union* [2013], para 50.

concern' to the applicants, the Court first makes note that the second limb of the fourth paragraph of Article 263 TFEU corresponds to the second limb of the fourth paragraph of Article 230 EC. Then the Court states that the *authors of the Lisbon Treaty did not have intention* to alter 'the scope of the conditions of admissibility already laid down in the fourth paragraph of Article 230 EC'. Lastly the Court also noted that 'it is clear from the *travaux préparatoires* relating to Article III-365(4) of the proposed treaty establishing a Constitution for Europe that the scope of those conditions was not to be altered', concluding that therefore 'the General Court did not err in law applying the assessment criteria'.[196] In this case the Court made two important statements relative to the status of the *travaux* of the Treaties as a means of interpretation. Firstly, and most importantly, the Court explicitly stated in paragraph 50 of the judgment that the origins of a provision may also provide information relevant to the interpretation of EU law, including EU primary law. In stating this, the CJEU expressly accepts the utilization of the *travaux* of the Treaties as an interpretative aid and method. Since the Court also referred to the earlier Pringle case when stating this, it seems that the Court's intention is to start building a new line of interpretation method to the EU law. Secondly, the origins of Article 263 TFEU had a large impact in assessing the appropriateness of the General Court's judgment.

In the *Gauweiler* case[197] the request for a preliminary ruling concerned the validity of decisions of the Governing Council of the European Central Bank of 6 September 2012 on a number of technical features regarding the Eurosystem's outright monetary transactions in secondary sovereign bond markets ('the OMT decisions') and the interpretation of certain Treaty articles, including Article 123 TFEU.[198] When interpreting Article 123 TFEU, the CJEU referred to the *travaux* of the Maastricht Treaty. [199] First, the Court reviewed the wording of the article. This prohibits all financial assistance from the European System of Central Banks (the ESCB) to a Member State. However, it does not preclude the possibility of the ESCB purchasing bonds that were previously issued by a Member State from the creditors of the Member States. The Court then observes that 'the ESCB does not have authority to purchase government bonds on secondary markets under conditions which would, in practice, mean that its action has an effect equivalent to that of a direct purchase of government bonds from the public authorities and bodies of the Member States, thereby undermining the effectiveness of the prohibition in Article 123(1) TFEU'. To determine which kinds of purchases are compatible with Article 123(1) TFEU, the CJEU looked into the objective of that article. This objective was to encourage the Member States to follow a sound budgetary policy, and was found in the preparatory work to the Maastricht Treaty,[200] similarly as it found already previously in the Pringle case.

---

[196] Ibid., paras 70–71.

[197] Case C-62/14 *Gauweiler and others v Deutscher Bundestag* [2015].

[198] Ibid., para 1.

[199] Ibid., paras 99–100.

[200] Ibid., paras 93–100.

The most recent case C-286/14 concerned delegated acts. Article 290 TFEU establishes the Commission the competence either to adopt non-legislative acts of general application to supplement or to amend certain non-essential elements of the legislative act. In the case the Commission had done the latter, it had amended the Annex I to Regulation (EU) No 1316/2013 of the European Parliament and of the Council establishing the Connecting Europe Facility. The question was whether the Commission should have given the measure as a separate act that would have simply supplemented the given regulation.

The CJEU decided that due to the Commission's infringement of the rules of competence laid down in Article 290 TFEU, the Commission's contested regulation shall be annulled. The CJEU reasoned this by first looking at the provision of the Parliament's and Council's regulation where the delegation of power is established thus relying first to the contextual interpretation method.[201] Then the CJEU dealt with the issue of the two types of delegated powers laid down in Article 290 TFEU. The Court argued that the delegated power to supplement a legislative act is meant to authorize the Commission to flesh out that act whereas the delegated power to amend a legislative act authorizes the Commission to modify or repeal non-essential elements laid down by the legislature in an act. The Court stated that this interpretation is supported by the origins of Article 290 TFEU (the *travaux prépara-toires* relating to Article I-36 of the draft Treaty establishing a Constitution for Europe, the final report of Working Group IX on 'Simplification' of the European Convention of 29 November 2002, CONV 424/02, page 9). The Court even used the same exact wording that was used in that document.[202]

The Court's interpretation of the facts in the case was influenced by the *travaux préparatoires* of the Treaties. The *travaux* were used to determine that Article 290 TFEU in fact separates the two different types of delegated power and that the type of the delegated power must be determined in the act that gives the delegation of power. Here, the interpretation that relied on the *travaux* was static, it did not widen the delegated power laid down in Article 290 TFEU.

What impact have the Court's references to the *travaux préparatoires* of the Treaties had so far? Are the references restatements of the scope and meaning of the constitutional provisions (*ratio legis*) through intention of the constitutional legislator (the Member States as the Masters of the Treaties), or have they led to dynamic constitution building? The references to the *travaux préparatoires* of the Treaties made by Advocates General and the Court can be analysed and examined by using the following chart. This diagram identifies cases in which the CJEU has relied on the *travaux (these cases are highlighted in yellow)*. The Advocates General have relied on them more often than the Court itself.

---

[201] Case C-286/14 *European Parliament v European Commission* [2016], para 34 onwards.
[202] Ibid., paras. 40–46.

	Static – Aims to state the *original purpose*	Dynamic – Aims to fill gaps or otherwise *construct the* *constitution*
VCLT: '… to *confirm* the meaning …'	*Group 1: static/* *ascertaining* Trivial references: AG in C-427/12 AG in C-274/11 AG in C-95/12 Ascertaining references: AG in C-274/12 P AG in C-270/12 AG in C-114/12 AG in C-202/11	*Group 3: (hypothetical)*
VCLT: '…to *determine* the meaning, when meaning [would otherwise be] ambiguous or obscure, absurd or unreasonable'	*Group 2: static/extra* *value* References to clarify ambiguous meanings: **AG in C-61/03** **(EURATOM)** **AG in C-370/12** **(Pringle)** **AG in C-583/11 P** **(Inuit)** **AG in C-62/14** **(Gauweiler)**	*Group 4: dynamic/change* References to propose a constitutional construction by interpretation: AG in Joined Cases C-103/12 and C-165/12 (to fill a 'constitutional gap') **AG in C-286/14 (European** **Parliament v European** **Commission)**

Firstly, the Advocate Generals have referred to the *travaux* in a manner that only ascertains something that can be read from the text of the Treaties themselves, but if the reference to the *travaux* has not brought any extra value to the argumentation by clarifying ambiguous meanings of the Treaty provisions, the CJEU has not made references to them (in the above chart, Group 1 static/ascertaining).

Secondly, in Joined cases C-103/12 and C-165/12, AG Sharpston tried to fill a gap in the Treaties by proposing a dynamic Treaty interpretation. This would expand the Union's external competence through teleology and reference to the *travaux* (in the chart, Group 4 dynamic/change). In this case, the CJEU did not extend the Union's international competence in general nor did it make a reference to the *travaux*. Instead it merely concluded that the Union had the necessary competence in that particular case under the substantive decision-making power.

Third, the Advocates General have relied on the *travaux* in a static manner in order to determine the meaning and purpose of a Treaty provision (in the chart, Group 2 static/extra value). In these cases the Advocates General have made rather conservative references to the travaux, references that have had some extra value in their argumentation. In these cases, the Court itself has also referred to the *travaux*.

Maybe the most interesting use of the *travaux* is in the opinion of AG Jääskinen in C-286/14. In his opinion, AG Jääskinen first refers to the *travaux* but, contrary to the Court's later ruling, does not see the meaning of the difference of the two different types of delegated powers.[203] AG concludes that 'the legislature may leave it to the Commission's discretion whether to supplement or amend the basic act'.[204] Later, in its ruling, the CJEU argued based on the *travaux,* and to ensure the transparency of the legislative process, that Article 290 TFEU 'requires the legislature to determine the nature of the delegation that it intends to confer on the Commission'.[205] The conclusion of the AG was clearly more dynamic, whereas the CJEU's conclusion on the matter was much more static and stagnant because the Court's interpretation did not grant any wider powers or competence to the Commission than what the Article 290 TFEU and its *travaux préparatoires* establish. This means that the Court has made only static references to the *travaux.*

Since the Court has made only static references to the *travaux,* the *travaux* have not been used by the Court to reason interpretations that would entail dynamic primary law-building. This differs from the Court's general line of teleological jurisprudence which is highly dynamic.[206] In the context of interpreting EU primary law, it is understandable that the CJEU has used the *travaux* in a static manner since constitutions and constitutional law are usually meant to have stronger stability and fixity than statutory legislation. Also taking into account that the *travaux* of the Treaties are mainly used to ascertain the meaning or objective of the Treaty provision under interpretation, it is natural that the Court's interpretations based on the *travaux* have been conservative.

The CJEU uses different interpretation methods. It bases its reasoning on linguistic (textual), systematic (contextual) and teleological argumentation, as well as arguments from intention. Textual interpretation is a natural starting point for interpretation. Systemic arguments are used to interpret the provisions in question coherently with the EU legal system. Teleological arguments mean arguments on the purpose of the legal norms, their place in the overall legal structure and the effects of the chosen interpretation. The Court also refers to meta-purposes of the EU legal system, those of effectiveness, uniformity, protection of individual rights and legal certainty, for example. The arguments of intentions or *ratio legis* are close to systemic and teleological arguments because they can be used to justify the last-mentioned arguments. Since different interpretation methods can lead to different results, meta-rules concerning the interrelationship between these methods are necessary.[207] In *CILFIT*, the CJEU first explains the importance of the textual interpretation and then finds that Union law needs to be interpreted also in light of the contextual, systematic and teleological arguments.[208] Thus the linguistic

---

[203] AG Jääskinen in C-286/14, paras. 37–70.

[204] Ibid., para. 68.

[205] Case C-286/14 *European Parliament v European Commission* [2016], para. 46.

[206] Miettinen and Kettunen (2015) pp. 145–167.

[207] Komárek (2015), pp. 28–51, 45–49.

[208] Case C-283/81 *Srl CILFIT and Lanificio di Gavardo SpA v Ministry of Health* [1982] ECR p. 3415, paras 18–20.

argumentation method ought to have priority, supported by systemic and teleological interpretation.[209]

In the past, the CJEU, or the Advocates General for that matter, have not really given weight to the intention of the authors of the Treaties in the context of interpretation of EU primary law, but emphasized the spirit, the general scheme and the wording of the Treaties instead.[210] However, it is clear that during the recent years the Advocates General have actively started to base their argumentation on the *travaux* of the Treaties. The CJEU has indeed used the *travaux* of the Treaties as a basis of its argumentation in approximately a quarter of the cases in which an Advocate General had referred to them. In these cases, the CJEU has referred to the *travaux* as it refers to any other sources of law. References to the *travaux* are used to support historical (as was in the *EURATOM* case) or teleological purposive (as in the cases of *Pringle*, *Inuit* and *Gauweiler*) arguments. The Court has also referred to the *travaux* only when it has been necessary to find the *ratio legis* when textual interpretation led to unsatisfactory results. In general, the text and the *travaux* are used to form a picture of the *ratio legis*, the purpose and goal of the norms in question. The *travaux* do not only tell what the intention of the constitutional legislator was, they also tell more abstractly what the *ratio legis*, the purpose, scope, meaning and goal, of the norm in question is. The purpose of legislation is not an expression of someone's will, but rather a rational construction with the support of the legal preparatory work. Thus the *travaux*, together with other sources, can be used to construct the *ratio legis*. In this way, the interpretation relying on the *travaux* does not aim to construct the subjective will of the persons participating in the legislative process. Instead, such an interpretation aims to construct an objective and reasoned picture of the *ratio legis*.[211]

Because the different methods of interpretation are overlapping, it is difficult to distinguish interpretation relying on the *travaux* from the other methods of interpretation, in particular from historical or teleological interpretation. In addition to referring to the *travaux* of the Treaties, the Court has referred to the *travaux* of primary law in relation to the interpretation of the Member States' accession treaties. Not many references have as yet been made in the literature to this new method of interpretation. The few references that can be found deal with the matter only briefly. Some argue that the *travaux* could be used to support teleological

---

[209] Komárek (2015), pp. 28–51, 49.

[210] For example, Advocate General Roemer referred to the intention of the authors of the Treaties multiple times in his opinion in *Van Gend en Loos* as an argument against the direct effect of an Treaty provision (Case C- 26/62 *NV Algemene Transport- en Expeditie Onderneming van Gend & Loos v Netherlands Inland Revenue Administration* [1963] ECR p. 1, Opinion of AG Roemer 19–24). The CJEU did not refer to the intention nor the travaux of the Treaties in its judgment (Case C-26/62 *Van Gend en Loos* [1963] ECR 00001, pp. 12–13). In 1974, Advocate General Mayras even stated that all recourse to the preparatory work of the Treaties is excluded. See Case C-2/74 *Jean Reyners v Belgian State* [1974] ECR p. 631, Opinion of AG Mayras 666.

[211] Peczenik (1995), pp. 242–245; Peczenik (1989), pp. 406–407.

arguments,[212] and some say that the Court's argumentation gains legitimacy when the Court relies to the *travaux*.[213]

This work claims that reliance on the *travaux* enhances legitimacy also from the perspective of the Union's legislature when it is enacting criminal legislation. For example, when the choice of legal basis for criminal legislation is also considered from the perspective of the purpose and *ratio* of the legal basis, the legislative measure gains more legitimacy. If the *travaux préparatoires* of the Treaties are accessible, they can be used as a source of interpretation by the CJEU, and by researches and other actors as well. The *travaux* illustrate the *ratio* and purpose of the constitutional legislator, the Member States, and how and in what scope the autonomy of the Member States is meant to be limited.[214] As Beck argues, the Member States remain sovereign because the shift of competence limits their autonomy and not sovereignty. Article 50 TEU acknowledges this by stating that any Member State may withdraw from the Union in accordance with its own constitutional requirements. If cooperation does not respect the limits set for it, the Member States can, in extreme situations, even withdraw themselves from the Union. In the context of the approximation of substantive criminal law, the Member States have the possibility to rely on the emergency brake procedure, another mechanism to protect the Member States' sovereignty.

If not in other ways, the *travaux préparatoires* should be given emphasis in situations where the *travaux* indicate clearly that the primary law provision *ought* or *ought not* to be applied in certain situations. Thus far the CJEU has not relied on the *travaux préparatoires* of the Treaties when interpreting criminal law-related cases. However, taken into account that criminal law measures are highly intrusive to those individuals they are imposed to, and the principle of legality which demands strict interpretation of criminal legislation as well as the principle of *ultima ratio*, the *travaux préparatoires* of the Treaties ought not be utilised to support dynamic interpretations of the Union's substantive criminal law competence that would widen the scope or nature of the Union's substantive criminal law competence. The *travaux préparatoires* concerning the Union's substantive criminal law competence in addition to the Court's new interpretation method also support this kind of restrictive interpretation. This new method of interpretation is utilized in analysing whether substantive criminal legislation could be based on implicit legal bases (especially Chap. 3.7.3 and Chaps. 5.2.1.1 to 5.2.1.7) and in analysing the Union's accession to the ECHR (Chap. 5.1).

---

[212] Kornezov (2014), pp. 251, 257–258.

[213] Koedooder (2013), pp. 111, 123.

[214] On the idea of separating between autonomy and sovereignty, see, Beck (2002), pp. 39, 48–49.

References

A dictionary of modern legal usage (1995) OUP
Alexy R (2002) The argument from injustice: a reply to legal positivism. OUP
Arai-Takahashi Y (2002) The margin of appreciation doctrine and the principle of proportionality in the jurisprudence of the ECHR (Intersentia 2002)
Arnull A (2006) The European Union and its Court of Justice, 2nd edn. OUP
Ashworth A (2009) Principles of criminal law, 6th edn. OUP
Asp P (2012) The substantive criminal law competence of the EU (Stiftelsen Skrifter utgivna av Juridiska fakulteten vid Stockholms universitet). Jure
Avbelj M (2011) Supremacy or primacy of EU law – (why) does it matter? Eur Law J 17(6)
Balkin JM (2009) Framework originalism and the living constitution. Northwest Univ Law Rev 103(2)
Beck U (2002) The terrorist threat: world risk society revisited. Theory Cult Soc 19(4)
Boister N (2003) Transnational criminal law? Eur J Int Law 14(5)
Brauch AJ (2005) The margin of appreciation and the jurisprudence of the European Court of Human Rights: threat to the rule of law. Columbia J Eur Law 11
Cairney P (2012) Understanding public policy: theories and issues. Palgrave MacMillan
Christiansen T (2016) Governance in the European Union. In: Cini M, Borragán NP-S (eds) European Union politics, 5th edn. OUP
Craig P (2001) Constitutions, constitutionalism, and the European Union. Eur Law J 7(2)
Craig P, de Búrca G (2015) EU law: text, cases, and materials, 6th edn. OUP
Cryer R et al. (2011) Research methodologies in EU and International law (Hart Publishing 2011)
de Búrca G, Scott J (2006) Introduction. In: de Búrca G, Scott J (eds) Law and new governance in the EU and the US. Hart Publishing
de la Rasilla del Moral I (2006) The increasingly marginal appreciation of the margin-of-appreciation doctrine. German Law J 7(6)
de Wet E (2008) The reception process in the Netherlands and Belgium. In: Keller H, Sweet AS (eds) A Europe of rights – the impact of the ECHR on national legal systems. OUP
Duff RA, Green SP (2011) Introduction: searching for foundations. In: Duff RA, Green SP (eds) Philosophical foundations of criminal law. OUP
Fleming JE (2012) Living originalism and living consitutionalism as moral readings of the American constitution. Boston Univ Law Rev 92
Fuller L (1958) Positivism and fidelity to law – a reply to professor Hart. Harv Law Rev 71(4)
Galli F, Weyembergh A (eds) (2013) Approximation of substantive criminal law in the EU: The way forward (Editions de l'Universite de Bruxelles 2013)
Greer S (2006) The European Convention on Human Rights: achievements, problems and prospects. Clarendon University Press
Griffiths J (1986) What is legal pluralism? J Leg Pluralism Unoff Law 24
Grimm D (2010) The achievement of constitutionalism and its prospects in a changed world. In: Petra D, Martin L (eds) The twilight of constitutionalism? OUP
Halberstam D (2012) Local, global and plural constitutionalism. In: de Búrca G, Weiler JHH (eds) The worlds of European constitutionalism. CUP
Hart HLA (1958) Positivism and the separation of law and morals. Harv Law Rev 71(4)
Herlin-Karnell E (2012) The constitutional dimension of European criminal law. Hart Publishing
Hill M (2013) The public policy process, 6th edn. Pearson
Hirvonen A (2012) Post-positivist legal theory: the dual nature of law. In: Nuotio K, Melander S, Huomo-Kettunen M (eds) Introduction to Finnish law and legal culture. University of Helsinki, Forum Iuris
Huomo-Kettunen M (2014a) EU criminal policy at a crossroads between effectiveness and traditional restraints for the use of criminal law. New J Eur Crim Law 5(3)
Huomo-Kettunen M (2014b) Kolmas tie – Euroopan unionin aineellisen rikosoikeuden toimivallan palasia SEUT 83 artiklan ulkopuolella? Lakimies 112(1)

Jääskinen N (2007) Euroopan unioni – Oikeudelliset perusteet. Talentum

Jacobs FG, White RCA, Ovey C (2010) The European Convention on Human Rights. OUP

Keller H, Stone Sweet A (2008) Assessing the impact of the ECHR on national legal systems. In: Keller H, Sweet AS (eds) A Europe of rights – the impact of the ECHR on national legal systems. OUP

Klip A (2016) European criminal law: an integrative approach, 3rd edn. Intersentia

Koedooder C (2013) The *Pringle* judgment: economic and/or monetary union. Fordham Int Law J 37(1)

Kolehmainen E (2008) Kuuluuko perustuslain tulkintatoimen teoriaan synteettisten tulkintapropositioiden välttämisen periaate? Business Law Forum, Helsingin yliopiston yksityisoikeuden laitoksen julkaisuja

Komárek J (2015) Legal reasoning in EU law. In: Arnull A, Chalmers D (eds) The Oxford handbook of EU law. Oxford handbooks in law. OUP

Kornezov A (2014) Shaping the new architecture of the EU system of judicial remedies: comment on *Inuit*. Eur Law Rev 2

Krisch N (2007) The open architecture of European human rights law, LSE law, society, and economy working papers 11/2007, London School of Economics and Political Science Law Department 15

Krisch N (2012) The case for pluralism in the postnational law. In: de Búrca G, Weiler JHH (eds) The worlds of European constitutionalism. CUP

Lambert Abdelgawad E, Weber A (2008) The reception process in France and Germany. In: Keller H, Sweet AS (eds) A Europe of rights – the impact of the ECHR on national legal systems. OUP

Lappi-Seppälä T (1994) Miksi rikosoikeus? In: Hirvonen A (ed) Kohti 2000-luvun rikosoikeutta. Helsingin yliopiston rikos- ja prosessioikeuden laitoksen julkaisuja A:8

Lenaerts K, Van Nuffel P (2011) In: Robert B, Nathan C (eds) European Union law. Sweet & Maxwell

Licková M (2008) European exeptionalism in international law. J Int Law 19(3)

Loughlin M (2010) What is constitutionalisation? In: Dober P, Loughlin M (eds) The twilight of constitutionalism? OUP

Maduro MP (2007) Interpreting European law: judicial adjudication in a context of constitutional pluralism. Eur J Leg Stud 1(2)

Melander S (2010) EU-rikosoikeus. WSOYpro

Melander S (2011) Europeiseringen av straffrätten och den nationella strafflagstiftningens "suveränitet". Tidskrift utgiven av Juridiska föreningen i Finland 147(3)

Melander S (2013) Ultima ratio in European criminal law. Oñati Socio-Leg Ser 3(1)

Menkel-Meadow C (2011) Why and how to study "transnational" law. UC Irvine Law Rev 1(1)

Michaels R (2016) Does Brexit spell the death of transnational law? German Law J 17 (Brexit Suppl)

Miettinen S (2013a) Criminal law and policy in the European Union. Routledge

Miettinen S (2013b) Implied ancillary criminal law competence after Lisbon. Eur Crim Law Rev 3(2)

Miettinen S (2013c) Onward transfer under the European Arrest Warrant: is the EU moving towards the free movement of prisoners? New J Eur Crim Law 4(1–2)

Miettinen S (2015) The Europeanization of criminal law: competence and its control in the Lisbon era. University of Helsinki

Miettinen S, Kettunen M (2015) *Travaux* to the EU treaties: preparatory work as a source of EU law. Camb Yearb Eur Leg Stud 17. https://doi.org/10.1017/cel.2015.6

Mortenson JD (2013) The travaux of travaux: is the Vienna convention hostile to drafting history? Am J Int Law 107

Nuotio K (2007) Criminal law of a transnational polity. In: Müller-Dietz H, Müller E, Kunz K-L, Radtke H, Britz G, Momsen C, Koriath H (eds) Festschrift für Heike Jung: zum 65. Geburtstag am 23. April 2007. Nomos

Nuotio K (2011) European criminal law under the developing constitutional setting of the European
    Union. In: Neil Walker – Jo Shaw – Stephen Tierney (eds) Europe's constitutional mosaic. Hart
    Publishing
Nuotio K (2014) European criminal law. In: Dubber MD, Hörnle T (eds) The Oxford handbook
    of criminal law. OUP
Öberg J (2014) Limits to EU powers: a case study on individual criminal sanctions for the enforce-
    ment of EU law. European University Institute
Paunio E, Lindroos-Hovinheimo S (2010) Taking language seriously: an analysis of linguistic
    reasoning in EU law. Eur Law J 16(4)
Peczenik A (1989) On law and reason. Kluwer Academic Publishers
Peczenik A (1995) Vad är rätt? Om demokrati, rättssäkerhet, etik och juridisk argumentation.
    Fritzes
Peczenik A (2005) Scientia Juris, legal doctrine as knowledge of law and as a source of law. In:
    Pattaro E (ed) A treatise of legal philosophy and general jurisprudence. Springer
Pellonpää M (2012) Euroopan ihmisoikeussopimus. Talentum
Peters A (2005) Global constitutionalism revisited. Int Leg Theory 11:39–41
Piris J-C (2006) The constitution for Europe: a legal analysis. CUP
Pitkänen M (2013) Euroopan ihmisoikeussopimuksen valtion positiiviset toimintavelvoitteet ja
    suhteellisuusperiaatteen huomioiminen. Lakimies 111(1)
Raz J (1999) Intention in interpretation. In: George RP (ed) The autonomy of law: essays on legal
    positivism. Oxford Scholarship Online
Redish MH, Arnould MB (2012) Judicial review, constitutional interpretation, and the democratic
    dilemma: proposing a 'constrolled activism' alternative. Fla Law Rev 64(6)
Rosas A, Armati L (2010) EU constitutional law: an introduction. Hart Publishing
Scheeck L (2006) The relationship between the European courts and integration through human
    rights. Zeitschrift für ausländisches öffentliches Recht und Völkerrecht 65
Schiff Berman P (2007) Global legal pluralism. South Calif Law Rev 80
Soriano MC (2008) The reception process in Spain and Italy. In: Keller H, Sweet AS (eds) A
    Europe of rights – the impact of the ECHR on national legal systems. OUP
Stone Sweet A (2007) The politics of constitutional review in France and Europe. Int J Const Law
    5(1)
Stone Sweet A (2009) Constitutionalism, legal pluralism, and international regimes. Indiana J
    Global Leg Stud 16(2)
Stone Sweet A (2012) The European Convention on Human Rights and national constitutional
    reordering. Cardozo Law Rev 33(5)
Teubner G (1991–1992) The two faces of janus: rethinking legal pluralism. Cardozo Law Rev 13
Thurnherr D (2008) The reception process in Austria and Switzerland. In: Keller H, Sweet AS
    (eds) A Europe of rights – the impact of the ECHR on national legal systems. OUP
Tulkens F (2011) The paradoxical relationship between criminal law and human rights. J Int Crim
    Justice 9
Tümay M (2008) The "margin of appreciation doctrine" developed by the case law of the European
    Court of Human Rights. Ankara Law Rev 5(2)
Tuori K (2002) Critical legal positivism. Ashgate
Tuori K (2008) Two challenges to normative legal scholarship. In: Wahlgren P (ed) Law and soci-
    ety. Stockholm Institute for Scandinavian Law: Jure, Scandinavian Studies of Law
Tuori K (2010) The many constitutions of Europe. In: Tuori K, Sankari S (eds) The many constitu-
    tions of Europe. Ashgate
Tuori K (2015) European constitutionalism. CUP
Van Hoecke M (2011) Legal doctrine: which method(s) for what kind of discipline? In: Van
    Hoecke M (ed) Methodologies of legal research: which kind of method for what kind of disci-
    pline? Hart Publishing

von Bogdandy A (2009) Founding principles. In: von Bogdandy A, Bast J (eds) Principles of
    European constitutional law, 2nd edn. Hart Publishing – Verlag CH Beck, reprinted in paper-
    back 2011
Walker N (2002) The idea of constitutional pluralism. Mod Law Rev 65(3)
Walker N (2003) Late sovereignty in the European Union. In: Walker N (ed) Sovereignty in transi-
    tion. Hart Publishing
Walker N (2008) Taking constitutionalism beyond the state. Polit Stud 56
Walker N, Tierney S (2011) Introduction: a constitutional mosaic? Exploring the new frontiers
    of Europe's constitutionalism. In: Walker N, Shaw J, Tierney S (eds) Europe's constitutional
    mosaic. Hart Publishing
Weiler JHH (1999) The Constitution of Europe. CUP
Wiklund O (2008) The reception process in Sweden and Norway. In: Keller H, Sweet AS (eds) A
    Europe of rights – the impact of the ECHR on national legal systems. OUP

Chapter 2
The Nature of Traditional Criminal Law

2.1 Criminal Law as an Expression of State Power and Sovereignty

Defining crime or criminal law is a difficult task. From a legalistic perspective, one could simply state that crime is conduct that is punishable by law. Building on such an approach, criminal law could be defined, in a circular manner, as 'a branch of law which deals with those acts, attempts and omissions of which the state may take cognisance by prosecution in the criminal courts'.[1] This kind of legalistic or positivistic definition does not say much about the nature of criminal law.

Criminal justice systems symbolise states' national identity and culture. Criminal law, as a part of public law, is a closed system. The parties of a criminal case cannot develop their own set of penal norms.[2] Penal provisions are societal norms because crime is seen to influence the society at large in addition to the victim. Because criminal law is in this way public law, the norms have to be fixed in advance and equal in all criminal cases. Criminal law needs to determine and publicly announce what types of conduct are prohibited, or required in some situations, in order to appropriately instruct not to engage in certain types of action or to instruct how to act in some types of situations. In this sense criminal law is about rule articulation. Criminal law thus gives individuals fair warning beforehand with the aim of preventing undesirable conduct.[3] The prevention can work either through deterrence in the sense that provisions of criminal law create a threat of punishment, or through positive general prevention in the sense that provisions of criminal law create or

---

[1] Farmer (1996), p. 58, citing Gordon's (1978), p. 15.

[2] Klip (2016), p. 40.

[3] Robinson (1994), pp. 857–858.

© Springer International Publishing Switzerland and G. Giappichelli Editore 2020
M. Kettunen, *Legitimizing European Criminal Law*, Comparative, European and International Criminal Justice 2, https://doi.org/10.1007/978-3-030-16174-3_2

strengthen morals or habits amongst the individuals. In this sense, the rule articulation function is also communicative in nature.

The criminal justice systems of the member states of the ECHR and the EU are
different. Even though individual provisions that state the essential elements of a
crime and the threat of punishment might seem equivalent at a first glance, norms of
the general part of the criminal justice system, such as norms concerning the
application of mitigating and aggravating circumstances, affect the application of
the individual crime provisions and often lead to outcomes that are different from
their severity.[4] The general part of criminal law consists of doctrines and generaliza-
tions of criminal law, some of which can be derived from the special part of criminal
law.[5] The general part of criminal law reflects the criminal law's function to determine and assess the conditions of criminal liability. The norms of the general part
determine justifications and defences as well as mitigating and aggravating circumstances. The courts then evaluate the blameworthiness of the offender and execute
the grading function in individual cases by assessing the relative seriousness of the
particular offence.[6]

The German Constitutional Court (later the GCC) has assessed the special nature
of criminal law in its so-called Lisbon judgment. Criminal law is seen as 'particularly sensitive' for the ability of a constitutional state to democratically shape itself'.[7]
Criminal law is highly culturally specific branch of law which is affected by historical developments and determined by language.[8] We can see that the GCC sees criminal law as a key element in determining the identity of the society and the state.
Since criminal law expresses these, it is no wonder that national criminal justice
systems are all unique.

Each criminal justice system has its own general part that has gained its shape
over time. Some states might have more commonalities between their general parts,
as is the case with Nordic criminal justice systems.[9] Many legislative reforms in
Finland, for example, are inspired by reforms first adopted in Sweden. Even though
the Nordic systems share a rather similar perspective on criminal policy focusing on
general prevention, the moral and habit-creating effects of the criminal law, and on
treating everyone as an equal member of society and *vice versa* also as a potential
offender,[10] they also have quite large differences in their general parts. For example,
Denmark, Iceland and Norway have adopted a rather broad concept of perpetration

---

[4] Klip (2016), p. 43.

[5] Husak (2002), pp. 13 and 14.

[6] Robinson (1994), pp. 857–858.

[7] Lisbon judgment: BVerfG, 2 BvE 2/08 vom 30.6.2009, Absatz-Nr. (1–421), para 252. Available
in English: http://www.bverfg.de/entscheidungen/es20090630_2bve000208en.html, accessed 25
June 2018.

[8] Lisbon judgment: BVerfG, 2 BvE 2/08 vom 30.6.2009, Absatz-Nr. (1–421), para 253. Available
in English: http://www.bverfg.de/entscheidungen/es20090630_2bve000208en.html, accessed 25
June 2018.

[9] Melander (2007).

[10] Melander (2007), p. 119.

whereas Sweden and Finland have quite clear distinction between perpetration and other forms of participation.[11]

Larger differences can be found between the continental and common law legal cultures, for example, identification of the doctrine of criminal liability. In Germany and many other continental systems criminal liability is determined by a tripartite analysis of crime (definition of the offence, wrongdoing, culpability). In common law jurisdictions criminal liability is determined by bipartite analysis of crime (*actus reus* or the objective element of crime, and *mens rea* or the subjective element of crime).[12]

In addition to differences in the general parts of the criminal law, there are also differences in what criminal law (or penal law) is seen to consist of: whether it is only about reacting to criminal behaviour by means of punitive sanctions or by other means also (for example treatment or educational measures).[13] Criminal law determines what is criminal behaviour, how criminal liability is determined and *the different ways* society can react to crime. In turn, penal law only focuses to criminal behaviour and on the imposition of *state punishment*. In this sense, the concept of criminal law is broader than penal law.[14] Even though these concepts imply slightly different things, criminal-oriented or punishment-oriented perspectives, the concepts of criminal and penal law are used interchangeably in this research. However, the concept of penal law, as explained above, captures the idea behind the research task better since this research centers on the issue of criminal law competence. This study focuses on explaining who has, and under which terms, the competence to enact criminal legislation by determining the essential elements of crime provisions[15] and/or by enacting penalties.

Criminal law is often seen to have a close relationship to national sovereignty. Criminal law is described as an expression of state power,[16] an indicator of state sovereignty,[17] and vice versa, from a traditional perspective, the sovereign state is also seen as the penal sovereign.[18] Sovereignty as a concept can be divided into internal and external sovereignty. Internal sovereignty means the competences a state has over its society and is understood from the perspective of constitutional law. External sovereignty is about states' external relations to other states and inter-

---

[11] Nuotio (2007), p. 129.

[12] On the difference of tripartite and bipartite analysis of structure of crime, see for example, Fletcher (2007), pp. 43–57; Fletcher (1998), pp. 74–92; Russell (2007), p. 2675.

[13] Fletcher (2007), p. 73.

[14] Ibid., p. 69.

[15] Crime provisions consist of the name of the offense, the essential elements of the crime and the punishment threat. The term penal provision is wider and refers to different kinds of criminal law provisions, also to such as provisions concerning rules of sentencing etc.

[16] See, for example, Whitman (2003–2004), p. 901.

[17] Case C-440/05 *Commission of the European Communities v Council of the European Union* [2007] ECR p. I-9097, Opinion of AG Mazák, para 72; Garland (1996), pp. 445 and 450–460; Ashworth and Zedner (2008), pp. 21 and 40; Nuotio (2014b).

[18] Garland (1996), pp. 445 and 450–460.

national legal persons, and is thus perceived in terms of international law.[19] Sovereignty refers to ultimate (legal and political) authority or command over objects and individuals.[20] In the EU context criminal law is also seen as a sovereignty-sensitive branch of law as the remnants of the intergovernmental nature of criminal law cooperation illustrate.

Relative to state sovereignty, the GCC has stated that criminal law is and always has been a central duty of state authority. Criminal provisions protect the basic values of community life and thus places social and ethical judgment of unworthiness on the types of conduct that is penalized. Since criminal law expresses the values of the society, the choice of what conduct to criminalize is a fundamental decision. The GCC sees that the core content of criminal law is sensitive decision-making on legal ethical minimum-standards.[21] The sensitive nature of criminal law derives from the fact that criminal law is value-laden and imposes highly intrusive limitations on individuals.

The close interrelationship between criminal and constitutional law[22] also reflects how criminal law mirrors state sovereignty. The interrelationship between criminal and constitutional law is about balancing: criminal law is used to ensure fundamental rights and values enshrined in the constitution and simultaneously constitutional law restricts the excessive use of criminal law. Criminal law is special by its nature, since criminalization represents the ultimate social disapproval of certain types of conduct. The use of criminal sanctions, especially the loss of personal freedom through imprisonment, means greater forfeiture of rights for the sentenced than non-criminal sanctions, partly also due to the moral stigma, the attribution of blame attached to the use of criminal punishments. In its expressive function, punishment symbolises disapproval and condemnation. Criminal punishment is not only about 'hard treatment' (imprisonment etc.), it is essentially also about the expression of censure.[23]

The role of the state is not only to suppress violence between individuals but also in a way to exercise violence on behalf of individuals through the imposition of criminal sanctions.[24] This sounds harsh, but the use of criminal penalties—restriction of liberty, or ultimately even the death penalty—can be perceived as a form of violence or coercion exercised by the states. Max Weber famously defined the states

---

[19] Peters (2009), pp. 513 and 515–517; Oppenheim (1912), p. 167; Walker (2003), p. v.

[20] Walker (1998), pp. 355 and 357; Walker (2002), pp. 317 and 345; Preuss (2010), p. 26.

[21] Lisbon judgment: BVerfG, 2 BvE 2/08 vom 30.6.2009, Absatz-Nr. (1–421), paras 355 and 358. Available in English http://www.bverfg.de/entscheidungen/es20090630_2bve000208en.html, accessed 25 June 2018.

[22] On the interrelationship between criminal and constitutional law, see, for example, Fletcher (2007), pp. 97–106.

[23] Feinberg (1970), p. 98. In Case C-240/90 *Federal Republic of Germany v Commission of the European Communities* [1992] ECR p. I-5383, Opinion of AG Jacobs, para 11, Advocate General found that penal sanction is about deterrence, stigma of social disapproval, and attribution of blame, the stigma being the distinguishing feature between penal and non-penal sanctions.

[24] Whitman (2003–2004), pp. 901 and 903.

to have a monopoly on the legitimate use of physical force or violence.[25] Weber's idea of the monopoly of violence covers of course also other state institutions than solely criminal law, but the idea of the state being the sole user of violence, as a main rule,[26] is the key here. Criminal law is a social institution that is used to control vengeance[27] and to preserve peace within the society.[28] Following the idea of social contract, in order for the state to have legitimacy to deny the use of force by individuals the state has an obligation to protect its citizens.[29] Whereas the individual's obligation is to obey the law as a consequence of tacit consent to be governed under the state's laws, the state's duty is to protect the individual from threats and to prevent harm from occurring to them.[30] By means of criminal justice, states can protect their citizens by aiming to prevent crimes from occurring and by solving conflicts caused by crime. Following the same logic, the state's obligation to punish an offender can be derived from its own failure to prevent the crime and to protect the victim. And since the state has prohibited personal vengeance, the obligation to punish remains with the state.[31]

Acts and omissions forbidden by criminal law are not only moral or private wrongs. Crimes are wrongs in the sense that they need to be forbidden by law, and *public wrongs* in the sense that they cannot be settled between individuals by means of private law, such as tort law.[32] Criminal law protects both private and public interests against the wrongdoing of others, and in this sense it protects public and private jurisdictions,[33] the sphere of autonomy or the individual's right to decide on her own property, and in this way promotes individual's autonomy.[34] It is essential to emphasise that rather than protecting morality, criminal law protects these public and private jurisdictions. For example, doctors have a responsibility to respect their patients' will, her jurisdiction, even if a medical procedure, such as a blood transfusion for example, might be morally defensible in the doctor's opinion. Regardless of the doctor's view, the choice remains within the jurisdiction of a competent patient. From this public law account, criminal law is more centred on protecting public and private jurisdictions, and less centred in identifying moral wrongs.[35] However, a strong connection remains between criminal law and morals, since even the word wrong or wrongdoing has a moral connotation. Also, criminal law protects individuals' basic rights and freedoms that are entrenched with moral significance.

---

[25] Weber (1978), p. 54.

[26] Individuals can use violence legitimately in situations of self-defence, for example.

[27] Whitman (2003–2004), pp. 901 and 902.

[28] Wessels and Beulke (2012), pp. 1–2.

[29] Whitman (2003–2004), p. 901.

[30] Ashworth and Zedner (2014a), p. 7.

[31] Council of Europe, Explanatory Report on the European Convention on the Compensation of Victims of Violent Crimes (ETS No. 116), para 9; Ashworth and Zedner (2014b), p. 14.

[32] Dagger (2011), p. 50.

[33] Thorburn (2011), p. 31.

[34] Dagger (2011), p. 57.

[35] Thorburn (2011), pp. 33–34.

Offences that are inherently wrongful, such as murder or torture (*mala in se*), are a good example of the connection between morals and criminal law. These types of offences are close to the core of both criminal and constitutional law, and they protect the intrinsic values of the society. The matter is more complicated in regard to the regulatory offences *mala prohibita*, conduct that is wrong simply because it has been criminalized. Nevertheless, reducing the strong association of morals with criminal law is welcomed due to the multiculturalism which poses challenges to criminal justice systems, since criminal law ought to accommodate the cultural differences present in everyday life. Criminal law can try to accommodate different views on values in multicultural contexts, but in situations where multicultural societies cannot find consensus on values, criminal law turns into a more political issue.[36] The distinction between a moralized notion of crime as wrong (*mala in se*) and a legalized notion of crime as an infraction (*mala prohibita*)[37] describes how crime can be a moral wrong, but is not necessarily one.[38] Even though criminal law has a strong connection to morals, individual provisions of criminal law do not protect morals as such, but instead 'real' interests such as individual autonomy.[39]

Crimes can be understood as public wrongs also in terms of the community sharing the wrongs. Here, the difference between civil and criminal wrongs is made by determining which wrongs are wrongs against the community as much as they are wrongs against the victims. Relative to wrongs that are crimes, the members of the community thus associate and identify themselves with the victim. This requires some sense of shared values. From this perspective, the crime (the wrong) does not cease from being a wrong against the victim, it simply widens to being a wrong against the community because the wrong was directed against its member.[40]

We can see that the role of criminal law as a reflection of state sovereignty can be drawn from the interrelationship of criminal law with constitutional law, morals, society and community. Each legal system is unique. Each criminal justice system is also unique. Criminal law directly reflects state sovereignty because it is the ultimate means of control to ensure the compliance with laws that are enacted in a democratic process. Criminal law also protects those very basic values of the society that are reflected in the constitutions.

Criminal law is about ensuring the freedom and autonomy of individuals by simultaneously restricting their freedom on the basis of law. Thus criminal law is merely one aspect of public law. The use of public power is not just about a restriction of individuals' rights but rather about strengthening individual autonomy. The justification of the institution of criminal law as a part of public law is about how the exercise of public power by means of criminal law can be reasoned in general. Following H.L.A. Hart, this level of justification is called the general justifying

---

[36] Nuotio (2014a), pp. 67–71.

[37] Lacey (2013), p. 14.

[38] Farmer (1996), pp. 57 and 58.

[39] Hassemer (1989), pp. 388 v 396.

[40] Marshall and Duff (1998), pp. 7 and 18–21.

aim.[41] In turn, the justification of the use of criminal law at the level of criminalization is about expressing what is considered undesirable conduct and what limits there should be for governance by means of criminal law. Those limits for criminalization are referred to as the criminalization principles, and by following them, the legislature can enact legitimate criminal laws.[42] At least some of the limits for the use of criminal law, such as proportionality or protection of fundamental rights, can be derived from constitutional law, which as such brings legitimacy to the use of criminal law. All criminal law theory or justifications for the use of criminal law cannot be derived from constitutional law, however. For example, not all legitimate interests that are protected by means of criminal law are necessarily constitutionally protected rights.[43] The justification for imposing criminal sanctions on individuals is often derived from the desert principle, meaning that the justification to punish individuals stems from the crime committed.

We can see that the justification of criminal law can be divided into different levels. For example, John Rawls argued that the use of punishment as a practice and the use of that practice in particular cases should be reasoned with different arguments.[44] Also H.L.A. Hart has distinguished the general justification aim of the criminal justice system from the justification of the use punishment. The latter justification relates to the distribution of punishment: who may be punished and how much.[45] Next, these two levels of justification for criminal law are elaborated in more detail.

2.2 Justifying the Use of Criminal Law as an Institution: The General Justifying Aim

2.2.1 Looking Ahead

The difference between consequentialist and deontological moral theories is a good starting point to illustrate the main two approaches on justification of criminal law. Theories of punishment are used to justify the entire criminal justice system, in addition to justifying the use of punishment.[46] The classical debate between retribution and deterrence as the rationale for punishment in criminal theory can also be seen from the perspective of moral theories as a difference between deontological

---

[41] See, Hart (1992), pp. 8–12.

[42] On criminalization theory, see, for example, Melander (2008), p. 7.

[43] On the interrelationship between criminal law theory and constitutional law, see du Bois-Pedain (2014), pp. 307 and 324.

[44] Rawls (1995), pp. 3 and 5.

[45] Hart (1958), pp. 8–12.

[46] Lappi-Seppälä (1994), pp. 20–21.

and consequentialist approaches to moral problems.[47] In different levels of criminal law (justification of the institution of criminal law, criminalization, sentencing, and execution of punishment) the emphasis varies between the two. For example, the legislator is more likely to focus on the deterrent effect of the criminalization and thus adopts a consequentialist moral approach, whereas the judge needs to adopt also a backward-looking deontological approach to ensure equal treatment in sentencing. Because sentencing represents the condemning function of criminal law that is mainly centered around the criminal act and blameworthiness of the individual, it ought not to be justified only by references to general deterrence.[48]

The basic aim of utilitarianism is to improve the well-being of all, or at least the greatest possible amount of people. Utilitarianism as a moral theory suggests that a universal aim of well-being, the producing of human happiness and the avoidance of suffering, should be adopted as the moral standard guiding the decision-making, but no legal order can be totally utilitarian: each legal order seeks to protect its own interests. International legal regimes, such as the International Criminal Court for example, could be seen as exceptions to this, since their aims and reason for being seem genuinely universal.[49]

Amongst the wide spectrum of literature on utilitarianism, Jeremy Bentham's and John Stuart Mill's works are classics.[50] Relative to criminal law, utilitarianism starts from the premise that since the use of punishment brings harm to the convicted, the use of punishment would be legitimate only if it prevents more harm than it produces. Jeremy Bentham has famously phrased the idea as follows: '[A]ll punishment is mischief: all punishment in itself is evil. Upon the principle of utility, if it ought at all to be admitted, it ought only to be admitted in as far as it promises to exclude some greater evil.'[51] Cesare Beccaria also found that deterrence is the only appropriate justification for punishment. Beccaria used utilitarianism as the basis of his analysis on policy, because he found utility was a principle on which people with different views could agree.[52] Thus utilitarianism is deterrence-oriented. The deterrent effect of punishment is connected to both general and special deterrence, meaning that the use of punishment as an institution should in general deter people from committing crimes, and that punishing an individual should deter the offender from reoffending.

Of course, utilitarianism is a multidimensional concept that can be used to mean slightly different things. For example, from an economist's perspective, one could argue that based on utilitarianism all policies should be assessed purely on their (economic) effects on individuals' welfare. This might diminish the role of fairness

---

[47] Fletcher (2000), pp. 687 and 697.

[48] Hart (1992), pp. 1–3; Jareborg (2002), pp. 90–91.

[49] Fletcher (2007), pp. 193–198.

[50] Jeremy Bentham (2000) and Mill (1974, 1979).

[51] Jeremy Bentham (2000), available in internet http://www.efm.bris.ac.uk/het/bentham/morals. pdf, accessed 25 June 2018, Chapter XIII: Cases Unmeet for Punishment, § 1, para II.

[52] Beccaria (1764), pp. 52, 60, and 115; Binder (2002), pp. 321 and 335.

in decision-making, such as granting procedural rights for the accused.[53] But from another perspective, ensuring fairness can be seen to increase the well-being of an individual and society by creating happiness amongst the citizens in that they know they are treated fairly. Needless to say, it is improbable that any criminal justice system would have adopted purely economic efficiency for its foundation.[54]

Both Bentham and Beccaria are said to have adopted their approach from Baron Helvétius who saw punishment *as an institution of government* rather than as a moral question. Helvétius emphasized the role of the government as a subject of moral philosophy to ensure the principles of ethics through legislation. This is well captured in the following quotation.[55]

'[A]nd I say, that all men tend only towards their happiness; that it is a tendency from which they cannot be diverted; that the attempt would be fruitless, and even the success dangerous; consequently, it is only by incorporating personal and general interest, that they can be rendered virtuous. This being granted, morality is evidently no more than a frivolous science, unless blended with policy and legislation: whence I conclude that, if philosophers would be of use to the world, they should survey objects from the same point of view as the legislator. Though not invested with the same power, they are to be actuated by the same principle. The moralist is to indicate the laws, of which the legislator insures the execution, by stamping them with the seal of his authority.'[56]

When punishment is seen as an institution of government, the legitimacy of punishment is evaluated through political legitimacy rather than morality. The emphasis is then on the legitimacy of the decision-making process. As Binder has put it, 'the utilitarian imperative is not for individuals to maximize the aggregate happiness of society as they see it; [it] is for polities to realize the institutional conditions for public utility'.[57] Thus, legislation can be perceived legitimate when it is enacted in a procedure that maximizes a good. In terms of criminal law, this means that the criminal legislative procedure ought to balance the restrictions of individual freedoms with the protection of individual freedoms. For example, the legislative procedure ought to ensure that the restrictions of individual freedoms are clear and foreseeable (principle of legality), or that the freedoms are not disproportionately limited.

As an alternative approach to consequentialism, Kant's deontological moral theory focuses on the need to act in a particular way, as opposed to focusing on the end results of different choices of conduct. Respect for human dignity, the intrinsic equality of all, is a core element of Kantian deontologicalism. To Kant, human dignity is an absolute value that needs to be respected by others. Respect for human dignity means that no one should act in a way that they would not wish to become an universal law. Respect for human dignity can be found from several modern

---

[53] Kaplow and Shavell (2003), p. 331.

[54] Fletcher (2007), p. 198.

[55] Binder (2002), pp. 321 and 334; Baron Claude Adrien Helvétius (1807), pp. 124–125.

[56] Baron Claude Adrien Helvétius (1807), pp. 124–125.

[57] Binder (2002), pp. 321, 338, and 342–349.

constitutions.[58] For example, the German and the Finnish constitutions, as well as the EU Charter of fundamental rights, hold human dignity as a basic value.[59] The ECHR regime also represents a Kantian approach by acknowledging human dignity and human freedom as the very essence of the ECHR, protected by the Convention rights and freedoms.[60] The Convention does not only protect human dignity as an *individual right*, it also protects it as an *objective value*.[61] When human dignity is protected as an objective value, the individual cannot freely consent to conduct that infringes human dignity.[62] In short, even though human freedom is a part of the very essence of the ECHR, it is limited by respect for human dignity.

Kant's theory on punishment does not seem to pursue the respect for human dignity in every detail. In Kant's view, retribution (*jus talionis*, the eye for an eye principle) is essential to ensure that the deed and the punishment correspond. Some argue that Kant's focus on the retribution also meant that the theory was not interested in what effects the punishment would have on the external world.[63] Others claim that since the theory found the literal interpretation of the *jus talionis* deeply immoral in some cases, since then the punishment would not respect the person-hood and humanity of the offender, the theory would actually support the use of proportionality in judging and would thus also have place for the deterrent effect.[64] In this sense, Kant speaks of justice as a necessary element in deterring potential lawbreakers.[65]

Perhaps the most well-known writings on the justification of the criminal justice system in general are those of John Rawls and H.L.A. Hart. Both Rawls and later Hart started from the premise that the justification of the criminal justice system in general and the use of punishment in individual cases must be separated from another. To them, the general justification for the use of criminal law lies in the preventive function of criminal law. Whereas Rawls argued that utilitarian arguments justify the use of punishment as a practice,[66] Hart considered that the beneficial (utilitarian) consequences of punishment can be used to justify the use of

*

---

[58] Fletcher (2007), pp. 198–201.

[59] Some EU Member States have explicit references to human dignity in their constitutional documents. For example, constitutions of Belgium, Germany, Estonia, Greece, Spain, Ireland, Italy, Latvia, Lithuania, Hungary, Austria, Poland, Portugal, Slovenia, Slovakia, and Finland. European Parliament, *Charter of Fundamental Rights in the European Union Article 1 Human Dignity*, 6. National Laws http://www.europarl.europa.eu/comparl/libe/elsj/charter/art01/default_en.htm, accessed 25 June 2018.

[60] *Pretty v. The United Kingdom* App no 2346/02 (ECtHR, 29 April 2002), para 65. See also Foster (2011), p. 97. See also European Committee of Social Rights Complaint No. 14/2003 by the *International Federation of Human Rights Leagues (FIDH) v. France*, para 31.

[61] Hörnle and Kremnitzer (2011), pp. 143 and 148.

[62] Ibid.

[63] Fletcher (2007), p. 205.

[64] Murphy (1987), pp. 509 and 531.

[65] Hill (1999), pp. 407 and 414.

[66] Rawls (1995), pp. 3 and 5.

punishment in general.[67] Utilitarianism and prevention are justifications for the institutions of punishment and criminalization (justification of the use of criminal law in general).

Justifying the use of criminal law at the general level is best explained by prevention theories than by backward looking retributivist theories. The purpose of criminal law include the general deterrent function that criminal legislation produces, and the distributive function of criminal law. The general deterrent function means that through its expressive function criminal legislation conveys information on society's values and morals to individuals who can then choose to adopt these values. This is called the moral-creating or educational function of criminal law. When individuals also choose to respect these norms and to not violate them, criminal law creates habits for individuals. Naturally, individuals can also respect the law out of fear of punishment.[68] In its distributive function, criminal law is applied in the courts to react to a crime in an appropriate way. Whereas backward-looking theories explain the distributive function on criminal law,[69] prevention theories fit better to justify the use of criminal law and the existence of the criminal justice system in general.

The level of criminalization is often justified by positive and negative general prevention. The threat of punishment, negative general prevention, has an apparent role in justifying the practice of criminalizing certain types of conduct because the main purpose of criminalization is to prevent individuals from acting in certain ways.[70] How well the threat of punishment works as a deterrent depends on the severity of penalties and, perhaps even more importantly, on the likelihood or certainty of getting caught and being punished. This presumption starts from the premise that the potential offenders act rationally and consider their options. In this consideration the likelihood of getting caught and the certainty of being punished has more deterrent effect than the severity of punishment. Even if a certain type of crime was punishable by a threat of severe punishment, the threat means nothing if committing the offense does not result in punishment.[71] For example relative to economic crime, offenders usually have a certain economic and social position due to which even a relatively low punishment threat can deter them from committing the crime. For them, the probability of getting caught works as a stronger preventive incentive. However, relative to some types of so-called moral crimes, such as the criminalization of homosexuality, or political crimes, such as terrorism, the threat of punishment is not seen to have influence on individuals' behaviour.[72] We can see that the effectiveness of the preventive effect of criminal law varies amongst different types of crime.

---

[67] Hart (1992), pp. 8–10. See also, Lacey (1988), p. 47; Lessnoff (1971), pp. 141 and 143.

[68] Andenaes (1974), pp. 7–8.

[69] Hart (1992), pp. 8–10.

[70] Jareborg (2002), pp. 90–91; Melander (2008), pp. 180–181.

[71] Lappi-Seppälä (2000), pp. 50–52.

[72] Andenaes (1974), pp. 14–15 and 19–21.

Positive general prevention means that the law is obeyed because compliance with the law is perceived as right, or has become habitual. If individuals internalize the norms and adopt the values that are conveyed by criminal law, they will not commit crimes because the penalized conduct is considered wrong as such.[73] In this sense the moral-creating function of criminal law is an expression of the educational or socio-pedagogical function of criminal law. Habitual lawfulness stems from internalization of norms. When an individual internalises the prohibitions expressed in the law either out of fear of punishment or its moralizing effect, he will obey the law even though there would be no risk of getting caught.[74] Individuals can obey the laws also because they find the laws legitimate. The norms are considered as binding products of democratic process and as such they represent the rules of society. The laws are perceived legitimate if they are within reasonable and appropriate limits, but laws can be obeyed because they are considered formally legitimate simply because they are laws. In this sense, obedience of the law becomes a habit. This is called the normative commitment to law, or the moral or habit-creating function of criminal law.[75]

In order for positive general prevention to work, in addition to sufficient severity and certainty of punishment, individuals need to perceive the punishment as censure. Punishment should convey blame in order to either create or strengthen the personal moral opinions of the individuals.[76] Whereas each provision of criminal law expresses censure concerning the type of conduct in the abstract, criminal judgment expresses it in individual cases. Criminal punishment differs from other types of sanctions, such as a tax surcharge for example, in that punishment conveys social disapproval. Crimes are considered blameworthy, as a type of action that is somehow seen to be more wrong than other types of conduct. In judging, censure is directed towards the offender, but criminalization also addresses third parties and communicates censure to them by advising them to refrain from engaging in conduct that constitutes crime. Last, but not least, censure speaks to the victim. Whereas the judgment acknowledges that injury or other harm happened to her, the censure conveyed by criminal law states that the perpetrator wronged the victim. Criminal law censures the conduct of the perpetrator and places blame on him due to that conduct.[77] We can see that criminal law has a communicative function that works through censure.

The effectiveness of criminal law or its preventive effect is sometimes challenged. It is true that every offender or prisoner is a proof that general prevention has not worked in his case. This, however, does not prove that general prevention does not work. Similarly, it could be argued that criminal law is unnecessary because it is highly value-laden and people already refrain from committing crimes on moral

---

[73] Tyler (1990), pp. 3–7 and 25–26; Lappi-Seppälä (2000), pp. 56–57.

[74] Andenaes (1974), pp. 35–36.

[75] Tom R Tyler (1990), pp. 3–7 and 25–26; Lappi-Seppälä (2000), pp. 56–57; Melander (2008), pp. 180–181.

[76] Lappi-Seppälä (2000), p. 59.

[77] von Hirsch (2003), pp. 9–11.

grounds. Even though this argument also has some truth in it, in particular relative to crimes that constitute *mala in se*, the same does not apply to prohibited forms of conduct of a more regulatory nature but which are still necessary in order to ensure the peaceful functioning of the society. A good example of the effectiveness of criminal law is the increase in the number of abortions after it has been legalized or liberalized in different countries. Even though the criminal prohibition of abortion probably has no effect on the individual's desire to have an abortion, it nevertheless has other effects, such as an unwillingness to be socially judged for having such a procedure done.[78] We can see that even though no perfect statistics are available to prove the effectiveness of the preventive or deterrent function of criminal law, it is still reasonable to argue that criminal law works to prevent crime even though the reasons for its effectiveness vary between different types of crime and between individuals depending on how risk-aversive they are.

2.2.2   More than Words

The communicative or expressive theory of punishment mixes consequentialist and deontological approaches. On the one hand, censure aims at prevention. Criminal punishments should communicate that the conduct is wrong and something that should be avoided. In this sense punishment communicates with the public at large in its forward-looking dimension. On the other hand, at the level of conviction, censure focuses on the past act and condemns it. Here, the punishment communicates to the perpetrator: the punishment is something that he deserves based on his past conduct.[79] Censure and communication have thus both forward- and backward-looking dimensions.

There is a difference of connotation between the communicative and expressive function criminal law. Whereas the expressive function of criminal law or punishment suggests that the criminal law one-sidedly expresses condemnation and censure to the offender and to the public at large, communication entails that someone, such as the perpetrator, takes part in the dialogue. Communication requires that someone actively participates in the discussion that happens in the criminal trial (and the execution of punishment). From this approach, the offender is seen as a rational and responsible moral agent, whose criminal act ought to be appropriately recognised and who has a right to be punished.[80] In their consequentialist dimensions, censure and communication aim to affect the future behaviour of the convicted as well as others. Censure communicates that the criminal act is wrong, or at least a mistake from which one should refrain. *But ultimately, the aim of the com-*

---

[78] Andenaes (1974), pp. 41–46 and 53.

[79] Duff (1986), pp. 235–236; Duff (2003), pp. 49–50.

[80] Duff (1986), p. 263.

municative function of criminal law is that individuals would accept norms of criminal law as justified.[81]

Criminalization theory is about the limitations on criminalization. It sets normative requirements for new criminalizations. The criminalization principles work as restrictions that should be taken into account when new criminal legislation is considered in order to ensure the legitimacy of criminal legislation.[82] A normative theory of criminalization sets restrictions on criminalization, meaning that the so-called criminalization principles demand that the legislation is of certain type of legal quality. *Because criminalizations are generally considered to restrict fundamental rights*, either by forbidding certain acts or by imposing punishment threats, a *theory of criminalization can be anchored in norms of constitutional law.* And simply because the criminal law restricts fundamental rights, the legislature's power to criminalize must also be restricted.[83] Because theories of criminalization are normative theories that express what kind of criminal legislation ought to be enacted, the theories do not need to be changed simply because some legal realities do not perfectly fit them.

Criminalizations gain their contextual legitimacy by following the criminalization principles. The legitimacy of the legislature's power to criminalize within a polity also derives from its adherence to criminalization theory.[84] From this perspective, this book is highly topical because the normative framework of criminalization in the European context has not really been theorized.

Even though criminalization is of great importance and a key element of criminal law, theory has not really focused on it as thoroughly as it has focused on other topics of the general part of criminal law.[85] There are exceptions, however. To mention a few, in the UK Andrew Ashworth has examined the topic of criminalization in his *Principles of Criminal Law*. Ashworth does not attempt to establish a general theory of criminalization, but makes certain arguments that might speak for or against of criminalization. He concludes that criminal legislation should be kept to a minimum in order to ensure individuals' autonomy. Thus criminalizing '1) offensive behaviour unless certain further criteria are fulfilled; 2) the use of paternalistic reasons to justify criminalization, except to protect the vulnerable; 3) criminal liability for omissions, except in strong cases; 4) extending criminal sanction to minor harms; 5) criminal liability based on remote harms; and 6) the creation of so-called victimless crimes' ought to be limited.[86] In the USA, based on the doctrines of the general part, Douglas Husak has argued that only conduct worthy of condemnation should be criminalized, innocent conduct should not be criminalized, only criminalizations

---

[81] Duff (2003), pp. 80–81.

[82] Husak (2002), p. 17.

[83] Nuotio (2010), p. 254.

[84] Lacey (1995), p. 25.

[85] Husak (2002), p. 20; Lacey (1995), p. 2; Melander (2008), p. 1.

[86] Ashworth (2003), pp. 24–25 and 55–57.

that cause more good than harm should be enacted, criminal law should be used as only a last resort and it should protect essential interests.[87]

In Germany, the justification for the existence of criminal law in general is said to be the need for prosperous coexistence. By protecting legal goods (the *Rechtsgütern*) criminal law fulfills its function. German criminal law is based on and fulfils the objectives of the Basic Law.[88] The protection of legal interests together with the principles of *ultima ratio*, proportionality and legality restrict the scope of the use of criminal law and criminalization.[89] Similar principles have also been presented in the Nordic jurisprudence that is heavily influenced by the German jurisprudence as limitations to criminalization power. According to Nils Jareborg, criminalizations ought to be limited by certain principles to restrict the powers of the legislature. Criminal legislation ought to protect legal interests and respect the principle of culpability. Criminal law ought to be focused on conduct instead of individuals. This also means that the criminalizations ought to be general in nature. Criminal law ought to respect the principles of legality and *ultima ratio*. There should be inner coherence and proportionality between the different crime provisions as well as in sentencing.[90] Similarly Sakari Melander has identified five criminalization principles: the principle of legality, respect for human dignity, the principle of protected interests, the *ultima ratio* principle, and social cost-benefit evaluation (the costs and benefits of criminalization ought to be evaluated and criminalizations that cause more harm than benefits to society ought not to be enacted).[91]

We can see that different theories of criminalization have different emphases, but that some common elements can be seen at a very abstract level.[92] They seem to attach great importance to criminalization protecting some important interest. Criminal law should not be used to forbid behavior that is not likely to cause any harm. The use of criminal law should be proportionate because if everything is punishable, the preventative dimension of criminal law's communicative function is less likely to work. Also from a fundamental rights perspective, criminal law ought not to have too broad a scope. If there are other means that could be used to achieve the same results as effectively, criminal law measures should not be used. Out of respect for fundamental rights and individual autonomy, criminal liability ought also to be based on guilt, which means that the innocent should not be punished. For example, involuntary action should not lead to criminal liability. Criminal law should also be predictable and foreseeable, and therefore the principle of legality ought to be respected.

We can also see that, depending on one's approach to constitutional law, many if not all of the criminalization principles can be derived from constitutional law. Fundamental rights protection is part of constitutional law. The principle of pro-

---

[87] Husak (2002), p. 45.

[88] Wessels and Beulke (2012), p. 2.

[89] Markus Dirk Dubber (2005), pp. 1–11.

[90] Jareborg (2002), pp. 94–95. See also, Asp et al. (2013).

[91] Melander (2008).

[92] On the Theories of criminalization in Europe, see Nuotio (2010).

portionality, and hence also the principle of *ultima ratio*, can be derived from constitutional law.[93] The principle of legality is enshrined in many constitutions and also in the ECHR which is binding law in all of the European states. Since the criminal law simultaneously protects and restricts fundamental rights, it is only natural that the theory of criminalization has been linked to the norms of constitutional law.[94]

2.3   Justifying the Use of Punishment in Individual Cases

Whereas the primary general justification for criminal law can be found in its utilitarian and preventive effects, it is generally considered that the use of punishment in individual cases cannot be *solely* or *primarily* justified on these grounds.[95] If for example purely utilitarian purposes would be used to guide conviction, criminal punishment could even be inflicted on the innocent if that would lead to satisfactory results, for example to avoid rebellions or lynching. Even though punishing the innocent could cause greater utility (prevention of lynching) than harm (the suffering of the innocent), this would also cause several disutilities such as the possible reoffending of the person who was actually guilty, the criminal justice system's inability to protect law-abiding people, and feelings of insecurity if it was known that an innocent was punished.[96]

Threats of disproportionately harsh punishment might also cause feelings of insecurity and dissatisfaction. In the utilitarian idea according to which punishment is needed in order to produce greater overall well-being in the society, punishments can only be regulated and measured to a level that is effective in producing the desired utilitarian outcome.[97] However, in the abstract, unequal or disproportionate punishments could be rationalized through greater overall utility which is why consequentialism is said to have an equity problem.[98] For these reasons, punishing individuals should be based on retributive reasons. The individual should be punished due to the crime committed.[99] Even though punishing the offender might simultaneously achieve general deterrence amongst the public in general, the primary justification for punishing the offender is backward-looking and is based on the past act. The justification for the use of punishment in individual cases is thus twofold, the prevailing reason being retributive.

---

[93] Tuori (2013), p. 6; Melander (2013), p. 42.

[94] Nuotio (2010), p. 254.

[95] See, for example, Rawls (1995), pp. 3 and 5; Hart (1992), pp. 1–3 and 11–12; Lacey (1988); Jareborg (2002), pp. 90–91.

[96] Lacey (1988), pp. 38–39.

[97] Lacey (1988), pp. 39–42.

[98] Dolinko (2014), p. 407; Hoffman and Graham (2009), pp. 149–151.

[99] Hart (1992), pp. 11–12.

Retributivism, also referred to as the absolute or deontological theory of punishment, justifies the use of punishment based on the committed crime. It sees punishment as payback or restitution. It is a deserved or even required reaction from the state. Punishment is seen in a way to negate the crime.[100] The notion of the desert principle has been explained in several ways, for example by connecting it to different reasonings such as the culpability principle, the eye for an eye-principle, the choosing of forfeiture of rights when committing the crime, the unfair advantages gained by crime, and the restoration of a moral equilibrium.[101] Retributivism seeks to establish an equivalence between the crime and punishment. The punishment ought not to be more than that to which the crime gives reason to sentence the offender. Naturally, relative to some offences, suitable punishment is sometimes hard to find. For example in relation to treason or forgery it might be difficult to assess how much harm the conduct has caused.

However, strict equivalence between the crime and punishment is not necessary. Punishments only need to be proportional between different crimes.[102] This means that the legislature needs to evaluate the relative harmfulness of different types of crime by enacting suitable and proportional penalties. The levels of punishment express the degree of the society's disapproval towards the criminalized acts, and thus the sanction levels also suggest a relative severity of the act.[103] Thus the legislature aims to achieve inner coherence between the different types of crime. This legislator's task is sometimes referred to as the *inner dimension of the ultima ratio principle* according to which different criminal and penal provisions need to create a coherent whole that emphasizes the proportional seriousness of different types of conduct.[104] The legislative framework then works as the applicable framework for the courts. At the level of conviction, the courts then need to evaluate the specifics of the individual crime-act and sentence appropriate punishment to fit the crime. Here, mitigating and aggravating circumstances, and possible excuses, are also taken into consideration.

From the retributivist perspective, crime is seen as a conflict between the offender and society. The crime is perceived as an egoist act that represents coercion against other citizens and a violation against shared public values. In turn, punishment negates the egoistic criminal act also by coercion. Where the egoistic criminal act is seen as a false universalization of will, and as such to violate the universalized moral will of the society, punishment is correspondingly seen as a universalization of the offender's act. The offender might not necessarily want to get punished but her actions are seen to implicitly tell otherwise. Therefore punishment only recognizes the offender as a responsible moral agent who deserves to be punished. The offender has a right to be punished and to be recognized by the state as a responsible

---

[100] Neumann (2014), pp. 67–84 and 70; Dolinko (2014), p. 412.

[101] Lacey (1988), pp. 16–27.

[102] Hoffman and Graham (2009), pp. 147 and 149.

[103] Andenaes (1974), p. 25.

[104] On the inner dimention of the ultima ratio principle, see Melander (2008), p. 407.

moral agent.[105] We can see that the retributivist theory represents a Kantian deontological approach. The reason for punishing an individual cannot solely or primarily rest on its good consequences such as reducing the amount of crime through deterrence (whether special or general deterrence), treatment or prevention, because then the offender would be punished merely to achieve the desired consequentialist objective.

However, general prevention has played and still plays a role in the sentencing practices of the courts.[106] For example, criminal judgments reinforce the prohibitions set by the criminal legislature and in this way perhaps strengthen the educational or communicative effect of punishment in general. Still, it should be argued that hopes for general prevention ought not to increase the severity of a penalty in individual cases. This would lead to unequal treatment of the offenders if one perpetrator were to be treated in a harsher way as a warning to others. Even if and when sentencing has preventive aims and effects, it should always be based on the principle of culpability and proportionality, thus simultaneously justifying the punishment with backward- and forward-looking arguments.

We can see that the so-called mixed theories or compromise theories combine the consequentialist and retributive approaches, usually emphasizing the consequentialist argument as the appropriate justification for the use of criminal law or punishment in general. Mixed theories make a 'distinction between justifying a practice and justifying a particular action falling under it.'[107] Some theories are based more on utilitarian arguments and others on the desert principle.[108] For example, John Rawls has argued that utilitarian arguments justify the use of punishment as a practice and that retributive arguments justify the use of these practices in particular cases.[109] Similarly H.L.A. Hart's theory of punishment sees the beneficial consequences of the punishment (utilitarianism) as the general justifying aim of punishment, but recognizes the desert principle to be necessary in justifying the issue of *who* may be punished and *how much* (the distributive principle).[110]

References

Andenaes J (1974) Punishment and deterrence. The University of Michigan Press
Ashworth A (2003) Principles of criminal law, 4th edn. OUP
Ashworth A, Zedner L (2008) Defending the criminal law: reflections on the changing character of crime, procedure, and sanctions. Crim Law Philos 2
Ashworth A, Zedner L (2014a) Preventive justice. OUP

---

[105] Hoffman and Graham (2009), pp. 148–149.

[106] Andenaes (1974), p. 39; Neumann (2014), pp. 67–84.

[107] Rawls (1995), p. 3.

[108] Lacey (1988), p. 46.

[109] Rawls (1995), pp. 3 and 5.

[110] Hart (1992), pp. 8–10. See also, Lacey (1988), p. 47. See also, Lessnoff (1971), pp. 141 and 143.

Ashworth A, Zedner L (2014b) The role of preventive state. In: Simester A, du Bois-Pedain A, Neumann U (eds) Liberal criminal theory. Hart Publishing

Asp P, Magnus U, Nils J (2013) Kriminalrättens grunder. Iustus Förlag

Beccaria C (1764) Rikoksesta ja rangaistuksesta, Kai Heikkilä tr, Edita 1998, the original 'Dei delitti e delle pene'

Binder G (2002) Punishment theory: moral or political? Buffalo Crim Law Rev 5(2)

Dagger R (2011) Republicanism and the foundations of criminal law. In: Duff RA, Green SP (eds) Philosophical foundations of criminal law. OUP

Dolinko D (2014) Punishment. In: Deigh J, Dolinko D (eds) The Oxford handbook of philosophy of criminal law. OUP

du Bois-Pedain A (2014) Criminal law theory in the constitutional state. In: Simester A, du Bois-Pedain A, Neumann U (eds) Liberal criminal theory. Hart Publishing

Duff A (1986) Trials and punishments. CUP

Duff A (2003) Punishment, communication, and community. OUP

Farmer L (1996) The obsession with definition: the nature of crime and critical legal theory. Soc Leg Stud 5

Feinberg J (1970) The expressive function of punishment. In: Feinberg J (ed) Doing & deserving: essays in the theory of responsibility. Princeton University Press

Fletcher GP (1998) Basic concepts of criminal law. OUP

Fletcher GP (2000) The nature and function of criminal theory. Calif Law Rev 88(3)

Fletcher GP (2007) The grammar of criminal law: American, comparative and international, volume one: foundations. OUP

Foster C (2011) Human dignity in bioethics and law. Hart publishing

Garland D (1996) The limits of the sovereign state: strategies of crime control in contemporary society. Br J Criminol 36(4)

Gordon GH (1978) The criminal law of Scotland, 2nd edn. W.Green & Son Ltd

Hart HLA (1958) Positivism and the separation of law and morals. Harv Law Rev 71(4)

Hart HLA (1992) Punishment and responsibility: essays in the philosophy of law. Clarendon Press, first published in 1968

Hassemer W (1989) Symbolinen rikosoikeus ja oikeushyvien suojelu. Oikeus 18(5)

Hill T (1999) Kant on wrongdoing, desert, and punishment. Law Philos 18

Hoffman J, Graham P (2009) Introduction to political theory, 2nd edn. Routledge

Hörnle T, Kremnitzer M (2011) Human dignity as a protected interest in criminal law. Isr Law Rev 44

Husak DN (2002) Limitations on criminalization and the general part of criminal law. In: Shute S, Simester AP (eds) Criminal law theory: doctrines of the general part. OUP

Jareborg N (2002) Scraps of penal theory. Iustus Förlag

Kaplow L, Shavell S (2003) Fairness versus welfare: notes on the pareto principle, preferences, and distributive justice. J Leg Stud 32(1)

Klip A (2016) European criminal law: an integrative approach, 3rd edn. Intersentia

Lacey N (1988) State punishment. Routledge

Lacey N (1995) Contingency and criminalisation. In: Loveland I (ed) Frontiers of criminality. Sweet & Maxwell

Lacey N (2013) What constitutes criminal law? In: Duff RA, Farmer L, Marshall SE, Renzo M, Tardos V (eds) The constitution of the criminal law. OUP

Lappi-Seppälä T (1994) Miksi rikosoikeus? In: Hirvonen A (ed) Kohti 2000-luvun rikosoikeutta. Helsingin yliopiston rikos- ja prosessioikeuden laitoksen julkaisuja A:8

Lappi-Seppälä T (2000) Rikosten seuraamukset (WSLT 2000)

Lessnoff M (1971) Two justifications of punishment. Philos Q 21(83)

Marshall SE, Duff RA (1998) Criminalization and sharing values. Can J Law Jurisprud XI(1)

Melander S (2007) Nordic criminal justice policy – single path or separate ways? In: Husa J, Nuotio K, Pihlajamäki H (eds) Nordic law – between tradition and dynamism. Intersentia

Melander S (2008) Kriminalisointiteoria – rangaistavaksi säätämisen oikeudelliset rajoitukset. Suomalaisen lakimiesyhdistyksen julkaisuja

Melander S (2013) Ultima ratio in European criminal law. Oñati Socio-Leg Ser 3(1)

Mill JS (1974) In: Himmelfarb G (ed) On liberty. Penguin Books, first published 1859

Mill JS (1979) Utilitarianism. Hackett Publishing Company, first published 1863

Murphy JG (1987) Does Kant have a theory of punishment? Columbia Law Rev 87(3)

Neumann U (2014) The 'deserved' punishment. In: Simester A, Du Bois-Pedain A, Neumann U (eds) Liberal criminal theory: essays for Andreas von Hirsch. Hart Publishing

Nuotio K (2007) Participation in crime in Nordic criminal laws: variations on a theme. In: Husa J, Nuotio K, Pihlajamäki H (eds) Nordic law – between tradition and dynamism. Intersentia

Nuotio K (2010) Theories of criminalization & the limits of criminal law. In: Duff RA, Farmer L, Marshall SE, Renzo M, Tadros V (eds) The boundaries of the criminal law. OUP

Nuotio K (2014a) Between denial and recognition: criminal law and cultural diversity. In: Kymlicka W, Lernestedt C, Matravers M (eds) Criminal law and cultural diversity. OUP

Nuotio K (2014b) European criminal law. In: Dubber MD, Hörnle T (eds) The Oxford handbook of criminal law. OUP

Oppenheim L (1912) International law, a treatis, vol 1, 2nd edn. Longmans, Green, and Co

Peters A (2009) Humanity as the A and the Ω of sovereignty. Eur J Int Law 20(3)

Preuss UK (2010) Disconnecting constitutions from statehood – is global constitutionalism a viable concept. In: Dobner P, Loughlin M (eds) The twilight of constitutionalism? OUP

Rawls J (1995) Two concepts of rules. Philos Rev 64(1)

Robinson PH (1994) A functional analysis of criminal law. Northwest Univ Law Rev 88

Russell CL (2007) Tripartite structures of criminal law in Germany and other civil law jurisdictions. Cardozo Law Rev 28(6)

Thorburn M (2011) Criminal law as public law. In: Duff RA, Green SP (eds) Philosophical foundations of criminal law. OUP

Tuori K (2013) Ultima ratio as a constitutional principle. Oñati Socio-Leg Ser 3(1)

von Hirsch A (2003) Censure and sanctions. Clarendon Press

Walker N (1998) Sovereignty and differentiated integration in the European Union. Eur Law J 4(4)

Walker N (2002) The idea of constitutional pluralism. Mod Law Rev 65(3)

Walker N (2003) Preface. In: Walker N (ed) Sovereignty in transition. Hart Publishing

Weber M (1978) Economy and society: an outline of interpretative sociology. University of California Press

Wessels J, Beulke W (2012) Strafrecht Allgemeiner Teil: Die Straftat und ihr Aufbau. C.F. Müller

Whitman JQ (2003–2004) Between self-defense and vengeance/between social contract and monopoly of violence. Tulsa Law Rev 39

Chapter 3
Features of European Criminal Law

3.1 Dimensions of European Criminal Law

The concept of European criminal law is used in a broad sense, referring to the influences the EU law and the ECHR regime have on criminal law. European criminal law consists of EU criminal law (directives, framework decisions, conventions, CJEU case law etc.) and ECtHR case law that is criminal law-related. In turn, the concept of EU criminal law is used to refer to the criminal law measures enacted within the EU framework. European criminal law is thus multileveled. Norms are created at the European level, either in the Council of Europe or the EU framework, and then implemented, applied and enforced at the domestic level.[1] However the European Public Prosecutor's Office will enforce EU criminal law directly within the limits of its competence.

We can see that the concept of European criminal law does not refer to supranational criminal law that would be applicable Europe-wide. Instead the concept refers to the creation of criminal norms at European transnational level and to a process in which national criminal laws are Europeanized. This means that national authorities have to implement the European influences into their criminal justice systems. Amendments to existing laws or new penal provisions are required as well as modifications in the interpretation of criminal laws.[2] Interpretation needs to be human rights-oriented as well as EU-law-sensitive. However, due to the principle of legality, interpretation cannot go beyond what the wording of national penal provisions enables.

The attribute *criminal* in European criminal law—context needs to be understood in the light of the ECtHR's Engel-case law (as explained above in Sect.

---

[1] Klip (2016), pp. 1–2.
[2] Satzger (2012), p. 43.

© Springer International Publishing Switzerland and G. Giappichelli Editore 2020
M. Kettunen, *Legitimizing European Criminal Law*, Comparative, European and International Criminal Justice 2, https://doi.org/10.1007/978-3-030-16174-3_3

1.3.3.2),[3] according to which the only decisive criterion in determining something under criminal law is not the national legal classification, but also the nature of the offence and the severity of the punishment.[4] This means that the meaning of classifications of branches of law lessens. For example, following the ECtHR case law, the division between criminal and administrative penalties has started to dissolve. In this work, following the Engel-criteria, European criminal law refers to norms that can be regarded to have a punitive nature.

Advocate Generals have also adopted the ECtHR's view on what differentiates penal sanctions from non-penal sanctions. In AG Jacobs' opinion penal sanctions do not only dissuade or deter from undesired conduct but also involve social and moral stigma and blame.[5] AG Mazák has explicitly stated that criminal law cannot be given a uniform definition since the criminal justice systems of the Member States all have their own special characteristics. However, he sees that criminal law in general reflects social disapproval and that the ECHR represents a common point of departure in identifying the core of criminal law. He refers to the case law of the ECtHR on the definition of criminal offence and to the notion that the punitive purpose differentiates criminal punishment from other types of sanctions.[6]

Also AG Kokott has referred to the Engel criteria and to the punitive nature of criminal penalties. She finds that punishment entails '*infliction of inconvenience which is intended to make amends for the culpable wrong which has been committed*, as differentiated from restitution, which is intended to restore the situation which existed before the infliction of damage' (emphasis added).[7] Here, she referred to the ECtHR judgment in Jussila, in which the ECtHR evaluated that a tax surcharge was not intended as pecuniary compensation for damage but instead as deterrence against re-offending and as such it was to be considered a criminal penalty with a purpose of being deterrent and punitive.[8]

Following AG Kokott, the CJEU itself has explicitly distinguished criminal penalties from administrative penalties by reference to the Engel-criteria and to the fact of whether a penalty has a punitive nature.[9] In this sense, criminal law is seen to mirror moral and social blame, which differentiates criminal law from other branches of law and gives it its special nature recognized also by the Advocate Generals, the CJEU and the ECtHR.

---

[3] Klip (2016), p. 2.

[4] *Engel and Others v. the Netherlands* App no 5100/71, 5101/71, 5102/71, 5354/72, 5370/72 (ECtHR, 8 June 1976), para 82; *Sergey Zolotukhin v. Russia* App no 14939/03 (ECtHR, 10 February 2009), para 53.

[5] Case C-240/90 *Federal Republic of Germany v Commission of the European Communities* [1992] ECR p. I-5383, Opinion of AG Jacobs, para 11.

[6] Case C-440/05 *Commission of the European Communities v Council of the European Union* [2007] ECR p. I-9097, Opinion of AG Mazák, paras 67–71.

[7] Case C-489/10 *Criminal proceedings against Łukasz Marcin Bonda*, Opinion of AG Kokott, paras 42–58.

[8] *Jussila v. Finland*, App no 73053/01 (ECtHR, 23 November 2006), para 38.

[9] Case C-489/10 *Criminal proceedings against Łukasz Marcin Bonda* [2012], paras 37–41.

Even though this work accepts this substantive-oriented perspective on what European criminal law is as described above, normative claims will be made concerning the kind of normative framework EU criminal legislative proposals ought to respect and under what legal basis they ought to be adopted. As this work will argue in greater detail in the following chapters, substantive EU criminal law ought to be based on Article 83 TFEU since the other possible implicit legal bases for substantive criminal law do not include appropriate normative safeguards to ensure the protection of national sovereignty.

3.2 History of European Criminal Law

Europeanization began in the aftermath of the Second World War. The concept can be used to refer to the change where European national policies started to have more pan-European commonalities.[10] Europeanization usually refers to the interaction of the EU legal order with the Member States and other actors. A top-down perspective describes how the EU shapes the policies of the Member States (and third countries that interact with the EU, such as Norway, for example). A bottom-up perspective on Europeanization explains how the Member States and other domestic actors shape the EU policies. States that have most votes in the EU Council and states that use the most convincing arguments are seen to have the best opportunities to shape EU policies. A sequential approach to Europeanization combines the top-down and bottom-up approaches by explaining the interaction and its effects as a series of top-down and bottom-up influences. Following the sequential approach Member States are likely to be able to adopt EU policies more successfully and with less problems if they can successfully participate in the shaping of EU policies.[11] In this work, Europeanization is simply used to refer to the interaction amongst the European Union legal order, the ECHR regime and the national legal orders.

The purpose of the Europeanization development was to promote peace in Europe through economic and human rights cooperation. The process that originally started as a peace project[12] has today developed into something extraordinary: the European states have shifted some of their competences to the European Union, and have chosen to grant the CJEU and the ECtHR the jurisdiction to evaluate the state authorities' actions from the perspective of these European legal systems.

Cooperation in the field of criminal law started in the framework of the Council of Europe. The Council of Europe was founded in 1949 by the signing of the Treaty of London.[13] Article 1 of the Statute stated that 'the aim of the Council of Europe is to achieve a greater unity between its members for the purpose of safeguarding and

---

[10] Ojanen (2013), p. 97.

[11] Börzel and Panke (2016), pp. 111–120.

[12] Statute of the Council of Europe (London, 5 May 1949) European Treaty Series No. 1, preamble; Treaty establishing the European Economic Community, 25 March 1957, preamble.

[13] Statute of the Council of Europe (London, 5 May 1949) European Treaty Series No. 1.

realizing the ideals and principles which are their common heritage and facilitating their economic and social progress'. In 1950, the members of the Council of Europe signed the Convention for the Protection of Human Rights and Fundamental Freedoms (the ECHR) which aims at 'the achievement of greater unity between its members' by 'the maintenance and further realization of human rights and fundamental freedoms'. This can best be achieved 'by an effective political democracy' and adherence to the rule of law.[14] Cooperation within the framework of the Council of Europe promotes the fundamental values shared by the states. This cooperation works in an intergovernmental basis.

The work done within the Council of Europe has established common grounds for further pan-European cooperation against cross-border crime. There are several conventions that are defined as part of the European Union's *acquis*,[15] which means that new applicant countries to the EU have to adopt those Council of Europe conventions to their national legal orders in order to fulfil the obligations deriving from EU accession. The frameworks built within the Council of Europe in relation to fight against terrorism[16] and organised crime[17] have also been used as the basis for later agreements within the Union. Cooperation within the Council of Europe framework also gave the European states experience in cooperation and an understanding of the differences amongst them which later facilitated criminal law cooperation within the European Union framework. Because the cooperation was geographically broad and it took place in purely intergovernmental structures, the negotiations and ratifications of the conventions took quite a lot of time. This might have created a need for other ways of cooperation outside the intergovernmental structures.[18]

Within the EU framework, cooperation between the Member States' law enforcement was explored already before the Maastricht Treaty, which gave the Union its explicit competence in criminal cooperation.[19] In 1976, an informal arena for discussion for the law enforcement officials, the Trevi group, was established to counter terrorism and to coordinate policing in the European Community. The Trevi group's work was based on intergovernmental cooperation outside the formal

---

[14] European Convention for the Protection of Human Rights and Fundamental Freedoms (signed in Rome 4 November 1950, entered into force 3 September 1953) European Treaty Series No. 5, preamble.

[15] These are: European Treaty Series No. 24, European Convention on Extradition, Paris 13 December 1957 and its additional protocols; European Treaty Series No. 70, European Convention on the International Validity of Criminal Judgments, The Hague, 28 May 1970; European Treaty Series No. 73, European Convention on the Transfer of Proceedings of Criminal Matters, Strasbourg 15 May 1972; European Treaty Series No. 112, Convention on the Transfer of Sentenced Persons, Strasbourg 21 March 1983.

[16] European Treaty Series No. 90, European Convention on the Suppression of Terrorism, Strasbourg 27 January 1977.

[17] European Treaty Series No. 141, Convention on Laundering, Search, Seizure and Confiscation of the Proceeds from Crime, Strasbourg 8 November 1990.

[18] Mitsilegas et al. (2003), pp. 19–21.

[19] Craig and de Búrca (2011), p. 3.

structure of the European Communities (the EC).[20] In 1985, the informal cooperation under the Trevi group was expanded to cover drugs offences and organised
crime.[21] Trevi cooperation aimed at ensuring EC internal security. The EC's cooperation in criminal matters before the Maastricht Treaty was not entirely informal.
In 1988, the then European Community signed the United Nations Convention
against Illicit Traffic in Narcotic Drugs and Psychotropic Substances.[22]

In 1985, the Commission conveyed concerns concerning the effects of the abolition of internal frontiers especially in relation to terrorism and the organised trafficking of illicit drugs in its White Paper on Completing the Internal Market.[23] The
creation of the internal market created new types of cross-border criminality that
needed to be addressed. The EU's competences in other policy fields created the
need for EU criminal law competence in order to tackle criminality. EU criminal
law competence is described as a spill-over of power which refers to the idea that
'the original goal can be assured only by taking further actions'.[24] EU criminal law
measures are necessary for the better realization of the internal market[25] and the
integration process in general.

Along with the Maastricht Treaty (Article K.1), cooperation in criminal matters
became a part of the Union's primary law. The cooperation took place in an intergovernmental legal framework under the third pillar (cooperation in the fields of
justice and home affairs).[26] The establishment of the pillar structure was a compromise in order to avoid including the sovereignty sensitive policy areas—foreign and
security policy (second pillar) and justice and home affairs (third pillar)—in the
supranational first pillar and under the Community's competence. The competences
under first and third pillar were different. The third pillar instruments had weaker
legal effects.[27] Maastricht Treaty also explicitly stated that nothing in the EU Treaty
was to affect the EC Treaty.[28] This meant that legislative proposals given under third
pillar competences could not include any regulation that affected or could have
affected the use of competences under the first pillar.

The EU institutions had limited roles in the third pillar. Before the Lisbon Treaty
entered into force, criminal legislation required unanimity in the Council and only a

---

[20] Tony Bunyan, *Trevi, Europol and the European State* http://www.statewatch.org/news/hand-
book-trevi.pdf, p. 1, accessed 25 June 2018; Mitsilegas (2009), p. 6.

[21] Tony Bunyan, *Trevi, Europol and the European State* http://www.statewatch.org/news/hand-
book-trevi.pdf, p. 3, accessed 25 June 2018; Mitsilegas (2009), p. 6; Miettinen (2013a), p. 20.

[22] United Nations Treaty Series vol. 1582, status of the Treaty; see also Mitsilegas (2009), s. 6.

[23] COM (85) 310, White Paper on Completing the Internal Market, Brussels, 14 June 1985, for
example paras 26–29.

[24] Lindberg (1963), pp. 10–11.

[25] Fletcher et al. (2008), p. 28.

[26] Craig and de Búrca (2015), p. 965; Melander (2010), p. 3; Mitsilegas (2009), p. 9.

[27] Miettinen (2013a), p. 24.

[28] The then Article M (during the era of Maastricht Treaty) and later Article 47 EU (during the era
of Amsterdam Treaty) concerned solving conflicts of competence between the Community and the
Union.

consultation with the European Parliament. Only one disagreeing Member State could force a change in the criminal legislation.[29] The Commission did not have a right of initiative in criminal matters. The European Parliament had only a small role, since it was only to be kept informed of the discussions in third pillar matters or simply consulted. The Parliament could only give recommendations or ask questions in these areas.[30] The CJEU had only limited competence to review cases relating to criminal matters. Most of the Conventions established a competence for the CJEU to interpret the Conventions and to solve conflicts regarding their application. Article K.3(2)(c) of the Maastricht Treaty enabled the Member States to give competence to the Court regarding the application of the Conventions but the primary law did not make it possible to give competence to the Court regarding the interpretation of the Joint Actions.[31] However at a more general level, based on Article M of the Maastricht Treaty, the CJEU had competence to examine whether the Joint Actions given in the policy fields mentioned in Article K.1 extended to the areas of competence that belong to the EC, and even annul them if the acts extended the Union's competence to areas of the Community's competence.[32]

The Amsterdam Treaty meant relatively big changes to the Treaty framework. Only provisions on police and judicial cooperation in criminal matters were left to the third pillar, while matters of immigration, asylum, borders and civil law were transferred to the first pillar and hence communitarised. Law-making remained strongly within the hands of the Member States and in the intergovernmental framework. The right of initiative changed, since the Member States shared it with the Commission. European Parliament was still to be merely consulted in the adaption of third pillar instruments. Amendments to the Amsterdam Treaty made in the Nice Treaty allowed enhanced cooperation in criminal law matters. Article 42 TEU also included a passarelle provision, which made it possible for the Council to transfer the provisions concerning criminal cooperation to the EC Treaty under the first pillar, but the provision was never used.[33]

The Commission did not have powers to launch infringement procedures against Member States in cases of mis- or non-implementation of third pillar law that was promulgated before the Lisbon Treaty entered into force. Also according to the then Article 35 TEU the CJEU had jurisdiction to give preliminary rulings on the validity and interpretation of framework decisions, decisions and interpretation of conventions and on the validity and interpretation of the measures implementing them only if a Member State had declared its acceptance of the Court's jurisdiction. Not all Member States had given such an acceptance.[34] Currently the Union's institutions

---

[29] Nowell-Smith (2012), pp. 381, 382.

[30] Mitsilegas (2009), pp. 9–11.

[31] Melander (2010), p. 8.

[32] Case C-170/96 *Commission of the European Communities v Council of the European Union* [1998] ECR p. I-2763, paras 12–18. See also Sakari Melander (2010), p. 8.

[33] Mitsilegas (2009), pp. 14–17.

[34] Ibid., pp. 18–19.

have better chances to react if the Member States have not fulfilled their obligations in the field of criminal law (more about this in Sect. 3.4).

After the failed Constitutional Treaty,[35] treaty amendments were made into a form of reform treaty, the Lisbon Treaty, that entered into force on 1 December 2009. It followed heavily the outline and changes of the Constitutional Treaty. All terminological references to constitution or constitutional symbolism were stripped away and a clause concerning the primacy of EU law that was included in the Constitutional Treaty was replaced by a declaration. Otherwise, the reform treaty maintained a constitutional nature.[36] Two treaties remained; The Treaty on the European Union (TEU) and the Treaty of the Functioning of the European Union (TFEU, the former TEC). After the Lisbon Treaty, criminal legislative measures are given in the form of directives instead of framework decisions. Because directives are not directly applicable and need to be implemented into the Member States' legal systems, directives alone cannot determine or aggravate criminal liability. Otherwise, the principle of conforming interpretation applies normally.

The Lisbon Treaty also brought essential changes to the Union's criminal law competence. The Union and the Member States now have shared competence over the cooperation in criminal matters (Article 4(2)j TFEU). Cooperation in criminal matters was described as becoming 'communitarised'[37] or 'normalized'[38] The majority decision-making procedure—the ordinary legislative procedure—is used also in relation to criminal legislative measures and the Parliament's position in the legislative procedure grew stronger. EU criminal law competence has however maintained some of its intergovernmental nature. In the fields of shared competence, draft legislative acts are forwarded to national Parliaments for them to review whether the draft legislative act is in compliance with the principle of subsidiarity.[39] The subsidiarity control threshold for legislative proposals based on legal bases of the AFSJ is lower than in other fields of Union policies. If at least a quarter of the

---

[35] The Laeken European Council adopted a Declaration on the future of European Union and set the following aims: to better divide and define the competences of the Union, to simplify the Union's instruments, to becoming more democratic, transparent and effective, and to create a Constitution for the European citizens for the purposes of transparency and simplification of the Treaty structure (Laeken Declaration on the Future of the European Union, Annex I to the presidency conclusions—Laeken, 14 and 15 December 2001). In the summer of 2003 the Draft Treaty establishing a Constitution for Europe was agreed by the Convention and submitted to the European Council (CONV 850/03, Draft Treaty establishing a Constitution for Europe, Brussels, 18 July 2003). After the Intergovernmental Conference amended few provisions, an agreement was reached on the draft Constitutional Treaty in 2004 (Presidency Conclusions of Brussels European Council, 17 and 18 June 2004, 10,679/2/04 REV 2, Brussels, 19 July 2004, paras 4–5). The Constitutional Treaty never became in force, because the ratification was stopped when France and Netherlands rejected the Treaty in their referenda (See for example Craig and de Búrca (2015), p. 18.

[36] Craig and de Búrca (2015), p. 20.

[37] Mitsilegas (2009), p. 39.

[38] Melander (2010), p. 15.

[39] Protocol on the Application of the Principles of Subsidiarity and Proportionality [2012] OJ C326/206, Article 6.

votes given to the Parliaments declare that proposed criminal legislation concerning the area of freedom, security and justice does not comply with the principle of subsidiarity, the draft will be reviewed, as opposed to the regular threshold of at least one third of the votes.[40] The legal bases for the Union's explicit criminal law competence—Articles 82 (procedural cooperation) and 83 (substantive criminal law) TFEU—include clauses requiring the so-called emergency brake procedure. In this procedure, if a Member State would consider that 'a draft directive would affect fundamental aspects of its criminal justice system', it can ask for a referral in the Council. The Council then needs to find unanimity on the controversial issue before the draft can be approved.

The Lisbon Treaty also gave the Charter of Fundamental Rights of the European Union (the Charter)—which was originally introduced in 2000 at the Nice European Council where the Charter gained political approval from the Member States[41]—a binding nature. The Charter is now part of the Union's primary law. Before the Lisbon Treaty entered into force, the CJEU had a strong role in fundamental rights protection at the Union level. The CJEU has found that the protection of fundamental rights is a general principle of EU law. The Court found that the Community/EU law ensures the respect for fundamental rights and draws inspiration from the constitutional traditions common to the Member States. However, protection for these rights in the then Community legal framework was based on the fact that the Court recognised that fundamental rights protection had the status of a general principle of EU law.[42] The CJEU has also widely referred to the ECHR and the ECtHR's case law as a source of law, even if not as a binding source of law.[43] The CJEU has competence to interpret the compatibility of Community/Union law with obligations deriving from the ECHR, but it does not have competence to evaluate the compatibility of national law and the ECHR in situations where the national law is not implementing EC/EU law (either through legislation or application of law).[44]

---

[40] Ibid. Article 7(2).

[41] Craig and de Búrca (2015), p. 17.

[42] Case C-29/69 *Erich Stauder v City of Ulm – Sozialamt* [1969] ECR p. 419, para 7; Case C-11/70 *Internationale Handelsgesellschaft mbH v Einfuhr- und Vorratsstelle für Getreide und Futtermittel* [1970] ECR p. 1125, paras 3–4; Case C-4/73 *J. Nold, Kohlen- und Baustoffgroßhandlung v Commission of the European Communities* [1974] ECR p. 491, para 13; Case C-112/00 *Eugen Schmidberger, Internationale Transporte und Planzüge v Republik Österreich* [2003] ECR p. I-5659, para 71.

[43] Case C-222/84 *Marguerite Johnston v Chief Constable of the Royal Ulster Constabulary* [1986] ECR p. 1651, para 18; Case C-36/02 *Omega Spielhallen- und Automatenaufstellungs-GmbH v Oberbürgermeisterin der Bundesstadt Bonn* [2004] ECR p. I-9609, para 33; Case C-112/00 *Eugen Schmidberger, Internationale Transporte und Planzüge v Republik Österreich* [2003] ECR p. I-5659, para 71; Case C-60/00 *Mary Carpenter v Secretary of State for the Home Department* [2002] ECR p. I-6279, paras 40–46; Case C-413/99 *Baumbast and R v Secretary of State for the Home Department* [2002] ECR p. I-7091, paras 65–67.

[44] Case C-12/86 *Meryem Demirel v Stadt Schwäbisch Gmünd* [1987] ECR p. 3719, para 28; Case C-112/00 *Eugen Schmidberger, Internationale Transporte und Planzüge v Republik Österreich* [2003] ECR p. I-5659, para 75.

The Union's primary law now considers the interrelationship between the ECHR regime and the Union law. Article 52(3) of the Charter stipulates that those rights guaranteed in the Charter that correspond to the rights guaranteed in the ECHR have the same scope and meaning as the rights guaranteed in the ECHR. In addition to this, Article 53 of the Charter states that the Charter offers at least the same level of protection as the other international agreements—especially the ECHR—to which the Union or the Member States are parties. Article 51 of the Charter stipulates that the field of application of the Charter is limited in the sense that it is addressed to the Union's institutions, bodies, offices and agencies and to the Member States when they are implementing Union law. This means that the Charter is applicable to all situations governed by EU law, but not outside such situations.[45] The Charter is applicable at least to the extent that the EU has exercised its competence.[46] It is unclear however, if it applies to situations where the Union has competence but has not acted based on it. The Charter's field of application varies from that of the ECHR, since the Member States have to respect their obligations stemming from the ECHR in all of their action or inaction, and in all situations when they are applying national law, EU law or fulfilling their other obligations.

3.3 Basic Values of European Criminal Law

3.3.1 Protection of Human Dignity as a Precondition for European Criminal Law

Pluralistic democracy, rule of law and human rights are the core values of the Convention. They are also core values of the EU.[47] This chapter explains the meaning of these three principles since they also set standards for European criminal policy. The principles are prerequisites for each other.[48] On one hand, the respect of human rights is a prerequisite for democracy since democracy cannot function

---

[45] Case C-617/10 *Åklagaren v Hans Åkerberg Fransson* [2013], para 19.

[46] Marguery (2013), pp. 282, 287.

[47] According to Article 2 TEU the founding values of the Union are respect for human dignity, freedom, democracy, equality, the rule of law and respect for human rights.

[48] Ronald Dworkin has distinguished legal principles from legal rules. Whereas rules are applied in all-or-nothing fashion, principles 'do not set out legal consequences that follow automatically when the conditions provided are met.' Principles are weighed and balanced against each other, and each applicable principle is to be given relative weight, or to put in other words, optimized. See, Dworkin (1977), pp. 24–26. Constitutional norms are often characterisized as principles. However, some principles can also be applied as absolute rules in the sense that their violation cannot be excused by any argument. For example, if human dignity is violated, the violation will not be evaluated in terms of other conflicting human rights or other principles, but instead the violation is acknowledged and prohibited. In other words, the violation cannot be excused, and in this manner, the principle of human dignity for example is absolute in its rule-like function. See, Alexy (2010), pp. 44, 62–63.

without the respect for the equal worth of individuals. On the other hand, democracy is the only political model that is compatible with the respect of human rights because democracy guarantees political equality. Democratic governance must respect the rule of law principle in order to guarantee the protection of fundamental and human rights and the equal and predictable application of law.

The principles of rule of law, democracy and human rights are constitutional principles. Constitutional principles are usually used as weighing and balancing instruments as opposed to strict rules, and they have a dual nature since they usually can be used to argue cases from different perspectives. For example, human rights can be used either in favour or against the criminalization of abortion, assisted suicide, active euthanasia, and so on.[49] General constitutional principles describe the basic choices of the polity and place constitutional regulations into a coherent whole. General constitutional principles can be written specifically into constitutional documents or they can be deduced from other constitutional provisions. Their field of application is vast, since they are often applied when individual constitutional provisions do not give specific answers.[50]

Rule of Law Principle   The core of the rule of law principle has been described to hold 'that all persons and authorities within the state, whether public or private, should be bound by and entitled to the benefit of laws publicly made, taking effect (generally) in the future and publicly administered in the courts'.[51] The rule of law principle also requires that laws are accessible, clear and predictable. This is essential especially in relation to criminal law. Penal provisions need to be clear so that everyone can know that a punishment can be passed due to certain forms of behaviour. The principle of legality in criminal law is a specific expression of the rule of law principle. The predictability of laws is also necessary in other fields of law. Individuals need to be able to know their rights and obligations before they act. Predictability creates infrastructure for trade, business, and welfare. As such questions of legal rights and liability should be resolved by application of the law and not by the exercise of discretion. This implies that similar cases ought to be treated alike and vice versa. However, discretion is necessary part of law. It is especially in criminal cases so that the judge can take into account the differences between the offences. All application of law naturally contains some degree of discretion.[52]

The rule of law principle requires equality of individuals. Exceptions to this can be made based on objective differences. For example, age can affect criminal liability. In general, the law must adequately protect fundamental human rights and the state must comply with its obligations in international law as it does its own national law. The rule of law principle also means that the exercise of public powers should be used only for the purpose for which the powers were conferred on them. Public

---

[49] Roach (2011), pp. 91, 99. On the nature of constitutional rights norms, see Alexy (1986), pp. 44–48.

[50] Tuori (1983b), p. 444.

[51] Bingham (2011), p. 37.

[52] Ibid., pp. 37–54.

authorities should not exceed the limits of conferred powers and this power should be used fairly. The state should offer dispute resolution to the parties who are unable to resolve their disputes together and there should not be prohibitive costs or inordinate delays. The state should also provide a fair trial.[53]

The ECtHR has referred to the principle of rule of law in several occasions. In *Sunday Times* the Court emphasised that the law must be accessible. The law needs to be precise enough for individuals to foresee the consequences that a given action may entail.[54] Within the ECHR regime, Article 6 ECHR fulfils the requirements of the rule of law principle but the principle is not exhausted in that article. The ECtHR has found the principle of rule of law as 'inherent in all the Articles of the Convention'.[55] In this sense the rule of law principle is similar to the principles of democracy and human dignity; they all are considered as inherent attributes or underlying values of the Convention rights and freedoms. This means that they are general constitutional principles of the ECHR.

The Inviolability of Human Dignity The ECtHR has stated that human dignity and human freedom are the very essence of the ECHR.[56] Human dignity is protected through other Convention rights and freedoms. In this sense, human dignity plays a role in the interpretation of the other Convention rights and freedoms. In some national constitutions human dignity is seen to be a general constitutional principle in addition to its possible rule-natured functions. For example, in Germany the principle of human dignity represents the highest value and the value basis of the constitution. The German Basic Law states that human dignity is inviolable. The principle of human dignity cannot be amended since it is an absolute and a paramount value of the nation.[57] In addition to its status as a founding principle behind the other constitutional provisions, it is also seen as a binding norm. Its position as a substantive right is debated, but the German Constitutional Court has affirmed that it is at least an objective right. This means that if another fundamental right has been breached, the violation of human dignity in its objective sense can also be reviewed.[58] In Finland, human dignity is a constitutional principle that primarily protects human individuals but it also stretches to more abstract situations. For example, medical research that uses embryos and foetuses need to follow certain rules. Human dignity also provides a foundation for other fundamental rights provisions.[59]

---

[53] Ibid., pp. 55–129. Elements of fair trial are, for exmaple: equality of arms for the both sides, impartial and independent courts, public trials, presumption of innocence, the defendant should have a right to know on what crime he is accused of and examine witnesses of the prosecution, and a right to legal assistance and interpretation, and a right to attend the trial.

[54] *The Sunday Times v. The United Kingdom* App no 6538/74 (ECtHR, 26 April 1979), para 49.

[55] *Ukraine-Tyumen v Ukraine* App no 22603/02 (ECtHR, 22 November 2007), para 49.

[56] *Pretty v. The United Kingdom* App no 2346/02 (ECtHR, 29 April 2002), para 65. See also Foster (2011), p. 97. See also European Committee of Social Rights Complaint No. 14/2003 by the *International Federation of Human Rights Leagues (FIDH) v. France*, para 31.

[57] Bendor and Sachs (2011), pp. 25, 31–32.

[58] Heun (2011), p. 201.

[59] Scheinin (1998), pp. 59–60, 66–67.

General constitutional principles are elements of legal culture.[60] As being general constitutional principles, the principles of democracy and respect for human dignity belong at the level of legal culture, but they also penetrate the surface level and the deep structure of law.[61] Human dignity is also an absolute constitutional principle, meaning that it cannot be overridden by other principles. In addition, it is also a rule, since a violation of human dignity cannot be excused.[62] The principle of human dignity cannot be weighed and balanced against other principles in order to make the breach justifiable. Thus it works as a rule. In contrast, other fundamental rights protected by the constitution can be balanced against each other and fulfilled as far as possible, or optimized. The human dignity norm works in an 'either – or'—way. It cannot be balanced against other rights or satisfied only partly. The requirements it sets must be fulfilled completely.

The principle of human rights requires that states protect human rights by restraining themselves from human rights infringements and by taking measures in fulfilling the rights. What kind of influences does the principle of human rights have in relation to *substantive* criminal law? This is examined by analysing the principle of human dignity as an example, since the other fundamental rights are based on it. It is necessary to keep in mind that in addition to the following expressions of human dignity each fundamental and human right has its own sphere of influence in criminal law.

Human Dignity, Ultima Ratio and Proportionality as Criminalization Principles Criminal law ought to be used only if there is no other less intrusive means that could be used to achieve the wanted results. Thus criminal law ought to be used only when the criminal law measures are proportionate, necessary, and effective. Different kinds of disproportionate uses of criminal law could be seen to ultimately infringe the principle of human dignity. The disproportionate use of criminal law violates the fundamental rights of individuals since the freedom of individuals would be restricted more than necessary. The influence of human dignity can be seen to be especially strong in the core area of fundamental rights and human rights[63] and thus conduct that fits into the core area of fundamental right ought not to be criminalized.[64] Some argue that the concept of human dignity is not the best concept to be used in the field of criminal law because of its vagueness. Instead, other concepts such as proportionality could fulfil the same function.[65] Whichever concept is used (human dignity, proportionality, *ultima ratio*) the main idea remains the same. Criminal law should be used in a rational and humane way.

---

[60] Tuori (1983b), p. 670; Tuori (1983a), pp. 74–77.

[61] Tuori (2000), p. 211.

[62] Alexy (1986), pp. 62–63.

[63] Melander (2008), p. 302.

[64] *Pretty v. The United Kingdom* App no 2346/02 (ECtHR, 29 April 2002), para 65; Statement of the Constitutional Law Committee of the Finnish Parliament, PeVL 23/1997 vp, 2.

[65] Roach (2011), p. 91.

Unnecessary and purely symbolic criminalization ought to be avoided, and the threat of penalty ought to be proportionate to the criminal conduct.

All criminalizations have some symbolic functions through their communicative properties. Criminalization communicates to individuals what kind of behaviour ought to be avoided. However, some criminalizations might be purely symbolic. The function of purely symbolic criminalizations is solely to govern risks or to protect interests. However, they are not efficient even in terms of the communicative function of criminal law. Toothless criminalizations, that are not efficient and would be enacted solely to promote moral, popular or ideological reasons, should be avoided. These purely symbolic criminalizations could be given for hidden reasons, such as to appease the people or to demonstrate the strength or power of the state.[66] Symbolic criminalization is nevertheless acceptable to some extent. Criminalizations are always somewhat symbolic at least through their communicative nature. It is not clear at which point this symbolic nature and the lack of efficacy of a provision of criminal law becomes troublesome.[67] For example, even if provisions criminalizing terrorism, genocide or torture might not be effective deterrents, their existence is defensible because when such crimes occur, society must have appropriate means to react to such offences.[68]

All this means that criminalization ought to protect 'real' interests. For example, sex crime provisions ought not to protect sexual morality, but instead individual autonomy, self-determination, and the young.[69] Seen from this perspective, it is easy to argue that for example rape, marital rape and child sexual abuse should all be criminalized, where as homosexual behaviour should not. If broad or vague common interests, such as 'security', are protected by criminal law, the individual provisions of criminal law ought to be formulated as precisely as possible, with respect for the principles of legality and predictability.[70]

Human Dignity as a Protected Interest   Human dignity can also be seen as the protected interest of some criminal provisions.[71] It might be problematic to say that all crime provisions protect human dignity directly. However, at least a few types of crime provisions, such as torture and crimes against humanity, seem to directly protect human dignity.[72] One way of analysing the status of human dignity as a protected interest is to separate human dignity into an *individual right* and an *objective value*.[73] The prohibition of so-called 'peep-shows' in Germany[74] and the

---

[66] Hassemer (1989), pp. 388, 390–395; Melander (2008), pp. 364–367.

[67] Hassemer (1989), pp. 388, 393–394.

[68] Melander (2008), pp. 366–367; Hassemer (1989), pp. 388, 393.

[69] Hassemer (1989), pp. 388, 396.

[70] Similarly, Hassemer (1989), pp. 388, 397.

[71] Hörnle and Kremnitzer (2011), p. 143. Human dignity as a protected interest of certain serious crimes such as genocide and torture, see Melander (2008), pp. 272–276.

[72] Melander (2008), pp. 272–276.

[73] Hörnle and Kremnitzer (2011), pp. 143, 148.

[74] Ibid.

prohibition of dwarf-tossing in France[75] are good examples of cases where human dignity has been protected as an objective value. These prohibitions have a common factor: when human dignity is protected as an objective value, the individual cannot freely consent to the conduct that infringes the human dignity. Penal provisions prohibiting hate speech, incitement to violence and negationism can also be classified as protecting the objective value of human dignity. Examples of types of crime that violate human dignity as an individual right are torture and rape. Torture infringes rights to physical autonomy and rape infringes person's right to sexual autonomy. In contrast, some argue that rape infringes human dignity because of its social meaning, its use to humiliate and instrumentalize its objects, which explains why rape is so commonly used as a means of warfare. Some offences are seen to violate both elements of the inviolability of human dignity. For example, trafficking of human beings has elements of both: it infringes individual rights and the objective value of human beings.[76]

Human Dignity as a Limitation to the Use of Criminal Sanctions   Human dignity affects the use of certain type of sanctions both in general and in relation to specific crimes. In general, Article 3 ECHR prohibits torture and other inhuman or degrading treatment or punishment. According to Article 15(2) ECHR the prohibition is unconditional. The prohibition includes the prohibition to use certain types of punishments, such as shaming punishments. Article 3 ECHR also sets minimum standards for conditions of punishment and detention.[77] For example, in *Muršić v Croatia* the Court stated that 'the State must ensure that a person is detained in conditions which are compatible with respect for human dignity, that the manner and method of the execution of the measure do not subject him or her to distress or hardship of an intensity exceeding the unavoidable level of suffering'. In this case the ECtHR found, relative to the requirement of having some personal space in detention for example, that 'the requirement of 3 sq. m of floor surface per detainee in multi-occupancy accommodation should be maintained as the relevant minimum standard for its assessment under Article 3 of the Convention'.[78]

> the personal circumstances of the condemned person, the proportionality to the gravity of the crime committed and the conditions of detention pending execution of the sentence are examples of factors capable of bringing the treatment or punishment received by the condemned person within the proscription under Article 3.[79]

Even more difficult problems of interpretation arise from the phrasing of 'other inhuman or degrading treatment or punishment'.[80] In a case of *Tyrer v UK* the applicant was sentenced to three strokes of birch. The ECtHR did not find the

---

[75] On human dignity and dwarf-tossing, see for example Foster (2011), pp. 95–97.

[76] Hörnle and Kremnitzer (2011), pp. 143, 148, 152, 158–160.

[77] *Mayzit v. Russia* App no 63378/00 (ECtHR, 20 January 2005).

[78] *Muršić v. Croatia* App no 7334/13 (ECtHR, 20 October 2016), paras 99 and 110.

[79] *Ilaşcu and Others v. Moldova and Russia* App no 48787/99 (ECtHR, 8 July 2004), para 429.

[80] Melander (2008), pp. 308–309.

punishment as torture. It was not inhuman punishment either, because the suffering did not attain a particular level. The Court found that the punishment was degrading and that there was a violation of Article 3 of the Convention. The Court found that one of the main purposes of Article 3 is to protect person's dignity and physical integrity,[81] referring for the first time to the principle of human dignity.[82] The Court interpreted the *Tyrer* case in the light of present-day conditions and drew influences from the 'standards in the penal policy of the member States of the Council of Europe in this field.'[83] The Court interpreted the Convention as a living instrument and utilized a comparative legal method (see Sect. 1.3.3.1 above). The *Tyrer* case shows that corporal punishments violate human dignity and personal physical integrity and are not acceptable forms of punishments in modern European criminal justice systems.

As for the life sentence, the Court has distinguished three types of life sentences, which all need to be evaluated slightly differently. The first type, a life sentence with eligibility for release after a minimum period has been served, raises no issues under Article 3 ECHR. The second type, a discretionary sentence of life imprisonment without the possibility of parole, does not raise an issue under Article 3 at the time of sentencing, but it can raise an issue under Article 3 if 'the applicant's continued imprisonment can no longer be justified on any legitimate penological grounds (such as punishment, deterrence, public protection or rehabilitation)' or 'the sentence is irreducible *de facto* and *de jure*'. The third type, a mandatory sentence of life imprisonment without the possibility of parole, is problematic because it must be used irrespective of the level of culpability of the defendant and irrespective of whether the sentencing court considers the sentence to be justified. The Court did not find the third type to be incompatible with the Convention *per se* but it did note that it 'is much more likely to be grossly disproportionate than any other of the types of life sentence, especially if it requires the sentencing court to disregard mitigating factors which are generally understood as indicating a significantly lower level of culpability on the part of the defendant, such as youth or severe mental health problems'.[84]

It depends on the type of the life sentence and the facts of a particular case whether a life sentence could be acceptable under Article 3 ECHR. In jurisprudence, the life sentence as a form of punishment has been criticized because of the indeterminate length of the sentence. Respect for human dignity requires precise criminal sanctions.[85] In line with the ECtHR's case law, it has also been argued that

---

[81] *Tyrer v. The United Kingdom* App no 5856/72 (ECtHR, 25 April 1978), paras 9–10, 29–35.

[82] European Parliament, Charter of Fundamental Rights in the European Union Article 1 Human Dignity, 5. Case Law, internet-address www.europarl.europa.eu/comparl/libe/elsj/charter/art01/default_en.htm, accessed 25 June 2018.

[83] *Tyrer v. The United Kingdom* App no 5856/72 (ECtHR, 25 April 1978), para 31.

[84] *Babar Ahmad and Others v. The United Kingdom* App no 24027/07, 11,949/08, 66,911/09 and 67,354/09 (ECtHR, 10 April 2012), paras 239–242.

[85] See for example Melander (2008), pp. 310–312.

human dignity would be violated if a prisoner needs to give up hope of ever being released even though there would not be justifications to keep her in prison.[86]

The ECtHR has not had cases in which it had evaluated the correctness of shaming penalties (such as pillory or the modern phenomenon of self-debasement[87]). Even though the shaming penalties have been familiar in American law even fairly recently,[88] such penalties are not in active use in Europe. However, there were two intertwined cases in which the ECtHR evaluated whether the conditions of criminal proceedings constituted inhumane or degrading treatment under Article 3 ECHR.[89] The evaluation of the form and nature of the trials in these cases might be the closest thing the Court has had which has verged on the issue of acceptability of shaming punishments. The two cases concerned the same circumstances where two ten-year-old boys had abducted a two-year-old boy, battered him to death, and left him on a railway line to be run over. Their trial was public, and it gained much publicity nationally and internationally. The boys were convicted of murder and abduction. The judge allowed the boys' names to be published. The boys were sentenced to detention during Her Majesty's pleasure (meaning a kind of substitute for life sentence with minimum terms). The trial had caused the boys to fear that they would be attacked. In relation to the setting of the tariff, 278,300 people had signed a petition according to which the boys should never be released, and tens of thousands other people were supporting harsher punishment than what was the judicial recommendation. A tariff of 15-years was fixed, which devastated the boys.[90]

The ECtHR referred to the United Nations Standard Minimum Rules for the Administration of Juvenile Justice ('the Beijing Rules', General Assembly on 29 November 1985) concerning *inter alia* the protection of the juvenile's privacy. According to paragraph 8, harm caused by undue publicity or labelling should be avoided. Information that could lead to the identification of a juvenile offender should not be published. Article 40 of the United Nations Convention on the Rights of the Child (1989) resembles the paragraph 8 of the Beijing Rules.[91]

Criminal proceedings with shaming elements could perhaps be compared with the idea of shaming penalty. The nature of the trial might have been seen as inhuman or degrading because the trial was public and the boys' identities were released to the public regardless of their young age. Even though trial in itself is not a punishment, the trial might be able to constitute equivalent harm to the defendant comparable to inhuman or degrading treatment. Revealing the children's identity could be argued to resemble a shaming punishment. The Court, however, did not find a

---

[86] See for example Appleton and Grover (2007), pp. 597, 609–610.

[87] Kahan (1996), pp. 591, 633. See also Melander (2008), p. 314.

[88] Kahan and Posner (1999), p. 365.

[89] *V. v. The United Kingdom* App no 24888/94 (ECtHR, 16 December 1999); *T. v. The United Kingdom* App no 24724/94 (ECtHR, 16 December 1999).

[90] *V. v. The United Kingdom* App no 24888/94 (ECtHR, 16 December 1999), paras 7, 9, 15–17, 20–24, 35–40.

[91] Ibid., paras 45–46.

violation of Article 3 ECHR.[92] According to the joint partly dissenting opinion of judges Pastor Ridruejo, Ress, Makarczyk, Tulkens and Butkevych, the complaint under Article 3 was well-founded and the trial reached the minimum level for inhuman and degrading treatment. However, they found that a lack of privacy of juvenile defendants could not be decisive for the question whether the trial in public amounted to treatment attaining the minimum level of severity under Article 3. Instead, they found that the relevant criterion was the effect of the treatment on the children.

Human dignity is a vague concept. The Kantian conception of human dignity is taken here as the starting point for the study.[93] The core idea of human dignity lies in individual self-determination and the equal self-worth of all human beings.[94] Equality and autonomy are the core ideas of the concept of human dignity. According to Kant, all human beings have an intrinsic value that is based on the idea of individual autonomy. The principle of morality requires that persons ought not to be treated as means to an end, but always as an end itself.[95] At the minimum, human dignity is essentially just about being,[96] which is why the concept of human dignity expresses the equality of all human beings. The intrinsic worth of others should be recognized and respected by all.[97] The core of human dignity consists of individuals' freedom to decide on their own autonomy and the obligation of others to restrain themselves from infringing that right.[98] Robert Alexy has explained this interrelationship between human dignity and negative liberty. If the principle of negative liberty would not apply, human dignity could not be respected.[99] Thus human dignity sets limits on the use of individual autonomy as well.[100] This aspect has been described as 'human dignity as a constraint'.[101] The dichotomy of human dignity as an individual right and as an objective value is used to describe the two dimensions of human dignity.[102] Human dignity as an objective value can restrict an individual's autonomy to decide on conduct that infringes an objective standard of human dignity. For example dwarf tossing is prohibited because it violates human dignity objectively even though the individual herself would not mind this treatment.

Equality as the basic idea of human dignity is the core idea of the democracy principle and has been presented above. Regardless of whether or not human dignity

---

[92] Ibid., para 80.

[93] See for example Dan-Cohen (2011), p. 9; McCrudden (2008), p. 655; Foster (2011); On the religious conception see for example Dan-Cohen (2011), pp. 9, 11.

[94] Glensy (2011), pp. 65, 67–68. In relation to freedom of speech see Robert Post (2011).

[95] Immanuel Kant, *Groundwork of the Metaphysics of Morals* (Jonathan Bennett tr), ch 2, pp. 33–34 www.stolaf.edu/people/huff/classes/GoodnEvil/Readings/kantgw.pdf, accessed 25 June 2018.

[96] McCrudden (2008), pp. 655, 679; Foster (2011), pp. 5–6, 10.

[97] McCrudden (2008), pp. 655, 679.

[98] Nieminen (2005), pp. 49, 54–55.

[99] Alexy (1986), p. 246.

[100] Nieminen (2005), pp. 49, 54–55.

[101] Beyleveld and Brownsword (2001), p. 11.

[102] Hörnle and Kremnitzer (2011), pp. 143, 148.

is explicitly mentioned in national constitutions,[103] the principle of human dignity is a common value throughout Europe because it is a fundamental value behind the ECHR regime. Human dignity is not mentioned in the Convention but the ECtHR has recognized its status in its case law as has been explained above. Human dignity is protected through other fundamental and human rights provisions and is concretized in those provisions.[104] Because human dignity is also an underlying value of democracy, it has implicit expression in constitutions through the democracy principle. The status of human dignity as a pan-European value is undisputable regardless of explicit expressions at the surface level of law.

The former president of the European Court of Human Rights, Jean-Paul Costa, has explored the links between democracy and human rights under the case law of the ECtHR. He analysed the elements of democracy in the light of the Convention rights. First he mentions the accountability of states. The states are accountable to guarantee the Convention rights and democracy for their citizens.[105] In literature, democratic governance is even seen as an emerging right; democracy is seen as a condition without which governance cannot be validated or legitimate.[106]

In the ECHR context, the states' responsibility to guarantee the Convention rights and democracy means two things. Firstly, the states are obliged to guarantee freedom from the state. This is expressed in various forms, such as in freedom from torture, slavery, invasion of privacy, or unjust trial. Secondly, the states must guarantee the equal opportunity to engage in political activity. The Convention ensures this through Article 10 ECHR concerning the *freedom of expression*, Article 11 ECHR concerning the *freedom of assembly and association*, and Article 3 of the First Protocol concerning the *right to free elections*. Next, these elements will be studied as expressions of protection human dignity as an objective value. After that, a compact study is carried out of the protection of human dignity as an individual right.

3.3.1.1 Protection of Democratic Rights: Human Dignity as an Objective Value

Freedom of Expression The ECHR protects the freedom of expression as a fundamental building block of democratic society. The governments of democracies are chosen by fair elections but these democratic processes cannot function without

---

[103] Some EU Member States have explicit references to human dignity in their constitutional documents, as do for example, the constitutions of Belgium, Germany, Estonia, Greece, Spain, Ireland, Italy, Latvia, Lithuania, Hungary, Austria, Poland, Portugal, Slovenia, Slovakia, and Finland. European Parliament, *Charter of Fundamental Rights in the European Union Article 1 Human Dignity*, 6. National Laws, www.europarl.europa.eu/comparl/libe/elsj/charter/art01/default_en.htm, accessed 25 June 2018.

[104] Nieminen (2005), pp. 49, 54–55.

[105] Jean-Paul Costa (2008).

[106] Franck (1992), pp. 46–47; Marks (2011), p. 507.

freedom of speech and freedom of association.[107] The core of the freedom of speech is political speech, the right to present competing views for political discussion and decision-making.

Freedom of the press plays crucial role in the democratic development. This is why the sanction policy in relation to limiting freedom of expression should not be too repressive. Imprisonment should be used only exceptionally and the use of other sanctions, such as fines and damages, should be proportionate when freedom of expression is restricted, keeping in mind that heavy sanctions and damages might influence negatively to the media's willingness to fulfil its functions (the so-called chilling effect).[108]

In relation to the freedom of expression, imprisonment as a form of sanction should be used only exceptionally. The use of a prison sentence is compatible with Article 10 ECHR only in exceptional circumstances, for example in cases of hate speech or incitement to violence.[109] Article 10 ECHR can be restricted as long as the doctrine of margin of appreciation is followed. The ECtHR has authority to evaluate whether the restriction or the interference is justified. The restrictions need to be *prescribed by law*, they need to have *legitimate aim*, and they need to be *necessary in democratic society*. The restriction can be seen as *necessary* if there is a *pressing social need* at hand. There is a certain margin of appreciation to decide if there is such a need, and if it is recognized, what kinds of restrictions are made. The restriction must *be proportionate to the legitimate aims pursued* and the reasons behind the restriction must be *relevant and sufficient*.[110]

Imprisonment is found to violate Article 10 ECHR relative to offences of freedom of expression as a main rule,[111] but a suspended prison sentence might not in the Court's opinion constitute a violation of Article 10 ECHR.[112] However, the Court finds that in classic cases 'of defamation of an individual in the context of a debate

---

[107] See for example Mirsky (2005), pp. 358, 360.

[108] For example Parliamentary Assembly Recommendation 1506(2001) Freedom of expression and information in the media in Europe, paras 1, 5, 12. See also Parliamentary Assembly Resolution 1535(2007) Threats to the lives and freedom of expression of journalists, paras 3, 6. See also Parliamentary Assembly Resolution 1577 (2007) Towards decriminalization of defamation, paras 1, 4–7, 11–14, 17. On the chilling effect, for example, *Cumpănă and Mazăre v. Romania* App no 33348/96 (ECtHR, 17 December 2004), para 119.

[109] *Cumpănă and Mazăre v. Romania* App no 33348/96 (ECtHR, 17 December 2004), paras 37, 48, 50, 112, 115–119; *Mariapori v. Finland* App no 37751/07 (ECtHR, 6 July 2010), para 67.

[110] *Lešnik v. Slovakia* App no 35640/97 (ECtHR, 11 June 2003), paras 41–52; *Mariapori v. Finland* App no 37751/07 (ECtHR, 6 July 2010), paras 50–55; *Žugic v. Croatia* App no 3699/08 (ECtHR, 31 August 2011), paras 40–44; *Lopuch v. Poland* App no 43587/09 (ECtHR, 24 July 2012), paras 51–58; *Skalka v. Poland* App no 43425/98 (ECtHR, 27 May 2003), paras 30–35; *Cumpănă and Mazăre v. Romania* App no 33348/96 (ECtHR, 17 December 2004), paras 84–90; *Saaristo and Others v. Finland* App no 184/06 (ECtHR, 12 October 2010), paras 52–57; *Otegi Mondragon v. Spain* App no 2034/07 (ECtHR, 15 March 2011), paras 52–57. See also Jussi Matikkala (2012), p. 153.

[111] *Skalka v. Poland* App no 43425/98 (ECtHR, 27 May 2003), paras 12, 17, 19, 39, 42.

[112] *Lešnik v. Slovakia* App no 35640/97 (ECtHR, 11 June 2003), paras 25, 64, 65.

on a matter of legitimate public interest—present no justification whatsoever for the imposition of a prison sentence' even if it was conditional.[113] Disqualification from exercising civil rights has also been considered as inappropriate sanction. A prohibition on working as a journalist has not been justifiable either, since it 'contravened with the principle that the press must be able to perform the role of a public watchdog in a democratic society'. Restraining the activities of journalists can be justified only exceptionally.[114] In its case law, the ECtHR has referred to the Parliamentary Assembly Resolution 1577(2007) *Towards decriminalization of defamation* in which it is urged to abolish the possibility of imprisonment for defamation from penal codes even if it is not used.[115]

It is clear that prison sentences can be used *at least* in the case of hate speech or incitement to violence or the promotion of negationism. The list is not exhaustive. From the perspective of predictability, open formulations such as *'in exceptional circumstances, notably where other fundamental rights have been seriously impaired, as, for example, in the case of hate speech or incitement to violence'*[116] or *'unless the seriousness of the violation of the rights or reputation of others makes it a strictly necessary and proportionate penalty, especially where other fundamental rights have been seriously violated through defamatory or insulting statements in the media, such as hate speech'*[117] are problematic. The contracting parties do not know exactly which conduct they can punish with imprisonment.

The freedom of speech is an essential foundation of a democratic society. The Court finds that pluralism, tolerance and broadmindedness require that the freedom of expression applies also to statements that 'offend, shock or disturb'. This pluralism is a prerequisite for democratic society. The freedom of political debate is 'at the very core of the democratic society which prevails throughout the Convention'.[118] Since Governments are accountable to their constituents, their conduct needs to be open for public discussion without a fear of the Government resorting to criminal proceedings.[119]

The ECtHR identifies tolerance and respect for equal dignity of all human beings as foundations of a democratic, pluralistic society.[120] Democratic constitutionalism protects the ideal of pluralistic society and cultural heterogeneity by protecting

---

[113] *Cumpănă and Mazăre v. Romania* App no 33348/96 (ECtHR, 17 December 2004), para 116; *Mariapori v. Finland* App no 37751/07 (ECtHR, 6 July 2010), para 68.

[114] *Cumpănă and Mazăre v. Romania* App no 33348/96 (ECtHR, 17 December 2004), paras 117–119.

[115] *Mariapori v. Finland* App no 37751/07 (ECtHR, 6 July 2010), para 69; *Saaristo and Others v. Finland* App no 184/06 (ECtHR, 12 October 2010), para 69; *Otegi Mondragon v. Spain* App no 2034/07 (ECtHR, 15 March 2011), para 31.

[116] For example *Mariapori v. Finland* App no 37751/07 (ECtHR, 6 July 2010), para 67.

[117] Committee of Ministers Declaration on freedom of political debate in the media 12 February 2004, para VIII).

[118] *Lingens v. Austria* App no 9815/82 (ECtHR, 8 July 1986), para 41–42.

[119] *Castells v. Spain* App no 11798/85 (ECtHR, 23 April 1992), para 46.

[120] Affaire *Erbakan c. Turquie* Requête no 59405/00 (ECtHR, 6 July 2006), para 56.

individual rights and group rights such as women's rights or minority groups' rights.[121] Thus, it is sometimes considered necessary to criminalize and prevent different forms of expressions, which spread, incite, promote or justify hatred-based intolerance.[122] For example hate speech focusing on race, sexual orientation or religion, negationism, and speech based on totalitarian doctrine are considered offensive and contrary to the Convention.[123] This particularly serious attitude towards hate speech, incitement to violence, and promotion of negationism stems from the principles of equality and human dignity.[124] Since hate speech aims to pinpoint that 'distinctions of race are distinctions of merit, dignity, status, and personhood' it injures the dignity of the person (or the group) that is the target of the speech.[125]

Democracy expresses human dignity and equality by aiming to achieve fair governance.[126] Examined from another perspective, respect for human dignity is a prerequisite for democracy.[127] Human dignity has vast consequences within the context of free speech. It affects the dignity of the speaker, the dignity of the target of the speech and the dignity of the individuals who should or should not hear or otherwise receive the information.[128] With respect to dignity, free speech can be evaluated from the perspectives of the speaker and the targets of the speech. From the perspective of the speaker, human dignity manifests itself through the autonomy for their opinion and through equal right to express the opinions. However hate speech, incitement to violence, and promotion of negationism violate the autonomy and equal worth of the targets of the speech.

When it is accepted that the core area of free speech is political speech, how can it be determined what kind of speech is wrong and thus does not fall under the category of acceptable political speech? The natural starting point is to notice Article 17 ECHR, which concerns the prohibition on abuse of rights. According to Article 17, the Convention cannot be interpreted in such a way that it would be allowed to destroy rights and freedoms guaranteed in the Convention or limit them to greater extent than what is provided for in the Convention. Article 10(2) ECHR also enables limitations to freedom of expression if they are necessary in democratic society. Since respect for human dignity is a prerequisite for democracy, destructive messages that violate the human dignity of others can be seen to target the core value of democracy at the same time. The next quotation from the Court's case law illustrates well how freedom of expression, democracy, and its underlying values such as human dignity are intertwined.

---

[121] Post (2000), pp. 185, 190–192.

[122] Affaire *Erbakan c. Turquie* Requête no 59405/00 (ECtHR, 6 July 2006), para 56.

[123] Factsheet – Hate speech, European Court of Human Rights, Press Unit, June 2012.

[124] Affaire *Erbakan c. Turquie* Requête no 59405/00 (ECtHR, 6 July 2006), para 56.

[125] Delgado (1982), pp. 133, 135–136.

[126] Catá Backer (2007–2008), p. 57. See also Glensy (2011), pp. 65, 10, 68.

[127] Möllers (2009), pp. 416, 432.

[128] Glensy (2011), pp. 65, 82; Greenawalt (1989), pp. 119, 153; Wright (2006), pp. 527, 529.

As has been stated many times in the Court's judgments, not only is political democracy a fundamental feature of the European public order but the *Convention was designed to promote and maintain the ideals and values of a democratic society. Democracy, the Court has stressed, is the only political model contemplated in the Convention and the only one compatible with it.* By virtue of the wording of the second paragraph of Article 11, and likewise of Articles 8, 9 and 10 of the Convention, *the only necessity capable of justifying an interference with any of the rights enshrined in those Articles is one that may claim to spring from "democratic society"*[…]

Referring to the hallmarks of a "democratic society", the Court has attached particular importance to pluralism, tolerance and broadmindedness. In that context it has held that, although individual interests must on occasion be subordinated to those of a group, democracy does not simply mean that the views of the majority must always prevail: a balance must be achieved which ensures the fair and proper treatment of minorities and avoids any abuse of a dominant position[…][129] (emphasis added).

This quote illustrates that the Convention system promotes democracy as the only acceptable political model and that the Convention protects its underlying values. Any derogation from Article 10 ECHR that undermines human dignity also undermines democracy. Thus following this logic, democracy needs to protect itself from threats that stem from inside the democracy and different opinions of people.

Militant democracy is described as 'a form of constitutional democracy authorized to protect civil and political freedom by pre-emptively restricting the exercise of such freedoms'.[130] Democracy has needed to become militant in order to protect democracy from the exploitation of the democratic ideology, such as fascism. Tolerant confidence in democratic ideology and its blindness has been a weakness of democracy, thus making democracy itself the Trojan horse. In the 1920s and the 1930s anti-fascist legislation was the means of militant democracy to protect democracy itself (from itself) and the fundamental rights of individuals.[131] Today anti-hate-speech legislation, the banning of certain political parties, and anti-terrorism legislation, among others, are seen as manifestations of militant democracy.[132] Also the restriction criterion of fundamental and human rights, according to which interference with a right is possible if it is necessary in a democratic society, can be seen as the means of democracy to protect itself from the harms that democracy enables.

Hate speech, the incitement of violence, and promotion of negationism are seen to have potential to expose democracy to danger[133] because these types of speech target groups of people and label them explicitly as less worthy in terms of human dignity and implicitly also by their democratic competence. Even though human dignity is important in relation to individual autonomy and freedom of speech, '[a] constitutional democracy cannot allow for a graded hierarchy of the basic dignity of

---

[129] *Gorzelik and Others v. Poland* App no 44158/98 (ECtHR, 17 February 2004), paras 89–90.

[130] Macklem (2006) 4, p. 488. See also Loewenstein (1937a), p. 417; Loewenstein (1937b), p. 638.

[131] Loewenstein (1937a), pp. 423–424, 430–431.

[132] Macklem (2006), p. 488.

[133] Similar reasoning that hate speech and promotion of violence are a threats to democracy is also used in the United States, see Tsesis (2009), pp. 497, 502–503.

persons.'[134] The threat to democracy seems to be the ultimate reason behind the logic of imposing more intrusive sanctions in relation to hate speech, incitement of violence, and promotion of negationism. When compared to defamation for example, the act of defamation does not extend its consequences towards the ideology of democracy, whereas that is the case with hate speech.

Freedom of Assembly and Association and Right to Free Elections Freedom of assembly and association protected by Article 11 ECHR are closely connected to the freedom of expression protected by Article 10 ECHR.[135] The ECtHR has opened up the concept of pluralistic democracy in the *Refah* case by stating that political parties ensure pluralism and the functioning of democracy. Without pluralism there cannot be democracy. In addition to freedom of expression, pluralism depends on the freedom of thought, conscience and religion protected by Article 9 ECHR.[136]

According to the prohibition of abuse of rights enshrined in Article 17 ECHR, convention rights cannot be used in a way that aims at the destruction of the Convention rights and freedoms. Political parties ought to act using only legal and democratic means and their agenda ought to be in line with fundamental democratic principles. Policies or agendas cannot include incitement to violence or other incompatibilities with democracy.[137] Thus fundamental democratic principles include at least the equal worth of individuals and equal political rights. Article 3 of the first Protocol ensures the right to free elections at reasonable intervals by secret ballot. The Article ensures the right to vote and the right to stand for election to the legislature. The right to vote should be based on universal suffrage. Right to free elections guarantees the free expression of the opinion of the people in the choice of legislature. However, every contracting party can decide how they build their democratic system.[138] Even though Article 3 of the first Protocol does not include an explicit limitation clause with a list of legitimate aims, the Article is not absolute. Implied limitations are acceptable.[139] The contracting parties have a wide margin of appreciation in choosing how to mould their own democratic vision. The Court finds that '[t]here are numerous ways of organising and running electoral systems and a wealth of differences'.[140] The Convention system does not aim to fit its contracting parties into a single mould. It would not even fit into the Court's mandate to determine an exact meaning of democracy, nor can the Court examine national electoral laws in the abstract.[141] The Court can evaluate in specific cases whether democratic Convention rights have been breached or not. The case *Yumak and Sadak v*

---

[134] Wright (2006), pp. 527, 557.

[135] Jean-Paul Costa (2008).

[136] *Refah Partisi (The Welfare Party) and Others v. Turkey* App no 41340/98 (ECtHR, 13 February 2003), paras 88–90.

[137] Ibid., para 98.

[138] Jean-Paul Costa (2008).

[139] *Yumak and Sadak v. Turkey* App no 10226/03 (ECtHR, 8 July 2008), para 109.

[140] *Hirst v. the United Kingdom* (no. 2) App no 74025/01 (ECtHR, 6 October 2005), para 61.

[141] *Yumak and Sadak v. Turkey* App no 10226/03 (ECtHR, 8 July 2008), para 73.

Turkey had a special nature since the complaints were directed against Turkey's entire electoral system.[142]

3.3.1.2 Protection of Human Dignity as an Individual Right: Observations Concerning Articles 3 and 4 ECHR

Article 3 ECHR prohibits torture and inhuman or degrading treatment or punishment. The Court has defined torture in the case of *Ireland v. the United Kingdom*, in which it stated that torture is the 'deliberate inhuman treatment causing very serious and cruel suffering',[143] and thus a form of conduct that infringes human dignity.[144] According to the Court, "Article 3 enshrines one of the most fundamental values of democratic societies".[145]

In the case of *Aksoy v Turkey*, for the first time the Court evaluated treatment amounting to torture.[146] During detention, the applicant's hands had been tied behind his back and the applicant was then hung from his hands (Palestinian hanging). While hanging, he had been given electric shocks. He had also been hit and verbally abused. The methods were used in order to try to get information from the applicant. The Court found that the treatment was serious and cruel by its nature and that it could only be described as torture.[147]

In the case of *Selmouni v France* the Court has referred to the United Nations Convention against Torture and Other Cruel, Inhuman or Degrading Treatment or Punishment[148] when assessing if the conduct in the case constituted torture.[149] The UN definition of torture can be divided in three elements. First, the intentional act of torture must inflict severe mental or physical pain or suffering. Second, the purpose of the act is to obtain information or confession, to punish, to intimidate or coerce, or to discriminate. And three, the pain or suffering is inflicted by or at the instigation of or with the consent or acquiescence of a public official or other person acting in an official capacity. The Court notes that because the Convention is a living

---

[142] *Yumak and Sadak v. Turkey* App no 10226/03 (ECtHR, 8 July 2008), para 125. The applicants complained that since the political parties had to receive at least 10% of the given votes in order to get into Parliament, the Turkish electoral system breached Article 3 of the first Protocol. As a result of the threshold, 45% of the voters were not represented at the Parliament. The Court found that the 10% threshold system of the Turkish electoral system had legitimate aim of avoiding excessive parliamentary fragmentation and strengthening governmental stability. The Court found that any specific maximum percentage limit for the possible thresholds cannot be abstractly set.

[143] *Ireland v. The United Kingdom* App no 5310/71 (ECtHR, 18 January 1978), para 167.

[144] Kidutuksen kriminalisointi, Oikeusministeriön työtyhmämietintöjä 2008:1, 38.

[145] See for example *Ilaşcu and Others v. Moldova and Russia* App no 48787/99 (ECtHR, 8 July 2004), para 424; *Selmouni v. France* App no 25803/94 (ECtHR, 28 July 1999), para 95.

[146] Pellonpää (2012), p. 348.

[147] *Aksoy v. Turkey* App no 21987/93 (ECtHR, 18 December 1996), paras 14, 59–64.

[148] United Nations Convention against Torture and Other Cruel, Inhuman or Degrading Treatment or Punishment (26 June 1987), UNTS Vol. 1465, I-24841.

[149] *Selmouni v. France* App no 25803/94 (ECtHR, 28 July 1999), para 97.

instrument, certain acts which are not classified as torture today may be classified as torture in the future.[150]

The contracting parties have to ensure that the rights guaranteed in the Convention are not theoretical and illusory but practical and effective. Thus, if an individual makes a complaint that she has suffered from treatment that infringes Article 3 ECHR, the state must conduct an effective official investigation. Such investigation 'should be capable of leading to the identification and punishment of those responsible'.[151] This means that the contracting parties do not only have negative obligation to restrain their officials from acting in a way that would fall under Article 3 ECHR, they also have positive obligation to ensure effective legal remedies.[152] One way for a contracting party to fulfil its obligations stemming from Article 3 ECHR is to explicitly criminalize torture and other types of conduct that can be classified as inhuman or degrading treatment under other crime provisions.

The contracting parties also need to have effective legal remedies for ill-treatment administered by private individuals that falls under Article 3 ECHR. To fall within the scope of Article 3 ECHR, the ill-treatment must attain a minimum level of severity. The assessment depends on 'all the circumstances of the case, such as nature and context of the treatment, its duration, its physical and mental effects, and in some instances, the sex, age and state of health of the victim'. In the case of *A v the United Kingdom*, the Court found that the respondent state was responsible to a violation because English law did not provide adequate protection against treatment contrary to Article 3 ECHR. The applicant was beaten by his stepfather and English law protected parents when they 'administer punishment which is moderate and reasonable in the circumstances' in that parental role. The burden of proof to satisfy the jury as to the fact that the punishment did not constitute a lawful punishment is on the prosecution.[153] It can be concluded from this that in order to fulfil their obligations under Article 3 ECHR, the contracting parties need to have comprehensive provisions of criminal law and effective legal remedies against different kinds of ill treatment administered by private individuals.

The ECtHR has found that rape conducted by a state official can be deemed torture,[154] and that threats of rape combined with beating and other threats by state officials have constituted torture.[155] Rape may also constitute a crime against

---

[150] Ibid., para 101. See also Kidutuksen kriminalisointi, Oikeusministeriön työtyhmämietintöjä (2008), pp. 1, 23.

[151] *Selmouni v. France* App no 25803/94 (ECtHR, 28 July 1999), para 177. See also Kidutuksen kriminalisointi, Oikeusministeriön työtyhmämietintöjä (2008), pp. 23–24.

[152] Kidutuksen kriminalisointi, Oikeusministeriön työtyhmämietintöjä (2008), pp. 1, 23.

[153] *A. v. The United Kingdom* App no 25599/94 (ECtHR, 23 September 1998), paras 14, 20–24.

[154] *Aydin v. Turkey* App no 23178/94 (ECtHR, 25 September 1997), para 86; *Maslova and Nalbandov v. Russia* App no 839/02 (ECtHR, 24 January 2008), para 106.

[155] *Menesheva v. Russia* App no 59261/00 (ECtHR, 9 March 2006), paras 14, 58–63. See also *Gäfgen v. Germany* App no 22978/05 (ECtHR, 1 June 2010), paras 94–101, in which the applicant had claimed he had been threatened with sexual and physical abuse during his interrogation. The Court however did not found his claims concerning the threats of sexual abuse being proved without reasonable doubt. The other aspects of the conduct during his interrogation was however seen to fall under inhuman treatment (Article 3 ECHR).

humanity, as the essential protected interest is human dignity.[156] More than 15 years ago, the International Criminal Tribunal for Rwanda established that the coercive nature was a decisive element of rape rather than the lack of consent. Use of physical force is not a necessary element of coercion: threats, intimidation, or simply the environment of armed conflict is sufficient to fulfil the requirement of coercion.[157] Shortly after, in *Kunarac, Kovac and Vukovic* the International Criminal Tribunal of the former Yugoslavia (ICTY) emphasized the lack of genuine consent as an essential element of rape.[158] In *M.C. v Bulgaria*, the ECtHR refers to several of judgments of the ICTY, including the case of *Kunarac, Kovac and Vukovic*.[159]

In *M.C. v Bulgaria* the ECtHR evaluated if the definition of rape could be relevant in evaluating state responsibility.[160] The issue was whether the respondent state had provided effective legal protection against rape and sexual abuse. The applicant claimed to be raped twice during one night (31 July 1995-1 August 1995). Police had made an initial inquiry on the matter in August 1995 and forwarded the matter to the prosecutor, who did not press charges. The investigations were resumed in November 1996. In December 1996 the investigator stated that there was no evidence that the suspects had threatened the applicant with violence and proposed that the prosecutor close the case. From January 1997 to March 1997 an additional investigation was undertaken. It ended in the discontinuation of the criminal investigation because it found the use of force or threats had not been established beyond reasonable doubt. Article 152 §§ of the Bulgarian criminal code defined rape as 'sexual intercourse with a woman (1) incapable of defending herself, where she did not consent; (2) who was compelled by the use of force or threats; who was brought to a state of helplessness by the perpetrator.' The ECtHR referred to paragraph 35 of the Recommendation Rec (2002)5 of the Committee of Ministers of the Council of Europe on the protection of women against violence, according to which the contracting parties should penalize any sexual act committed against non-consenting persons, even if they do not show signs of resistance.[161]

As shown above, human dignity is about equality and autonomy. In rape, the autonomy of the victim is violated, thus showing that provisions criminalizing rape do not protect only the sexual and physical integrity of individuals, but their dignity as well. Similarly, in the United States, sexual assault committed by a prison guard

---

[156] Rome Statute of the International Criminal Court Article 7, Statute of the International Criminal Tribunal for Rwanda (ICTR) Article 3, ICTR-96-4-T *The Prosecutor v. Jean-Paul Akayesu* (ICTR 2 September 1998).

[157] ICTR-96-4-T *The Prosecutor v. Jean-Paul Akayesu* (ICTR 2 September 1998), para 688. See also Jokila (2010), pp. 65–66.

[158] IT-96-23-T & IT-96-23/1-T *Prosecutor v. Dragoljub Kunarac, Radomir Kovac and Zoran Vukovic* (ICTY 22 February 2001), para 464. See also Jokila (2010), p. 66.

[159] *M.C. v Bulgaria* App no 39272/98 (ECtHR, 4 December 2003), paras 102–107.

[160] Pitea (2005), p. 447.

[161] *M.C. v Bulgaria* App no 39272/98 (ECtHR, 4 December 2003), paras 3, 11–31, 44–46, 51–64, 74, 101; Recommendation Rec (2002)5 of the Committee of Ministers of the Council of Europe on the protection of women against violence, para 35.

has been seen as offensive to human dignity.[162] The United Nations Committee on the Elimination of Discrimination against Women has also associated gender-based violence such as rape and sexual assault with questions of human integrity and dignity.[163] The ECtHR referred to this recommendation in its judgment[164] thus linking the rape offence to human dignity. Paragraph 165 of the judgment reflects the central elements of dignity—equality and autonomy—especially well by stating that 'the development of law and practice in that area reflects the evolution of societies towards effective *equality* and respect for each individual's sexual *autonomy*' (emphasis added). The Court refers to both of the sub-elements of dignity, equality and autonomy, in this paragraph. Already in its previous case law, the ECtHR has connected rape to human dignity. In the cases of *S.W. v the United Kingdom* and *C.R. v the United Kingdom* concerning marital rape, the ECtHR stated that '[w]hat is more, the abandonment of the unacceptable idea of a husband being immune against prosecution for rape of his wife was in conformity not only with a civilised concept of marriage but also, and above all, with the fundamental objectives of the Convention, the very essence of which is respect for human dignity and human freedom.'[165]

In *M.C. v Bulgaria*, the ECtHR found that the contracting parties have an obligation to enact effective criminal law provisions against rape and to apply them in practice through effective investigation and prosecution. The Court also notices that the contracting parties have a certain margin of appreciation, which is limited by Convention provisions.[166] As noted above in Sect. 1.3.3.1, the more there is a consensus on particular issue, the narrower the margin of appreciation is concerning that issue.[167] However, according to Article 15(2) ECHR, Articles 2, 3, 4(1), and 7 ECHR contain absolute rights, which means that national authorities do not have discretion to determine the scope of these rights.[168] It is noteworthy that in *M.C. v Bulgaria* the Court referred to the margin of appreciation when it analysed Article 3 ECHR in conjunction with Article 8 ECHR (right to respect for private and family life). It did so even though according to Article 15(2) ECHR contracting parties cannot make derogations to Article 3 ECHR. This provision should have meant that there is no margin of appreciation relative to Article 3 ECHR in itself.

Different opinions have been introduced in literature on the matter. In his article on the role of margin of appreciation in the Convention's interpretation, Steven

---

[162] Case of *Douglas W. Schwenk v. James Hartford; Steve Sinclair; Robert Mitchell* No. 97-35870 United States Court of Appeals for the Ninth Circuit 204 F.3d, paras 17–18. See also Wright (2006), pp. 527, 533.

[163] General Recommendation 19 (29 January 1992) of the United Nations Committee on the Elimination of Discrimination against Women, para 24.

[164] *M.C. v Bulgaria* App no 39272/98 (ECtHR, 4 December 2003), para 108.

[165] *S.W. v. the United Kingdom* App no 20166/92 (ECtHR, 22 November 1995), para 44; *C.R. v. the United Kingdom* App no 20190/92 (ECtHR, 22 November 1995), para 42.

[166] *M.C. v Bulgaria* App no 39272/98 (ECtHR, 4 December 2003), paras 153–155.

[167] Brauch (2005), pp. 113, 128; de la Rasilla del Moral (2006), pp. 611, 617.

[168] See also Greer (2000), pp. 26–27.

Greer shows that the limits of applicability of the doctrine of margin of appreciation relative to different Convention rights is not clear. While some commentators argue that there is no limit to the doctrine, some emphasise that the doctrine has not been applied with respect to Article 2 ECHR (right to life), Article 3 ECHR (prohibition of torture and inhuman and degrading treatment), or Article 4 (prohibition of slavery and forced labour).[169] According to Howard Davis, the contracting parties have either little or no margin of appreciation at all relative to Article 3 ECHR.[170]

As a general rule, it is clear that the margin of appreciation doctrine applies to express limitations, in other words to limitations which are expressly mentioned in the Articles of the Convention (such as those in the second paragraphs of Articles 8 to 11 ECHR). Some other Convention rights, such as Article 3 of Protocol 1, leave a margin of appreciation to the contracting parties even though they do not contain express limitation clauses. These are often referred to as implied limitations. However, articles 2, 3, 4(1), and 7 ECHR have special position in the Convention system because contracting parties cannot derogate from them even in a time of emergency. Thus they are special compared to the other rights of the Convention. The use of the margin of appreciation doctrine in the context of Article 3 ECHR in *M.C. v Bulgaria* seems possible only because the Court interprets Article 3 ECHR in conjunction with Article 8 ECHR. The case of *M.C. v Bulgaria* seems to be the first case where the Court has used the margin of appreciation doctrine in conjunction with Article 3 ECHR.[171]

Later however, in only one other case, the ECtHR has spoken about margin of appreciation in conjunction with Article 3 ECHR alone. The admissibility case of the application by John Wilkinson concerned medical treatment against a patient's will. The patient was seen by the state officials to be incapable to decide on his own treatment. When the Court assessed the state's obligations under Article 3 ECHR, it noted that 'the decision as to what therapeutic methods are necessary is principally one for the national medical authorities: those authorities have a *certain margin of appreciation* in this respect since it is in the first place for them to evaluate the evidence in a particular case'.[172] Whether to use coercive medical treatment or not is an issue that needs to be decided by the contracting parties. Here the assessment does not focus on the quality of the medical treatment but whether or not the medical treatment is used, which of course is a medical decision. State responsibility relating to the issue can be evaluated by assessing if the state has offered legal remedies for the patient by ensuring proceedings in which the medical decision on coercive treatment can be evaluated; whether the treatment is necessary and in the best interest of the patient. The use of the doctrine on margin of appreciation in conjunction with Article 3 ECHR could be criticized because Article 15 ECHR recognizes Article 3 ECHR as non-derogable, and thus margin of appreciation ought not to

---

[169] Greer (2010), pp. 1, 4.

[170] Davis (2007), p. 116.

[171] Pitea (2005), pp. 447, 456.

[172] Decision as to the admissibility of Application no. 14659/02 by *John Wilkinson against the United Kingdom* (ECHR, 28 February 2006) 20–21.

apply to its scope. Also, the issue could have been assessed from the point of view of Article 8 (right to privacy) in conjunction with Article 13 (right to effective remedy). Lastly, even if the circumstances were evaluated to fall under the scope of Article 3 ECHR, there was no need to use the margin of appreciation doctrine.

However, what would it mean from the perspective of criminal law if rights that are enshrined in Article 3 ECHR are accepted as absolute rights? Would it mean, for example, that because the contracting parties have both negative and positive obligations to fulfil the rights guaranteed in the Convention, that excuses, such as command from superior officer, could not be used in relation with some types of offences, such as torture? Could the absolute nature of rights enshrined in Article 3 ECHR affect the theory of criminal liability?

Use of the doctrine of margin of appreciation in the case of *M.C. v Bulgaria* can be argued to be inconsistent with the Court's previous jurisprudence according to which implied limitations are not allowed in relation to positive obligations under articles containing a limitation clause.[173] This means that restrictions 'to Articles 8–11 must be justified under the provisions of the second paragraph of the article in issue'.[174] Due to this, the Court's use of margin of appreciation in *M.C. v Bulgaria* could only have focused on Article 3 ECHR, not in Article 8 ECHR. *In Golder v the United Kingdom* the Court has stated that '[t]he restrictive formulation used at paragraph 2 (art. 8-2) ('There shall be no interference … except such as …') leaves no room for the concept of implied limitations,'[175] meaning that implied limitations are acceptable only in regard to articles that do not have express limitation clauses. Then again, if implied limitations would be possible in connection to Article 3 ECHR, would the prohibition of torture be absolute? One can only say that there has to be certain margin of appreciation for the contracting parties to decide on the measures they use to ensure that the rights protected in Article 3 ECHR are effectively fulfilled.

In the past, the Convention has not had much effect on the special part of criminal law,[176] except for the overall obligation of the contracting parties to criminalize the most serious forms of conduct that violates human rights. The case of *X and Y v the Netherlands* concerned a rape of a resident of a mental institution. The domestic legislation did not enable holding the abuser criminally liable. The ECtHR found that 'the protection afforded by the civil law in the case of wrongdoing of the kind inflicted on Miss Y is insufficient' since 'this is a case where fundamental values and essential aspects of private life are at stake'. The Court also stated that 'effective deterrence is indispensable in this area and it can be achieved only by criminal-law provisions'.[177] More recently the ECtHR has often stated that the contracting parties

---

[173] Cesare Pitea (2005), p. 447.

[174] Jacobs et al. (2010), pp. 309–310.

[175] *Golder v. the United Kingdom* App no 4451/70 (ECtHR, 21 February 1975), para 44.

[176] Sakari Melander (2011), pp. 239, 256.

[177] *X and Y v. the Netherlands* App no. 8978/80 (ECtHR, 26 March 1985), para 27.

have an obligation to criminalize certain types of conduct, such as taking someone's life unlawfully,[178] forced labour, slavery or servitude,[179] or human trafficking.[180]

However, the case of *M.C. v Bulgaria* is different in that it narrows the margin of appreciation. The contracting parties have to define the essential elements of the rape offence.[181] The case also gives guidelines on how national criminal law on rape ought to be interpreted and emphasizes the importance of effective investigation and prosecution procedures. This kind of argumentation used by the ECtHR indicates, according to Petter Asp, that the case of *M.C. v Bulgaria* does not necessarily require reform of national laws concerning sexual offences into a form that would explicitly state that non-consent is a sufficient requirement for establishing the rape offence. More important than the wording of the crime provision is the result of the investigation, prosecution, and court processes, and that non-consensual sexual acts are and can be efficiently dealt with in the legal systems of the Contracting parties.[182]

The ECtHR established that there is a European (and international) consensus on the definition of rape. The Court found that a requirement of physical resistance is not a part of that European consensus. As result of this observation, the ECtHR found that 'the member States' positive obligations under Articles 3 and 8 of the Convention must be seen as requiring the penalisation and effective prosecution of any non-consensual sexual act, including in the absence of physical resistance by the victim'.[183] In other words, definitions of rape or processes of investigation and

---

[178] *Nachova and Others v. Bulgaria* App no. 43577/98 and 43579/98 (ECtHR, 26 February 2004), para 157, where the ECtHR stated that "compliance with the State's positive obligations under Article 2 of the Convention requires that the domestic legal system must demonstrate its capacity to enforce criminal law against those who unlawfully took the life of another, irrespective of the victim's racial or ethnic origin"; *Branko Tomasic and Others v. Croatia* App no 46598/06 (ECtHR, 15 January 2009), para 49, where the ECtHR states that "... a primary duty on the State to secure the right to life by putting in place effective criminal-law provisions to deter ..."; *Opuz v. Turkey* App no 33401/02 (ECtHR, 9 June 2009), para 128.

[179] *Siliadin v. France* App no 73316/01 (ECtHR, 26 July 2005); *C.N. v. the United Kingdom* App no 4239/08 (ECtHR, 13 November 2012), paras 81–82, where the ECtHR found that investigation of the applicant's complaints concerning domestic servitude was "ineffective due to the absence of specific legislation criminalising such treatment" constituting a violation of Article 4 ECHR; *C.N. and V. v. France* App no. 67724/09 (ECtHR, 11 October 2012), para 104, the ECtHR stating that the contracting parties have a "positive obligation to penalise and effectively prosecute actions in breach of Article 4".

[180] *Rantsev v. Cyprus and Russia* App no. 25965/04 (ECtHR, 7 January 2010), para 285, where the ECtHR referred to case of *Siliadin* and found that the ECtHR has confirmed that Article 4 ECHR entails "a specific positive obligation on member States to penalise and prosecute effectively any act aimed at maintaining a person in a situation of slavery, servitude or forced or compulsory labour" and that "in order to comply with this obligation, *member States are required to* put in place a legislative and administrative framework to *prohibit and punish trafficking*".

[181] Melander (2011), pp. 239, 257–258.

[182] Asp (2010), pp. 229, 232–234.

[183] *M.C. v Bulgaria* App no 39272/98 (ECtHR, 4 December 2003), paras 156–159, 162–163, 166.

the consideration of charges which require that physical resistance is used violate Article 3 ECHR.[184]

Thus the Court has established a specific obligation for the contracting parties to meet the European standards in the formulation of the penal provision on rape. If absence of consent is not *explicitly* mentioned as an essential element of the crime, the rape provision should cover situations of non-consensual sexual acts at least by leaving room for interpretation. Article 7 ECHR needs to be taken into account. Article 7 ECHR would require in this context that penal provisions on rape can be interpreted in the manner the Court requires within the limits and requirements of the principle of legality. In other words, the European constitutional principles of respecting human integrity and dignity require certain kinds of penal provisions, and more specifically in this context, a penal provision of rape that enables investigation, prosecution, and conviction based on circumstances where a lack of consent is at hand. If the wording of a national provision on rape does not allow room for prosecution of a *non-consensual sexual act,* the contracting party needs to reconsider and reform the wording of provision. Taking into account the requirement of precision of penal provisions and the aim of predictability, it might be advisable for the contracting parties to explicitly mention the lack of consent as an essential element of the provision on rape.

Similarly as in *M.C v Bulgaria* where the ECtHR imposed obligation to effectively criminalize rape, in case of *Siliadin v France*, the ECtHR has imposed an obligation to criminalize servitude and forced labour. In *Siliadin*, the applicant had arrived in France when she was 15 years old with a person 'who had agreed with her father that she would work until her air ticket had been reimbursed, that her immigration status would be regularized and that she would be sent to school'. The labour lasted about 15 h a day every day of a week and she had not made the decision concerning the work by herself. Being underage, she had no other resources, was forced to live in the house where she worked and was forbidden to leave the house.[185]

The ECtHR found that the applicant was held in servitude, in domestic slavery, as meant in Article 4 ECHR, and that 'positive obligations under Article 4 of the Convention must be seen as requiring the penalization and effective prosecution of any act aimed at maintaining a person in such a situation'.[186] Conduct that forces another person to work for which the person has not offered himself voluntarily under the threat of any penalty is considered by the ECtHR as forced labour that should be penalized by the contracting parties. The contracting parties ought to also criminalize servitude which for the purposes of the Convention means 'an obligation to provide one's services that is imposed by the use of coercion'.[187] The Court referred to its previous judgment in *M.C. v Bulgaria* when it imposed the criminalization obligation.[188] Based on *Siliadin*, and the following judgements of *C.N. v the*

---

[184] Pellonpää (2012), p. 345.

[185] *Siliadin v. France* App no 73316/01 (ECtHR, 26 July 2005), paras 109, 126.

[186] Ibid., paras 129, 111–112.

[187] Ibid., paras 116–117, 124.

[188] Ibid., para 112.

United Kingdom,[189] *C.N. and V. v France*,[190] and *Rantsev v Cyprus and Russia*[191] it is clear that Article 4 ECHR imposes obligations to criminalize variety of types of conduct. In *C.N. v the United Kingdom*[192] the ECtHR found that investigation of the applicant's complaints concerning domestic servitude was 'ineffective due to the absence of specific legislation criminalizing such treatment' constituting a violation of Article 4 ECHR. In *C.N. and V. v France*[193] the ECtHR stated that the contracting parties have a 'positive obligation to penalise and effectively prosecute actions in breach of Article 4'. In *Rantsev v Cyprus and Russia*[194] the ECtHR referred to case of *Siliadin* and found that the ECtHR has confirmed that Article 4 ECHR entails a specific obligation to penalize and prosecute human trafficking and any act aimed at maintaining a person in a situation of slavery, servitude or forced or compulsory labor.

In two cases, one concerning the definition of rape and the other the essential elements of crime provisions of servitude, the ECtHR has now set clear criminalization obligations for the contracting parties that not only require the criminalization itself, but that also set substantive minimum criteria for the national criminal laws. The ECtHR does not necessarily require changes in national law depending on whether the national provisions can be interpreted in a way that shows respect to human dignity and whether national procedural rules on investigation, prosecution and conviction can be used effectively.[195]

The states' positive obligation to protect the Convention rights requires that the contracting parties aim to deter individuals from violating the rights of others. According to the ECtHR, particularly relative to serious human rights violations, criminal law can be used in trying to achieve the aim of deterrence.[196] Some commentators have argued that the doctrine of positive obligations is concerned only with general deterrence.[197] This might be the primary aim of the criminalizations. However, taking into account the Court's strong emphasis on the requirement of effective legal remedies which requires that a finding of criminal-liability is possible in individual cases,[198] it seems that the states' positive obligation to criminalize contains elements of specific deterrence focusing on the perpetrator,[199] but also a retributive element in that conduct that violates others' human dignity, the very

---

[189] *C.N. v. the United Kingdom* App no 4239/08 (ECtHR, 13 November 2012), paras 81–82.

[190] *C.N. and V. v. France* App no. 67724/09 (ECtHR, 11 October 2012), para 104.

[191] *Rantsev v. Cyprus and Russia* App no. 25965/04 (ECtHR, 7 January 2010), para 285.

[192] *C.N. v. the United Kingdom* App no 4239/08 (ECtHR, 13 November 2012), paras 81–82.

[193] *C.N. and V. v. France* App no. 67724/09 (ECtHR, 11 October 2012), para 104.

[194] *Rantsev v. Cyprus and Russia* App no. 25965/04 (ECtHR, 7 January 2010), para 285.

[195] Similarly, see, Stoyanova (2014), pp. 407, 431.

[196] *Branko Tomasic and Others v. Croatia App no 46598/06 (ECtHR, 15 January 2009)*, para 49; *Opuz v. Turkey* App no 33401/02 (ECtHR, 9 June 2009), para 128.

[197] Rogers (2003), pp. 690, 695.

[198] *X and Y v. the Netherlands* App no. 8978/80 (ECtHR, 26 March 1985), para 27.

[199] Stoyanova (2014), pp. 407, 414.

fundamental value of the Convention, cannot be dealt with by only civil law measures.[200]

3.3.2 Pluralistic Democracy as a Precondition for European Criminal Law

Pluralistic democracy is a concept that is used to describe democracy where individuals are seen as political equals. All members of the society ought to have an equal and effective opportunity to vote and all votes need to be counted as equal (voting equality). All adults should also have full citizenship rights and everyone ought to be treated as political equals (inclusion of adults). Even though there can be different kinds of democratic constitutions, one element ought to be common to all democracies: the principle of political equality.[201] Political equality refers to the intrinsic equality of all members of the society in the sense that everyone has equal intrinsic worth (human dignity). This dimension expresses a moral judgment concerning all human beings.[202] In pluralist democracy, the different groups ought to have equal opportunity to participate to the political discussion.[203]

In the ECHR regime, the concept of pluralistic democracy refers to two elements. Firstly, different kinds of democratic governance can meet the democracy standard. Article 3 of the first Protocol to the Convention stipulates a right to 'free elections at reasonable intervals by secret ballot, under conditions which will ensure the free expression of the opinion of the people in the choice of the legislature' ensuring the right to vote and the right to stand for election to the legislature. However, every member state can decide how they build their democratic system.[204] The ECtHR has found that Article 3 of the first Protocol enshrines a 'characteristic principle of democracy' and is of great importance in the Convention system. The Court has also stated that the Contracting Parties have a wide margin of appreciation in how they arrange their democratic system. Naturally the Court has the ultimate competence to determine whether the requirements of Protocol No. 1 (P1) have been complied with. According to the Court, 'any electoral system must be assessed in the light of the political evolution of the country concerned; features that would be unacceptable in the context of one system may accordingly be justified in the context of another, at least so long as the chosen system provides for conditions which will ensure the "free expression of the opinion of the people in the choice of the legislature"'.[205]

---

[200] *X and Y v. the Netherlands* App no. 8978/80 (ECtHR, 26 March 1985), para 27.

[201] Dahl (1998), pp. 36–38.

[202] Dahl (1998), pp. 62–65, 69–77.

[203] Barton and Johns (2013), p. 12.

[204] Jean-Paul Costa (2008).

[205] *Mathieu-Mohin and Clerfayat v. Belgium* App no 9267/81 (ECtHR, 2 March 1987), paras 47, 52, 54.

Even though Article 3 of the first Protocol does not include an explicit limitation clause with a list of legitimate aims, the article does not constitute absolute rights, since implied limitations are acceptable.[206] The contracting parties have wide margin of appreciation in choosing how to mould their own democratic vision. The Court finds that '[t]here are numerous ways of organising and running electoral systems and a wealth of differences'.[207] The Convention system does not aim to fit its member states into a single mould. It would not be compatible with the Court's mandate to determine an exact meaning of democracy, nor can the Court examine national electoral laws in the abstract.[208]

Secondly, the concept of pluralistic democracy seems to mean that different groups of people ought to have an *equal possibility* to try to promote their own interests. The Court can evaluate in specific cases whether or not Convention democratic rights have been breached. The case *Yumak and Sadak v Turkey* was unusual since the complaints were directed against Turkey's entire electoral system.[209] The applicants complained that since the political parties had to receive at least 10% of the given votes in order to get into Parliament, the Turkish electoral system breached Article 3 of the first Protocol. As a result of the threshold, 45% of the voters were not represented in Parliament. The Court found that the 10% threshold system of the Turkish electoral system had legitimate aim of avoiding excessive parliamentary fragmentation and strengthening governmental stability. The Court found that any specific maximum percentage limit for the possible thresholds could not be set in the abstract.

3.3.2.1   Influence of the Type of Democracy to Criminal Policy

The ECHR regime does not set any specific requirements on how democracy ought to be established in the legal systems of the contracting parties beyond the rights to vote and to stand for an election. However, the political arrangements in democracies affect the development and evolution of the criminal justice systems and criminal justice policies.[210] The level of democracy and the way democracy is conceptualized also affects rates of imprisonment. Consensus democracies are associated with having more lenient penal policy than majoritarian democracies.[211]

Arend Lijphart has studied the patterns of democracy and identified dimensions that imply whether the political model in a society is closer to a majoritarian or a consensus model. Majoritarian models and consensus models are classifications of types of democracy that are at the opposite ends of a continuum. Polities can situate themselves anywhere on this continuum and they can evolve over time. A

---

[206] *Yumak and Sadak v. Turkey* App no 10226/03 (ECtHR, 8 July 2008), para 109.

[207] *Hirst v. the United Kingdom* (no. 2) App no 74025/01 (ECtHR, 6 October 2005), para 61.

[208] *Yumak and Sadak v. Turkey* App no 10226/03 (ECtHR, 8 July 2008), para 73.

[209] Ibid., para 125.

[210] See, e.g., Snacken and Dumortier (2012), p. 8.

[211] Lappi-Seppälä (2012), pp. 55–58.

majoritarian model of democracy finds that in a situation of conflict and difference of opinion, the government should be responsive to the opinion of the majority of people, whereas the consensus model of democracy claims that the government should be responsive to as many people as possible. As Lijphart has put it, 'the majoritarian model of democracy is exclusive, competitive, and adversarial, whereas the consensus model is characterized by inclusiveness, bargaining, and compromise'.[212]

The general political culture affects the likelihood of radical policy changes. The so-called conflict systems (majoritarian systems) that usually have two major political parties, are more sensitive to big policy changes than the consensus systems which usually have several political parties and more consistent criminal policy aims regardless of the changes in the composition of the government. Consensus systems typically have stronger policy continuity.[213] Lijphart finds that consensus democracies (political systems) have achieved more humane criminal justice polices. This is shown in the fact that most of the consensus democracies have lower imprisonment rates than democracies in which power is more concentrated (majority democracies).[214]

In Europe, the UK is the best example of a majoritarian democracy. However, both of the UK's two biggest political parties, the Labour party and the Conservative party, situate policy-wise in the middle of the political value field.[215] Ireland has also been described as majoritarian democracy.[216] Most of the western European countries, the Nordic countries, Switzerland, Belgium and others, represent consensus democracies.[217] The EU itself has been categorised as a consensus democracy.[218]

Since the EU's constitutional framework means cooperation amongst different national and cultural traditions, it is no wonder that the Union's democratic and political model can be classified under consensus democracy. There are flexible structures in the Union's constitution to ensure the protection and respect of fundamental aspects of national legal orders and identities. In the field of criminal law, the so-called emergency brake procedure is a prime example of this. It enables the use of unanimity requirement in relation of criminal legislative proposals concerning which a Member State has concerns of its suitability with the essential elements of its national criminal justice system. Thus the emergency brake procedure in its own way manifests a consensus ideology.

Regarding policy-making, one should ask how much emphasis is given to public opinions and attitudes, and to professional knowledge and experience.[219] As illustrative extremes, consensus political cultures (or democracies) could be linked with an

---

[212] Lijphart (1999), pp. 1–3.
[213] Tonry (2007), pp. 18–19.
[214] Lijphart (1999), pp. 297, 298, 301.
[215] Lijphart (1999).
[216] Lappi-Seppälä (2012), p. 57.
[217] Lijphart (1999), Tonry (2007), p. 9.
[218] Lijphart (1999).
[219] Tonry (2007), p. 32; Bell (1992), p. 77.

expert-based policy-making process. Similarly conflict political cultures (or majoritarian democracies) could be linked with populist-based policy-making processes.[220] This kind of categorical classification serves only a pedagogical purpose. The intention is not to suggest that this clear a distinction exists.

Expert-based policy-making means that a specific group of people who share a common background or profession is given power to make decisions in a democratic society.[221] Experts, for example of people who represent certain professional and expert knowledge in a policy area, can be utilised in policy-making in order to achieve rational decisions for the general good. The tension between the idea of political equality and the desirability of expertise is inherent in democracy.[222] In most Western countries that are consensus democracies, quite a lot of weight is given to the professional expert opinion as a basis for policy-making.[223]

Conflict political cultures (or majoritarian democracies) can be linked to policy-making processes based on populism.[224] In majoritarian democracies, power concentrates through confrontation and competition into the hands of the majority.[225] Populist ideology or expressions can be used to gather the votes of the majority. Whereas pluralistic democracy includes different groups of people,[226] populism can be described 'by the negation of pluralism'.[227] Populist politics use direct, simple and common-sense language in order to gain votes from a large group of people.[228] Populism is often related to hostility towards representative politics and the mistrust of expert opinion.[229] Penal populism—populism that is directed to criticize the criminal justice establishment[230]—can be used amongst other populist themes to gain votes. Usually penal populist politics are punitive in their nature because the politicians *assume* that public opinion would favour more punitive criminal justice policies.[231]

However, research shows that when individuals are given more detailed information concerning criminal cases, they tend to lean toward a more lenient punishment. This contrasts with situations when they are given only general information on the crime committed and were prone to adopt a harsher line on punishment. In the abstract, people generally believe that sentences are too lenient, but when given more information, this belief shifts towards the less punitive approach.[232] Information

---

[220] Tonry (2007), p. 34.

[221] Barton and Johns (2013), p. 13.

[222] Bell (1992), p. 66.

[223] Tonry (2007), p. 32.

[224] Ibid., p. 34.

[225] Lappi-Seppälä (2012), p. 56.

[226] Barton and Johns (2013), p. 12.

[227] Snacken (2012), p. 250.

[228] Canovan (1999), pp. 2, 9, 17.

[229] Snacken (2012), p. 250.

[230] Pratt (2007), p. 12.

[231] Pratt (2007).

[232] Gelb (2008), Balvig et al. (2015), pp. 342, 350–355.

concerning sanctions and sentencing is received mostly from the media, which tends to focus particularly on violent crime. The media does not really write about sentencing norms or practices and the alternatives to imprisonment. All this contributes to the public tendency for distorted views of sentencing in the abstract *before* receiving detailed information.[233]

When given similar information as the courts, people would impose very similar or even more lenient sentences than the courts.[234] Thus the assumption that the public supports more punitive line of sentencing when given all the facts of individual cases is a myth, or at least an overstatement.[235] The same shift in attitudes applies also to attitudes towards recidivists. In the abstract, 88 percent of the respondents chosen randomly from amongst the residents in Ohio (USA) supported the so-called three strikes law. When the respondents were given specific cases to consider, only 17% of the respondents favoured the imposition of life imprisonment on three-time offenders.[236]

The public also favours other ways for reducing crime than the increased use of imprisonment, for example by non-criminal law measures such as improving the level of unemployment,[237] or education and youth programs.[238] When people are asked what kind of criminal sanctions would be appropriate for a specific crime, those people who are given full information on sentencing practices and alternatives are more inclined to choose alternative criminal sanctions rather than imprisonment. To be precise, only one half of the people that were offered a 'sentencing menu' would have imposed imprisonment when evaluating a specific crime, whereas two-thirds of the group that had not been given the 'sentencing menu' chose the imprisonment as appropriate sanction.[239]

3.3.2.2 Distinction Between Constitutional and Populist Conception of Democracy: Significance on Criminal Policy

Democracy can be perceived from constitutional or populist perspective. The adopted perspective on democracy affects greatly to the perspective on criminal policy. A constitutional perception on democracy emphasises certain values. These include democracy, rule of law, equality and the respect for human and fundamental rights. In contrast, populists tend to regard themselves as the voice of the people or as a representation of true democracy. Populists claim to speak for ordinary people,

---

[233] Roberts and Doob (1989), pp. 491, 500.

[234] Gelb (2009), p. 288; Gelb (2008); Roberts and Doob (1989), pp. 491, 501.

[235] Roberts and Doob (1989), pp. 491, 509–511; Gelb (2009), p. 288; Gelb (2008).

[236] Roberts (2003), pp. 483, 493.

[237] Hough and Roberts (1999), pp. 11, 19; Roberts and Doob (1989), pp. 491, 502–504.

[238] Peter D Hart Research Associates, Inc. for The Open Society Institute (2002), p. 3.

[239] Hough and Roberts (1999), pp. 11, 19; Roberts and Doob (1989), pp. 491, 502–504.

and strive for the power to make decisions instead of the experts who are seen to override the 'public' opinion.[240]

A constitutional perception of democracy in criminal policy-making context is seen necessary in order to avoid the tyranny of majority and to establish moderate penal policies in Europe. Because punishment is essentially about state authority using its power, the rule of law principle has a pivotal role in guaranteeing equal and foreseeable procedure because it requires impersonal laws which are to be applied without emotional commands.[241] It is clear that if courts were to take public or populist opinions into account when deciding on individual cases, the courts would not be independent and impartial as required by Article 6 ECHR.

The populist perception of democracy emphasises the importance of the assumed will of the majority. In this sense the populist conception of democracy is not interested in the interests and rights of unpopular minorities such as criminals or prisoners.[242] Penal populism generates fear and feelings of insecurity. It can lead to bad (criminal) political decisions. The ultimate risk it produces falls upon democracy itself,[243] since populism could turn into the tyranny of a majority,[244] which could jeopardise the humaneness of criminal policy. The Council of Europe and the EU have adopted the constitutional conception of democracy, which requires respect for human rights, the rule of law and tolerance. This means that the rights of unpopular minorities are protected from the opinion of majority. Practical examples of this approach are the abolition of the death penalty and the improved protection of prisoners' rights.[245] From a majoritarian perspective, it has been argued that the European approach on abolishing the death penalty would be less democratic than the American approach that takes into account the opinion of the majority of the population.[246] However, pluralistic democracy requires tolerance in respect of all members of the society.

3.3.3   ECHR Regime and Criminal Policy

When speaking of the ECHR regime and criminal policy one needs to ask if the ECHR regime supports any specific type of criminal policy? The ECtHR has answered this question in its case law. In the case of *Kafkaris* the applicant alleged that Articles 3, 5, 7 and 14 of the Convention had been violated as a result of his life sentence and continuing detention. The applicant had been found guilty of three counts of premeditated murder. The life sentence had been given in respect of each

---

[240] Canovan (1999), pp. 2, 4–5.

[241] Snacken (2012), p. 248.

[242] Ibid., p. 249.

[243] Salas (2010), pp. 12–18, 40.

[244] Pettit (1999), p. 8.

[245] Snacken (2012), pp. 250–257.

[246] Joshua Micah Marshall (2000).

count. The applicant wanted to know if his sentence meant three consecutive life sentences for the rest of his life as provided in the Criminal Code, or of imprisonment for a period of 20 years since the Prison Regulations provided that imprisonment for life in practice meant imprisonment for 20 years. The sentencing court had confirmed that the sentence meant imprisonment for the rest of his life. However, the applicant had been given a date of release by the prison authorities according to which he would be released after 20 years of imprisonment. When that date arrived, he was not released. The Supreme Court of Cyprus evaluated his situation after the date of his release had elapsed and came to the same conclusion as the sentencing court.[247]

The applicant claimed that 'framework for protection of the rights of persons serving life-imprisonment sentences in Cyprus was contrary to the practices in most other member States of the Council of Europe and that there was an obvious need to establish a common policy'.[248] The ECtHR stated that

> it is clear from the relevant case-law that the existence of a system providing for consideration of the possibility of release is a factor to be taken into account when assessing the compatibility of a particular life sentence with Article 3. In this context, however, it should be observed that *a State's choice of a specific criminal-justice system, including sentence review and release arrangements, is in principle outside the scope of the supervision the Court carries out at European level, provided that the system chosen does not contravene the principles set forth in the Convention.*[249] (emphasis added)

The applicant also claimed that a harsher penalty had been imposed on him than had been described by law since, in practice, according to the Prison Regulations applicable at the time of sentencing life imprisonment was tantamount to 20 years of imprisonment. The ECtHR stated that '[a]lthough the changes in the prison legislation and in the conditions of release may have rendered the applicant's imprisonment effectively harsher, these changes cannot be construed as imposing a heavier 'penalty' than that imposed by the trial court'. The Court also stated that 'issues relating to release policies, the manner of their implementation and the reasoning behind them fall *within the power of the Member States in determining their own criminal policy'.*[250] Similarly in *Achour* the Court stated that

> [t]he applicant complained that he had been deemed to be a recidivist when tried for, and convicted of, the offence committed in 1995. It is clear, therefore, that the Court must examine the rules on recidivism and the way in which they were applied in the circumstances of the case. It considers, however, that *matters relating to the existence of such rules, the manner of their implementation and the reasoning behind them fall within the power of the High Contracting Parties to determine their own criminal policy, which is not in principle a matter for it to comment on.*[251] (emphasis added)

---

[247] *Kafkaris v. Cyprus* App no 21906/04 (ECtHR, 12 February 2008), paras 3, 12, 13, 30, 42, 85.

[248] Ibid., para 82.

[249] Ibid., para 99; *Archour v. France* App no 67335/01 (ECtHR, 29 March 2006), para 51.

[250] *Kafkaris v. Cyprus* App no 21906/04 (ECtHR, 12 February 2008), paras 126, 151.

[251] Case of *Achour v. France* App no 67335/01 (ECHR, 29 March 2006), para 44.

As a main rule, it seems that the Court finds that the basic choices concerning the criminal justice systems made by the member states of the Council of Europe do not as such fall within the scope of the ECtHR's competence. The ECtHR can only review the conformity between elements of criminal justice systems and the Convention in relation to a specific case and question at hand. This means that the ECHR regime does not support any specific view on criminal policy nor does it aim to import any specific criminal policy into the criminal justice systems of the Contracting Parties.

According to Article 46 ECHR, the ECtHR's rulings are binding upon the Contracting Party in that particular issue. In other words, under a strict interpretation the contracting parties must correct the situation in question in particular cases when the ECtHR finds that there has been a breach of convention right. The problem can also have a more general nature. Sometimes judgments give reason to tackle the problem through general legislative changes. Sometimes the ECtHR gives rulings in which it refers to a more *general incompatibility* with the Convention or to *systemic or structural* problems. If there is a violation that had 'originated in a systemic problem affecting a large number of people, *general measures at national level could be called for in the execution* of its judgments'. This is called a 'pilot-judgment procedure'. It is designed to help the Contracting Parties fulfil their obligations and to resolve problems at national level.[252] The pilot judgment procedure is a technique that is used to tackle structural problems that are revealed through repetitive cases which stem from a common dysfunction at national level. The Court can guide the governments to solve the structural or systemic problem and the contracting parties can then decide how they will fulfil their obligations deriving from the (pilot) judgments. The Council of Ministers supervises the execution of the judgments.[253] The examination of the other related cases can be adjourned for a set period of time on the condition that the respondent state fulfils its obligations based on the pilot judgment.[254]

The ECHR regime has impact on the choices the Contracting Parties make in their criminal justice systems regardless of whether the ECtHR has not required systemic changes, and regardless of whether the judgment is technically directed to another state. This is demonstrated for example in the case of *M.C. v Bulgaria*. One could say therefore that the ECHR regime affects the criminal policy of the Contracting Parties indirectly and implicitly. The case law of the ECtHR inevitably and unavoidably shapes the criminal policy of the Contracting Parties and brings the criminal justice systems of the Contracting Parties closer to each other at some level.

---

[252] *Sejdovic v. Italy* App no 56581/00 (ECtHR, 1 March 2006), para 120; *Broniowski v. Poland* App no 31443/96 (ECtHR, 22 June 2004), paras 188–194 and 34–35.

[253] European Court of Human Rights, *Factsheet – Pilot Judgments* (July 2013) www.echr.coe.int/Documents/FS_Pilot_judgments_ENG.pdf, accessed 25 June 2018.

[254] European Court of Human Rights, *The Pilot Judgment Procedure*—Information note issued by the Registrar, www.echr.coe.int/Documents/Pilot_judgment_procedure_ENG.pdf, accessed 25 June 2018.

The ECtHR has stated that the ECHR regime does not support any specific type of criminal policy. Yet, the ECHR regime has a pronouncedly high impact on criminal procedure and on the use of sanctions. It has influence on substantive criminal law as can be seen from the judgments in *M.C. v Bulgaria, Siliadin, Rantsev* and other similar cases. Even though the ECtHR acknowledges the lack of criminal policy within the Convention framework, the Committee of Ministers of the Council of Europe has given several recommendations, some concerning more specific topics than others, to the contracting parties on criminal policy. The recommendations only guide the member states' policies. In 1996 the Committee of Ministers gave a recommendation named 'crime policy in Europe in a time of change'. One accelerator amongst others for giving the recommendation was the creation of the single market and opening of the internal borders of the EU. The Committee of Ministers saw that since cross-border crime will increase, the ever more international dimension in crime will need coherent and concerted European crime policy to respond to it.[255] The Committee of Ministers took the initiative in ensuring coherence in European criminal policy even though the need for doing so originated in the EU framework.

The fundamental values of the Convention, the principles of rule of law, pluralistic democracy and human rights (human dignity), have their expressions in the Recommendation 96(8) on Crime policy in Europe in a time of change given by the Committee of Ministers. Crimes that offend human dignity can be seen to offend democracy as well, since respect for human dignity is a prerequisite for democracy. Democracy cannot function in a society where the equal worth of individuals is not respected. The criminal justice systems of the contracting parties ought to respect democracy as the political model. This also means they must respect and protect cultural pluralism and tolerance and provide penal provisions that would provide protection to the values of human dignity and democracy.

The principles of rule of law, democracy, and the respect of human rights are seen as paramount elements that need to be taken into account in every response to crime. Due to these principles, criminal policy ought to be rational and the emphasis should be on general deterrent effects and on the prevention of crime. In addition to criminal policy measures, crime prevention also consists of social prevention (such as educational means) and situational prevention (such as reducing the opportunities and means of committing offences). Social reintegration of offenders and the possibility of alternatives to custodial sentences are considered crucial to the prevention of recidivism. The contracting parties are also guided to contemplate the cost-effectiveness of crime control measures. The costs of crime should be weighed against the costs of crime control.[256]

---

[255] Council of Europe, Committee of Ministers, Recommendation No R (96) 8 on crime policy in Europe in a time of change, 5 September 1996; Council of Europe, Committee of Ministers, Explanatory memorandum to Recommendation Rec(1996) 8.

[256] Council of Europe, Committee of Ministers, Recommendation No R (96) 8 on crime policy in Europe in a time of change, 5 September 1996; Council of Europe, Committee of Ministers, Explanatory memorandum to Recommendation Rec(1996) 8.

Human rights have a dual role in the field of criminal law, a defensive role and an offensive role. Human rights work in their defensive role when they are used to protect individuals from the use of criminal law. The defensive role is most pronounced and obviously expressed in procedural safeguards, and in the principle of legality. The offensive role of human rights refers to them as the driving force to argue for the use of criminal law measures. Sometimes only the use of criminal law is seen to be a satisfactory means to protect the fundamental values of the society, the fundamental rights being one central element of this, as the ECtHR's case law shows.[257] For example, in the case of *M.C. v Bulgaria* the ECtHR found that 'effective protection against rape and sexual abuse requires measures of a criminal-law nature'.[258] It follows from this offensive role that the contracting parties have positive obligations, criminalization obligations, also in the field of criminal law. This offensive role of human rights is not to be confused with the offensive role of criminal law which refers to the widening of the use of criminal law to situations that are not necessarily close to individuals. For example, merely a potential threat of violation against rights are seen as sufficient reason, instead of being merely a necessary reason, for criminalization. Criminalizations that protect state machinery or anonymous public, such as security at large, are typical to offensive criminal law. Also, the penalty threats are increased.[259] We can see that the concept of offensive role has different meaning relative to human rights protection and criminal law.

Human rights protection guides criminal policy choices in two diverging directions. Human rights-oriented views on criminal policy are often described as defensive criminal policy. According to Nils Jareborg, defensive criminal policy supports a reserved approach on the use of criminal law and emphasizes the need to protect individuals against the state's use of power and especially excessive repression. Legal certainty and procedural safeguards are essential in fulfilling this task. Because defensive criminal law aims to cool down conflicts, respect for the values of legal certainty and justice are paramount; the defensive approach is built upon *Rechtsstaat* ideology.[260] Several elements of the ECHR regime express the defensive role of human rights in criminal policy.

The ECHR regime limits substantive criminal law by limiting the state actors from criminalizing certain types of conduct or using certain types of sanctions and sanctioning practices in relation to certain types of offences.[261] In relation to freedom

---

[257] *X and Y v. the Netherlands* App no. 8978/80 (ECtHR, 26 March 1985), para 27; *Nachova and Others v. Bulgaria* App no. 43577/98 and 43579/98 (ECtHR, 26 February 2004), para 157; *Branko Tomasic and Others v. Croatia* App no 46598/06 (ECtHR, 15 January 2009), para 49; *Opuz v. Turkey* App no 33401/02 (ECtHR, 9 June 2009), para 128; *Siliadin v. France* App no 73316/01 (ECtHR, 26 July 2005); *C.N. v. the United Kingdom* App no 4239/08 (ECtHR, 13 November 2012), paras 81–82; *C.N. and V. v. France* App no. 67724/09 (ECtHR, 11 October 2012), para 104; *Rantsev v. Cyprus and Russia* App no. 25965/04 (ECtHR, 7 January 2010), para 285; Tulkens (2011), p. 577.

[258] *M.C. v Bulgaria* App no 39272/98 (ECtHR, 4 December 2003), para 186.

[259] Jareborg (2002), p. 98.

[260] Ibid., pp. 92, 94–95.

[261] Dumortier et al. (2012), pp. 117–120.

of expression, the use of imprisonment has been restricted by the Court to cases concerning hate speech, incitement to violence and promotion of negationism, all of which are seen by the ECtHR to violate human dignity.[262] The use of sanctions in relation to offences concerning freedom of expression is limited because heavy sanctions, as well as heavy damages, might negatively influence the media's willingness to fulfil its functions, especially its role in the democratic processes in society (the so-called chilling effect).[263]

The Convention system also restricts criminalizing certain types of conduct. For example, criminal law should not in principle be applied in the case of consensual sexual practices which fall under the protection of Article 8 ECHR on the right to private and family life.[264] The ECtHR has found that criminalization of homosexual acts also infringes the right to private life as guaranteed in Article 8 ECHR. According to the Court, penal provisions criminalizing homosexual acts between consenting adults capable of valid consent cannot be justified as being necessary or proportionate in a democratic society.[265]

Human rights do not only limit the power of the national legislators and authorities applying the law, they also require active human rights protection from national authorities. In other words, states have also positive obligations to protect human rights in addition to their negative obligations to refrain from infringing human rights. In this sense, human rights have a more offensive role in criminal policy decision-making. Criminal law measures should be used in order to protect individuals from serious violations directed toward their rights by other individuals.[266] Human rights can thus legitimize the use of criminal law and its punitive logic.[267] Many penal provisions protect human and fundamental rights or protected interests

---

[262] See for example *Cumpănă and Mazăre v. Romania* App no 33348/96 (ECtHR, 17 December 2004), paras 37, 48, 50, 112, 115–119; *Mariapori v. Finland* App no 37751/07 (ECtHR, 6 July 2010), para 67.

[263] For example Parliamentary Assembly Recommendation 1506(2001) Freedom of expression and information in the media in Europe, paras 1, 5, 12. See also Parliamentary Assembly Resolution 1535(2007) Threats to the lives and freedom of expression of journalists, paras 3, 6. See also Parliamentary Assembly Resolution 1577(2007) Towards decriminalization of defamation, paras 1, 4–7, 11–14, 17. On the chilling effect, for example *Cumpănă and Mazăre v. Romania* App no 33348/96 (ECtHR, 17 December 2004), para 119.

[264] *K.A. and A.D. v. Belgium* App no 42758/98 and 455558/99 (ECtHR, 17 February 2005).

[265] *Dudgeon v. the United Kingdom* App no 7525/76 (ECtHR, 22 October 1981), para 60; *Norris v. Ireland* App no 10581/83 (ECtHR, 26 October 1988), paras 38, 46; *A.D.T. v. the United Kingdom* App no 35765/97 (ECtHR, 31 July 2000), para 38.

[266] *X and Y v. the Netherlands* App no. 8978/80 (ECtHR, 26 March 1985), para 27; *Nachova and Others v. Bulgaria* App no. 43577/98 and 43579/98 (ECtHR, 26 February 2004), para 157; *Branko Tomasic and Others v. Croatia* App no 46598/06 (ECtHR, 15 January 2009), para 49; *Opuz v. Turkey* App no 33401/02 (ECtHR, 9 June 2009), para 128; *Siliadin v. France* App no 73316/01 (ECtHR, 26 July 2005); *C.N. v. the United Kingdom* App no 4239/08 (ECtHR, 13 November 2012), paras 81–82; *C.N. and V. v. France* App no. 67724/09 (ECtHR, 11 October 2012), para 104; *Rantsev v. Cyprus and Russia* App no. 25965/04 (ECtHR, 7 January 2010), para 285.

[267] Tulkens (2012), p. 156.

that derive from these rights. Decriminalization of certain conduct, such as rape or murder, would then clearly violate fundamental and human rights.

The ECtHR has sometimes required the use of criminal law measures in its case law.[268] In the case of *Öneryildiz v Turkey* the Court found that life-endangering offences should not go unpunished. Judicial systems should ensure that criminal penalties are applied when lives are lost as a result of dangerous activity. The use of the criminal penalties is justified due to the states' positive obligation to protect lives as enshrined in Article 2 ECHR.[269] The Court has also stated that as required by Article 2, effective judicial systems 'may, and in under some circumstances must, include recourse to the criminal law'. As a limitation to this main rule, when 'the infringement to the right to life or physical integrity is not caused intentionally, the positive obligation imposed by Article 2 to set up an effective judicial system does not necessarily require the provision of a criminal-law remedy in every case'.[270] These cases demonstrate the ECHR regime requires that criminal law measures are adopted in relation to serious human rights violations and that the contracting parties provide an effective criminal justice system for their citizens. More specifically, intentional infringements of the right to life or personal integrity ought to be criminalized in the contracting parties of the ECHR.

The ECtHR has emphasised the deterrent effect of the criminal justice system as a means to protect human rights.[271] In *X and Y v the Netherlands*, the Court found that *civil law measures are not sufficient to produce effective deterrence against rape* or to produce sufficient protection for the fundamental values violated by that type of criminal conduct.[272] In *Branko Tomasic and Others v Croatia* and in *Öneryildiz v Turkey*, the Court has also found that the contracting parties have a positive obligation *to deter individuals in the form of criminal law measures* from violating others' right to life.[273]

The ECtHR has not specified if by deterrence it refers to the general deterrence that concerns all members of society or to specific deterrence which focuses on the offenders and aiming at the prevention of recidivism. It would seem logical that the Court has both dimensions of deterrence in mind, keeping in mind the reason for

---

[268] See, for example, *M.C. v Bulgaria* App no 39272/98 (ECtHR, 4 December 2003); *X and Y v. the Netherlands* App no. 8978/80 (ECtHR, 26 March 1985), para 27; *Nachova and Others v. Bulgaria* App no. 43577/98 and 43579/98 (ECtHR, 26 February 2004), para 157; *Branko Tomasic and Others v. Croatia* App no 46598/06 (ECtHR, 15 January 2009), para 49; *Opuz v. Turkey* App no 33401/02 (ECtHR, 9 June 2009), para 128; *Siliadin v. France* App no 73316/01 (ECtHR, 26 July 2005); *C.N. v. the United Kingdom* App no 4239/08 (ECtHR, 13 November 2012), paras 81–82; *C.N. and V. v. France* App no. 67724/09 (ECtHR, 11 October 2012), para 104; *Rantsev v. Cyprus and Russia* App no. 25965/04 (ECtHR, 7 January 2010), para 285.

[269] *Öneryildiz v. Turkey* App no 48939/99 (ECtHR, 30 November 2004), paras 94–96.

[270] *Vo v. France* App no 53924/00 (ECtHR, 8 July 2004), para 90; *Calvelli and Ciglio v. Italy* App no 32967/96 (ECtHR, 17 January 2002), para 51.

[271] See, for example, *Opuz v. Turkey* App no 33401/02 (ECtHR, 9 June 2009), para 128.

[272] *X and Y v. the Netherlands* App no. 8978/80 (ECtHR, 26 March 1985), para 27.

[273] *Branko Tomasic and Others v. Croatia* App no 46598/06 (ECtHR, 15 January 2009), para 49; *Öneryildiz v. Turkey* App no 48939/99 (ECtHR, 30 November 2004), para 96.

which the ECtHR requires the use of criminal law measures, the prevention of human rights violations amongst individuals. It seems that the criminalization obligations the ECtHR has set are also at some level related to a backward-looking deontological justification that emphasizes the reprehensible and blameworthy nature of the types of conduct it has required to be criminalized effectively since the Court has emphasised the fundamental value of human dignity as the reason for the criminalizations.

Effective criminal law measures must also be used, at least in situations in which a Convention right is seriously violated. In the case of *M.C. v Bulgaria* the ECtHR found that 'effective protection against rape and sexual abuse requires measures of a criminal-law nature'.[274] This judgment is unique in the sense that the Court implicitly outlined how the penal provision on rape ought to be formulated in the member states since the ECtHR concluded that criminal prosecution determination of criminal liability ought to be possible in matters of sexual violence also in situations which are based on the lack of consent. In other words, rape could not be defined in penal provisions so that the existence of physical resistance would be one of the determining factors.[275] This judgment is a text–book example in illustrating that ECtHR case law may contain explicit instructions for the contracting parties to use effective criminal law and procedural measures to tackle a certain type of crime.

The ECtHR has stated in *Kafkaris* and *Achour* that the member states' choice on a type criminal justice system does not as such fall under the Court's supervision as long as the system does not contravene the Convention principles. As a main rule, the contracting parties have the power to determine the type of their criminal justice system and criminal policy. The ECHR regime does not support any specific type of criminal policy choices. The only limitation is that the criminal policy they choose to follow and the criminal justice system they build must comply with the Convention. This also means that an abolitionist legal system without any kind of criminal justice system is not a choice for the contracting parties, since the ECtHR has required that the member states provide criminal law protection for certain values, as has been explained above.

3.4 Difference Between National Criminal Law and European Criminal Law

In terms of the functions of criminal law, European and national criminal law differ from one and other in that European criminal law is about criminal policy creation and the enactment of criminal legislation. Naturally the ECtHR can examine individual cases brought to it, but still the contents of the judgments need to be enforced at the national level. Also, it is up to the national authorities to decide how to react

---

[274] *M.C. v Bulgaria* App no 39272/98 (ECtHR, 4 December 2003), para 186.

[275] See for example Dumortier et al. (2012), p. 126.

to the judgments that guide national criminal policies on more general level and what measures they possibly need to take due to the ECtHR case law.

In Sect. 2.1 the different functions of criminal law were briefly described. Whereas national criminal laws are about rule articulation, liability assignment, and grading, European criminal law is only about rule articulation, and not about the liability assignment and grading that are tasks of the national courts applying the law. National authorities are in charge of sentencing and the enforcement of the sentence. Naturally European norms affect national criminal justice systems more broadly, but the European systems do not have institutions of their own to enforce the European criminal law. For example, the Union does not have a criminal court of its own. The establishment of the European Public Prosecutors' Office (later the EPPO) will be an exception.

The discussion on the establishment of a European public prosecutor started along with the *Corpus Juris* academic study founded by the Commission.[276] The proposed Constitutional Treaty included a provision[277] on the establishment of an EPPO inspired by which a similar article (Article 86 TFEU) was included in the Lisbon Treaty. Article 86 TFEU was a compromise provision originating from the deliberations of the Justice and Home Affairs Working Group at the Convention on the Future of Europe working for to shape the Constitutional Treaty.[278] Article 86 TFEU enables the establishment of the EPPO to combat crimes affecting the financial interests of the Union. It also includes a possibility to expand the EPPO's competence in the future 'to include serious crime having a cross-border dimension',[279] linking the EPPO to the AFSJ in more general,[280] and to the so-called euro-crimes in particular.

EU criminal law has been described by mirroring it against models of federal criminal law. In the dual model, there are two autonomous systems—federal and local—that regulate both the substantive and procedural criminal law that establish their own criminal systems in which their own norms apply. Such a system exists in the USA for example. In the plural model state criminal law has full autonomy in each of its constituent countries. In the plural model as adopted in the UK, there is no supra-jurisdictional level of criminal law. The plural model is seen most suited to describe the proposals for the EPPO since national legislation has a crucial role in the functioning of the EU criminal law. The proposals, at least thus far, are all based on the idea that the cases prosecuted by the EPPO are tried in the competent national judicial organs and decided by the national judges, meaning that the Member States' judges would continue to apply relevant EU law.[281]

There were different options of the EPPO's organizational structure. The Commission compared four different policy options: an EPPO within Eurojust, a

---

[276] *Sous la direction de Mireille Delmas-Marty* (1997).

[277] Article III-274 of the Constitutional Treaty.

[278] Mitsilegas (2009), p. 231.

[279] Article 86(4) TFEU.

[280] Ligeti (2013), p. 75.

[281] Martín et al. (2013), pp. 784–787.

College-type EPPO, a decentralized EPPO and a centralized EPPO. The first option would have meant that the EPPO would have been a non-independent entity within Eurojust. In this model, the EPPO would not have competence to prosecute suspects in the national courts.[282] A centralized model represents the opposite to the EPPO-within-Eurojust model. In the centralized model a central EPPO at the EU level would have autonomous powers and would have operated in the Member States' territories. The centralized model would have taken integration the furthest,[283] and would have represented a hierarchical model where the EPPO as an EU body would work to protect the EU 'federal' financial interests. The centralized EPPO would have been separate from national systems since the EPPO would not have depended on national prosecution or investigation services.[284]

The Commission proposed establishing the EPPO in a decentralized integrated model that represents intermediate level of integration.[285] The EPPO would be integrated into national systems. There would be a central office which would make the decisions on investigations and prosecutions concerning offences directed against the Union's financial interests. Delegated European Public Prosecutors would work at the national level carrying out investigations and prosecuting offenders. The two levels would create a single body with an internal hierarchy where the chief European Public Prosecutor would supervise the European Delegated Prosecutors.[286] The integrated model was considered feasible because it would build on existing structures, most prominently on national prosecution authorities and Eurojust. The model does not have too heavy an impact on national legal systems, since their main characteristics can be preserved, with only a need for some new adaptions of the EPPO's competence.[287]

The Council favored the college model which represents a low level of integration. The EPPO would be comprised of a College of national members appointed by the Member States. The EPPO would be in charge of investigations and prosecutions, but the trial would be run by a delegated national prosecutor who would be acting in the name of the EPPO, and the EPPO could give binding instructions to

---

[282] SWD(2013) 274 final, Commission Staff Working Document Impact Assessment Accompanying the Proposal for a Council Regulation on the establishment of the European Public Prosecutor's Office, Brussels, 17 July 2013, 32–33.

[283] Ligeti and Simonato (2013), pp. 7, 13–14.

[284] SWD(2013) 274 final, Commission Staff Working Document Impact Assessment Accompanying the Proposal for a Council Regulation on the establishment of the European Public Prosecutor's Office, Brussels, 17 July 2013, 34.

[285] Article 6, COM(2013) 534 final, A proposal for a Council's Regulation on the establishment of the European Public Prosecutor's Office, Brussels, 17 July 2013.

[286] SWD(2013) 274 final, Commission Staff Working Document Impact Assessment Accompanying the Proposal for a Council Regulation on the establishment of the European Public Prosecutor's Office, Brussels, 17 July 2013, 33. See also Ligeti and Simonato (2013), pp. 7, 15–16.

[287] SWD(2013) 274 final, Commission Staff Working Document Impact Assessment Accompanying the Proposal for a Council Regulation on the establishment of the European Public Prosecutor's Office, Brussels, 17 July 2013, 50.

national authorities.[288] The collegial structure would slightly resemble the structure of Eurojust,[289] at least if the Council's view of the College is taken as a point of reference. The Council considers that the College would only decide on strategic matters and issues of general application arising from individual cases to ensure consistency in the prosecution policy throughout the Union, and would not participate in operational (investigative or prosecutional) decision-making.[290] The European Parliament has stressed the importance of effectiveness in the EPPO's work, but also the importance of in-depth knowledge of the Member States's legal systems. The EP supported the Commission's proposal to establish the EPPO on the basis of a decentralized and integrated model.[291] In the Commission's original proposal the College was understood to take majority decisions as regards to investigations and prosecutions. The Commission found the College structure too cumbersome for the purpose of rapid decision-making.[292]

The Council's approach to collegial decision-making seems to differ of that of the Commission's in that collegial decision-making would not be used in basic operational decisions in individual cases. Rather, the Council's approach seems to aim at consensus decision-making in more principled matters that might have more in-depth effects on the Member States' judicial systems. According to the Council's suggestion, the College would be the organ making larger policy choices, keeping in mind national differences.

In June 2017 20 EU Member States found a political agreement on the establishment of the EPPO under enhanced cooperation.[293] The cooperation will be organized in a decentralized model where there will be a central office at the EU level and European Delegated Prosecutors in the Member States. The Delegated Prosecutors would still be national prosecutors as well.[294] The Council's regulation (EU) 2017/1939 implementing enhanced cooperation on the establishment of the EPPO has entered into force but according to Article 120 of the Regulation the

---

[288] SWD(2013) 274 final, Commission Staff Working Document Impact Assessment Accompanying the Proposal for a Council Regulation on the establishment of the European Public Prosecutor's Office, Brussels, 17 July 2013, 33. See also Ligeti and Simonato (2013), pp. 7, 13–14.

[289] Ligeti and Simonato (2013), pp. 7, 13–14.

[290] Council document 16993/14, Proposal for a Council Regulation on the establishment of the European Public Prosecutor's Office – Report on the State of Play, Brussels, 18 December 2014), Article 8.

[291] P7_TA-PROV(2014)0234, European Parliament resolution of 12 March 2014 on the proposal for a Council regulation on the establishment of the European Public Prosecutor's Office (COM(2013)0534 – 2013/0255(APP)), paras 7, 21.

[292] SWD(2013) 274 final, Commission Staff Working Document Impact Assessment Accompanying the Proposal for a Council Regulation on the establishment of the European Public Prosecutor's Office, Brussels, 17 July 2013, 33 and 45.

[293] European Commission, Press release, 'Commission welcomes decision of 20 Member States to establish the European Public Prosecutor's Office', Brussels, 8 June 2017.

[294] Council of the European Union, Interinstitutional File 2013/0255 (APP), 5766/17 LIMITE, Brussels, 31 January 2017.

EPPO shall not start its investigative and prosecutorial tasks before at least 3 years after the entry into force of the Regulation.[295]

A more fundamental difference between national and European criminal law, relating to the above described difference, is that European criminal law does not indicate that the European legal orders would be sovereign whereas national criminal law is often considered to reflect national sovereignty, as described in Sect. 2.1. Norms of both EU criminal law and the ECHR are implemented and enforced in national criminal justice systems. National criminal laws are needed to implement European norms, and national criminal laws remain those that are primarily applied when criminal liability is determined in national courts. In this sense European criminal law is not autonomous. It is dependent on national criminal laws and justice systems, and in this sense it is subordinate to national criminal law.

When the dependence of European criminal law on national criminal laws is viewed from an opposite perspective, from a national perspective, we can see that European criminal law increases national sovereignty because European criminal law improves the EU Member States' ability to tackle cross-border crime. Ulrich Beck has studied state sovereignty vis-à-vis modern cosmopolitan relations. To him, it is important to differentiate between the state's autonomy and the state's sovereignty. Beck argues that the state's sovereignty actually increases as a result of cooperation with other states, but at the same time the state's autonomy decreases. As a result of cooperation between states, the impact of one state is greater on the world stage than it would be without such cooperation.[296] Beck's theory is interesting because he sees cooperation between states, the impact of globalization or Europeanization, as a factor which increases sovereignty. When sovereignty of the EU Member States, for example, is viewed from this perspective, Union membership seems to increase the sovereignty of the Member States. Thus criminal law cooperation in the EU framework increases the legitimacy of both the EU legal order and the national legal orders.

Even though EU criminal law is dependent on national criminal laws, and has to operate within national criminal justice systems, Member States still ought to fulfil their obligations stemming from their EU membership as the principle of sincere cooperation requires. Previously, the Commission did not have the power to intervene if the Member States had not fulfilled their obligations in the field of criminal law.

Before the Lisbon Treaty entered into force, the Commission did not have power to launch infringement procedures against Member States in cases of mis- or non-implementation of third pillar law. Also according to the then Article 35 TEU,[297] the CJEU had limited jurisdiction to give preliminary rulings on the validity and interpretation of EU criminal legislative measures or on the validity and interpretation of

---

[295] Council Regulation (EU) 2017/1939 of 12 October 2017 implementing enhanced cooperation on the establishment of the European Public Prosecutor's Office ('the EPPO') [2017] OJ L 283, 31.10.2017, pp. 1–71.

[296] Beck (2002), pp. 39, 48–49.

[297] Article 35 TEU, OJEU C 321E, 29 December 2006.

the measures implementing them. The CJEU had this jurisdiction only after a Member State had declared its acceptance of the Court's jurisdiction, but not all Member States had given such an acceptance.[298]

Since the Lisbon Treaty entered into force, the Commission and the CJEU have had competence relative to criminal law measures that are enacted after the Lisbon Treaty entered into force. It is noteworthy, however, that relative to some criminal legislative measures that were given before the Lisbon Treaty in a form of a directive under the first pillar,[299] the Commission and the CJEU have had competence to address mis- or non-implementation already prior to the Lisbon Treaty.

As of 1 December 2014 the transitional phase of the Lisbon Treaty came to an end and lifted the previous limitations to the judicial control by the CJEU and to the Commission's power to launch infringement proceedings relative to framework decisions given before Lisbon Treaty entered into force.[300] In other words, currently, under Article 258 TFEU, the Commission has full right to start infringement procedures against Member States concerning the implementation of any EU criminal law instrument regardless when it has entered into force, and under Article 267 TFEU, the CJEU has full competence to give preliminary rulings on the validity and interpretation of any EU criminal law measure.

The strengthened role of the Commission and the CJEU in the field of criminal law as 'the guardian of the Treaties'[301] naturally limits the Member States' autonomy in deciding what kind of criminal legislation they enact. However, simultaneously their ability to confront cross-border crime occurring in Europe that affects their interests is increasing. In practice, the criminal procedural instruments (such the FD EAW) facilitate the cooperation between national authorities, but the more the substantive criminal legislation is approximated, the easier the use of the procedural instruments becomes. In this sense, European criminal law strengthens the sovereignty of the EU Member States.

---

[298] Mitsilegas (2009), pp. 18–19.

[299] For example the directive on the protection of the environment through criminal law (Directive 2008/99/EC of the European Parliament and of the Council of 19 November 2008 on the protection of the environment through criminal law (Text with EEA relevance) [2008] OJ L 328, 6.12.2008, pp. 28–37) and the directive on the ship-source pollution (Directive 2009/123/EC of the European Parliament and of the Council of 21 October 2009 amending Directive 2005/35/EC on ship-source pollution and on the introduction of penalties for infringements (Text with EEA relevance) [2009] OJ L 280, 27.10.2009, pp. 52–55).

[300] Commission, SWD(2014) 109 final, Commission staff working document, Preliminary list of the former third pillar acquis, Brussels, 14 March 2014, www.statewatch.org/news/2014/mar/eu-com-draft-third-pillar-acquis-swd-109-2014.pdf, accessed 25 June 2018, p. 1.

[301] SWD(2014) 109 final, Commission staff working document, Preliminary list of the former third pillar acquis, Brussels, 14 March 2014, www.statewatch.org/news/2014/mar/eu-com-draft-third-pillar-acquis-swd-109-2014.pdf, accessed 25 June 2018, 1.

3.5 Difference Between General EU Law and EU Criminal Law

This chapter examines general principles and doctrines of EU law (direct applicability, direct effect, primacy, conforming interpretation/indirect effect) and explains how the application of these principles and doctrines differs in general EU law and in the field of EU criminal law.

3.5.1 Vertical Direct Effect

The direct effect doctrine stems from the doctrine of direct application of Regulations. Article 288 TFEU explicitly stipulates that regulations are binding in their entirety and directly applicable in all Member States. The CJEU has defined the meaning of direct applicability by stating that '[t]he direct application of a Regulation means that its entry into force and its application in favour of or against those subject to it are independent of any measure of reception into national law.'[302] Even though direct applicability and direct effect are similar doctrines, there is a clear difference. EU regulations do not need any implementation acts in order to be in force in national legal systems, whereas directives need to be implemented into national legal systems as a main rule. In *van Duyn*, the CJEU stated that also other categories of acts than regulations can be applied directly, and invoked by individuals, if 'the nature, general scheme and wording of the provision' enable this. The provision must also *confer rights to individuals* 'which the national courts must protect'.[303] Vertical direct effect of an EU provision is possible when it is unconditional, clear, and sufficiently precise.[304]

Directives ought to have vertical direct effect because '[i]t would be incompatible with the binding effect attributed to directive by Article 189 (the current Article 288 TFEU) to exclude, in principle, the possibility that the obligation which it imposes may be invoked by those concerned'. Secondly, '[t]he useful effect of such an act would be weakened if individuals were prevented from relying on it before their national courts and if the latter were prevented from taking it into consideration as an element of community law'.[305] Thirdly, 'a Member State which has not adopted the implementing measures required by the directive in the prescribed periods may not rely, as against individuals, on its own failure to perform the obligations

---

[302] Case C-34/73 *Fratelli Variola S.p.A. v Amministrazione italiana delle Finanze* [1973] ECR 00981, para 10.

[303] Case C-41/74 *Yvonne van Duyn v Home Office* [1974] ECR p. 1337, paras 7, 12.

[304] Case C-26/62 *NV Algemene Transport- en Expeditie Onderneming van Gend & Loos v Netherlands Inland Revenue Administration* [1963] ECR 00001.

[305] Case C-41/74 *Yvonne van Duyn v Home Office* [1974] ECR p. 1337, para 12.

which the directive entails'.[306] The overarching attribute of these reasons is clearly the efficiency of EU law.

The term of vertical direct effect is used of the consequence that manifests in the interrelations between a state and individuals.[307] Because criminal law is a legal institution where a state solves criminal conflicts that are directed against the state itself in addition to other individuals, the consequence of direct effect in the field of criminal law is vertical. As presented above (in Sect. 1.3.3.2), the general EU law doctrine of direct effect does not apply normally *in the field of EU criminal law*. Criminal liability or the aggravation of criminal liability cannot be based on directives or framework decisions alone. These types of instruments cannot have direct effect to the detriment of the accused,[308] because they are not considered *law* in the sense that the criminal law principle of legality requires. A state cannot establish or aggravate criminal liability independently based on a directive or a framework decision. Criminal liability or aggravation of it must always be based on law, and due to the nature of the EU criminal law instruments, national criminal provisions are always needed to convict an individual. If a state had a need to act against an individual based solely on a directive, it would mean that the state had not implemented it properly or on time. All this means that a state cannot act against individuals on the fact that they have not implemented the measures that the directive requires accordingly or on time.

Vertical direct effect also means that individuals can invoke an EU provision in relation to a state. *In the field of criminal law*, the kind of situation where vertical direct effect could be considered is where a directive obliges Member States to decriminalize certain acts or omissions, if a directive mitigates the scope of criminal liability, or if a directive would mitigate a penalty scale. The CJEU has explicitly stated that Member States cannot rely *against individuals, who have acted according to a directive*, on the fact that they have not implemented the measures that the directive requires on time. Without this norm the Member States could avoid their obligations simply by not implementing directives which would lead to ineffectiveness of EU law.[309] If a Member State would not have fulfilled the obligations deriving from a criminal law directive that would mitigate criminal liability, the authorities of the Member State could not act against the rights of individuals which would be protected in the directive: charges could not be pressed, the individual could not be convicted and any harsher penalty scale could not be applied.[310]

---

[306] Case C-148/78 *Criminal proceedings against Tullio Ratti* [1979] ECR p. 1629, para 1 (summary).

[307] As opposed to horizontal direct effect that is a consequence between individuals. See, for example, http://europa.eu/legislation_summaries/institutional_affairs/decisionmaking_process/l14547_en.htm, accessed 25 June 2018.

[308] Case C-14/86 *Pretore di Salò v Persons unknown* [1987] ECR p. 2545, para 20; Case C-80/86 *Criminal proceedings against Kolpinghuis Nijmegen BV* [1987] ECR p. 3969, para 14; Case C-105/03 *Criminal proceedings against Maria Pupino* [2005] ECR p. I-5285, paras 44–45.

[309] Case C-148/78 *Criminal proceedings against Tullio Ratti* [1979] ECR p. 1629, paras 21–22.

[310] Ibid., para 4; Melander (2010), p. 86.

It is also noteworthy that according to ex-Article 34(2)b EU (as amended in the Treaty of Nice) *framework decisions* cannot have direct effect. In addition, the framework decision cannot establish or aggravate criminal liability independently from national criminal provisions. This means that, in principle, individuals cannot invoke provisions of framework decisions in order to try to exclude or mitigate criminal liability. The exclusion of the direct effect of framework decisions can be criticized because of this latter situation. However, the mitigating EU norm could be given an effect in those national legal systems in which the prosecutors have the discretion to not to file charges or in which the court has discretion not to sentence the individual.[311]

3.5.2   Primacy of EU Law

The jurisprudence on the principle of primacy[312] is based on the direct applicability of regulations as well. The CJEU stated that

[t]the obligations undertaken under the Treaty establishing the Community would not be unconditional, but merely contingent, if they could be called in question by subsequent legislative acts of the signatories.—The precedence of Community law is confirmed by Article 189, whereby a regulation 'shall be binding' and 'directly applicable in all Member States'. This provision, which is subject to no reservation, would be quite meaningless if a State could unilaterally nullify its effects by means of legislative measure which could prevail over Community law. It follows from all these observations that the law stemming from the Treaty, an independent source of law, could not because of its special and original nature, be overridden by domestic legal provisions, however framed—.[313]

According to the principle of primacy, national legislation, including constitutions, cannot override EU law. National legislation must be in accordance with EU law. In situations of conflict between national law and EU law the provision of EU law needs to be applied. However, *in the field of substantive criminal law, principle of primacy does not apply in this manner to the detriment of the accused.* This brings us to the next principle of EU law, namely to the principle of conforming interpretation.

3.5.3   Indirect Effect/Conforming Interpretation

Conforming interpretation (more commonly referred as indirect effect) means that Member States have an obligation to interpret national law harmoniously and in conformity with EU law as far as it is possible. If national law cannot be applied in

---

[311] Melander (2010), p. 87.

[312] In academic literature often referred as the principle of supremacy.

[313] Case C-6/64 *Flaminio Costa v E.N.E.L.* [1964] ECR p. 1195.

conformity with EU law, such domestic law must be held inapplicable.[314] Conforming interpretation cannot lead to interpretation of national law *contra legem*. If national law 'cannot receive an application which would lead to a result compatible with that envisaged by' EU law, conforming interpretation cannot be used.[315] In all cases where EU-influenced national law is applied, the indirect effect of EU law ought to be at hand regardless whether the national law in question has or has not been amended as a result of implementation of EU law into national law.[316] Conforming interpretation applies to all EU law[317] including provisions which are directly applicable or have direct effect. The meaning of conforming interpretation is however particularly relevant relation to directives. When EU law is given indirect effect, the national provision maintains its position as the provision that is applied primarily.[318] As already mentioned, in the field of substantive criminal law the principle of legality restricts indirect effect because criminal liability cannot be determined or aggravated on the basis of framework decision or directive alone to the detriment of the accused.[319] Thus, the interpretation of penal provisions is possible only within the limits of the wording of a national penal provision.[320]

The principle of primacy, the principle of legality, direct effect, and the principle of conforming interpretation work differently in situations where the EU legislation is not implemented on time and national legislation is conflicting with EU legislation, depending on whether an EU provision would establish or aggravate criminal liability or if EU provision would mitigate criminal liability. When national legislation does not allow conforming interpretation, the principles cannot be applied to establish or aggravate criminal liability. In situations where an EU provision would mitigate liability but in which the national legislation does not allow conforming interpretation, the principles could still lead to the mitigation of criminal liability. In these cases national legislation is not applied and the mitigation of criminal liability could be based on either direct effect (directives) or the principle of primacy (framework decisions).

Based on what is said of the difference of the application of the doctrines of vertical direct effect, primacy and indirect effect in general EU law on one hand and in EU criminal law on the other hand, *it can be concluded that there is a difference in how legal effects are formed in general EU law and in EU criminal law. In general EU law, legal effects result from the EU itself.* Even though EU law is enforced at

---

[314] Case C-157/86 *Mary Murphy and others v An Bord Telecom Eireann* [1988] ECR p. 673, para 11.

[315] Case C-105/03 *Criminal proceedings against Maria Pupino* [2005] ECR p. I-5285, paras 43, 47.

[316] Melander (2010), p. 91.

[317] Case C-157/86 *Mary Murphy and others v An Bord Telecom Eireann* [1988] ECR p. 673, para 11.

[318] Raitio (2006), pp. 199–201.

[319] Case C-105/03 *Criminal proceedings against Maria Pupino* [2005] ECR p. I-5285, paras 44–45; Case C-14/86 *Pretore di Salò v Persons unknown* [1987] ECR p. 2545, para 20; Case C-80/86 *Criminal proceedings against Kolpinghuis Nijmegen BV* [1987] ECR p. 3969, para 14.

[320] Melander (2010), p. 92.

the domestic level, EU law itself can establish legal effects that the relevant national authorities have to grant and recognise. *In EU criminal law, legal effects to the detriment of the accused cannot be constituted without national law.* This is a result of the key criminal law principle of legality. The establishment and aggravation of criminal liability always needs to be based on *law*, and directives (and framework decisions) simply do not count as law in this sense due to their nature as instruments of approximation.

3.6 Criminal Law Decision-Making in the EU

The ordinary legislative procedure applies to criminal law decision-making. The criminal law initiatives are either proposals of the Commission or initiatives presented by a quarter of the Member States (Article 76 TFEU). Thus far the Member States have not initiated substantive criminal legislative proposals.[321] Following Article 4 of Protocol No 2 on the application of the principles of subsidiarity and proportionality, the Commission sends its legislative proposals to the national Parliaments at the same time as they are forwarded to the Union's legislator. If national Parliaments find that the draft in question does not comply with the principle of subsidiarity, they have 8 weeks of time to send reasoned opinions to the presidents of the European Parliament, the Council and the Commission. If the opinions representing one quarter of the votes allocated to the national Parliaments find that the criminal legislative proposal is not given in compliance with the principle of subsidiarity, the draft must be reviewed by the Commission (the so-called yellow card mechanism, Article 7 of the Protocol no 2), and decided whether to maintain, amend or withdraw the draft.

In the ordinary legislative procedure (Article 294 TFEU) the Commission gives a legislative proposal to the Union's legislator, the European Parliament and the Council. After this the Parliament and Council can adopt the measure either in the first or second reading by accepting each other's amendments and positions relative to the proposal. The Council acts in a qualified majority. If the Parliament and the Council have not come to a consensus during the first and second reading, the proposal will be dealt in the Conciliation Committee that is formed by an equal number of members of the Council or their representatives and the Parliament. The Committee's aim is to reach an agreement on a joint text in 6 weeks of time. If consensus cannot be found, the proposal will not be adopted. If the Committee approves a joint text, both the Parliament and the Council have to adopt the proposal in 6 weeks, or otherwise the proposed act shall not be adopted.

The Parliament's equal participation in the legislative process with the Council is a turn towards EU-level criminal legislation with democratic legitimacy. The

---

[321] Weyembergh (2013), p. 22. However, on the criminal procedural side, the Directive 2011/99/EU of the European Parliament and of the Council of 13 December 2011 on the European protection order [2011] OJ L 338, 21.12.2011, pp. 2–18 was initiated by the Member States.

legislative process is easier than before, now that the Council acts with a qualified majority as opposed to the pre-Lisbon era's unanimity-requirement. However, even in situations where qualified majority would suffice, decisions are often made in the Council without voting due to the strong aspiration for consensus amongst the Member States.[322] The criminal legislative process with its subsidiarity control threshold requirements as well as the legislative practice aiming at unanimity represent a consensus-seeking atmosphere and the mutual accommodation of interests in the decision-making process. As also mentioned above, the emergency brake procedure of Article 83(3) TFEU still represents a remnant of the era of intergovernmental cooperation in criminal legislation and reminds us of the sovereignty-sensitive nature of criminal law.

In addition to these rather big changes in the legislative procedure towards democratic legitimacy and the 'normalization' of criminal law as an EU policy, a lot has happened and contines to happen also in the preparatory stages of the legislative work. There are different preparatory bodies and mechanisms that have quite significant effects on the legislative outcomes.

The Commission has several departments referred to as Directorate-Generals, which prepare legislative proposals in their own areas.[323] Criminal legislation, among them fundamental rights, civil justice, citizenship and equality issues, is generally prepared in the Commission's Directorate General Justice. The Commission has set up an expert group on EU criminal policy (henceforth the Expert group)[324] 'to assist the Commission in the preparation of legislation or in policy definition'.[325] The expert group gives the Commission advice concerning substantive criminal law proposals and the development of EU criminal policy. The advice can relate to any relevant legal question or 'gathering of factual evidence for the assessment whether EU criminal law measures are essential to ensure the effective implementation of a Union policy' (Article 2 of the Decision). The establishment of this kind of group that has expert members who either are legal practitioners or come from scientific or research institutions is definitely a step in a good direction and illustrates that the Commission aims to give legislative proposals that fit different traditions in national criminal justice systems.

The opinions of the Expert group have not been published. Only agendas and key findings of each meeting are published on the internet.[326] Since the expert group on EU criminal policy is established to help the Commission in developing of the EU criminal policy, in order to evaluate the Commission's focus or problem points in the EU criminal policy creation, it would be helpful to know what the problem areas

---

[322] Lewis (2016), pp. 142–153.

[323] Commission's internet site http://ec.europa.eu/about/ds_en.htm, accessed 25 June 2018.

[324] Commission decision of 21 February 2012 on setting up the expert group on EU criminal policy (OJEU 23.2.2012, C 53).

[325] Commission's internet site -> register of Expert Groups and Other Similar Entities http://ec.europa.eu/transparency/regexpert/index.cfm?do=groupDetail.groupDetail&groupID=2760, accessed 25 June 2018.

[326] Ibid.

are, how the Expert group has evaluated them and on what grounds, and how the Commission has taken the advice presented by the Expert group into account.

The first meeting of the Expert group concerned sanctions. The experts discussed the interplay between administrative and criminal sanctions and found that the Member States' approaches to the issue varied significantly, and that the effectiveness of the sanctions (regardless of whether they are administrative or criminal sanctions) is more dependent on the probability of getting caught and the effectiveness and certainty of prosecution and procedures than on sanction severity. The Expert group has also found that the approximation of sanctions is more difficult than the approximation of definitions of criminal offences. It was questioned, and the expert opinions varied, on whether setting minimum levels of maximum sanctions would have added value. The expert group considered whether setting of minimum sanctions would lead into full harmonization of sanctions. It was also brought up that the approximation of sanction types would lead to different treatment in different Member States since the rules on the execution of the sanctions vary significantly. The Expert group presented alternative ways of phrasing the requirements concerning the sanctions that could perhaps be used, such as focusing on the 'normal' result that would follow from effective enforcement of certain sanctions.[327] Many experts have also considered that as regards proper EU legal interests (such as fraud against the Union's financial interests) the EU would have more legitimacy to determine minimum sanctions.[328]

The Expert group has also focused on criminal procedure, namely on the concept of presumption of innocence and the establishment of the EPPO.[329] Regarding the future of EU criminal justice and mutual recognition, differences in how criminal justice systems sentence offenders and execute those sentences were seen as the aspects that cause most difficulty in the approximation of sanctions. Some experts even proposed that instead of approximating sanction levels, perhaps it would be feasible to define the 'actual' levels of imprisonment. This was not generally accepted as appropriate way to deal with the problem since such legislation could not be based on Article 83 TFEU.[330] The Expert group has also discussed the mutual recognition of freezing and confiscation orders and pre-trial detention. Here, the experts raised concerns regarding human rights protection and the principle of *ne*

---

[327] The Expert group on EU criminal policy, Meeting 19 June 2012, available in internet http://ec.europa.eu/transparency/regexpert/index.cfm?do=groupDetail.groupDetail&groupID=2760, accessed 25 June 2018.

[328] The Expert group on EU criminal policy, Meeting 16 October 2013, available in internet http://ec.europa.eu/transparency/regexpert/index.cfm?do=groupDetail.groupDetail&groupID=2760, accessed 25 June 2018.

[329] The Expert group on EU criminal policy, Meetings 23 January 2013 and 16 October 2013, available in internet http://ec.europa.eu/transparency/regexpert/index.cfm?do=groupDetail.groupDetail&groupID=2760, accessed 25 June 2018.

[330] The Expert group on EU criminal policy, Meeting 12 March 2014, available in internet http://ec.europa.eu/transparency/regexpert/index.cfm?do=groupDetail.groupDetail&groupID=2760, accessed 25 June 2018.

bis in idem.[331] The last meeting focused on the cooperation relative to evidence (e-evidence, admissibility of evidence, interconnection of criminal records) which was seen relevant also regarding the establishment of the EPPO.[332]

In the Commission, legislative proposals also go through inter-service consultation preferably at an early stage, to make the Commission's work efficient and to ensure that all Directorate Generals concerned are consulted on the matter.[333] Within the Commission's Legal Service, which needs to be consulted on all draft legislation, during the Inter-Service Consultation a lawyer specialized in the branch of law in question goes through the legislative draft.[334] The Commission has also created an inter-service coordination group on criminal law whose role is to coordinate the initiatives on criminal law measures.[335]

The European Parliament does not have a committee to coordinate proposals containing criminal law provisions. In general, the Civil Liberties committee deals with Justice and Home Affairs issues. In 2011, in the hearing concerning the Parliament's document on the EU approach on criminal law, the Parliament's Legal Service said it could theoretically provide 'legal advice on the quality and coherence of proposed criminal law-related legislation'. This kind of new task for the Legal Service would require more resources for it.[336]

In the Council, the JHA ministers try to coordinate the legislative process of proposals containing criminal law provisions. The Working Party on substantive criminal law (DROIPEN) considers typical JHA-related proposals such as initiatives regarding substantive criminal law, but in practice has competence to discuss any criminal law provision regardless on which policy field it belongs to, such as initiatives regarding criminal procedure.[337] The Coordinating Committee in the area of police and judicial cooperation in criminal matters (CATS, previously Committee for Article 36) also prepares the work of the Council in the field of criminal law. CATS deals with proposals that have already been discussed in the relevant Council

---

[331] The Expert Group on EU criminal policy, Meeting 29 September 2016, available in internet http://ec.europa.eu/transparency/regexpert/index.cfm?do=groupDetail.groupDetail&groupID=2760, accessed 25 June 2018.

[332] The Expert Group on EU criminal policy, Meeting 23 March 2017, available in internet http://ec.europa.eu/transparency/regexpert/index.cfm?do=groupDetail.groupDetail&groupID=2760, accessed 25 June 2018.

[333] Commission, Communication from the president (2010), available in internet http://ec.europa.eu/commission_2010-2014/president/news/documents/pdf/c2010_1100_en.pdf, accessed 25 June 2018, 8.

[334] William Robinson, 'Drafting EU legislation' (European Parliament) http://www.europarl.europa.eu/RegData/etudes/note/join/2012/462442/IPOL-JURI_NT(2012)462442_EN.pdf, accessed 25 June 2018.

[335] European Parliament, Report on an EU approach on criminal law, A7-0144/2012, 24 April 2012, 9; Vervaele (2013), p. 65.

[336] European Parliament, Report on an EU approach on criminal law, A7-0144/2012, 24 April 2012, 9.

[337] http://eu2013.ie/ireland-and-the-presidency/abouttheeu/theeuexplained/councilworkingparties/, accessed 25 June 2018; European Parliament, Report on an EU approach on criminal law, A7-0144/2012, 24 April 2012, 9.

working parties (such as DROIPEN) by discussing the issues 'from a more strategic and coordinating perspective' before they go to COREPER and the Council.[338]

COREPER is the Council's main preparatory body; it is not a decision-making body. JHA matters, and naturally criminal law matters, are dealt in COREPER II configuration. It is composed of the permanent representatives of the governments of the Member States (ambassadors to the EU).[339] COREPER II deals with politically sensitive and important issues, such as criminal law matters. COREPER aims to achieve unanimity on the draft proposal before the issue will be dealt in the Council.[340] The work done at the preparatory stages is important, since the Council configuration deciding on criminal legislative proposals is not necessarily the JHA Council. It can be any of the Council's configurations.[341] In addition to this, most of the legislative issues are discussed and 'effectively closed at the working party level or at the latest in Coreper'.[342]

We can see that even though majority decision-making applies to the EU criminal legislative process, in practice the Council aims for unanimity. This suggests that there still is a strong intergovernmental element in the criminal law decision-making. Neo-functionalism, the polar opposite to intergovernmentialism, explains the integration process from a euro-centric approach. It flourished between the 1950s and 1970s, and went through a revival in the 1990s and the 2000s. Today, it is not the most widely used theoretical framework in EU studies, but it is still used as a point of reference in the understanding 'how political integration in the EU might be explained as a result of the unintended consequence of cooperation among countries'.[343] Neo-functionalism centred explaining the integration process itself but not its goals or nature. According to this theory, cooperation in one policy area creates pressure in a neighbouring policy area, which is then placed on the political agenda for further integration. The integration process is mostly seen driven by national and international elites. It is strongly influenced by supranational institutions, such as the Commission or the European Parliament, and interest groups such as the European political parties.[344]

Neo-functionalists explain the unintended policy transfer by the concept of spill over, which means that political cooperation in one area leads to formulation of new goals in another policy area in order to achieve the original goals. There are different types of spill over. Functional spill over refers to this above-explained policy spill over where the policy agenda widens from its original goal to other goals. Political

---

[338] http://eu2013.ie/ireland-and-the-presidency/abouttheeu/theeuexplained/councilworkingparties/, accessed 25 June 2018; See also, Melander (2010), p. 61.

[339] Article 16(7) TEU; Council's internet site http://www.consilium.europa.eu/en/council-eu/preparatory-bodies/coreper-ii/, accessed 25 June 2018.

[340] Melander (2010), pp. 63–64.

[341] A reply from Päivi Leino-Sandberg (counsellor of legislation in the Ministry of Justice, Finland) on 18 September 2014 to my e-mail concerning the matter.

[342] Päivi Leino (2014), p. 4.

[343] Jensen (2016), p. 63.

[344] Ibid., pp. 54–59.

spill over refers to the situation where national political groups find supranational cooperation necessary in order to solve certain problems. In turn, cultivated spill over means that supranational actors, such as the Commission, the Members of the European Parliament or even the CJEU, drive the integration process forward when the Member States are less active.[345] Today, spill over is a relevant concept in regard to EU criminal law because it is used to describe the birth of EU criminal law as a response to increasing free movement that brought along with it also unwanted cross-border criminality. When the integration process is viewed from today's perspective, it is evident that the supranational institutions, particularly the CJEU, have had a great deal of impact in the integration process.

Whereas neo-functionalism is a rather euro-centric approach, intergovernmentialism is a competing state-centric approach that gives national governments a central role in the integration process. It emerged in the 1960s as a critique to the neo-functionalism. The theory starts from a pragmatic premise according to which the states cooperate simply because they need to resolve common problems. The supranational institutions, such as the Commission, are seen rather as servants to the Member States since they are not seen to have any independent role within the integration process. Liberal intergovernmentalism starts from the premise that all decisions made by the EU are result of bargaining amongst the Member States and that the EU is motivated purely by national interests. This premise is questioned, since the premise seems to describe the decision-making in the EU only relative to the unanimous decision-making, most evidently relative to constitutional changes in the EU, but it does not describe the day-to-day decision-making in the EU.[346] This critique seems even stronger after the entry into force of the Lisbon Treaty increased the policy areas in which majority voting is used as a main rule, including criminal law.

The intergovernmentalist critique of the neo-functionalism's spill over thesis is that it could occur only in low politics, such as economic integration, but not in high politics, such as common foreign policy or sovereignty-sensitive policy issues. However, developments in the integration process seem to have disproved this critique.[347] Also, in a way, the very existence of EU criminal policy as such seems to shake this critique since criminal law is a highly sovereignty-sensitive policy area. Nevertheless, the criminal law decision-making process has a strong intergovernmental dimension in the sense that the Council seeks to establish unanimity between the national representatives for new legislative measures. The consensus-seeking nature of decision-making is good in terms of legitimacy. This way the political outcomes, such as legislative measures, are more likely to be implemented and enforced efficiently by the national authorities.

---

[345] Jensen (2016), pp. 55–59.
[346] Cini (2016), pp. 66–76.
[347] Ibid., p. 75.

3.7 Legal Basis Determines the Union's Competence to Enact Substantive Criminal Legislation

Criminal law became an EU policy when the Maastricht Treaty entered into force. As is well known, the Union's criminal law competence is seen to derive from the so-called spill-over of power. Since the disappearance of internal borders in the EU has facilitated unwanted cross-border criminal activities, the EU needs to have a competence and means to counter that crime.[348] Leon Lindberg has formulated the idea of the spill-over as follows

> 'Spill-over' refers to a situation in which a given action, related to a specific goal, creates situation in which the original goal can be assured only by taking further actions, which in turn create a further condition and a need for more action ... integrating one sector of the economy—for example coal and steel—will inevitably lead to the integration of other economic and political activities. ... [T]he initial task and grant of power to the central institutions creates a situation or series of situations that can be dealt with only by further expanding the task and the grant of power. ... 'Spill-over' assumes the continued commitment of the Member States to the undertaking.[349]

According to the spill-over argument, EU measures in the field of criminal law are necessary for the better realization of the internal market.[350] Cooperation in criminal matters can be seen as a natural continual of the integration process and constitutionalization in the EU framework, as also Kaarlo Tuori's theory[351] on the many constitutions of the EU suggests. The building of the AFSJ could even be seen as a requirement for the effective functioning of the internal market.

Article 83 TFEU includes legal basis for two types of substantive criminal law competence. Article 83 TFEU reads as follows:

1. The European Parliament and the Council may, by means of directives adopted in accordance with the ordinary legislative procedure, establish *minimum rules concerning the definition of criminal offences and sanctions in the areas of particularly serious crime with a cross-border dimension* resulting from the nature or impact of such offences or from a special need to combat them on a common basis.
   These areas of crime are the following: terrorism, trafficking in human beings and sexual exploitation of women and children, illicit drug trafficking, illicit arms trafficking, money laundering, corruption, counterfeiting of means of payment, computer crime and organised crime.
   On the basis of developments in crime, the Council may adopt a decision identifying other areas of crime that meet the criteria specified in this paragraph. It shall act unanimously after obtaining the consent of the European Parliament.
2. If *the approximation of criminal laws and regulations of the Member States proves essential to ensure the effective implementation of a Union policy in an area which has been subject to harmonisation measures, directives may establish minimum rules with*

---

[348] Fletcher et al. (2008), pp. 21–23. On the concept of spill-over, see Lindberg (1963), p. 10.

[349] Lindberg (1963), pp. 10–11.

[350] Fletcher et al. (2008), p. 28.

[351] Tuori (2010).

regard to the definition of criminal offences and sanctions in the area concerned. Such directives shall be adopted by the same ordinary or special legislative procedure as was followed for the adoption of the harmonisation measures in question, without prejudice to Article 76.

3. Where a member of the Council considers that a draft directive as referred to in paragraph 1 or 2 *would affect fundamental aspects of its criminal justice system, it may request that the draft directive be referred to the European Council. In that case, the ordinary legislative procedure shall be suspended.* After discussion, and in case of a consensus, the European Council shall, within four months of this suspension, refer the draft back to the Council, which shall terminate the suspension of the ordinary legislative procedure.

   Within the same timeframe, in case of disagreement, and if at least nine Member States wish to establish *enhanced cooperation* on the basis of the draft directive concerned, they shall notify the European Parliament, the Council and the Commission accordingly. In such a case, the authorisation to proceed with enhanced cooperation referred to in Article 20(2) of the Treaty on European Union and Article 329(1) of this Treaty shall be deemed to be granted and the provisions on enhanced cooperation shall apply. (emphasis added).

The first paragraph of the article defines the Union's competence to enact criminal legislation in areas of particularly serious crime with a cross-border dimension. These are called the 'euro-crimes'. The second paragraph defines the Union's express ancillary criminal law competence. The Union has competence to approximate national criminal legislation when it is essential to ensure the effective implementation of a Union policy in an area, which has already been subject to harmonization measures.

Even though Article 83 TFEU offers the Union a clear legal basis to enact criminal law measures, there has been plenty of debate whether the Union has implicit substantive criminal law competence.[352] This chapter focuses to briefly present the key rules on the choice of legal basis (Sect. 3.7.1). Then the pre-Lisbon situation is examined since at that time the CJEU had found that the Union had implicit criminal law competence at least to certain extent.[353] This is examined in Sect. 3.7.2. Lastly, the nature of Article 83 TFEU is examined thoroughly in Sect. 3.7.3. The possibility that the Union could have implicit substantive criminal law competence and what that would entail is analysed in Sects. 5.2.1.1–5.2.1.7.

---

[352] See, for example, Mitsilegas (2009), Satzger (2012), Asp (2012); Miettinen (2013b), p. 194; Miettinen (2015); Öberg (2014), Huomo-Kettunen (2014), p. 23.

[353] See, the so-called *environmental crimes* Case C-176/03 *Commission of the European Communities v Council of the European Union* [2005] ECR p. I-7879 and the so-called *ship-source pollution* Case C-440/05 *Commission of the European Communities v Council of the European Union* [2007] ECR p. I-9097.

3.7.1   Rules on the Choice of Legal Basis

The choice of legal basis is first and foremost an issue of EU constitutional law because it inseparably relates to a question of the Union's competences. The question of EU competence is usually divided into two separate issues: the conferral of powers and to the exercise of those powers.[354] The choice of legal basis has extensive effects on the limits and proportions of EU substantive criminal law competence and on the respect for fundamental aspects of national criminal justice systems. The choice of legal basis influences the possibilities of deciding what type of legislative instrument to use, and to what extent sanctions can be harmonised. It also determines if the emergency brake procedure can be applied, and through that, what possibilities the Member States have to protect the fundamental aspects of their criminal justice systems. Because of this, the choice of legal basis has been described as a criminal policy issue.[355] Since EU criminal policy is strongly related to competence issues, EU criminal policy also has a constitutional dimension.

There is a vast number of cases concerning the choice of legal basis. The integration- or effectiveness-oriented view seems to be the prevailing approach in the CJEU's case law. Since the Union only has competence that is conferred upon it, the Union's legislator must reason the legislation. The obligation to state reasons includes the obligation to determine the appropriate legal basis for the legislative acts. The choice of legal basis is often a subject of disagreement between the Commission and the Member States, which illustrates the political nature of the choice of the legal basis.

Objective factors, the aim and the content of the legislative act, determine the choice of appropriate legal basis. In its so-called titanium-dioxide judgment and later judgments, the CJEU found that the choice of legal basis cannot rest solely on an institution's conviction as to the objective pursued. Instead, the objective factors, such as the aim and content of the act, which can be judicially reviewed by the Court, are determining factors.[356]

In its *ECOWAS* judgment the CJEU also found that 'the legal basis for an act must be determined having regard to its own aim and content and not to the legal basis used for the adoption of other Union measures which might, in certain cases, display similar characteristics',[357] meaning that only the CJEU can evaluate the *judicial* appropriateness of the choice of the legal basis. Any *legal* conclusions about the appropriateness of the choice of legal basis cannot be drawn from the fact that a legislative act previously has been based on certain legal basis and an action for annulment has not been lodged relating to that choice of legal basis. At most, one

---

[354] Rosas and Armati (2010), pp. 17–26.

[355] Frände (2013), pp. 78–92, 82; Huomo-Kettunen (2014), p. 23.

[356] For example Case C-300/89 *Commission of the European Communities v Council of the European Communities* [1991] ECR p. I-2867, para 10 and Case C-209/97 *Commission of the European Communities v Council of the European Union* [1999] ECR p. I-8067, para 13.

[357] Case C-91/05 *Commission of the European Communities v Council of the European Union* [2008] ECR p. I-3651, para 106.

can determine that the legal basis that was used has enjoyed *political* acceptance since act for annulment has not been initiated.

As a main rule, Union legislative acts ought to have only one legal basis. If the act 'pursues number of objectives or has several components that are indissociably linked, without one being secondary and indirect in relation to the other, such an act will have to be founded on the various corresponding legal bases'.[358] There is a limitation to this rule however. If the legislative procedures are not compatible with each other, various legal bases cannot be used simultaneously.[359] If the legislative act has twofold purpose, the act ought to be based on the main or predominant purpose of component if the other purpose is merely incidental.[360] The aim and content is evaluated based on both the explanatory memorandum and on the legislative text itself. In addition to these rules, it should be considered whether the legislative act is necessary to fulfil the objectives and aims of the Union policy in question.[361]

Due to the special nature of criminal law the matter of choice of legal basis is not as unproblematic as it might be the case with other branches of law. The special nature of criminal law manifests in the role of criminal law in societies as a minimum normative basis for shared values and behaviour, expressed at least in the core of criminal law, in criminal law provisions such as provisions prohibiting homicides or theft, the principle of legality and so on. Criminal law also is closely linked to national sovereignty, as explained in Sect. 2.1.[362] Legal norms affect individuals' freedoms, and penal norms, in particular the criminal punishment, restrict individual freedoms more profoundly than other legal norms. Criminal law and particularly the state's right to punish are manifestations of state power because punishments always restrict a person's fundamental rights which, in turn, are established to determine the interrelation between the state and the individuals.

Moreover, criminal legislation has criminal policy objectives but it simultaneously aims to protect interests that can be derived from different policy areas. In the abstract, criminal law protects peaceful social life and interaction between individuals. From this perspective, it is difficult to evaluate what exactly could be identified as predominantly criminal law objectives and contents. In this light, the Union's ancillary competence enshrined in Article 83(2) TFEU seems particularly problematic in the light of its wording.

> If the approximation of criminal laws and regulations of the Member States proves essential to *ensure the effective implementation of a Union policy in an area which has been subject*

---

[358] Case C-411/06 *Commission of the European Communities v European Parliament and Council of the European Union* [2008] ECR p. I-7585, para 47.

[359] For example in cases Case C-300/89 *Commission of the European Communities v Council of the European Communities* [1991] ECR p. I-2867, paras 18–21; Case C-490/10 *European Parliament v Council of the European Union* [2012], para 47.

[360] For example Case C-411/06 *Commission of the European Communities v European Parliament and Council of the European Union* [2008] ECR p. I-7585, paras 45–46.

[361] Case C-490/10 *European Parliament v Council of the European Union* [2012], para 68.

[362] For example Opinion of Advocate General Mazák in Case C-440/05 Commission v Council, delivered on 28 June 2007, paras 71–72; Melander (2013), pp. 42, 47.

> *to harmonisation measures*, directives may establish minimum rules with regard to the defi-
> nition of criminal offences and sanctions in the area concerned. (emphasis added)

The phrasing gives the ancillary competence an instrumental nature in comparison to Union's substantive legislation in other policy fields. This naturally raises a
question: in which situations the article is meant to be used as a legal basis for
Union's legislative acts? It seems clear that it could be a legal basis for legislative
acts where the predominant aim and content is criminal law–driven, like in the case
in the directive proposal for the protection of the Union's financial interests in criminal law measures. But what if the legislative act would include only one or few
criminal provisions and the predominant content would consist of other than criminal provisions. Could the entire legislative proposal be based on an article other than
Article 83(2) TFEU? Or should the proposal be based on two legal bases eve though
the Union's legislative acts ought to have only one legal basis as a main rule? Or
should the legislative proposal be divided into two proposals? Could Article 83(2)
TFEU be used as a legal basis for legislative acts that do not have any crime or penal
provisions in them but the aim and purpose of the act were linked to criminal law?

3.7.2   Implicit Substantive Criminal Law Competence Pre-Lisbon and Its Meaning Today[363]

In the so-called *environmental crimes* case,[364] the CJEU evaluated whether the competence to take criminal law measures relative to Community legislation on environmental protection belonged to the Community or the Union. The Commission,
with the support of the European Parliament, brought an action for annulment
against Council Framework Decision 2003/80/JHA on the protection of the environment through criminal law. The Framework Decision was based on criminal law
legal bases, ex-Article 34 EU in conjunction with ex-Articles 29 EU and 31(e)
EU. The Commission claimed that the appropriate legal basis was ex-Article 3(1)
EC and ex-Articles 174–176 EC on environmental policy and that the legislation
should be given by the Community, not the Union, in a form of a directive.

Ex-Article 47 EU was crucial to solving conflicts of competence between the
Community and the Union. The Article stated that nothing in the EU Treaty is to
affect the EC Treaty. The Court found that the competence to take criminal law
measures relative to the environmental protection belonged to the Community. The
Court reasoned this by stating that environmental protection is one of the essential
objectives of the Community and that it has a crosscutting nature amongst the other
Community policies. The Court then stated that 'as a general rule, neither criminal

---

[363] Some observations presented in this chapter and in Sect. 3.7.4 are first published in Huomo-
Kettunen (2014).

[364] Case C-176/03 *Commission of the European Communities v Council of the European Union*
[2005] ECR p. I-7879.

law nor the rules on criminal procedure fall within the Community's competence'. This however does not

> prevent the Community legislature, when the application of effective, proportionate and dissuasive criminal penalties by the competent national authorities is an essential measure for combating serious environmental offences, from taking measures which relate to the criminal law of the Member States which it considers necessary in order to ensure that the rules which it lays down on environmental protection are fully effective.[365]

The so-called *ship-source pollution* case resembles the *environmental crimes* case in terms of conflict of competence. The CJEU evaluated whether the competence to give legislative acts concerning environmental protection in relation to maritime transport, including setting an obligation for the Member States to use criminal penalties to give fully effective protection for the environmental protection, belonged to the Community (first pillar) or to the Union (third pillar). The Council considered that criminal law competence belonged to the Union based on the EU Treaty. The Council also pointed out that the Commission had based its directive proposal on the article that was a legal basis for legislative acts concerning maritime transport (ex-80.2 EC) and not on the legal basis concerning the environmental protection (ex-175 EC). The purpose of the directive was to improve maritime transport safety and to promote environmental protection. The Council had enacted a framework decision 2005/667/JHA that supplemented Directive 2005/35/EC and it also aimed to promote maritime safety. The Framework Decision contained penal provisions to ensure safety in maritime transport and a high level of environmental protection. Legal bases for the Framework Decision were ex-31.1.e EU and ex-34.2.b EU, which concerned criminal law cooperation. The legislation concerning the safety of maritime transport and environmental protection was thus divided into two instruments. Substantive norms on maritime transport were in the Commission's Directive based on the legal basis of common transport policy. Penal provisions—including the obligation for the Member States to criminalize certain conduct and to set certain minimum levels of maximum sanctions following those crimes—were given in the Framework Decision based on the legal bases concerning cooperation in criminal matters.

The question in the ship-source pollution case was whether the Community had competence to enact criminal legislation in situations where it was essential in order to ensure effective realization of the Community's policy, meaning that the case was concerned with the question of whether criminal law competence was exhaustively defined in the EU Treaty. From a political perspective, implicit criminal law competence in connection with the Community policies benefitted the Community and the Commission in the effective realization of the Community policies. Understanding criminal law competence to be exhaustively defined in the EU Treaty would have kept criminal law decision-making closer to the Member States and emphasised the status of criminal law as a manifestation of the Member State's sovereignty. At the time of the case, criminal law decision-making required unanimity in the Council,

---

[365] Case C-176/03 *Commission of the European Communities v Council of the European Union* [2005] ECR p. I-7879, paras 41–42, 47–48.

which expressed respect for the special nature of criminal law and its close relation to national sovereignty.[366] Thus the case also concerned the division of competences between the Communities (EC and EU) and the Member States. Nineteen Member States supported the Council in the case.

Both the common transport policy and criminal law cooperation were shared competences, but their legislative procedures differed. The Community used competence in the transport policy in which field the decision-making took place in a co-decision procedure (ex-Article 251 EC). In the co-decision procedure, the Commission gave a draft legislative act to the Council and the European Parliament, which the Council then approved by qualified majority voting after obtaining the opinion of the Parliament. The Union had competence in criminal law cooperation. Either the Commission or a Member State initiated a legislative process. Ex-Article 39 EU required the Council to hear the Parliament's opinion before deciding unanimously on the legislative act. We can see that the legislative procedures differed in quite a significant way. The co-decision procedure under the first pillar gave more power to the Parliament than the procedure that was followed in the criminal law framework. In this light it is not surprising that the Parliament supported the Commission's act for annulment of the Council's Framework decision. Also, the co-decision procedure did not require unanimity in the Council and thus, politically speaking, criminal legislation could have been enacted more easily under the co-decision procedure than within the criminal law framework.

Ex-Article 47 EU had once again a crucial role in solving the conflict of competence between the Community and the Union. According to ex-Article 47 EU, the criminal law competence established in the EU Treaty could not intrude on the powers established in the EC Treaty.[367] The CJEU found that the Community legislator had broad legislative powers to enact measures in order to improve safety and 'any other appropriate provisions'. Even though the legislative act was not based on Treaty provisions concerning environmental protection, environmental protection was considered to be an objective of the common transport policy in addition to being one of the essential objectives of the Community. The aims of the Framework Decision were considered essentially the same as the aims of the Directive and thus the Court found that the Community had the competence to oblige the Member States to set effective, proportionate and dissuasive criminal penalties for combating serious environmental offences and to ensure that the rules concerning safety in maritime transport are fully effective. Even though the Community legislator had the power to set this obligation, it did not have the competence to determine the type or level of the criminal penalties. Regardless, the Court concluded that the legislation on the matter was to be given entirely in a Directive under the first pillar, because the substantive provisions and the setting of the obligation to place effective,

---

[366] Reservedness in criminal law cooperation has often been linked to conceptions of the state sovereignty and to repressive nature of criminal law measures in the core of that sovereignty. See for example Salminen (2010), pp. 159–163.

[367] Case C-440/05 *Commission of the European Communities v Council of the European Union* [2007] ECR p. I-9097, paras 52–53.

proportionate and dissuasive criminal penalties were inseparably linked to each other.[368]

Thus, in the pre-Lisbon era, it was clear that the Community had implicit substantive criminal law competence under the first pillar in situations where criminal law measures were necessary to effectively fulfil the objectives of the Community's policies—at least for the purpose of environmental protection. It is necessary to ask what the meaning of these two cases is after the Lisbon Treaty entered into force since the new Treaty structure abolished the pillar structure and the division of competences between the Community and the Union.

The wording of Article 83(2) TFEU resembles the legal status before the Lisbon Treaty entered into force when the CJEU gave the two judgments[369] recognising criminal legislative powers in the first pillar. Article 83(2) TFEU is said to have codified this line of interpretation into the basic Treaties.[370] When this is viewed from a historical perspective, one can notice that the Article *does not* codify the Court's case law. Instead, preparations for the current Article 83(2) TFEU were started and developed well before the two judgments were given. The first of the two cases, the action for annulment in the *environmental crimes* case was brought on April 2003 and the judgment of the Court was given in September 2005. In the ship-source pollution case, the action for annulment was brought on 2005 and the judgment was given on 2007. The preparations of the then prepared Article III-172 of the so-called Constitutional Treaty (TCE) from June 2003 contain wording that very much resembles the current Article 83(2) TFEU: the wording is almost identical.[371]

In the final report of Working Group X 'Freedom, Security and Justice' given on December 2002 the content of the current Article 83(2) TFEU has already started to take its current shape.[372] When the Court's stand on the ship-source pollution case is taken into account as well—according to which a directive that was given under the first pillar could only contain an obligation to the Member States to enact effective, proportionate and dissuasive criminal penalties but the Community legislator could not specify the type or scale of the penalties—the wording of Article 83(2) TFEU which enables the Union legislator to establish '*minimum rules* with regard to the *definition of* criminal offences and *sanctions*' does not seem to codify the Court's pre-Lisbon case law. Instead, Article 83(2) TFEU establishes wider competence to

---

[368] Case C-440/05 *Commission of the European Communities v Council of the European Union* [2007] ECR p. I-9097, paras 58–74.

[369] The so-called *environmental crimes* Case C-176/03 *Commission v Council* [2005] ECR I- 7907 and the so-called *ship-source pollution* Case C-440/05 *Commission of the European Communities v Council of the European Union* [2007] ECR p. I-9097.

[370] Asp (2012), p. 127.

[371] For example, see the drafts of Article III-172 in following documents; The European Convention CONV 850/03, Draft Treaty establishing a Constitution for Europe, Brussels 18 June 2003, p. 139; Conference of the Representatives of the Governments of the Member States, CIG 4/1/03, IGC 2003—Editorial and legal comments on the draft Treaty establishing a Constitution for Europe—Basic Document, Brussels 6 October 2003, p. 326.

[372] The European Convention, CONV 426/02, WG X 14, Final report of Working Group X "Freedom, Security and Justice", Brussels, 2.12.2002, pp. 9–10.

the Union to set *minimum rules on sanctions* than what the pre-Lisbon case law had established for the Community.

Article 83 TFEU is different to what the Community's *implicit* criminal law competence was based on the two above described judgments before Lisbon Treaty entered into force. In the context at hand, both the first and the second paragraph of Article 83 TFEU give the Union the competence to 'establish minimum rules concerning the definition of criminal offences and sanctions'. In comparison, the judgments clearly demonstrate that the Community's implicit substantive criminal law competence did not include the possibility of establishing minimum rules on criminal sanctions. This means that the pre-Lisbon case law cannot today be applied as such in the field of criminal law.

3.7.3 Travaux Préparatoires *Advocate That Article 83 TFEU Was Intended to Exhaust Union's Substantive Criminal Law Competence*

The literature has presented diverging views on whether Article 83 TFEU is meant to be considered exhaustive. It has been asked whether Article 83(2) TFEU is independently sufficient as a legal basis for the Union's criminal legislation or whether another non-criminal law legal basis should support it.[373] It has also been argued that even after the Lisbon Treaty entered into force the Union could not set rules on the type or level of the criminal penalties based on implied substantive criminal law competence due to the requirements deriving from the principle of legality, but also because the state's right to punish has such a close connection to national sovereignty.[374] Article 83 TFEU is also argued to exhaust the Union's substantive criminal law competence but this argument has not been backed by a thorough historical overview of the legislative progress.[375]

It has been argued that Article 83(2) TFEU had been intended by the Member States to exhaust ancillary substantive criminal law competence.[376] An opinion of the Council's legal service (CLS) supports this argument. A few former Treaty provisions, such as Article 280 EC on the protection of the Community's financial interests and 135 EC on the customs cooperation, contained so-called exception clauses according to which the articles were not to be used for 'the application of national criminal law or the national administration of justice'. The Lisbon Treaty deleted these exception clauses. According to the CLS, the deletion of these exception clauses cannot be argued to lead into an *a contrario* conclusion, meaning that the CLS finds that the current articles 325(4) TFEU on the protection of the Union's

---

[373] Mitsilegas (2009), pp. 108–109.

[374] Melander (2012), pp. 509, 521.

[375] Piris (2010), pp. 181–187.

[376] Miettinen (2013b), pp. 194, 203–204.

financial interests and 33 TFEU on the customs cooperation could not be used as legal bases for the 'approximation of criminal law through the definition of criminal offences and sanctions'. Instead, the CLS finds that *the deletion of the restriction clauses 'should be read in conjunction with the insertion of the new legal basis in Article 83(2) TFEU* which was meant to tackle all cases where the EU legislature needs to harmonise the definition of criminal offences and sanctions in order to make other (non-criminal law) EU harmonized measures more effective'.[377] (emphasis added).

In his fairly recentarticle 'Implied ancillary criminal law competence after Lisbon', Samuli Miettinen has conducted a thorough study on the issue. He explains that in the light of the preparatory documents of the European Convention working on the provisions of the Constitutional Treaty, the provisions of which, including the corresponding to Article 83 TFEU were basically copy-pasted onto the Lisbon Treaty. Article 83 TFEU seems to have been intended to exhaust the substantive criminal law competence. However, by analysing the CJEU's case law on the rules of the choice of legal basis and few recent legislative proposals, he concludes that implied substantive criminal law competence might still be possible.[378] This chapter utilizes the data concerning the legislative history of Article 83 TFEU presented in Miettinen's article, but develops the idea further by following the CJEU's new line of interpretation based on the use of *travaux préparatoires* to the Treaties (on the Court's new line of interpretation, see Sect. 1.3.3.3.2).

It is noteworthy that the Treaties do not *as such* rule out the possibility of using some other article than 83(2) TFEU as a legal basis for the Union's criminal legislation. However, as explained above in Sect. 1.3.3.3.2 concerning the status of the *travaux préparatoires* of the Treaties, the CJEU's interpretation concerning the *ratio legis* is changing. In addition of taking preparatory work into consideration in interpreting the secondary law, the Court has recently also used the *travaux préparatoires* of the Treaties as a means of interpretation in its case law in trying to establish the *ratio legis* of primary law.[379] The Court has not drawn dynamic conclusions by reference to the *travaux* of the Treaties. Instead, preparatory works are used to support static interpretation.

Even though the CJEU has not yet relied on the *travaux préparatoires* of the Treaties when analysing *criminal law-related cases*, this line of interpretation based on the intent of the constitutional legislator could be used also to interpret the scope

---

[377] Opinion of the Council's Legal Service, 15309/12, paras 12–14.

[378] Miettinen (2013b), p. 194.

[379] On the case law where the Court has used the *travaux préparatoires* of the treaties in interpreting the Treaties, see Case C-61/03 *Commission of the European Communities v United Kingdom of Great Britain and Northern Ireland* [2005] ECR p. I-2477, para 25; Case C-370/12 *Thomas Pringle v Governement of Ireland, Ireland and The Attorney General* [2012], paras 135–136; Case C-583/11 P *Inuit Tapiriit Kanatami and Others v European Parliament and Council of the European Union* [2013], paras 50, 59, 69; Case C-62/14 *Gauweiler and others v Deutscher Bundestag* [2015], paras 93–100; Case C-286/14 *European Parliament v European Commission* [2016]. On the Court's use of *travaux préparatoires* of the secondary legislation, see Arnull (2006), pp. 614–615; Miettinen (2013c), pp. 99, 106.

of Article 83(2) TFEU. When the preparatory work adds value to the interpretation, it ought to be utilized. If and when Article 83(2) TFEU is interpreted in the light of that intention it seems that articles other than Article 83 TFEU should not be used as a legal basis for EU-level substantive criminal legislation.

In the *environmental crimes* and the *ship-source pollution* cases the CJEU followed the general rule on the choice of legal basis according to which the legal basis is chosen based on the aim and content of the measure and that as a main rule the measure should have only one legal basis. In these two cases, non-criminal law legal bases were seen appropriate. Also, ex-Article 47 EU was crucial to evaluating the appropriate legal basis *at that time*. However, the dismantling of the pillar-structure, and the rising of the new line of cases where the CJEU takes into account the *travaux préparatoires* of the Treaties and the intent and purpose behind the Treaty provisions is likely to change the interpretation in similar cases in the future, because Article 83 TFEU seems to be intended to exhaust the Union's substantive criminal law competence. Still, it is good to remember that the intention of the Union's constitutional legislature is more difficult to find out than, for example, the intention of national legislature enacting ordinary laws. The reason for this is that there is a lot of preparatory material and preparations are conducted in different working groups. The preparatory documents of the European Convention that worked on the provisions of the Constitutional Treaty can also be used to interpret the provisions of the Lisbon Treaty, at least those relevant to the issue at hand, because the provisions prepared for the Convention were later used as such or at least inspired comparable provisions in the Lisbon Treaty.

Working Group X, which prepared the substantive criminal law provision, was given a mandate limited to new AFSJ provisions and which excluded the possibility of fully considering the implicit substantive criminal competence.[380] In its final report, the Working Group X considered that it was necessary to clearly define the legal basis for criminal law and achieve legal certainty on the issue.[381] The issue of legal certainty relates with the democratic dimension of legislative procedure. *Travaux préparatoires* should be taken into account in legal interpretation together with *binding* sources of law (written and unwritten law), and other sources of law that *should* be taken into account (precedents, *travaux préparatoires*). Paying attention to the *travaux préparatoires* is likely to lead to predictability and continuity.[382]

Constitutions are generally meant to be stable and of long duration. They are not supposed to undergo significant changes very often, even though naturally they can be amended. The purpose of a constitution is to provide a stable framework for political and legal institutions and decision-making. Even though EU primary law is not a constitution in the same sense that the constitutions of nation states, nevertheless, EU primary law has some features similar to those of national constitutions. It is higher law than statutory law, and it provides the framework that constitutes the

---

[380] Miettinen (2013b), pp. 194, 200.

[381] CONV 426/02, WG X 14, Final report of Working Group X "Freedom, Security and Justice", Brussels, 2.12.2002, p. 9.

[382] Peczenik (1989), pp. 352 and 348.

Union's political and legal structures.[383] The preparatory documents date back only slightly over 10 years and are easy to perceive as up to date. The *travaux* to the Constitutional Treaty are in practice also the *travaux* to the Lisbon Treaty that entered into force only 8 years ago.

In the present EU context, it follows from the democratic dimension of the constitution-building that individuals ought to be able to know under which terms their freedoms can be restricted by means of criminal law. The conditions under which individuals' rights can be restricted vary greatly between the possible different substantive criminal law legal bases. From this fundamental rights perspective, it would be necessary to know in advance the legal basis for EU-level substantive criminal law competence.

The Working Group X also stated that ancillary substantive criminal law competence (the current Article 83(2) TFEU) should be used as a legal basis in the protection of the Union's financial interests or counterfeiting of euro.[384] This clearly shows that the deletion of the exception clause from the article concerning the protection of the Union's financial interests took place because Article 83(2) TFEU was developed. Later, this was also expressed in the Convention document concerning the AFSJ. A few other areas of crime that could be approximated under the explicit ancillary competence were also listed in the Convention document, including environmental crime.[385] This shows that Article 83(2) TFEU is to be used also in relation to environmental crime, also showing that the *environmental crimes* case and the *ship-source pollution* case are no longer relevant to the current Treaty framework.

Moreover, the limitation clauses of articles ex-280 EC concerning the financial interests (the current 325(4) TFEU) and ex-135 EC concerning the customs cooperation (the current 33 TFEU) were removed as 'a result of the provisions concerning an area of freedom, security and justice',[386] also suggesting that the article constituting the Union's substantive criminal law competence was intended to be exhaustive. Some national governments were of the belief that the limitation clauses previously existing in ex-280 EC and ex-135 EC were removed because they became unnecessary due to the new express provisions on Union's criminal law competence.[387]

These documents show that the ancillary competence enshrined in the current Article 83(2) TFEU is meant to cover several types of criminalization, including the protection of the Union's financial interests by means of criminal law, or, for that

---

[383] Craig (2001), pp. 125, 126–127; Raz (1998), pp. 153–154.

[384] CONV 426/02, WG X 14, Final report of Working Group X "Freedom, Security and Justice", Brussels, 2.12.2002, p. 9; Samuli Miettinen, 'Implied Ancillary Criminal Law Competence after Lisbon' (2013) 3(2) European Criminal Law Review 194, 201.

[385] CONV 614/03, Brussels, 14 March 2003, p. 26.

[386] CONV 821/03, Brussels, 27 June 2003, p. 161; Miettinen (2013b), pp. 194, 204.

[387] See, for example, Government's proposal (Finland) concerning the approval of the Lisbon Treaty, HE 23/2008 vp, Hallituksen esitys Eduskunnalle Euroopan unionista tehdyn sopimuksen ja Euroopan yhteisön perustamissopimuksen muuttamisesta tehdyn Lissabonin sopimuksen hyväksymisestä ja laiksi sen lainsäädännön alaan kuuluvien määräysten voimaansaattamisesta, 181 II.

matter, future environmental crimes. This means that substantive criminal legislation *is intended*, by the constitutional legislature, to be based on Article 83 TFEU *only*. The only exception to this that is evident from the *travaux* of the substantive criminal law competence is the possibility of using the ex-308 EC (the current 352 TFEU) as a legal basis for 'emergency action' (more on Article 352 TFEU in Sect. 5.2.1.4).[388]

3.7.4 Nature of the Substantive Criminal Law Competence of Article 83 TFEU

Article 4(2)j TFEU defines the Union's express criminal law competence as shared competence. Article 2(2) TFEU defines shared competence. Both the Union and the Member States may legislate in the criminal policy area. When the Union has exercised its competence on certain criminal law matters, the Member States shall not use their competences on those matters unless the Union has ceased exercising its competences on those matters. The Member States have full competence in those criminal law matters relating to which the Union has not exercised its competences. Even in these situations, the Member States have to follow the principle of sincere cooperation. This means that those measures that the Member States take cannot infringe the Union's interests in the policy field.

The first and second paragraphs of Article 83 TFEU read as follows:

1. The European Parliament and the Council may, by means of directives adopted in accordance with the ordinary legislative procedure, establish minimum rules concerning the definition of criminal offences and sanctions in the areas of particularly serious crime with a cross-border dimension resulting from the nature or impact of such offences or from a special need to combat them on a common basis.

   These areas of crime are the following: terrorism, trafficking in human beings and sexual exploitation of women and children, illicit drug trafficking, illicit arms trafficking, money laundering, corruption, counterfeiting of means of payment, computer crime and organised crime.

   On the basis of developments in crime, the Council may adopt a decision identifying other areas of crime that meet the criteria specified in this paragraph. It shall act unanimously after obtaining the consent of the European Parliament.

2. If the approximation of criminal laws and regulations of the Member States proves essential to ensure the effective implementation of a Union policy in an area which has been subject to harmonisation measures, directives may establish minimum rules with regard to the definition of criminal offences and sanctions in the area concerned. Such directives shall be adopted by the same ordinary or special legislative procedure as was followed for the adoption of the harmonisation measures in question, without prejudice to Article 76.

Because the Union's substantive criminal law competence is shared competence, the requirements of principles of subsidiarity and proportionality must be followed in the legislative procedure. These principles are described as 'federal' and

---

[388] CONV 426/02, WG X 14, Final report of Working Group X "Freedom, Security and Justice", Brussels, 2.12.2002, p. 9.

democratic safeguards within Europe.[389] TFEU defines that under the principle of subsidiarity 'the Union shall act only if and in so far as the objectives of the proposed action cannot be sufficiently achieved by the Member States' (Article 5(3) TEU). This means that '[u]nder the principle of conferral, the Union shall act only within the limits of the competences conferred upon it by the Member States— Competences not conferred upon the Union in the Treaties remain with the Member States" (Article 5(2) TEU). The subsidiarity principle understood in the terms of "federal" proportionality governs the sphere of the competence that remains with the Member States' exclusive competence.[390] The principle of proportionality requires that 'the content and form of Union action shall not exceed what is necessary to achieve the objectives of the Treaties' (Article 5(4) TEU).

Because the national parliaments exercise *political* control of subsidiarity, the principle of subsidiarity is also a democratic safeguard within Europe.[391] Article 12(b) TEU states that the national Parliaments contribute to the functioning of the Union "by seeing to it that the principle of subsidiarity is respected in accordance with the procedures provided for in the Protocol on the application of the principles of subsidiarity and proportionality". Thus the national parliaments are a kind of "watchdogs of subsidiarity" as explained in more detail above in Sect. 3.6.[392] The subsidiarity control mechanism is referred as a 'yellow card' mechanism because it is not a hard procedural rejection even though it may lead to a withdrawal of the draft.[393]

EU-level criminal legislative measures must be justified by the EU's legislator. The justification of the legislative acts can be read from the explanatory memoranda to legislative proposals. According to Article 5 of the Protocol on the application of the principles of subsidiarity and proportionality all draft legislative proposals should contain 'a detailed statement making it possible to appraise compliance with the principles of subsidiarity and proportionality'. Qualitative, and when possible quantitative, indicators should be used in the reasoning. The choice of legal basis is the pivotal element in the justification of Union's competence. The justification must contain reasoning why the Union measures are necessary due to the scale of the proposed action or the impact of the subject matter of the proposed legislation. The justification requirement is even more evident in relation to the ancillary competence than in relation to the so-called euro-crimes that are defined in the first paragraph of Article 83 TFEU. The first paragraph seems to imply that the listed so-called euro-crimes usually have a cross-border which is required for the Union to use that competence.

As for to the Union's ancillary substantive criminal law competence, this appears to be more instrumental by its nature since the use of ancillary competence is possible when it proves to be *'essential* to ensure the *effective implementation of a*

---

[389] Schütze (2009), pp. 525, 527.

[390] Ibid., pp. 525, 532.

[391] Ibid., pp. 525, 527.

[392] Cooper (2006), p. 281.

[393] Schütze (2009), pp. 525, 530.

Union policy that has been subject to harmonization measures' (emphasis added). This form of words suggests that criminal law measures would merely be means for effectively pursuing other Union policies. That provision requires that EU-level non-criminal law harmonisation measures have been enacted before criminal law measures are taken to ensure that 'too excessive or hasty recourse to criminal sanctions' would be avoided.[394] The idea behind the expression was thus to limit the use of EU criminal law following the principles of subsidiarity, proportionality and *ultima ratio*, instead of implying that the ancillary competence would be instrumental.

So far, only two legislative acts have been based on Article 83(2) TFEU. The regulation on insider dealing and market manipulation contains non-criminal law substantive norms which aim to increase market integrity and investor protection in order to increase the attractiveness of securities markets for raising capital. The regulation is based on Article 114 TFEU on competition and contributes to the functioning of the Single Market.[395] It also obliges the Member States to use administrative sanctions and determines the minimum levels of maximum pecuniary sanctions (Article 30).

The Directive on criminal sanctions for insider dealing and market manipulation imposes requirements for the Member States 'to provide for minimum rules on the definition of the most serious market abuse offences and on minimum levels of criminal sanctions attached to them'. The definition of the essential elements of insider dealing and market manipulation, the obligation to criminalize these conducts as well as inciting, aiding and abetting and attempt to such conduct, the obligation to ensure that legal persons can be held liable for these offences, and the obligation to set effective, proportionate and dissuasive criminal sanctions are all included in the directive.[396]

The Directive on the fight against fraud to the Union's financial interests by menas of criminal law establishes 'minimum rules concerning the definition of criminal offences and sanctions with regard to combatting fraud and other illegal activities affecting the Union's financial interests' The directive defines what conduct constitutes a fraud and other criminal offences affecting the Union's financial interests. The directive requires that these types of conduct are criminalized when

---

[394] CONV 727/03, Draft sections of Part Three with comments, Brussels, 27 May 2003, p. 32.

[395] Regulation (EU) No 596/2014 of the European Parliament and of the Council of 16 April 2014 on market abuse (market abuse regulation) and repealing Directive 2003/6/EC of the European Parliament and of the Council and Commission Directives 2003/124/EC, 2003/125/EC and 2004/72/EC Text with EEA relevance [2014] OJ L 173, 12.6.2014, pp. 1–61; COM(2011) 651 final, European Commission, proposal for a Regulation on insider dealing and market manipulation (market abuse), Brussels, 20 October 2011, pp. 1–5.

[396] Directive 2014/57/EU of the European Parliament and of the Council of 16 April 2014 on criminal sanctions for market abuse (market abuse directive) [2014] OJ L 173, 12.6.2014, pp. 179–189; COM(2011) 654 final, European Commission, proposal for a Directive on criminal sanctions for insider dealing and market manipulation, Brussels, 20 October 2011; COM(2012) 420 final, European Commission, Amended proposal for a Directive on criminal sanctions for insider dealing and market manipulation, Brussels, 25 July 2012.

conducted intentionally. Also incitement, aiding and abetting, and attempt of the crimes are to be criminalized, and the Member States must also ensure that legal persons can be held liable for the offences. Directive also stipulates sanctions with regard to natural and legal persons. Sanction levels do not include minimum levels for minimum penalties, but instead only minimum levels of maximum penalties.[397]

Since Article 83 TFEU only enables the establishment of *minimum rules* concerning definition of criminal offences and sanctions *by the means of directives*, full harmonization of criminal definitions and sanctions is not possible on the basis of Article 83 TFEU. This means that harmonisation cannot take place using regulations which would be directly applicable in the national courts. If EU criminal legislation would be given in the form of regulations, national courts would have to base their convictions directly on the applicable regulation. The reference to the minimum rules indicates that the national courts will base their judgments in the national provisions that implement Union legislation.

The requirement of minimum rules also means that the Union cannot exhaustively determine the scale of the punishment. However, there is disagreement on to what extent the sanctions can be harmonised. Some argue that the Union can set requirements of minimum levels for both minimum and maximum penalties. This is not seen as complete harmonisation of penalty scales, because the Member States could still impose harsher penalty scales. However, EU criminal legislation cannot require certain fixed levels for the minimum and maximum levels of penalties because that would mean full harmonisation of penalty scales.[398]

Some Member States, for example France, do not recognise minimum penalties, and thus they possibly rely on the emergency brake procedure to stop such legislative proposal from moving along since, to them, the issue concerns the structure of their criminal justice system.[399] Previously, Declaration 8 annexed to the Amsterdam Treaty clarified that 'Article K.3(e) of the Treaty on European Union shall not have the consequence of obliging a Member State whose legal system does not provide for minimum sentences to adopt them.'[400] The Declaration clearly stated that minimum penalties could not be harmonized.

In 2003, the secretariat of the Intergovernmental Conference sent all declarations annexed to the Final Acts of the intergovernmental conferences, including the Declaration 8, to a working group of legal experts to evaluate whether the declarations were still needed, or if some of them proved to be unnecessary in the planned

---

[397] Directive (EU) 2017/1371 of the European Parliament and of the Council of 5 July 2017 on the fight against fraud to the Union's financial interests by menas of criminal law OJ L 198, 28.7.2017, pp. 29–41.

[398] Asp (2012), pp. 125–126.

[399] Ibid., p. 125.

[400] For example, in France, the penalty scales simply state the maximum penalties but remain silent on the threshold of the minimum penalties (French Penal Code, english translation available in internet www.legifrance.gouv.fr/Traductions/en-English/Legifrance-translations, accessed 25 June 2018).

new treaty structure.[401] Nothing was mentioned later concerning Declaration 8.[402] The *travaux* do not say anything about why the Declaration 8 was not renewed. Equally interesting, the *travaux* do not clarify the meaning of minimum rules either.

Two legislative proposals have included minimum levels for minimum penalties,[403] the proposal for a directive on the fight against fraud to the Union's financial interests by means of criminal law[404] and the proposal for a directive on the protection of the euro and other currencies against counterfeiting by criminal law.[405] The emergency brake has not been pulled. The Directive against counterfeiting and the Directive on the fight against fraud to the Union's financial interests by menas of criminal law have both entered into force but the final versions of them *do not* provide for minimum levels for the minimum penalties.[406]

Some argue that since the wording of ex-Article 31(e) TEU ('measures establishing minimum rules relating to the constituent elements of criminal acts and to penalties') and Article 83 TFEU ('establish minimum rules concerning the definition of criminal offences and sanctions') are very much similar, their meaning and scope ought to be interpreted as corresponding, meaning that minimum penalties could not be required based on Article 83 TFEU.[407] However, the *travaux* being silent on the matter, the best guess is that Declaration 8 was not renewed because it was found unnecessary due to the new criminal law provisions. Thus far, legislative measures containing a requirement of minimum levels of minimum penalties have not been enacted.[408] So *at least in practice,* the Union has set only minimum levels for the

---

[401] CIG 47/03, IGC 2003, Declarations annexed to the Final Acts of the intergovernmental conferences which adopted the EC and EU Treaties and the Treaties and Acts which amended them, Brussels 10 November 2003, pp. 5, 109.

[402] Miettinen (2013b), pp. 194, 205.

[403] Anne Weyembergh (in collaboration with Serge de Biolley) (2013), p. 15.

[404] COM(2012) 363 final, proposal for a directive on the fight against fraud to the Union's financial interests by means of criminal law, Brussels, 11 July 2012, Article 8.

[405] COM(2013) 42 final, Proposal for a Directive on the protection of the euro and other currencies against counterfeiting by criminal law, and replacing Council Framework Decision 2000/383/JHA, Article 5(4).

[406] Directive 2014/62/EU of the European Parliament and of the Council of 15 May 2014 on the protection of the euro and other currencies against counterfeiting by criminal law, and replacing Council Framework Decision 2000/383/JHA [2013] OJ L 151, 21.5.2014, pp. 1–8, Article 5; Directive (EU) 2017/1371 of the European Parliament nad of the Council of 5 July 2017 on the fight against fraud to the Union's financial interests by menas of criminal law OJ L 198, 28.7.2017, pp. 29–41, Article 7.

[407] Judit Altena-Davidsen, 'Mandatory minimum sentences coming in through the back door?' (Leiden Law Blog http://leidenlawblog.nl/articles/mandatory-minimum-sentences-coming-in-through-the-back-door, accessed 25 June 2018.

[408] Directives enacted under Union's criminal law legal basis after Lisbon Treaty entered into force do not contain requirements of minimum levels of minimum penalties. These directives are Directive 2011/36/EU of the European Parliament and of the Council of 5 April 2011 on preventing and combating trafficking in human beings and protecting its victims, and replacing Council Framework Decision 2002/629/JHA [2011] OJ L 101, 15.4.2011, pp. 1–11; Directive 2011/92/EU of the European Parliament and of the Council of 13 December 2011 on combating the sexual abuse and sexual exploitation of children and child pornography, and replacing Council Framework

maximum penalties. This indicates that there is no political consensus amongst the Member States to set the levels of minimum punishments.

In addition to this implication concerning the sanctions, it also means that the Union cannot exhaustively stipulate the phrasing of the penal provisions. Minimum rules refer also to the fact that the Member States have to ensure those minimum requirements concerning the sanctions and the essential elements of the offence that the directive requires. In other words, the Member States cannot give lower standards of protection than that required in the directive, but if they want they can offer higher levels of protection to the protected interests by using higher sanction scales or wider definitions of the essential elements of the offence (resulting in a wider scale of criminalised conduct).[409] It is not clear, however, if the Member States could add other essential elements to the definition of the offence than what has been required in the directive. Additional essential elements might actually narrow the applicability of the penal provision in a way that would not follow the purpose and aim, the spirit, of the EU legislation.[410] This needs to be evaluated on a case by case basis.

The ordinary legislative procedure is used when Article 83(1) TFEU is used as the legal basis. Either the Commission or a Member State can start the legislative procedure. Majority voting is used, meaning that unanimity is no longer required from the Council. Article 83(3) TFEU however enables the use of the so-called emergency brake procedure that reads as follows.

> 3. Where a member of the Council considers that a draft directive as referred to in paragraph 1 or 2 would affect fundamental aspects of its criminal justice system, it may request that

---

Decision 2004/68/JHA [2011] OJ L 335, 17.12.2011, pp. 1–14; Directive 2013/40/EU of the European Parliament and of the Council of 12 August 2013 on attacks against information systems and replacing Council Framework Decision 2005/222/JHA [2013] OJ L 218, 14.8.2013, pp. 8–14; Directive 2014/57/EU of the European Parliament and of the Council of 16 April 2014 on criminal sanctions for market abuse (market abuse directive) [2014] OJ L 173, 12.6.2014, pp. 179–189; Directive 2014/62/EU of the European Parliament and of the Council of 15 May 2014 on the protection of the euro and other currencies against counterfeiting by criminal law, and replacing Council Framework Decision 2000/383/JHA [2013] OJ L 151, 21.5.2014, pp. 1–8; Directive (EU) 2017/541 of the European Parliament and of the Council of 15 March 2017 on combating terrorism and replacing Council Framework Decision 2002/475/JHA and amending Council Decision 2005/671/JHA OJ L 88, 31.3.2017, pp. 6–21; Directive (EU) 2017/1371 of the European Parliament nad of the Council of 5 July 2017 on the fight against fraud to the Union's financial interests by means of criminal law OJ L 198, 28.7.2017, pp. 29–41; Directive (EU) 2017/2103 of the European Parliament and of the Council of 15 November 2017 amending Council Framework Decision 2004/757/JHA in order to include new psychoactive substances in the definition of 'drug' and repealing Council Decision 2005/387/JHA, OJEU L 305/12, 21.11.2017. Directive 2014/42/EU of the European Parliament and of the Council of 3 April 2014 on the freezing and confiscation of instrumentalities and proceeds of crime in the European Union OJ L 127, 29.4.2014, pp. 39–50, is based on Articles 82(2) and 83(1) TFEU but naturally does not contain provisions of minimum levels of minimum penalties.

[409] This is seen as the "mainstream interpretation" of the term 'minimum rules', Anne Weyembergh (in collaboration with Serge de Biolley) (2013), p. 14. On the meaning of *minimum rules*, see for example Asp (2012), pp. 110–127; Klip (2016), pp. 178–185.

[410] Klip (2016), p. 182.

the draft directive be referred to the European Council. In that case, the ordinary legislative procedure shall be suspended. After discussion, and in case of a consensus, the European Council shall, within four months of this suspension, refer the draft back to the Council, which shall terminate the suspension of the ordinary legislative procedure.

Within the same timeframe, in case of disagreement, and if at least nine Member States wish to establish enhanced cooperation on the basis of the draft directive concerned, they shall notify the European Parliament, the Council and the Commission accordingly. In such a case, the authorisation to proceed with enhanced cooperation referred to in Article 20(2) of the Treaty on European Union and Article 329(1) of this Treaty shall be deemed to be granted and the provisions on enhanced cooperation shall apply.

If any of the Member States consider that the draft legislative act would affect fundamental aspects of its criminal justice system, the Member State can suspend the ordinary legislative procedure and transfer the matter to the European Council. This means that in a case of lack of unanimity in the European Council the Union cannot enact the rules as such.

As Sect. 3.6 above shows, criminal law decision-making is still very much consensus-seeking. For this reason, the emergency brake procedure is unlikely to be pulled without weighty reasons. Consensus-seeking decision-making seeks to achieve effective cooperation. Since the political culture is quite accommodating, arguably, the threshold to pull the emergency brake might be rather high.

In a case of lack of unanimity in the European Council, the Article enables the so-called enhanced cooperation. At least nine Member States which agree on the draft legislation can start enhanced cooperation on the matter. The legislative procedure enshrined in Article 83 TFEU is still a lighter procedure compared to the pre-Lisbon decision-making process that required unanimity as a starting point. The emergency brake procedure brings flexibility to the otherwise well-regulated ordinary legislative procedure and shows elasticity in the constitutional structures between the Union and the Member States. It also makes sure that the Member States do not have to accept substantive criminal legislation that would not fit into their existing criminal justice systems.

Finally, Article 83 TFEU as a legal basis differs from some other legal bases in that it has a limited geographic applicability. The UK and Ireland can choose to opt in to legislative instruments,[411] but of course after Brexit the situation changes all together relative to the United Kingdom.[412] Legislative measures based on Article 83 TFEU are not applicable in Denmark.[413]

---

[411] Protocol 21.

[412] For insights concerning the consequences of Brexit, see Weyembergh (2017), pp. 284–299.

[413] Protocol 22.

References

Alexy R (1986) A theory of constitutional rights. OUP, reprinted 2010
Appleton C, Grover B (2007) The pros and cons of life without parole. Br J Criminol 47
Arnull A (2006) The European Union and its Court of Justice, 2nd edn. OUP
Asp P (2010) Sex och Samtycke. Iustus Förlag
Asp P (2012) The substantive criminal law competence of the EU (Stiftelsen Skrifter utgivna av Juridiska fakulteten vid Stockholms universitet). Jure
Balvig F, Gunnlaugsson H, Jerre K, Tham H, Kinnunen A (2015) The public sense of justice in Scandinavia: a study of attitudes towards punishments. Eur J Criminol 12(3)
Barton A, Johns N (2013) The policy-making process in the criminal justice system. Routledge
Beck U (2002) The terrorist threat: world risk society revisited. Theory Cult Soc 19(4)
Bell J (1992) Populism and elitism: politics in the age of equality. Regnery Gateway
Bendor AL, Sachs M (2011) The constitutional status of human dignity in Germany and Israel. Isr Law Rev 44
Beyleveld D, Brownsword R (2001) Human dignity in bioethics and biolaw. OUP
Bingham T (2011) The rule of law. Penguin Books, first published by Allen Lane, 2010
Börzel TA, Panke D (2016) Europeanization. In: Cini M, Borragán NP-S (eds) European Union politics, 5th edn. OUP
Brauch AJ (2005) The margin of appreciation and the jurisprudence of the European Court of Human Rights: threat to the rule of law. Columbia J Eur Law 11
Canovan M (1999) Trust the people! Populism and the two faces of democracy. Polit Stud 47(1)
Catá Backer L (2007–2008) God(s) over constitutions: international and religious transnational constitutionalism in the 21st century. Miss Coll Law Rev 27
Cini M (2016) Intergovernmentalism. In: Cini M, Borragán NP-S (eds) European Union politics, 5th edn. OUP
Cooper I (2006) The watchdogs of subsidiarity: national parliaments and the logic of arguing in the EU. J Common Mark Stud 44(2):281
Craig P (2001) Constitutions, constitutionalism, and the European Union. Eur Law J 7(2)
Craig P, de Búrca G (2011) EU law: text, cases, and materials, 5th edn. OUP
Craig P, de Búrca G (2015) EU law: text, cases, and materials, 6th edn. OUP
Dahl RA (1998) On democracy. Yale University Press
Dan-Cohen M (2011) A concept of dignity. Isr Law Rev 44(1–2)
Davis H (2007) Human rights law: directions. OUP
de la Rasilla del Moral I (2006) The increasingly marginal appreciation of the margin-of-appreciation doctrine. German Law J 7(6)
Delgado R (1982) Words that wound: a tort action for racial insults, epithets, and name-calling. Harv Civil Rights-Civil Lib Law Rev 17
Dumortier E, Gutwirth S, Snacken S, De Hert P (2012) The rise of the penal state: what can human rights do about it? In: Snacken S, Dumortier E (eds) Resisting punitiveness in Europe? Welfare, human rights and democracy. Routledge
Dworkin R (1977) Taking rights seriously. Harvard University Press
Fletcher M, Lööf R, Gilmore B (2008) EU criminal law and justice. Edward Elgar Publishing
Foster C (2011) Human dignity in bioethics and law. Hart Publishing
Franck TM (1992) The emerging right to democratic governance. Am J Int Law 86(1)
Fründe D (2013) EU och finsk kriminalpolitik. In: Hinkkanen V, Mäkipää L (eds) Suomalainen kriminaalipolitiikka – Näkökulmia teoriaan ja käytäntöön. Tapio Lappi-Seppälän juhlakirja. University of Helsinki
Gelb K (2009) Myths and misconceptions: public opinion versus public judgment about sentencing. Fed Sentencing Rep 21(4)
Glensy RD (2011) The right to dignity. Columbia Hum Rights Law Rev 43
Greenawalt K (1989) Free speech justifications. Columbia Law Rev 89(1)
Greer S (2010) The interpretation of the European Convention on Human Rights: universal principle or margin of appreciation? UCL Hum Rights Rev 3
Hassemer W (1989) Symbolinen rikosoikeus ja oikeushyvien suojelu. Oikeus 18(5)

Heun W (2011) The constitution of Germany: a contextual analysis. Hart Publishing

Hörnle T, Kremnitzer M (2011) Human dignity as a protected interest in criminal law. Isr Law Rev 44

Hough M, Roberts JV (1999) Sentencing in Britain: public knowledge and public opinion. Punishment Soc 1(1)

Huomo-Kettunen M (2014) Kolmas tie – Euroopan unionin aineellisen rikosoikeuden toimivallan palasia SEUT 83 artiklan ulkopuolella? Lakimies 112(1)

Jacobs FG, White RCA, Ovey C (2010) The European Convention on Human Rights. OUP

Jareborg N (2002) Scraps of penal theory. Iustus Förlag

Jensen CS (2016) Neo-functionalism. In: Cini M, Borragán NP-S (eds) European Union politics, 5th edn. Oxford, OUP

Jokila H (2010) Tahdonvastainen suostumus ja liiallisen luottamuksen hinta. Suomalaisen lakimiesyhdistyksen julkaisuja

Kahan DM (1996) What do alternative sanctions mean? Univ Chic Law Rev 63(2)

Kahan DM, Posner EA (1999) Shaming white-collar criminals: a proposal for reform of the federal sentencing guidelines. J Law Econ 42(1)

Klip A (2016) European criminal law: an integrative approach, 3rd edn. Intersentia

Lappi-Seppälä T (2012) Explaining national differences in the use of imprisonment. In: Snacken S, Dumortier E (eds) Resisting punitiveness in Europe? Welfare, human rights and democracy. Routledge

Lewis J (2016) The Council of the Euroepan Union and the European Council. In: Cini M, Borragán NP-S (eds) European Union politics, 5th edn. OUP

Ligeti K (2013) Approximation of substantive criminal law and the establishment of the European Public Prosecutor's Office. In: Galli F, Weyembergh A (eds) Approximation of substantive criminal law in the EU: the way forward. Editions de l'Universite de Bruxelles

Ligeti K, Simonato M (2013) The European Public Prosecutor's Office: towards a truly European prosecution service? New J Eur Crim Law 4(1–2)

Lijphart A (1999) Patterns of democracy: government forms and performance in thirty-six countries. Yale University Press

Lindberg LN (1963) The political dynamics of European economic integration. Stanford University Press

Loewenstein K (1937a) Militant democracy and fundamental rights I. Am Polit Sci Rev XXXI(3)

Loewenstein K (1937b) Militant democracy and fundamental rights I. Am Polit Sci Rev XXXI(4)

Macklem P (2006) Militant democracy, legal pluralism, and the paradox of self-determination. Int J Const Law 4(3)

Marguery T (2013) European Union fundamental rights and member states action in EU criminal law. Maastricht J Eur Comp Law 20(2)

Marks S (2011) What has become of the emerging right to democratic governance. Eur J Int Law 22(2)

Martín AN, Wade M, de Morales MM (2013) Federal criminal law and the European Public Prosecutor's Office. In: Ligeti K (ed) Toward a prosecutor for the European Union, volume 1: a comparative analysis. Hart Publishing

Matikkala J (2012) Onko ilmaisurikoksia koskeva sääntelymme kohdallaan? In: Hyttinen T et al (eds) Rikoksesta rangaistukseen – Juhlajulkaisu Pekka Viljanen 1952 – 26/8 – 2012. Turun yliopiston oikeustieteellisen tiedekunnan julkaisuja

McCrudden C (2008) Human dignity and judicial interpretation of human rights. Eur J Int Law 19(4)

Melander S (2008) Kriminalisointiteoria – rangaistavaksi säätämisen oikeudelliset rajoitukset. Suomalaisen lakimiesyhdistyksen julkaisuja

Melander S (2010) EU-rikosoikeus. WSOYpro

Melander S (2011) Europeiseringen av straffrätten och den nationella strafflagstiftningens "suveränitet". Tidskrift utgiven av Juridiska föreningen i Finland 147(3)

Melander S (2012) EU ja talousrikosoikeus. Defensor Legis 93(4)

Melander S (2013) Ultima ratio in European criminal law. Oñati Socio-Leg Ser 3(1)

Miettinen S (2013a) Criminal law and policy in the European Union. Routledge

Miettinen S (2013b) Implied ancillary criminal law competence after Lisbon. Eur Crim Law Rev 3(2)

Miettinen S (2013c) Onward transfer under the European Arrest Warrant: is the EU moving towards the free movement of prisoners? New J Eur Crim Law 4(1–2)

Miettinen S (2015) The Europeanization of criminal law: competence and its control in the Lisbon era. University of Helsinki

Mirsky Y (2005) Human rights, democracy, and the inescapability of politics; or, human dignity thick and thin. Isr Law Rev 38(1–2)

Mitsilegas V (2009) EU criminal law. Hart Publishing

Mitsilegas V, Monar J, Rees W (2003) The European Union and internal security: guardian of the people? Palgrave Macmillan

Möllers C (2009) Democracy and human dignity: limits of a moralized conception of rights in German constitutional law. Isr Law Rev 42

Nieminen L (2005) Ihmisarvon loukkaamattomuus perus- ja ihmisoikeussuojan lähtökohtana. Lakimies 103(1)

Nowell-Smith H (2012) Behind the scenes in the negotiation of the EU criminal justice legislation. New J Eur Crim Law 3(3–4)

Öberg J (2014) Limits to EU powers: a case study on individual criminal sanctions for the enforcement of EU law. European University Institute

Ojanen T (2013) The Europeanization of Finnish law: observations on the transformations of the Finnish scene of constitutionalism. In: Nuotio K, Melander S, Huomo-Kettunen M (eds) Introduction to the Finnish law and legal culture. University of Helsinki, Forum Iuris

Peczenik A (1989) On law and reason. Kluwer Academic Publishers

Pellonpää M (2012) Euroopan ihmisoikeussopimus. Talentum

Pettit P (1999) Republicanism: a theory of freedom and government. OUP, reprinted 2002

Piris J-C (2010) The Lisbon Treaty: a legal and political analysis. CUP

Pitea C (2005) Rape as a human rights violation and a criminal offence: the European court's judgment in *M.C. v. Bulgaria*. J Int Crim Justice 3(2)

Post RC (2000) Democratic constitutionalism and cultural heterogeneity. Aust J Leg Philos 25(2)

Post RC (2011) Participatory democracy and free speech. Va Law Rev 97(3)

Pratt J (2007) Penal populism. Routledge

Raitio J (2006) Eurooppaoikeus ja sisämarkkinat. Talentum

Raz J (1998) On the authority and interpretation of constitutions: some preliminaries. In: Alexander L (ed) Constitutionalism. CUP

Roach K (2011) The primacy of liberty and proportionality, not human dignity, when subjecting criminal law to constitutional control. Isr Law Rev 44

Roberts JV (2003) Public opinion and mandatory sentencing: a review of international findings. Crim Justice Behav 30(4)

Roberts JV, Doob AN (1989) Sentencing and public opinion: taking false shadows for true substances. Osgood Hall Law J 27(3)

Rogers JW (2003) Applying the doctrine of positive obligations in the European Convention of Human Rights to domestic substantive criminal law in domestic proceedings. Crim Law Rev

Rosas A, Armati L (2010) EU constitutional law: an introduction. Hart Publishing

Salas D (2010) La volonté de punir – Essai sur le populisme pénal. Librairie Arthème Fayard/Pluriel, first published Hachette Littératures 2005

Salminen J (2010) Yksityisten oikeudellisen suojelun mahdollisuudet ja rajat Euroopan unionin kolmannen pilarin alla. In: Nuotio K, Malkki L (eds) Vapauden, turvallisuuden ja oikeuden Eurooppa. University of Helsinki, Forum Iuris

Satzger H (2012) International and European criminal law. C.H.Beck

Scheinin M (1998) Ihmisarvon loukkaamattomuus valtiosääntöperiaatteena. In: Van Aershot P, Ilveskivi P, Piispanen K (eds) Juhlakirja Kaarlo Tuori 50 vuotta. Helsingin yliopiston julkisoikeuden laitos

Schütze R (2009) Subsidiarity after Lisbon: reinforcing the safeguards of federalism? Camb Law J 68(3)

Snacken S (2012) Conclusion: why and how to resist punitiveness in Europe. In: Snacken S, Dumortier E (eds) Resisting punitiveness in Europe? Welfare, human rights and democracy. Routledge

Snacken S, Dumortier E (2012) Resisting punitiveness in Europe? An introduction. In: Snacken S, Dumortier E (eds) Resisting punitiveness in Europe? Welfare, human rights and democracy. Routledge

Sous la direction de Mireille Delmas-Marty (1997) Corpus Juris. ECONOMICA

Stoyanova V (2014) Article 4 of the ECHR and the obligation of criminalising slavery, servitude, forced labour and human trafficking. Camb J Int Comp Law 3(2)

Tonry M (2007) Determinants of penal policies. In: Tonry M (ed) Crime, punishment, and politics in comparative perspective crime and justice – a review of research, vol 36. The University of Chicago Press

Tsesis A (2009) Dignity and speech: the regulation of hate speech in a democracy. Wake Forest Law Rev 44

Tulkens F (2011) The paradoxical relationship between criminal law and human rights. J Int Crim Justice 9

Tulkens F (2012) Human rights as the good and the bad conscience of criminal law. In: Snacken S, Dumortier E (eds) Resisting punitiveness in Europe? Welfare, human rights and democracy. Routledge

Tuori K (1983a) Valtionhallinnon sivuelinorganisaatiosta 1. Suomalaisen lakimiesyhdistyksen julkaisuja

Tuori K (1983b) Valtionhallinnon sivuelinorganisaatiosta 2. Suomalaisen lakimiesyhdistyksen julkaisuja

Tuori K (2000) Kriittinen oikeuspositivismi. WSLT

Tuori K (2010) The many constitutions of Europe. In: Tuori K, Sankari S (eds) The many constitutions of Europe. Ashgate

Vervaele JAE (2013) Harmonised union policies and the harmonization of substantive criminal law. In: Galli F, Weyembergh A (eds) Approximation of substantive criminal law in the EU: the way forward. Editions de l'Universite de Bruxelles

Weyembergh A (2013) Approximation of substantive criminal law: the new institutional and decision-making framework and new types of interaction between EU actors. In: Galli F, Weyembergh A (eds) Approximation of substantive criminal law in the EU: the way forward. Serge de Biolley, Editions de l'Universite de Bruxelles

Weyembergh A (2017) Consequences of Brexit for European Union criminal law. New J Eur Crim Law 8(3)

Wright GR (2006) Dignity and conflicts of constitutional values: the case of free speech and equal protection. San Diego Law Rev 43

Chapter 4
Theoretical Ideals for European Constitutional Structures and Criminal Legislation

4.1 Heterarchical Constitutional Structures of the ECHR Regime[1]

4.1.1 Heterarchical Constitutional Structures Pertaining Between National Legal Orders and the ECHR Regime

> The margin of appreciation is a prime constitutional concept, particularly in relation to federal state structures.[2]

Some principles and doctrines of the ECHR regime, the subsidiarity principle, the doctrine of margin of appreciation (and proportionality analysis) and the doctrine on equivalent protection,[3] represent heterarchical flexible constitutional structures. Heterarchical constitutional structures between the national legal systems and the ECHR regime refer to constitutional structures that create an integrated and flexible constitutional system between the contracting parties and the ECHR regime.

The ECtHR has stated that the individual application procedure in the ECHR regime is subsidiary to the protection that is provided in the national systems. The Convention rights are left for the Contracting Parties to ensure and the ECtHR may take a case only after all domestic remedies have been exhausted.[4] This means the principle of subsidiarity is embedded in the human rights protection regime. The principle of subsidiarity of the ECHR regime is clearly stipulated in Article 1 ECHR,

---

[1] Some of the ideas presented in this chapter and in Sect. 4.2 are previously published in Huomo-Kettunen (2013).

[2] Alkema (2000), p. 50.

[3] The doctrine of equivalent protection is examined in Sect. 4.1.2 and Chap. 5.1.

[4] See, for example, *Handyside v. the United Kingdom* App no 5493/72 (ECtHR, 7 December 1976), para 48.

© Springer International Publishing Switzerland and G. Giappichelli Editore 2020   151
M. Kettunen, *Legitimizing European Criminal Law*, Comparative, European and International Criminal Justice 2, https://doi.org/10.1007/978-3-030-16174-3_4

according to which the State Parties shall ensure the rights and freedoms enshrined in the Convention. Article 13 adds to this by stipulating that everyone whose rights and freedoms under the Convention have been violated shall have an effective remedy before a national authority. Articles 34 and 35 concerning the individual application procedure in the ECtHR also demonstrate the role of subsidiarity in the ECHR regime by stipulating that the ECtHR has the competence to review cases only after all domestic remedies are exhausted. National authorities must have an effective opportunity to investigate the matter and tackle the problem, if there is one, before the ECtHR has jurisdiction in the matter. These articles say much about the nature of the Convention.

The ECHR is meant to guarantee a minimum standard for the protection of fundamental and human rights. The individual application procedure to the ECtHR is the last resort for individuals trying to protect their rights. This means that human and fundamental rights protection ought to take place at the national level and that the Convention leaves room for the national authorities to independently correct practices that violate the Convention rights. However, Articles 34 and 35 build a hierarchical court structure between the national courts and the ECtHR, because the ultimate competence to interpret the Convention is granted to the ECtHR. According to Article 46 ECHR, the contracting parties must abide by the final judgment of the ECtHR. However, the ECtHR is not a European 'supreme court'; it is not an appeal court because the ECHR regime is autonomous.

The ECHR regime itself is built upon an idea of a certain level of harmonization of human rights issues in the Contracting states. The margin of appreciation doctrine works in a slightly different direction; it respects differences between the national legal systems and preserves pluralism.[5] The margin of appreciation doctrine enables flexible cooperation between national legal systems and the ECHR regime when the State Parties restrict Convention rights. The doctrine leaves room for the Contracting Parties to strike a balance between common good of the society and the rights of individuals,[6] meaning that the national authorities have room to determine if an interference of the right is 'necessary in a democratic society'.[7] The margin of appreciation doctrine also leaves room for the discretion of the Contracting Parties to decide how to implement the Convention standards and how to fulfil obligations deriving from the ECHR.[8] However, the principle of proportionality imposes limits on the margin of appreciation. The doctrine has been developed in order to strike a balance between national views on human rights and the uniform application of the Convention.[9]

---

[5] Steven Greer (2000), pp. 20–21.

[6] Tümay (2008), p. 201.

[7] Brauch (2005), pp. 113, 116.

[8] *"Relating to certain aspects of the laws on the use of languages in education in Belgium" v. Belgium* (Merits) App no 1474/62, 1677/62, 1769/63, 1994/63, 2126/64 (ECtHR, 23 July 1968) para 10.

[9] Arai-Takahashi (2002), pp. 2–3.

Before the ECtHR adopted the doctrine of margin of appreciation in its jurisprudence, the European Commission of Human Rights used the doctrine especially relative to the interpretation of exigencies mentioned in Article 15 ECHR relating to the possibility to derogate from the Convention in a time of emergency.[10] In the case of *Lawless v Ireland* the Commission stated that 'certain discretion—a certain margin of appreciation—must be left to the Government in determining whether there exists a public emergency which threatens the life of the nation and which must be dealt with by exceptional measures derogating from its normal obligations under the Convention.'[11] The ECtHR relied on the doctrine of margin of appreciation for the first time in the case of *Ireland v UK*,[12] which also concerned the application of Article 15 ECHR. The ECtHR stated that

> It falls in the first place to each Contracting State, with its responsibility for "life of its nation", to determine whether that life is threatened by a "public emergency" and, if so, how far it is necessary to go in attempting to overcome the emergency. *By reason of their direct and continuous contact with the passing needs of the moment, the national authorities are in principle in a better position than the international judge to decide both on the presence of such an emergency and on the nature and scope of derogations necessary to avert it.* In this matter Article 15 para 1 (art. 15-1) leaves those authorities a wide margin of appreciation.[13] (emphasis added)

Later, the use of the doctrine evolved to also cover other articles of the Convention. The extent of the discretion varies in relation to different articles of the Convention depending on how detailed the text of the Article is.[14] Margin of appreciation also relates to a methodological issue concerning the interpretation of the Convention as a living instrument. This type of *evolutive interpretation* was developed in the backdrop of the World War II. The intention behind it was to give flexibility to the interpretation of the Convention bearing in mind that situations could evolve in the future which the drafters of the Convention could not have foreseen.[15] In the case of *Tyrer*, the ECtHR stated that 'the Convention is a *living instrument* which, as the Commission rightly stressed, must be interpreted in the light of present-day conditions'. The interpretation of the Convention can be described both dynamic and evolutive as well as practical and effective.[16] The evolutive and dynamic approach enables the use of the doctrine of margin of appreciation because if there were no room for discretion, the Contracting parties could not interpret the Convention in a dynamic and evolutive fashion. Naturally the dynamic and evolutionary interpretation must be tied to the text of the Convention.[17]

---

[10] Arai-Takahashi (2002), p. 5; Tümay (2008), p. 209.

[11] Report of the Commission, Application No 332/57, *Gerard Richard Lawless against the Republic of Ireland* (Adopted on 19th December 1959), paras 82, 85.

[12] Arai-Takahashi (2002), p. 5; Tümay (2008), p. 209.

[13] *Ireland v. The United Kingdom* App no 5310/71 (ECtHR, 18 January 1978), para 207.

[14] Brauch (2005), pp. 113, 120.

[15] Tümay (2008), pp. 209–210; Mowbray (2005), pp. 57, 58.

[16] *Christine Goodwin v. the united Kingdom* App no 28957/95 (ECtHR, 11 July 2002), para 74.

[17] Brauch (2005), pp. 113, 148.

The doctrine of the Convention as a living instrument covers the substantive Articles of the ECHR and also institutional Articles as stated in the case of *Loizidou v Turkey*. This case concerned the right to own plots of land. The applicant claimed to own a piece of land in northern Cyprus prior to the Turkish occupation of northern Cyprus in 1974. The applicant claimed there was a continuing violation of her right to access her property ever since 1974. Article 159 of the 1985 Constitution of the 'Turkish Republic of Northern Cyprus' stipulated that all immovable properties and buildings which were found abandoned on 13 February 1975 and which situated within the boundaries of the TRNC on 15 November 1983 shall be the property of the TRNC. On 22 January 1990 Turkey gave a declaration under Article 46 ECHR giving jurisdiction for the ECtHR to examine the matter. The declaration stipulated that the jurisdiction 'extends to matters raised in respect of facts, including judgments which are based on such facts which have occurred subsequent to the date of deposit of the present Declaration'.[18]

The Turkish Government claimed that the ECtHR lacked competence to consider the case because the matters complained did not fall within Turkish jurisdiction but within the jurisdiction of the TRNC, and that in accordance with their declarations they had not accepted the competence of the Commission or the ECtHR to examine acts and events outside their metropolitan territory.[19] The ECtHR found that

> [i]n interpreting these key provisions it must have regard to the special character of the Convention as a treaty for the collective enforcement of human rights and fundamental freedoms.—[and] that the Convention is a living instrument which must be interpreted in the light of present-day conditions—*Such an approach in the Court's view is not confined to the substantive provisions of the Convention, but also applies to those provisions, such as Articles 25 and 46, which govern the operation of the Convention's enforcement machinery.* It follows that these provisions cannot be interpreted solely in accordance with the intentions of their authors as expressed more than forty years ago.—In addition, the object and purpose of the Convention as an instrument for the protection of individual human beings requires that its provisions be interpreted and applied so as to make its safeguards *practical and effective*.[20]

The ECtHR stated also that "in accordance with the concept of 'jurisdiction' in Article 1 (art. 1) of the Convention, State responsibility may arise in respect of acts and events outside State frontiers".[21]

The Turkish Government claimed that taking the property in northern Cyprus was justified under the international law doctrine of necessity and that the applicant had lost her ownership of the land before the crucial date of 22 January 1990. The ECtHR found that while interpreting the Convention, one must keep in mind the Convention's special character as a human rights treaty (teleological interpretation). The ECtHR found that because a large number of Turkish troops had engaged in active duties in northern Cyprus, Turkey had control that entails responsibility for

---

[18] *Loizidou v. Turkey (Preliminary Objections)* Ap no 15318/89 (ECtHR, 23 March 1995), paras 12, 18, 24–25.

[19] Ibid., para 55.

[20] Ibid., paras 70–72.

[21] Ibid., paras 87–89.

the policies and actions of the TRNC. Turkey therefore had an obligation to secure to the applicant the rights and freedoms set out in the Convention which extended to the northern part of Cyprus (dynamic and evolutive interpretation). The ECtHR concluded that the continuous denial of access must be regarded as a breach of Article 1 of Protocol no. 1.[22]

There are also limitations to the margin of appreciation. The ECtHR has tried to bring clarity to the doctrine by introducing a balancing of the importance of the right with the importance of the restriction. The margin is narrower if, for example, free speech and in particular free political speech is restricted.[23] Conversely, the margin is wider when a state restricts a right in order to protect national security.[24] The more there is consensus on a particular issue, the narrower the margin of appreciation is on that issue. Vice versa, diversity in understanding a particular issue increases the margin of appreciation.[25] The margin of appreciation expresses an acceptance of the pluralism of legal systems[26] and their cooperation in a flexible format. Thus, the margin of appreciation could be seen to represent a heterarchical constitutional structure between the ECHR regime and national legal systems.

4.1.2   Heterarchical Constitutional Structures Pertaining Between the ECHR Regime and the EU Legal Order

The interrelationship between the Union (and its predecessors) and the ECHR regime has been under discussion from the 1950s. In 1953 a draft European Political Community Treaty included the ECHR as a part of Community law. This draft was never adopted due to its close relation to the Defence Community Treaty in 1954. This would have created an European Army to which France objected because it feared a loss of national sovereignty.[27] From the 1960s onwards, the CJEU started to recognize human rights as general principles of Community law.[28] Slowly thereafter the CJEU started to make references to the ECHR.[29] The idea for the EEC to

---

[22] Ibid., paras 35–36, 43, 56, 63–64.

[23] Brauch (2005), pp. 113, 126–127.

[24] *Klass and Others v. Germany* App no 5029/71 (ECtHR, 6 September 1978), paras 49–50, 59–60. See also Brauch (2005), pp. 113, 127.

[25] Brauch (2005), p. 128; de la Rasilla del Moral (2006), pp. 611, 617.

[26] Krisch (2007), p. 28.

[27] Craig and de Búrca (2015), p. 380.

[28] See, for example, Case C-6/64 *Flaminio Costa v E.N.E.L.* [1964] ECR p. 1195; Case C-29/69 *Erich Stauder v City of Ulm – Sozialamt* [1969] ECR p. 419; Case C-11/70 *Internationale Handelsgesellschaft mbH v Einfuhr- und Vorratsstelle für Getreide und Futtermittel* [1970] ECR p. 1125.

[29] See, for example, Case C-36/75 *Roland Rutili v Ministre de l'intérieur* [1975] ECR p. 1219, para 32; Case C-222/84 *Marguerite Johnston v Chief Constable of the Royal Ulster Constabulary* [1986] ECR p. 1651, para 18.

accede in the ECHR emerged in the 1970s.[30] In 1996, the CJEU gave an opinion on whether the EU Treaties included competence for the EU to accede to the ECHR.[31] At that time the CJEU found that the Treaty provisions could not be used to 'enact human rights provisions or to conclude international conventions in this field'.[32] Largely due to the fact that the accession would have 'fundamental institutional implications', a specific legal basis was necessary in order for the Union to have competence to accede to the ECHR.[33] The Lisbon Treaty introduced this specific legal basis. According to Article 6(2) TEU the Union shall accede to the ECHR.

At this point of time, the *ad hoc* negotiation group ("47+1") of the Steering Committee for Human Rights (CDDH) and the European Commission have given their final report to the CDDH (which works under the auspices of the Committee of Ministers) on the EU's accession to the ECHR.[34] The draft agreement suggests that, as far as possible, the Union ought to have same rights and obligations as the other Contracting Parties. The Union aspired to be equal to the other Contracting Parties, making only minimal adaptations, largely due to the fact that the EU is not a state.[35] This approach starts from the premise that all contracting parties to the ECHR ought to have equal obligations deriving from the Convention. The EU should not be granted special privileges merely because it is not a state.

According to the draft accession treaty, proceedings in the CJEU ought not to be understood as procedures of international investigation or settlement as meant in Articles 35(2b) and 55 ECHR.[36] This means that previous proceedings in the CJEU would not prohibit the ECtHR from investigating an individual application. The ECtHR could investigate both Inter-State (or Inter-Party) cases and individual applications in which the Union would be the respondent party, regardless of possible previous proceedings in the CJEU. The accession would thus mean that all acts, measures and omissions of the Union would be subject to the control exercised by the ECtHR. The decisions of the ECtHR in cases to which the EU is a party would

---

[30] Simone White (2011), p. 9.

[31] Opinion 2/94 Opinion of the Court of 28 March 1996. Accession by the Community to the European Convention for the Protection of Human Rights and Fundamental Freedoms [1996] ECR I-1783.

[32] Ibid., para 27.

[33] Ibid., para 35.

[34] 47+1(2013)008rev2, Fifth negotiation meeting between the CDDH ad hoc negotiation group and the European Commission on the accession of the European Union to the European Convention on Human Rights, Final report to the CDDH, Strasbourg, 10 June 2013. For previous versions of the draft agreement, see, for example, Steering Committee for Human Rights, CDDH(2011)009, Report to the Committee of Ministers on the elaboration of legal instruments for the accession of the European Union to the European Convention on Human Rights, Strasbourg, 14 October 2011; There were disagreements on the content of the draft, see, for example Friends of Presidency (FREMP) Accession of the EU to the ECHR: Working Document from the Presidency (DS 1675/11), Brussels 4 November 2011.

[35] 47+1(2013)008rev2, Final report to the CDDH, p. 17; CDDH(2011)009, pp. 16 and 19.

[36] 47+1(2013)008rev2, p. 8; CDDH(2011)009, p. 8.

be binding on all of the EU's institutions, including the CJEU.[37] The draft agreement thus presents the ECtHR with similar jurisdiction regarding the EU as it has regarding state contracting parties.

The proposed competence of the ECtHR would indicate that the scope of protection of fundamental rights in the EU would move towards more extensive protection of human rights emphasising the actual protection of human rights. On the one hand, from a criminal law perspective, this development might challenge the status of the principle of mutual recognition as the cornerstone principle in criminal matters. In the context of fundamental rights, the mutual trust means that Member States must recognize the level of protection of fundamental rights as sufficient in the other Member States.[38] In order to use instruments based on mutual recognition, mutual trust concerning the protection of fundamental rights must be accomplished.[39] After the Union's accession to the ECHR the focus ought to be in the actual realization of the substantial rights guaranteed in the ECHR instead of recognizing or assuming that the Convention rights are realized, even if there was a suspicion that they actually are not fully realized. From this perspective, there might be a need to adjust the doctrine of mutual recognition to fit human rights protection, for example by accepting human rights as grounds for refusal relative to all instruments that are based on mutual recognition. On the other hand, the Union's accession might build trust among the EU Member States as regards fundamental rights protection. However, since all of the EU Member States are already parties to the ECHR, the Union's accession might not have any impact on the trust amongst the EU Member States themselves. Rather, it seems more likely that the Union instruments based on the principle of mutual recognition would need adjustment to fit to the new level of human rights protection in the Union, as the CJEU has also recognized in its recent opinion concerning the accession (more on this topic in Chap. 5.1).

The case law concerning the presumption of equivalence established in *Bosphorus* would be likely to lose its meaning after the Union's accession to the Convention. If the presumption of equivalence would remain, it would establish unequal standing between the Union and the state parties because the EU would benefit from it unlike its Member States.[40] The ECtHR might renounce the *Bosphorus* case law after the Union's accession,[41] and bring the EU to the same standing with the state parties. This is seen as preferable also in the Draft Accession Agreement explanatory report, which states that the Convention control mechanism should as a rule be applied to the EU the same way as it is applied to the other contracting parties.[42] The Draft

---

[37] 47+1(2013)008rev2, Final report to the CDDH, pp. 16–20; CDDH(2011)009, pp. 16–18.

[38] Suominen (2011), pp. 37, 38–39.

[39] Ibid., pp. 37, 43.

[40] Fondation Robert Schuman Policy Paper by Xavier Groussot, Tobias Lock and Laurent Pech (2011), p. 4; Tobias Lock (2009), p. 395.

[41] Tobias Lock (2009), p. 396; Scheeck (2006), pp. 837, 862.

[42] 47+1(2013)008rev2, p. 27; CDDH(2011)009, p. 16.

Accession Agreement does not explicitly say anything about the presumption of equivalence, meaning that the ECtHR could decide the issue later.[43]

The Draft Accession Agreement would enable the ECtHR to review EU primary law.[44] The ECtHR can, however, only investigate whether EU law is compatible with the Convention. In other words, the ECtHR could not declare provisions of EU law invalid. This means that the exclusive jurisdiction and interpretative autonomy of EU law would remain with the CJEU.[45] The Draft Accession Agreement also clarifies in which circumstances the CJEU could review EU law-related cases before review by the ECtHR. The main rule is that the applicant must exhaust only the remedies in the legal order of the main respondent, whether it is the EU or a EU Member State, but not the remedies of the co-respondent. If the EU would be the main respondent, the applicant should exhaust all remedies of the EU legal order, which are the General court and the CJEU. If the EU would be a co-respondent— meaning that the main respondent would be a EU Member State and the Union would voluntarily want to join to the proceedings as a co-respondent—the CJEU could review the case before it is examined by the ECtHR. If the EU would not be co-respondent in a case where a EU Member State would be the main respondent, the CJEU could not review the case. In those situations the only way the CJEU could have reviewed the case would be if a national court had asked a preliminary ruling from the CJEU at an earlier stage during the national proceedings.[46] All this would mean that once the EU would accede to the Convention, the ECtHR would have the jurisdiction to evaluate the compatibility with the ECHR of EU-level measures and omissions.[47]

On the request of the Commission, the CJEU has given an opinion in which it evaluates whether the draft agreement on the accession of the EU to the ECHR is compatible with the Treaties (examined in more detail in Chap. 5.1).[48] The draft accession treaty would give the Union the same obligations as the State parties. This would mean changes in interpretation of some provisions of Union instruments. For example, human rights violations could be seen as an excuse to not to surrender a person to another state based on an European arrest warrant (EAW). Differences between national law or regional transnational law and the Convention are not

---

[43] Fondation Robert Schuman Policy Paper by Xavier Groussot, Tobias Lock and Laurent Pech (2011), p. 9.

[44] 47+1(2013)008rev2, Article 5; CDDH(2011)009, p. 7, Fondation Robert Schuman Policy Paper by Xavier Groussot, Tobias Lock and Laurent Pech (2011), p. 9.

[45] Fondation Robert Schuman Policy Paper by Xavier Groussot, Tobias Lock and Laurent Pech (2011), pp. 9–10.

[46] 47+1(2013)008rev2, p. 27; CDDH(2011)009, 24–25. Fondation Robert Schuman Policy Paper by Xavier Groussot, Tobias Lock and Laurent Pech (2011), pp. 14–15.

[47] 47+1(2013)008rev2, p. 27; CDDH(2011)009, pp. 15–18; See also, Huomo-Kettunen (2013), pp. 47, 61.

[48] Opinion 2/13 Opinion of the Court (Full Court) of 18 December 2014. (Opinion pursuant to Article 218(11) TFEU—Draft international agreement—Accession of the European Union to the European Convention for the Protection of Human Rights and Fundamental Freedoms— Compatibility of the draft agreement with the EU and FEU Treaties).

acceptable excuses for failing to comply with the Convention, since the basic idea of the Convention is to bring coherence to the protection of human rights in the European area. The Union's accession would enhance this coherence.[49] Union's accession to the ECHR following the terms as laid down in the draft accession treaty would mean that the Union's human rights protection would move towards actual and effective human rights protection. Also, when the acts of the EU institutions would be subject of the same human rights control as the Member States' organs are, the rights of individuals would be better protected.[50]

For now, the CJEU has decided in its opinion 2/13 that the draft accession agreement was not compatible with the Union's specific legal nature or with the Court's exclusive jurisdiction. New draft accession treaty has not been drafted.[51]

4.2 Heterarchical Constitutional Structures of the EU Law

4.2.1 Primacy of EU Law, Member States as the Masters of the Treaties, Principle of Sincere Cooperation

Whereas the idea of supremacy denotes hierarchical superiority to the exclusion of all other claims of authority, the idea of primacy suggests a more tentative claim of *primus inter pares* – a kind of precedence in the horizontal accommodation among equals.[52]

As briefly mentioned above, the European Union and the Member States could be described as having heterarchical constitutional structures. This chapter examines some of the principles that express the heterarchical nature of the constitutional structure formed by the Union together with the individual Member States. It is not implied here that the Union with all of its Member States is one big heterarchical structure. Instead, it is suggested that the heterarchical constitutional structure is formed by the Union and the individual Member States separately. The heterarchical constitutional framework is a system that consists of two or more polities that do not have any absolute hierarchy between them or their institutional structures. In this sense the legal systems of the Union and the individual Member States seem to be parallel and complementary to each other.[53] The principles of sincere cooperation, primacy and the Member States as 'Masters of the Treaties' illustrate the heterarchical constitutional nature of the Union.

Before these three principles are examined in detail, the idea of heterarchical constitutional structures is compared to a pluralist view on EU constitutionalism,

---

[49] 47+1(2013)008rev2, p. 27; CDDH(2011)009, p. 16.

[50] Lazowski and Wessel (2016), p. 212. For an opposing view, see Peers (2016), p. 222.

[51] European Parliament, EU accession to the European Convention on Human Rights (ECHR), 6 July 2017 http://www.europarl.europa.eu/RegData/etudes/BRIE/2017/607298/EPRS_BRI(2017)607298_EN.pdf, accessed 25 June 2018.

[52] Halberstam (2012), p. 202.

[53] Daniel Halberstam (2011), p. 13; Maduro (2003), p. 98.

which the heterarchical approach resembles. Constitutionalism is sometimes contrasted with pluralism. Constitutionalism is seen as a unity and hierarchy-orientated conception, whereas pluralism is seen as a dynamic, adaptive and heterarchy-oriented concept.[54] The heterarchial view builds on the pluralist premise according to which there are several legal systems in the European social and geographical area. From the perspective of each individual EU Member State, there are at least three applicable legal systems in the given geographical area: the national legal system of the Member State, the EU legal order and the ECHR regime. The idiosyncratic nature of the constitutional structure is examined here. This consists of the constitutions of the Union and the individual Member States. It is described using the term heterarchical constitutional structure.

The idea of a heterarchical constitutional structure differs from a pluralist view in at least one vital respect. The heterarchical structure can be seen as an hybrid legal order that is formed by the Union and individual Member States. It is important to understand the constitution of the EU as an integral part of the constitutions of the Member States and vice versa. This also means that the pictures of the heterarchical constitutional structures formed by the constitutions of the Union and each individual Member State can be somewhat different when compared to each other. The constitutional system of the Union is seen as the commonality found in these different heterarchical constitutional pictures. In a similar way, in his conception of European legal pluralism Miguel Poiares Maduro seems to accept national deviations as long as those deviations do not affect the set of norms shared with the broader European legal community. In other words, deviations can exist, but they need to be coherent and harmonious with the legal order of the European Union.[55]

The Court has recognized the principle of primacy in its case law. In the case of *Costa v ENEL*, the Court stated that the law stemming from the Treaty could not be overridden by domestic legal provisions, however they were framed. The Court's interpretation of the primacy of European Union law is based on the direct applicability of regulations. The Court found that the application of Union law would be contingent if Union law did not have primacy over national legislation.[56] The case has been interpreted in such a way that the primacy of Union law derives from the agreement already made by the Member States when they join the European Union.[57]

In the case of the *Internationale Handelsgesellschaft* the Court added that 'the validity of a community measure or its effect within a Member State cannot be affected by allegations that it runs counter to either fundamental rights as formulated by the constitution of that state or the principles of a national constitutional structure'.[58] In the case of *Simmenthal* the Court repeated that the scope of the

---

[54] See Krisch (2012).

[55] Maduro (2003), p. 99.

[56] Case C-6/64 *Flaminio Costa v E.N.E.L.* [1964] ECR p. 1195.

[57] Craig and de Búrca (2015), p. 268.

[58] Case C-11/70 *Internationale Handelsgesellschaft mbH v Einfuhr- und Vorratsstelle für Getreide und Futtermittel* [1970] ECR p. 1125, para 3.

primacy of European Union law extends over all of the Member States' legisla-tion.[59] The *Internationale Handelsgesellschaft* and *Simmenthal* cases demonstrate that primacy extends its effects over the constitutions as well as overall national legislation, regardless of whether the legislation was enacted prior to or subsequent to the European Union legislation.

A declaration concerning primacy is annexed to the Lisbon Treaty. There is no particular mention of primacy over constitutions. Instead, the declaration refers to the settled case law of the Court. The declaration also explicitly mentions the case of *Costa v ENEL*,[60] but not for example the *Internationale Handelsgesellschaft* or *Simmenthal* cases. However, the fact that there is a declaration concerning the pri-macy principle annexed to the Lisbon Treaty indicates that the principle is widely recognized by the Member States. Nevertheless, the status of the principle in rela-tion to the Member States' constitutions is not clearly defined in the declaration, which simply mentions that the Union law has primacy over the laws of the Member States. It is worth pointing out, however, that already in the *Costa v ENEL* case, the Court stated that primacy concerns national legislation *however framed* (emphasis added). Already in this quotation, the primacy of Union law can be seen to cover all national legislation, including constitutions.

The primacy of Union law does not, however, establish any absolute hierarchy of powers between the Union and the Member States. The principle of primacy simply expresses a rule concerning the *application* of law between the Union legislation and the legislation of Member States.[61] In situations of norm conflict between union law and national law, the union law will be applied. Union law prevails over national law, but national law will not be declared invalid by the Union Courts.[62] Therefore primacy of EU law does not mean supremacy of EU law. In a heterarchical model, the principle of primacy is not understood to be about the validity of law.[63]

Yet, the principle of primacy does not influence the division of powers between the Union and the Member States, as the principle of the Member States being Masters of the Treaties demonstrates. The division of powers, or the limitation of sovereignty as the Court describes it,[64] is regulated in the Treaties. The division of competences in the EU is not exhaustive; instead the Member States can add to Union competences to and from the Union. This means that the EU is not a federa-tion or federal state. These are characterised by a strict division of powers and hier-archical structures between the central federal-level government and state-level

---

[59] Case C-106/77 *Amministrazione delle Finanze dello Stato v Simmenthal SpA* [1978] ECR p. 629, para 24.

[60] Declarations, Annexed to the Final Act of the Intergovernmental Conference which Adopted the Treaty of Lisbon, 13 December 2007, A.17 Declaration concerning primacy, OJEU C 83/337, 30 March 2010, p. 10.

[61] In similar way see Preuss (2010), p. 39.

[62] Rosas and Armati (2010), pp. 55–56.

[63] Avbelj (2011), pp. 744, 750–751.

[64] Case C-6/64 *Flaminio Costa v E.N.E.L.* [1964] ECR p. 1195.

governance.[65] There are different types of competences listed in the Lisbon Treaty: exclusive competence, shared competence and supporting competence. These illustrate a rather flexible division of competences in the EU. From a constitutional law perspective, it is not exactly clear what form of government the EU represents. More important than categorizing the EU as any specific form of government is to simply recognize the key elements of the constitutional interrelationship between the EU and the Member States and understand their impact in different situations.

The primacy of Union law simply expresses a rule concerning the application of law in areas where the Member States have shifted their powers to the Union, but it does not alter the Member States' competence to amend the Treaties. The principle of primacy is similar to connecting factor rules, at least in situations where there is a clear norm collision between an EU law provision and a national law provision. However, the principle of primacy is not a true connecting factor rule, because it can also function as a weighing and balancing principle in cases where the norm conflict can be avoided by EU law-oriented interpretation of national law provisions. In situations of norm collision the principle of primacy can lead to two outcomes. First, it can lead to EU law-oriented interpretation (conforming interpretation) when national legislation can be interpreted in line with the union law. Or secondly, it can lead to the disapplication of a provision of national law, when the norm collision cannot be avoided simply through interpretation. In these cases the national law provision will remain valid but inapplicable in the particular case in question.

It is important to conceptually separate primacy from supremacy, because each has a different meaning. On one hand, supremacy refers to hierarchical structures between the Union and the Member States, to supreme legal acts and to the validity of norms. On the other hand, primacy refers to heterarchical structures and to the possible sidelining of norms when laws are applied.[66] But what difference does it make, which word is used? It is essential to understand the actual effects of this principle. The terminological issue is more theoretical and relevant to a deeper and more profound understanding of the Union legal system.

In the case law concerning the primacy of the Union law, the CJEU has used the English term *supremacy* or *supreme* only in three cases, briefly described here.[67] Even though there is plenty of case law concerning the principle of primacy, the CJEU has used the concept of supremacy in only a few cases. In the most recent of these cases given in 1973, the Court used the concept of *primacy* in its French language version—*primauté*. In the two other cases in the French language version the Court used the concept of *prééminent* (adjective) or *prééminence sur* (substantive + preposition), which translates into English as pre-eminent or pre-eminence (or superiority). In the *CILFIT* case the Court has stated that all language versions are equally authentic and that the interpretation of Community law requires comparison between the different language versions. In addition Community law needs to be interpreted in the light of both the provisions of Community law as a whole

---

[65] Nieminen (2004), p. 30.

[66] Likewise, Avbelj (2011), pp. 744, 746–751.

[67] See also Avbelj (2011), pp. 744–745.

and the objectives of the Community (today the Union).[68] However, the French language has a special position in that the judges of the Court use one common language in their deliberations, and it is French. Therefore, it is advisable to compare other language versions to the French version.

There are 24 official languages in the EU which poses a challenge to the legal system of the pluralistic Union. Because of the plurality of official languages teleological reasoning is essential in interpreting Union law. The indeterminacy of the meanings of words in the Union law is greater than in national legal systems due to multilingualism. Multilingualism makes italos difficult to determine precise meanings for words.[69] To some extent, vague language might even be considered to facilitate cooperation between the Member States, as long as the essential meanings of the terms are clear and the vagueness does not hinder predictability.

In the case of *Walt Wilhelm* the Court stated that 'que l'article 87 paragraphe 2, E, en attribuant a une institution de la communaute le pouvoir de definir les rapports entre les legislations nationales et le droit communautaire de la concurrence, confirme le *le caractère prééminent du droit communautaire*'. In the English language version the phrase is translated to read as follows: 'Article 87(2)(E), in conferring on a Community institution the power to determine the relationship between national laws and the community rules on competition, *confirm the supremacy of Community law*'. (emphasis added)[70] In Case 93/71 the term supremacy can be found only among the keywords in the judgement. The French language version of the decision uses the phrase '*prééminence sur le droit interne*',[71] referring to pre-eminence or supremacy because of the preposition *sur*, equivalent to the English prepositions on, over, upon. In the case of *Fratelli Variola* the Court used the following phrasing: '*le principle fundamental de la primauté de l'ordre juridique communautaire*'.[72] The English translation, 'the fundamental principle that the community legal system is supreme', does not correspond with the French phrasing because the French term *primauté* does not refer to supremacy, but to the primacy of the Community legal order instead.

English became Union's official language in 1973, which means that the English translations of these three cases have been made later on. Still, it is true that the Court used terminology (in French) that can be interpreted as referring to supremacy at least in Case 93/71. The Court has not used the English terms 'supreme' or 'supremacy' in this context since 1973, and the French-language version in the case from 1973 refers to primacy. In the 2000s, the Court has used the term *primacy of Community law* or, in French, *primauté du droit communautaire*,[73] and the term

---

[68] Case C-283/81 *Srl CILFIT and Lanificio di Gavardo SpA v Ministry of Health* [1982] ECR p. 3415, paras 17–20. See also Paunio and Lindroos-Hovinheimo (2010), pp. 395, 396.

[69] Paunio and Lindroos-Hovinheimo (2010), pp. 395, 397–399, 409.

[70] Case C-14/68 *Walt Wilhelm and others v Bundeskartellamt* [1969] ECR p. 1, para 5.

[71] Case C-93/71 *Orsolina Leonesio v Ministero dell'agricoltura e foreste* [1972] ECR p. 287.

[72] Case C-34/73 *Fratelli Variola S.p.A. v Amministrazione italiana delle Finanze* [1973] ECR p. 981, para 15.

[73] For example, Case C-314/08 *Krzysztof Filipiak v Dyrektor Izby Skarbowej w Poznaniu* [2009] ECR I-11049; Case C-2/08 *Amministrazione dell'Economia e delle Finanze and Agenzia delle*

primacy of Union law, or in French *principe de primauté du droit de l'Union*.[74] The declaration concerning primacy annexed in the Lisbon treaty also uses the term 'primacy' instead of 'supremacy.' It appears that the concept of 'primacy of Union law' should be used instead of the concept of 'supremacy of Union law'.

The principle of the Member States as Masters of the Treaties is set forth in Article 48 TEU, which regulates the amending of the Treaties. Amendments to the Treaties that are made at the Intergovernmental Conference (in an ordinary revision procedure) enter into force after being ratified by all the Member States (Article 48(4) TEU). The treaty amendments can either increase or reduce the Union's competences. When the simplified revision procedure described in Article 48(6) is followed, the decisions cannot increase the Union's competences. Also, Article 50 TEU stipulates that any Member State can withdraw from the Union. These provisions show that even though the EU law can have primacy over national law in particular cases, the Member States are the pouvoir constituants of the Treaties and that it is in States' own volition whether they want to continue to participate in the Union or not. The Member States have the ultimate power to amend the Union's constitution and to withdraw themselves from the Union.

Article 50 TEU is a novelty in the Lisbon Treaty. Because previous versions of the Treaties did not include a withdrawal clause, the issue of unilateral withdrawal from the Union was more ambiguous than it is now.[75] The right to withdraw has said to have symbolic value and expresses a continuing choice of a Member State to belong to the Union.[76] In the light of the UK preparing to leave the Union, it is clear that the right to withdraw from the Union has more indepth meaning than just symbolic statement. The UK is said to have been a fierce defender of its national sovereignty,[77] and its withdrawal from the EU is a clear demonstration of its sovereign powers. It could be argued that Article 50 TEU embodies a heterarchical structural idea. Belonging to the Union is voluntary for states. This shows that the Union's legal system does not rank higher than the legal system of an individual Member State which means that the Union's constitution (primary law, accession treaties) and the Member States' constitutions do not have hierarchical relationship. Thus the idea of constitutionalism in regard to the idea of norm hierarchy does not work in the transnational relationship between the Union and the Member States. This is also in line with the fact that the principle of primacy works as a rule to solve

---

entrate v Fallimento Olimpiclub Srl [2009] ECR p. I-7501; Joined cases C-392/04 and C-422/04 *i-21 Germany GmbH (C-392/04) and Arcor AG & Co. KG (C-422/04) v Bundesrepublik Deutschland* [2006] ECR p. I-8559; Case C-234/04 *Rosmarie Kapferer v Schlank & Schick GmbH* [2006] ECR p. I-2585; Case C-453/00 *Kühne & Heitz NV v Produktschap voor Pluimvee en Eieren* [2004] ECR p. I-837.

[74] Case C-409/06 *Winner Wetten GmbH v Bürgermeisterin der Stadt Bergheim* [2010] ECR p. I-8015.

[75] Malathouni (2008), pp. 118–120.

[76] Lenaerts and Van Nuffel (2011), p. 98. Voluntary withdrawal clause from the Union is sometimes referred as the sunset clause. Malathouni (2008), p. 115.

[77] Weyembergh (2017).

norm-conflicts. In this sense it could be described as trans-systemic principle.[78] It is not a supremacy clause, such as Article VI of the Constitution of the United States for example.[79] Given Article 50 TEU, which allows the withdrawal of a Member State from the European Union through the Member State's own decision, the idea of the supremacy of Union law and of a hierarchical structure of the Union and Member States does not seem logical as was demonstrated above. Instead, a heterarchical structure appears closer to reality.

Article 4(3) TEU stipulates the scope and substance of the principle of loyalty or the principle of sincere cooperation. Article 4(3) TEU stipulates that 'the Union and the Member States shall, in full mutual respect, assist each other in carrying out tasks which flow from the *Treaties*'. The loyalty principle applies to both the Union and the Member States. Because the commitment to loyalty does not concern only the Member States, the principle of loyalty can also be seen to express the heterarchical structure of the Union.

In addition, Member States have to take all appropriate measures to ensure the fulfilment of their obligations deriving from the Treaties. The Member States must also refrain from measures that could jeopardize the attainment of the Union's objectives. The principle of loyalty therefore involves both a positive and a negative obligation. The principle of loyalty is closely related to the effectiveness of Union law.[80] Without the principle of sincere cooperation the binding nature of Union law would lose its meaning, or in other words, experience inflation. The principle of primacy would also lose its impact. The principle of primacy and the principle of loyalty are closely connected, and both foster the effectiveness of Union law.

4.2.2 Criminal Law Specific Heterarchical Constitutional Structures

The principle of conforming interpretation gives an important role to national legislation and national authorities when applying EU law. The field of criminal law is sensitive from the perspective of national sovereignty. The use of conforming interpretation is therefore restricted in this context, as presented above in Chap. 3.5. A framework decision or a directive cannot independently determine or aggravate criminal liability.[81] Therefore the principle of primacy should not be considered

---

[78] Avbelj (2011), pp. 744, 750.

[79] In Article VI of the Constitution of United States, the second sentence reads: 'This Constitution, and the Laws of the United States which shall be made in Pursuance thereof; and all Treaties made, or which shall be made, under the Authority of the United States, shall be the supreme Law of the Land; and the Judges in every State shall be bound thereby, any Thing in the Constitution or Laws of any State to the Contrary notwithstanding.'

[80] Zuleeg (2011), p. 775; Lenaerts and Van Nuffel (2011), p. 151.

[81] Case C-14/86 *Pretore di Salò v Persons unknown* [1987] ECR p. 2545, para 20; Case C-80/86 *Criminal proceedings against Kolpinghuis Nijmegen BV* [1987] ECR p. 3969, para 14; Case C-105/03 *Criminal proceedings against Maria Pupino* [2005] ECR p. I-5285, paras 44–45.

absolute. The principle of primacy is applied only after determining that national legislation cannot be interpreted harmoniously with EU law in the case in question. However, in cases where national legislation and its EU law-oriented interpretation do not allow determining or aggravating criminal liability, the principle of primacy cannot be used as an alternative means to determine or aggravate criminal liability, and thus simultaneously to effectively enforce the norms of EU law. In cases like these, limits to conforming interpretation and the restriction on the principle of primacy expresses two of the sub-principles of the principle of legality: the principle of strict construction, also known as the prohibition of analogous application to the detriment of the accused (*nulla poena sine lege stricta*), and the requirement of precision (*lex certa*). The limits to the use of the principle of conforming interpretation and the restriction on the principle of primacy in the field of criminal law also represent the heterarchical structures between the EU legal order and the national legal orders since these restrictions show that strict pre-set hierarchical structures have not been established between the orders.

The Lisbon Treaty also introduced the so-called emergency brake procedure which is likely to prevent situations described in the paragraph above where the EU legislator might otherwise create criminal legislation which the Member States would consider excessive.[82] The emergency brake procedure can be seen as a more efficient manifestation of the general principle of subsidiarity and the subsidiarity control mechanism exercised by the national parliaments.

In the emergency brake procedure, where an EU Member State considers that 'a draft directive would affect fundamental aspects of its criminal justice system', it can ask for a referral to the European Council. This suspends the ordinary legislative procedure. The wording that is used, 'fundamental aspects of criminal justice system', seems to leave rather wide margin of appreciation for the Member States to use the emergency brake. Before the Lisbon Treaty, there was no need for an emergency brake because third pillar instruments required unanimity.[83] The wording of the emergency brake procedure now clearly acknowledges that there are differences between national criminal justice systems and that EU-level criminal law is not necessarily easy to enact due to those differences. The emergency brake procedure enables discussions concerning the proposed directive in the European Council. A consensus is required to continue the ordinary legislative process. Thus the procedure creates material legitimacy for the directive.

The limited scope for employing conforming interpretations or primacy in the field of criminal law as well as the emergency brake procedure show that cooperation within the EU framework is quite flexible and is also designed to take into account national specificities.

---

[82] Of course this does not affect to the possibility that the implementation acts by the Member States can be delayed.

[83] Asp (2012), p. 140.

4.3   Heterarchical Constitutional Pluralism in the European Legal Space

Constitutionalization in the European context is a more complex concept and phenomenon than it is in a state context. In the European Union context, constitutionalization includes both the formation of hierarchical structures within Union law and the formation of heterarchical structures between the Union and the Member States. The common constitutional picture of the Union and the Member States could be described as parallel, complementary or integral. To explain this, neither the Union nor the Member States occupy an absolutely higher hierarchical level in the constitutional structure in the sense that in any situation of norm collision always either the Union's constitution or the Member States' constitutions would prevail. The constitutional picture is parallel because when the Union law is applied, it is applied in the normative framework of the national law. The constitutional picture is integral because the Union law functions within the national legal systems. Norms that originate from the Union are applied parallel or complementary to national laws, or the Union norms are integrated to national legislation. As shown above, the Member States are the pouvoir constituant of the Union. However, in individual cases the Union law can sometimes prevail national law due to the principle of primacy. The constitutionalization of Union law is about defining what kind of a polity the Union is (ideological principles), the allocation of powers within the Union and between the Union and the Member States, and the heterarchical structures pertaining between the Union and the individual Member States. Heterarchical structures are embodied at least in the principles of primacy and sincere cooperation and in the principle of the Member States as Masters of the Treaties. Constitutionalization in a broader European context includes the evolution of heterarchical constitutional structures between the ECHR regime vis-á-vis the EU legal order and the national legal orders. These structures include the principle of subsidiarity and the doctrines of margin of appreciation and equivalent protection.

The heterarchical constitutional principles described above represent flexible co-existence between the different legal orders. They emphasize voluntary cooperation between the legal orders. The heterarchical principles have created a flexible interface between the legal systems that escapes the traditional hierarchical idea of constitutionalism. Heterarchical principles are also principles properly so called. They operate as balancing principles between the legal systems. Sometimes they can have a rule-like outcome however. For example, the principle of primacy cannot be applied contrary to the principle of legality of criminal law.

Flexible heterarchical constitutional structures do not clearly define the constitutional relationship between the Union, the Member States and the ECHR regime but nonetheless they contribute to the deepening of the cooperation by enabling the constitutionalization process within flexible limits. The heterarchical constitutional principles could be described as *communicative principles* since they do not suggest strict hierarchical structures between the legal orders. A concept of deep pluralism has been used to describe a situation 'where actors of each legal order proceed without systemic regard for the coherence of the whole'.[84] However some steps have been taken towards a more clearly defined relationship. For example, the declaration concerning primacy has been annexed to the Lisbon Treaty to clarify the interrelationship between the Union and the Member States, Article 6(2) TEU now explicitly stipulates that the Union shall accede to the ECHR, and even though not accepted an agreement for the Union's accession to the ECHR has been drafted.

Article 4(2) TEU states that the EU respects the national identities of the Member States. Article 50 TEU enables the Member States to leave the Union. Heterarchical constitutional principles, especially the possibility to withdraw from the Union, emphasise voluntariness in the relationship between the EU and the Member States. This in turn emphasises that the EU law must be materially acceptable to the Member States in order to legitimize its position in the national legal orders. Similarly, the ECHR regime leaves the manner of incorporation of the Convention open for the Contracting Parties to decide. The idea behind these heterarchical structures is for the member states and the European entities to accommodate their coexistence.

This also relates to the Beck's idea presented in the introductory chapter. Flexible heterarchical constitutional structures that are built upon voluntary compliance show how European cooperation in the EU and in the ECHR regime limits the autonomy of the member states but not their sovereignty. The Member States can withdraw themselves from the Union which means that they remain sovereign. They also have the power to amend the EU treaties which means that the Member States have the ultimate constitutional power in the Union. It also means that while being Member States in the Union, the Member States' sovereignty widens in this respect. Paradoxically, this simultaneously decreases the Member States' autonomy because the EU membership allows the CJEU to review the Member States' EU law related actions.

4.4   European Criminalization Principles

As noted above in Chap. 2.1, criminalization theory, the theory on the limitations on criminalization, is part of criminal law theory. The theory of criminalization is about contentual legitimation of criminalizations.[85] It is normative, meaning that the theory is not changed when new criminalizations are considered that do *not* follow the requirements of the theory. Rather, the requirements work as restrictions that *ought* to be taken into account when new criminal legislation is considered to be enacted. The European criminalization principles presented below[86] determine from a normative perspective *what the European legislature should take into account when*

---

[84] Kumm (2012), p. 40.

[85] Elholm (2014), pp. 71–73.

[86] Some of the ideas presented in Sects. 4.4.1 to 4.4.4 are previously published in Huomo-Kettunen (2014), p. 301.

criminal legislation is enacted and *how the legal basis for EU-level criminal legislation ought to be chosen.*

4.4.1 Subsidiarity and Proportionality: The Transnational Dimension of Ultima Ratio Principle

In the context of traditional criminal l aw, criminal law measures ought to be used only as a last resort (*ultima ratio*).[87] If the wanted outcome can be reached by using other than criminal law measures, the criminalization ought not to be enacted. The *ultima ratio* principle guides the legislator as to whether a particular type of conduct ought to be criminalized.[88] From the perspective of human and fundamental rights protection the principle of *ultima ratio* works toward the aim that such rights are not restricted more than is necessary.[89] Before criminalizing conduct, the legislator ought to establish that no other measures can sufficiently protect the legal interest at hand. Minimal use of criminalization and criminal sanctions is desirable since if used excessively, they lose their effectiveness because the desired standards of behaviour might not be achieved due to the overuse of criminalization.[90]

The traditional criminal law-oriented take on *ultima ratio* principle is acknowledged in EU criminal law. For example, Advocates General Ruiz-Jarabo Colomer and Mazák have referred to the nature of criminal law as *ultima ratio*[91] and *ultimum remedium*.[92] EU institutions exercising legislative powers also share a consensus on the *ultima ratio* principle as a central principle of EU criminal law. In 2009, the Council published model provisions that direct the Council's criminal law deliberations to ensure coherent and consistent use of criminal law provisions. In the document, the Council states that the need for criminal provisions ought to be assessed through the principles of protected interests, *ultima ratio*, conferral, subsidiarity, and proportionality. In the Council's view, substantive Union-level criminal legislation ought to be based only on the first or second paragraph of Article 83 TFEU.[93] The Commission and the Parliament have also found that the first step in assessing whether EU level criminal legislation ought to be enacted is to evaluate if criminal

---

[87] Husak (2004), p. 207.

[88] Ibid., p. 215.

[89] Ouwerkerk Jannemieke (2012), pp. 228, 238.

[90] The European Criminal Policy Initiative (2011), p. 88.

[91] Case C-297/07 *Klaus Bourquain* [2008] ECR p. I-9425, Opinion of AG Ruiz-Jarabo Colomer, para 70.

[92] See, for example, Case C-440/05 *Commission of the European Communities v Council of the European Union* [2007] ECR p. I-9097, Opinion of AG Mazák, para 71.

[93] Council Conclusions on model provisions, guiding the Council's criminal law deliberations, 2979th JUSTICE and HOME AFFAIRS Council meeting, Brussels, 30 November 2009, pp. 1–2.

law measures are essential and whether less intrusive means could be used.[94] The *ultima ratio* principle is also explicitly mentioned in the Stockholm Programme.[95]

The transnational dimension of the *ultima ratio* principle is different from the traditional criminal law dimension. Whereas national criminal policies concentrate on determining whether there is a need for criminal legislation and if new penal provisions can be justified, *EU criminal policy is more oriented to establishing whether criminal law measures are necessary at the Union level and choosing the appropriate legal basis for that legislation.*[96] The choice of legal basis is a pivotal element in the Union's justification for using its (criminal law) competence.

The EU criminal policy is not so much about the criminalization itself in the substantive sense but rather 'justifying the *harmonization* of substantive criminal law'.[97] The transnational dimension of the *ultima ratio* -principle is evident in the justification of Union level approximation measures, which emphasises 'federal' subsidiarity control instead of the substantive issue of the criminalization itself, at least in cases where similar conduct has already been criminalized at national level.

The principle of subsidiarity was constitutionalised in written form by the Maastricht Treaty (inserted as the then Article 3b EC) and is now enshrined in Article 5 TEU. The Union's express substantive criminal law competence is shared competence by its nature (Article 4(2)j TFEU). This means that both the EU and the Member States can create criminal legislation, but the Member States cannot exercise their competence if the Union has exercised its competence (Article 2(2) TFEU). According to the principle of subsidiarity the Union can act in areas which do not fall under the Union's exclusive competence only 'if and in so far as the objectives of the proposed action *cannot be sufficiently achieved by the Member States*—but can rather, by reason of the scale or effects of the proposed action, be better achieved at Union level' (Article 5(3) TEU, emphasis added). Union level criminal legislation must have extra value compared to dealing with the matter at the domestic level. This aspect of the principle of subsidiarity expresses a kind of 'federal level'[98] or transnational *ultima ratio*-principle.

The principle of subsidiarity also means that criminal legislative acts are assumed to be taken at primarily national level, and only secondarily at the EU-level, in order to bring criminal law decision-making as close to citizens as possible.[99] Subsidiarity is a principle that governs the use of power when power is divided or shared. It can be seen as a principle of good governance—'the basis of sound multi-level governance'[100] which requires, for example, that decision-making should occur as close

---

[94] COM (2011)573 final, p. 7; European Parliament, Report on an EU approach on criminal law, A7-0144/2012, 24 April 2012, p. 4.

[95] Stockholm Programme, OJ C 115 4.5.2010, 15.

[96] Huomo-Kettunen (2014), pp. 301, 313.

[97] Melander (2013), p. 46.

[98] Ibid., pp. 42, 51–52.

[99] The European Criminal Policy Initiative (2011), p. 91.

[100] Edward (2012), pp. 93–103, 93–96.

to the citizens as possible,[101] and that the subsidiarity principle ought to be read in the light of the aims and values of the Union.[102] From the perspective of legitimacy, it is important to make it possible for the citizens to participate in the criminal legislative discussions and to ensure criminal legislation is as culturally acceptable as possible. The possibility for citizens to participate in criminal legislative decision-making is essential because criminal law is a highly fundamental rights-sensitive branch of law. The subsidiarity control mechanism allows national parliaments, as closer representatives than the members of the European Parliament, to react to legislative proposals they consider do not fit with the fundamentals of national criminal justice systems.

National parliaments have a strong role in subsidiarity control. The national parliaments exercise *political* control of subsidiarity[103] by ensuring that the principle is respected in accordance with the procedures provided for in the Protocol on the application of the principles of subsidiarity and proportionality (Article 12(b) TEU). Protocol No 1 on the role of national Parliaments in the European Union and No 2 on the application of the principles of subsidiarity and proportionality set the framework for governance under the principle of subsidiarity. All legislative drafts must be justified with regard to the principles of subsidiarity and proportionality, including reasons *why the objective of the action can be better achieved at Union level.*

To a great extent the transnational dimension of the *ultima ratio*-principle deals with justifying the use of EU criminal law competence, and thus it is largely about subsidiarity and proportionality control. The CJEU and the Union's legislator can use the following questions as guidelines in assessing whether the Union legislative proposal complies with the principle of subsidiarity[104]:

1. Conferral: Does the Union have competence?
2. Subsidiarity: If it is shared competence, does the Union need to use it?

   a. What is the *objective* of the action?
   b. Can the objective be sufficiently achieved by the Member States?
   c. Can it by reason of the scale of the effects of the measure be better achieved at the Union level?

3. Proportionality: Could the Union use less intrusive means?

   a. Is the action or proposed action necessary to achieve the objective?
   b. Does the measure go further than is necessary to achieve it?

In the context of Article 83 TFEU, these guidelines should be taken into account in a following way:

---

[101] Schütze (2009a), p. 242; Edward (2012), pp. 93–103, 101, 96.

[102] Edward (2012), pp. 93–103, 101, 96.

[103] Schütze (2009b), pp. 525, 527; see also Ian Cooper (2006), p. 281.

[104] David Edward has suggested that these questions would be appropriate for the Court to use in assessing whether the principle of subsidiarity has been complied with. See Edward (2012), pp. 99–100.

1. Conferral: Is the area of crime that is proposed to be criminalized listed amongst the so-called euro-crimes, or has the Union enacted non-criminal law harmonisation measure relative to which also criminal legislative measures are necessary?
2. Subsidiarity: Is it necessary to enact this criminal legislative measure?

    a. Are the objectives and aims criminal-law embedded?
    b. Can the objectives be reached by measures taken at national level?
    c. Do Union-level measures add value?

3. Proportionality: Could the same objectives and aims be reached by using less intrusive means?

    a. Are other types of measures equally preventive? Would non-criminal law measures be sufficient to achieve the objectives and aims?
    b. Is the proposed criminal legislation proportionate in relation to the objectives and aims?

        i. Does the proposal restrict fundamental rights more than necessary?
        ii. Is the proposed sanction level defensible?
        iii. Is the proposed sanction level proportionate in relation to other EU-level criminal legislative measures?[105]
        iv. Is the proposed sanction-level proportionate in relation to the Member States' sanction-levels?

We can see that the question of conferral is not really as such a question of *ultima ratio* whereas the questions of subsidiarity and proportionality are. *The principle of subsidiarity and the first subquestion under the principle of proportionality represent the outer dimension of the ultima ratio principle*, referring to the choice of whether to take criminal or non-criminal legislative measures. Union-level criminal legislation ought to bring some extra value compared to taking measures at national level.

It has been argued that when deciding on EU-level criminalization, the legislature ought to focus on specific types of harmful conduct instead of general types of crime. This means that the Union's legislature ought to reason why specific types of conduct that are proposed for approximation require criminalization at the Union level. It is not sufficient to state that a certain type of crime should be criminalized at the Union-level.[106] This argument falls within the broader requirement that the EU-level criminal legislation ought to bring some added value in order to be justified.

Other questions falling within the principle of proportionality represent the inner dimension of the ultima ratio -principle. Two levels of inner coherence must be

---

[105] Also the Commission has found that the EU-level criminal law measures ought to "respect the consistency of the Union's system of criminal law [—] to ensure that criminal provisions do not become fragmented and ill-matched" (COM(2005) 583 final/2 Communication from the Commission to the European Parliament and the Council on the implications of the Court's judgment of 13 September 2005 (Case C-176/03 Commission v Council), Brussels 24 November 2005, p. 5).

[106] Melander (2008), pp. 464–465.

considered. First, the legislative measure ought to be in line with other EU-level criminal legislation in terms of determining the essential elements of crime and in terms of sanction levels. Second, the legislative measure needs to fit within the scheme of existing national criminal justice systems. EU-level criminal legislation ought not be manifestly disproportionate relative to the sanction levels in the Member States.

4.4.2 Respect for Fundamental Aspects of National Criminal Justice Systems

The need for the EU criminal law to respect fundamental aspects of national criminal justice systems is an EU-level constitutional principle enshrined in Articles 82 and 83 TFEU. Article 4(2) TEU stipulates a similar obligation by requiring that the Union respect the national identities of the Member States. Respect for national identities and the fundamental aspects of national criminal justice systems are related, because criminal justice is seen to reflect national identity.[107]

The subsidiarity control mechanism supports the requirement of respect for fundamental aspects of national criminal justice systems, because through the subsidiarity control mechanism national representatives are given the opportunity to protect their sovereignty. The emergency brake procedure could be seen as a derivative of the subsidiarity principle, only constituting a stronger procedural rejection than the subsidiarity control mechanism. Even though a Member State can prevent EU criminal legislation from affecting itself by relying on the emergency brake procedure, it cannot block it entirely if at least nine other Member States wish to start enhanced cooperation amongst themselves.

After the Lisbon Treaty entered into force, Article 83 TFEU has been used as a legal basis for several criminal law instruments. These are:

– Directive 2011/36/EU on preventing and combating trafficking in human beings and protecting its victims, and replacing Council Framework Decision 2002/629/JHA,[108]
– Directive 2011/92/EU on combating the sexual abuse and sexual exploitation of children and child pornography, and replacing Council Framework Decision 2004/68/JHA,[109]

---

[107] Lisbon judgment: BVerfG, 2 BvE 2/08 vom 30.6.2009, Absatz-Nr. (1-421), para 253. Available in English www.bverfg.de/entscheidungen/es20090630_2bve000208en.html, accessed 25 June 2018; Klip (2016), p. 40.

[108] Directive 2011/36/EU of the European Parliament and of the Council of 5 April 2011 on preventing and combating trafficking in human beings and protecting its victims, and replacing Council Framework Decision 2002/629/JHA [2011] OJ L 101, 15.4.2011, pp. 1–11.

[109] Directive 2011/92/EU of the European Parliament and of the Council of 13 December 2011 on combating the sexual abuse and sexual exploitation of children and child pornography, and replacing Council Framework Decision 2004/68/JHA [2011] OJ L 335, 17.12.2011, pp. 1–14.

- Directive 2013/40/EU on attacks against information systems and replacing Council Framework Decision 2005/222/JHA,[110]
- Directive 2014/42/EU on the freezing and confiscation of instrumentalities and proceeds of crime in the European Union,[111]
- Directive 2014/57/EU on criminal sanctions for market abuse (market abuse directive),[112]
- Directive 2014/62/EU on the protection of the euro and other currencies against counterfeiting by criminal law, and replacing Council Framework Decision 2000/383/JHA,[113]
- Directive (EU) 2017/541 on combating terrorism and replacing Council Framework Decision 2002/475/JHA and amending Council Decision 2005/671/JHA,[114]
- Directive (EU) 2017/1371 on the fight against fraud to the Union's financial interests by means of criminal law,[115] and
- Directive (EU) 2017/2103 amending Council Framework Decision 2004/757/JHA in order to include new psychoactive substances in the definition of 'drug' and repealing Council Decision 2005/387/JHA, OJEU L 305/12, 21.11.2017.[116]

So far, the emergency brake procedure has not been used.

However, it is useful to consider what might be fundamental aspects of national criminal justice systems such that the Member States could suspend the ordinary legislative procedure. At least the general doctrines of national criminal laws can be understood as a part of the fundamental aspects of national criminal justice systems.[117] For example, EU legislation affecting the basic principles and doctrines

---

[110] Directive 2013/40/EU of the European Parliament and of the Council of 12 August 2013 on attacks against information systems and replacing Council Framework Decision 2005/222/JHA [2013] OJ L 218, 14.8.2013, pp. 8–14.

[111] Directive 2014/42/EU of the European Parliament and of the Council of 3 April 2014 on the freezing and confiscation of instrumentalities and proceeds of crime in the European Union [2014] OJ L 127, 29.4.2014, pp. 39–50.

[112] Directive 2014/57/EU of the European Parliament and of the Council of 16 April 2014 on criminal sanctions for market abuse (market abuse directive) [2014] OJ L 173, 12.6.2014, pp. 179–189.

[113] Directive 2014/62/EU of the European Parliament and of the Council of 15 May 2014 on the protection of the euro and other currencies against counterfeiting by criminal law, and replacing Council Framework Decision 2000/383/JHA [2013] OJ L 151, 21.5.2014, pp. 1–8.

[114] Directive (EU) 2017/541 of the European Parliament and of the Council of 15 March 2017 on combating terrorism and replacing Council Framework Decision 2002/475/JHA and amending Council Decision 2005/671/JHA OJ L 88, 31.3.2017, pp. 6–21.

[115] Directive (EU) 2017/1371 of the European Parliament and of the Council of 5 July 2017 on the fight against fraud to the Union's financial interests by means of criminal law OJ L 198, 28.7.2017, pp. 29–41.

[116] Directive (EU) 2017/2103 of the European Parliament and of the Council of 15 November 2017 amending Council Framework Decision 2004/757/JHA in order to include new psychoactive substances in the definition of 'drug' and repealing Council Decision 2005/387/JHA, OJEU L 305/12, 21.11.2017.

[117] Melander (2014), pp. 274, 291.

on criminal liability, attempt and complicity might fall within the emergency brake procedure.[118]

Central principles of criminal law, such as the *ultima ratio* principle or legality principle, could also be understood as fundamental aspects of national criminal justice systems. If an approximation measure would affect the general doctrines of national criminal law, the emergency brake procedure might come into question. The general part of criminal law, including the key principles governing the use of criminal law, affect the different stages of the criminal justice system, from the stage of criminalization to the stages of conviction and execution of punishment. It is therefore only natural that the Member States have possibility to protect these elements, which are usually developed during a long period of time and represent fundamental choices in each society. Recourse to the emergency brake could possibly also come into question relative to approximation of sanctions,[119] if, for example, the approximation measure would require a transposition measure that would not be possible within the infrastructure of the national criminal justice system. An example of a situation where EU-level criminal legislation has led to a use of an unusual legislative method is the implementation of the Framework Decision on combating terrorism[120] in Finland, and more precisely, the criminalization obligation included in its Article 2(2)a concerning the directing of a terrorist group. Article 5(3) of the framework decision required that the directing of a terrorist group must be punishable by custodial sentences with a maximum sentence of not less than 15 years. The problem was that the Finnish penal code determines that the maximum period of fixed-term imprisonment for an offence is 12 years, and 15 years only when imposing a joint sentence.[121] In order to be able to implement the framework decision appropriately by imposing a penalty threat of at least 15 years of imprisonment, Finnish terrorist legislation now determines that a person who is sentenced for directing of a terrorist group shall *also* be sentenced for an offence that the terrorist group committed.[122]

This relates to the notion of the emergency brake procedure as reflecting the principle of proportionality. EU-level criminal legislative measures that would bring more harm than advantages could be challenged by recourse to the emergency brake procedure.[123] For example, a Member State could use the emergency brake procedure so that it would not need to enact penalties that would violate its obligations stemming from international agreements. For example, setting the minimum level of the maximum sanction excessively high might be questionable from the perspective of the coherent treatment of different types of offences.

---

[118] Satzger (2012), p. 81; Melander (2014), pp. 274, 277, 291.

[119] Weyembergh (in collaboration with Serge de Biolley) (2013a), p. 23.

[120] Council Framework Decision of 13 June 2002 on combating terrorism, OJ L 164, 22.6.2002, pp. 3–7.

[121] Finnish Penal Code, Chapter 2(c) Section 2.

[122] Finnish Penal Code, Chapter 34a Section 3(3).

[123] Melander (2008), p. 505.

4.4.3   The Principle of Legality: Transnational Dimension

The principle of legality governs the use of criminal law. It is a constitutional principle stemming from the rule of law principle. It is also enshrined separately in
different constitutional documents (Article 7 of the ECHR, Article 15 of the
International Covenant on Civil and Political Rights, Article 49 of the Charter, etc.).
Two of its sub-principles are examined in this chapter, because they impose requirements on the legislator and are therefore relevant from the EU criminal policy perspective.[124] These principles are the requirement of precision (*lex certa*) and the
requirement of *nullum crimen, nulla poena sine lege parlamentaria*.

4.4.3.1   The Formal Dimension of the Principle of Legality

By reference to Article 7 ECHR, the CJEU has stated that prohibition of retroactive
criminal legislation is a principle common to all the legal orders of the Member
States and a general principle of EU law.[125] Today, the requirement of *nullum crimen, nulla poena sine lege parlamentaria* is also enshrined in Article 49 of the
Charter, which restricts the enactment and application of retroactive criminal legislation as a main rule.

The requirement of *nullum crimen, nulla poena sine lege parlamentaria* gives
legitimacy for EU criminal legislation by guaranteeing that criminal legislation is a
product of democratic decision-making. The requirement that penal provisions take
the form of parliamentary law legitimizes the use of criminal law.[126] The democratic
element of the principle of legality ensures better chances for individuals and groups
to participate to the decision-making.[127] The democratic element of criminal law
making generate legitimacy for the criminal laws because democratic process
means that the laws are products of general will to which individuals including
potential offenders have agreed to. This general will represents the shared understanding of the community on balancing competing rights and interests. Criminal
law making in a democratic process is inclusive and criminal laws generated in this
way are more likely to be accepted by the individuals.[128]

The *democratic dimension of the legality principle* is also referred to as *the formal dimension of the principle of legality*.[129] Because national parliaments need to
comply with the harmonisation instruments the Union's legislator issues, the EU
law instruments must also be justifiable from the perspective of democracy and

---

[124] See, for example, ibid., p. 204.

[125] Case C-63/83 *Regina v Kent Kirk* [1984] ECR 2689, para 22. See also, Herlin-Karnell (2010),
pp. 1115, 1120.

[126] Roxin (2006), pp. 146–147; see also Melander (2008), p. 194.

[127] The European Criminal Policy Initiative (2011), p. 90.

[128] Peristeridou (2015), p. 45.

[129] Weyembergh (in collaboration with Serge de Biolley) (2013a), p. 22.

democratic governance. In this formal sense, EU-level criminal legislation fulfils the democratic dimension of legality principle when the EU-level penal provisions are enacted based on Article 83 TFEU. Subsidiarity control, with its lower threshold, and the emergency brake procedure involves the national governments and parliaments in legislative proceedings to ensure that decisions are taken as close to the individuals as possible.

The need for democratic legitimacy stems from the nature of criminal law as the most invasive state measure.[130] The co-decision procedure and the subsidiarity control exercised by the national parliaments lend EU criminal legislation its democratic legitimacy,[131] because the idea of representative democracy is maintained through the work of the European Parliament and the national parliaments. According to Article 83(1) TFEU criminal legislative approximation measures will involve the ordinary legislative procedure, in which the European Parliament has equal legislative powers with the Council (Article 294 TFEU).

The democratic element of the principle of legality demonstrates that criminal law in general and EU criminal law and policy in specific is dependent on its broader public acceptability. This raises the question which types of conduct should be subject to Union level approximation measures, and on what scale. Perhaps the public acceptability of the EU criminal policy and approximation of criminal law is linked to the EU criminal law's function of fostering a common European identity ('identity fostering effect') and 'giving citizens a common sense of justice throughout the Union'. In this sense the approximation of criminal law is not solely a manifestation auxiliary to mutual recognition, but instead approximation of criminal law seems to reinforce the notion of European citizenship,[132] and generally relates to the rights and duties of the EU citizens.[133]

Eurobarometer results show EU citizens think that the EU ought to tackle crime, placing it fourth in the list of areas that the European institutions ought to prioritise right after issues concerning the debt crisis and immigration and health policies.[134] This particular Eurobarometer data paints a very general picture which does not say much. It should be asked if the Union's actions in the field of criminal law respond to the citizens' expectations. In order to answer this question, more detailed research should be conducted relative to expectations concerning specific areas of crime and sanction policies. The questions need to be as specific and detailed as possible, perhaps including examples of specific cases, in order for them to give a precise picture of the citizens' sense of justice (on public opinion concerning criminal law, see Chap. 3.3.2.1 above).

---

[130] Satzger (2012), p. 84.

[131] The European Criminal Policy Initiative (2011), p. 90. The Manifesto has designated six guiding principles for EU criminal policy. These are the requirement of a legitimate purpose, and the principles of *ultima ratio*, guilt, legality, subsidiarity, and coherence.

[132] Weyembergh (in collaboration with Serge de Biolley) (2013a), p. 21.

[133] Vervaele (2013), p. 70.

[134] Eurobarometer 75, Spring 2011, p. 58 (available in internet http://ec.europa.eu/public_opinion/archives/eb/eb75/eb75_en.htm, accessed 25 June 2018; Herlin-Karnell (2012).

The democratic element of the principle of legality is not just about this formal or procedural legitimacy. Democracy in its substantive sense is about respecting human dignity and equality as was demonstrated above in Chap. 3.3. Even if legislation would have been enacted in democratic process, it might not be legitimate in substantive sense if it would violate human dignity. The democratic element is not exhausted in the democratic processes (right to self-governance), it also requires that the legislation respects the human dignity which is a prerequisite for democracy itself.[135]

4.4.3.2 Requirement of Precision

The requirement of precision is also interesting from the perspective of the Union legislator. The requirement of precision seeks to ensure the predictability and foreseeability of the criminal law. Both the objective and subjective prerequisites for criminal liability and sanctions for the criminalized conduct ought to be written clearly in the penal provisions in order for them to be foreseeable.[136]

The cases of *Taricco I* and *Taricco II* show how the principle of legality, a fundamental principle of the national criminal justice systems, proved difficult to be dealt within the CJEU. In the *Taricco* saga the question was mainly about application of law, but it would have had implications to the Italian national criminal legislation if the judgment in *Taricco II* would have had a different outcome.

The case of *Taricco I* was about how the CJEU had differentiated the applicability of the principle of legality in the fields of substantive criminal law and procedural criminal law and about the content and understanding of the principle of legality. In *Taricco I* the CJEU was asked if a limitation period in the rising of criminal charges relative to VAT frauds was compatible with EU law. The CJEU started its reasoning by stating that 'Article 325 TFEU obliges the Member States to counter illegal activities affecting the financial interests of the European Union through effective deterrent measures and, in particular, obliges them to take the same measures to counter fraud affecting the financial interests of the European Union as they take to counter fraud affecting their own interests'.[137] It continued by saying that 'the Member States must ensure that such cases of serious fraud are punishable by criminal penalties which are, in particular, effective and dissuasive. Moreover, the measures adopted in that respect must be the same as those which the Member States adopt in order to combat equally serious cases of fraud affecting their own financial interests.'[138] The Court continued by stating that 'it should be added that if the national court decides to disapply the national provisions at issue, it must also ensure that the fundamental rights of the persons concerned are respected. Indeed, in that case penalties may be imposed on those persons which, in all likelihood,

---

[135] Similarly, see, Peristeridou (2015), pp. 45–48.
[136] The European Criminal Policy Initiative (2011), pp. 89–90.
[137] Case C-105/14 *Taricco I* [2015], para 37.
[138] Ibid., para 43.

would not have been imposed if those provisions of national law had been applied.'[139] The Court argued that the disapplication of national laws on the limitation period would not infringe the rights of the accused as they are guaranteed by Article 49 of the Charter because it would not lead to a conviction of the accused for an act or an omission which did not constitute a criminal offence under national law at the time when it was committed.[140]

Taricco I shows that the CJEU made a rather noticeable distinction between substantive and procedural criminal law. The CJEU clearly considered that the principle of legality in the field of EU criminal law covers solely the retroactivity, preciseness and predictability of the essential elements of the crime and the sanctions, but not procedural elements of the crime provisions or criminal law, such as in *Taricco I* the limitation periods. Making this distinction, the CJEU understood the coverage of the principle of legality and its subprinciples entirely differently as they are understood in national criminal justice systems.[141] The fact that the CJEU is making this distinction between substantive and procedural criminal law is strange in the sense that the actual problem in the issue is that should the EU citizens be aware that such general provisions such as Article 325 TFEU walks over the more precise national criminal law provisions. Should the EU citizens be able to predict this kind of an outcome?[142] In addition to this, it should be noted that even though a norm could be classified as a procedural norm, such as the limitation period clause was classified by the CJEU differing form the Italian national understanding on the matter, it does not automatically mean that its application or non-application would not lead to aggravation of criminal liability.

The Italian Constitutional Court then asked the CJEU whether the *Taricco I* judgment requires the criminal court to disapply national legislation (in this case the limitation periods) even where such disapplication is at variance with the overriding principles of the constitution of the Member State concerned or with the inalienable rights of the individual conferred by the constitution of the Member State.[143] In *Taricco II* the CJEU stated that it is a task of the national legislatures, and not the courts, to lay down the rules on the limitation periods and in doing that, to make sure that the principle of assimilation is followed in the national law.[144] For their part, the national courts must make sure that the fundamental rights of the person being accused are being observed.[145] The CJEU found that 'it follows, first, that it is for the national court to ascertain whether the finding, required by paragraph 58 of the *Taricco* judgment, that the provisions of the Criminal Code at issue prevent the imposition of effective and deterrent criminal penalties in a significant number of cases of serious fraud affecting the financial interests of the Union leads to a situa-

---

[139] Ibid., para 53.

[140] Ibid., paras 55–56.

[141] Similarly, see Marco Bassini and Oreste Pollicino (2017).

[142] Michal Krajewski (2017).

[143] Case C-42/17 *Taricco II* (M.A.S. and M.B.) [2017], para 20.

[144] Ibid., para 41.

[145] Ibid., para 46.

tion of uncertainty in the Italian legal system as regards the determination of the applicable limitation rules, which would be in breach of the principle that the applicable law must be precise. If that is indeed the case, the national court is not obliged to disapply the provisions of the Criminal Code at issue.'[146] The CJEU seems to pull back a little by giving the national authorities a possibility to understand the content of the principle of legality in a flexible manner. The CJEU does not define the criteria of the legality principle but instead leaves it open.[147]

The *Taricco II* judgment is noteworthy also in that respect that the CJEU resolved the conflict between EU law and national constitutional law in the favor of the latter. The Court did not argue the case on the doctrine of primacy. Primacy was merely mentioned only once in the judgement ('the national authorities and courts remain free to apply national standards of protection of fundamental rights, provided that the level of protection provided for by the Charter, as interpreted by the Court, and the primacy, unity and effectiveness of EU law are not thereby compromised').[148] Thus, in *Taricco II* the principle of primacy is used by the Court as it should be used: with respect to the fundamental principles of national constitutional principles and tradition, and with respect to the fundamental aspects of national criminal justice systems. The CJEU left the Italian courts and authorities the possibility to interpret the principle of legality, which is a key principle of criminal law and constitutional law, in the manner as it is understood in the Italian constitutional and criminal law.

The requirement of precision also relates, as the other EU criminalization principles also do, to the choice of legal basis as outlined above. If the Union had implied substantive criminal law competence (for example, under Article 325(4) TFEU), it could promulgate criminal legislation in the form of regulations (more on this topic below in Chap. 5.2.2). As explained above, the Commission has considered such an option in relation to the proposal on the protection of the Union's financial interests. Since EU criminal legislation in the form of a regulation would be directly applicable in the national courts, the EU legislator would need to formulate the penal provisions as precisely as national legislatures. It might be difficult to achieve such EU level criminal legislation that would lead to a same outcome in different Member States because the definitions of offences are affected by the general part of the criminal law of the Member States. Similar provisions of criminal law could therefore lead to different norm application or to different levels of severity in different Member States. Moreover, even when the criminal legislation takes the form of a directive, the more precise provisions the EU legislator provides, the less of a margin of discretion the instrument leaves to the Member States,[149] thus emphasising the EU legislature's obligation under the principle of legality to ensure proportionality, or in other words the fulfilment of the inner dimension of the *ultima ratio* principle according to which criminal provisions ought to construct a coherent

---

[146] Ibid., para 59.
[147] Dana Burchardt (2017).
[148] Ibid.; Case C-42/17 *Taricco II* (M.A.S. and M.B.) [2017], para 47.
[149] The European Criminal Policy Initiative (2011), p. 89.

criminal justice system[150] within the domestic criminal justice systems. Ensuring this might be a difficult, if not impossible, task for the Union's legislature.

As explained in the Manifesto, the inner coherence of the criminal justice system is essential in order to establish the legitimacy of the criminal justice system. For example, according to the principle of coherence or the inner dimension of the *ultima ratio* principle the levels for the minimum-maximum criminal penalties set at the EU-level should not conflict with the criminal justice system infrastructures which already exist in the Member States. However, the EU legislator ought to also construct an internally coherent EU criminal law and policy.[151] Because there are at least as many different criminal law traditions as there are EU Member States, EU-level requirements on the levels of sanctions should be flexible to fit all traditions.

As explained above, the principle of legality limits the application of certain principles of general EU law. The CJEU has stated that even though national legislation has to be interpreted in conformity with the EU law that the domestic law implements, EU-level criminal legislation cannot determine or aggravate criminal liability. This simply means that criminal liability cannot be based on provisions that do not clearly define what kind of conduct is criminalized.[152] We can see that the principle of legality restricts the application of the principles of conforming interpretation (indirect effect) and the primacy of EU law in the substantive criminal law context. This supports the claim made above that the concept of primacy of EU law ought to be used instead of supremacy of EU law. EU law does not have supremacy over all national law, as the example of criminal law demonstrates. This also demonstrates that criminal law is different from general EU law and that it should be treated as such.

The situation is different relative to instruments based on the principle of mutual recognition, since they do not aim to approximate national legislation. For example, Article 2(2) of the Framework Decision on the European Arrest Warrant (FD EAW) consists of a list of types of crime. If they are punishable in the issuing Member State by a custodial sentence or a detention order for a maximum period of at least 3 years they give rise to surrender without verification of the double criminality of the act. What kind of conduct actually falls under the categories depends on how the issuing Member State has defined the essential elements of the so-called list offences. The aim of the framework decision is not to approximate the definitions of the criminal offences. The CJEU found that Article 2(2) FD EAW does not infringe the principle of legality, because the protection of fundamental rights, including the principle of legality, is a task of the Member State issuing the arrest warrant.[153]

---

[150] On the inner dimention of the *ultima ratio* principle, see Melander (2008), p. 407.

[151] The European Criminal Policy Initiative (2011), p. 91.

[152] Joined cases C-74/95 and C-129/95 *Criminal proceedings against X* [1996] ECR p. I-6609, paras 24–25; Case C-14/86 *Pretore di Salò v Persons unknown* [1987] ECR p. 2545, para 20; Case C-80/86 *Criminal proceedings against Kolpinghuis Nijmegen BV* [1987] ECR p. 3969, para 14; Case C-105/03 *Criminal proceedings against Maria Pupino* [2005] ECR p. I-5285, paras 44–45.

[153] Case C-303/05 *Advocaten voor de Wereld VZW v Leden van de Ministerraad* [2007] ECR p. I-3633, paras 48, 52–54.

Similarly, the Commission finds that the principle of legality imposes obligations primarily on the Member States when they are implementing the EU-level instruments which approximate substantive criminal law.[154]

The judgment in *Advocaten voor de Wereld* has been criticised as calling into question how genuinely the Union is committed to following the principle of legality since the Court found that this review is entirely a task of the Member States.[155] Because the CJEU found in *Advocaten voor de Wereld* that the protection of fundamental rights, including the principle of legality, is a task of the Member State issuing the arrest warrant, it would seem only logical that the EU could not enact criminal legislation in a form of regulations, because then the Union's legislative institutions would have to ensure the effective protection of fundamental rights including the requirements stemming from the principle of legality. However, *Advocaten voor de Wereld* was about the applicability of the principle of legality to the Union legislation that is based on the principle of mutual recognition, and not about approximation of substantive criminal law.

The cases of *Taricco I* and *Taricco II* that were described above, especially *Taricco I*, show that the CJEU has made a rather noteworthy difference in the applicability of the principle of legality in substantive and procedural criminal law. However, *Taricco II* shows that perhaps the CJEU has relaxed its approach on the matter and no longer makes such a strict differentiation between substantive and procedural criminal law in what comes to the application of the principle of legality. As argued above, the Member States have intended to exhaust the Union's substantive criminal law competence in Article 83 TFEU which allows only the use of directives as the form of measure of approximation. This also means that substantive provisions of criminal law cannot be completely harmonized. If the *travaux préparatoires* concerning Article 83 TFEU and its *ratio legis* are taken seriously following the Court's new line of interpretation, EU-level substantive criminal legislation could not be enacted in the form of regulations.

4.4.4 Respect of Fundamental Rights: Transnational Dimension

Originally, the protection of fundamental and human rights entered into EU law as a result of the primacy case law in order to make EU norms and the adaption of the primacy doctrine acceptable.[156] The Union assured Member States that it guarantees fundamental and human rights in its legislation and case law. EU criminal law must respect fundamental rights guaranteed in the Charter and give those rights at least the same level of protection guaranteed by the other international agreements— especially in the ECHR—to which the Union or the EU Member States are parties

---

[154]COM(2011) 573 final, p. 8.

[155]Herlin-Karnell (2007), pp. 1147, 1156; Melander (2010), pp. 131–132.

[156]Defeis (2007–2008), pp. 1, 2; see also Case C-29/69 *Erich Stauder v City of Ulm – Sozialamt* [1969] ECR p. 419.

(Article 53 of the Charter). EU primary law binds EU fundamental rights protection to the text and case law of the ECHR regime. Negotiations concerning the accession of the EU to the ECHR are in progress and once the EU accedes to the Convention, the ECtHR is proposed to have the jurisdiction to evaluate the compatibility of EU-level measures and omissions with the ECHR.[157] The Union's accession to the Convention seems rational only if the Union's obligations deriving from the ECHR correspond the obligations the State parties have.

In the criminal law framework, fundamental and human rights have a dual role—a defensive and an offensive role. In its offensive role human rights protection can act as the driving force for the use of criminal legislative measures. As has been established above, the ECHR regime expects that the member states have criminal justice systems and more specifically that in relation to some types of offences infringing individuals' physical or sexual integrity, there has to be deterrent criminal legislation. The defensive role protects individuals from an excessive use of criminal law.[158] For example, to illustrate the defensive role, both EU criminal policy and ECtHR case law start from the premise that criminal liability ought to be based on the principle of guilt,[159] which reflects respect for fundamental rights since this way of construing criminal liability respects human dignity.[160]

The CJEU has evaluated the scope of the Charter and the fundamental rights protection in the EU in several cases. In the case of *Melloni*, the CJEU examined whether, if necessary, a Member State could refuse to execute a European arrest warrant on the basis of Article 53 of the Charter. The applicant had not appeared in person at his trial (*in absentia*). The national constitution provided higher a standard than that deriving from the Charter. The CJEU found that such an interpretation of Article 53 of the Charter is not acceptable, because it would undermine the primacy of EU law. Providing higher level of fundamental rights protection on the basis of national constitution would allow the Member States 'to disapply EU legal rules which are fully in compliance with the Charter where they infringe the fundamental rights guaranteed by that State's constitution'. This interpretation would undermine the effectiveness of EU law and of the framework decision.[161]

---

[157] 47+1(2013)008rev2, Fifth negotiation meeting between the CDDH ad hoc negotiation group and the European Commission on the accession of the European Union to the European Convention on Human Rights, Final report to the CDDH, Strasbourg, 10 June 2013; Steering Committee for Human Rights (2011), pp. 15–18; see also Huomo-Kettunen (2013), pp. 47, 61.

[158] Tulkens (2011), p. 577; similarly, Maugeri (2013), p. 374.

[159] Affaire *Goktepe c. Belgique* Requete no 50372/99 (ECtHR, 2 juin 2005), paras 26, 29; The Council of the European Union, Council Conclusions on model provisions, guiding the Council's criminal law deliberations, 2979th JUSTICE and HOME AFFAIRS Council meeting Brussels, 30 November 2009; European Commission, COM(2011) 573 final, Towards an EU Criminal Policy: Ensuring the effective implementation of EU policies through criminal law, Brussels, 20 September 2011; European Parliament, Report on an EU approach on criminal law, A7-0144/2012, 24 April 2012.

[160] The European Criminal Policy Initiative (2011), p. 88.

[161] Case C-399/11 *Stefano Melloni v Ministerio Fiscal* [2013], paras 58–64.

In *Melloni* the CJEU accepted the Charter as the maximum level of fundamental rights protection in situations in which EU law is applied. From *Melloni*, we can see that the Charter does not constitute the minimum level of protection that needs to be provided in EU law related situations. It actually seems to set the maximum level of fundamental rights protection in these situations. This is evident in *Melloni* because the CJEU actually set aside Article 53 of the Charter[162] a provision of EU primary law, in order to ensure the effective application of the framework decision. The wording of Article 53 of the Charter indicates that the said provision would work as a kind of flexibility clause operating in the scene of the European constitutional pluralism mediating between the EU, the ECHR regime and the national legal orders. Article 53 of the Charter clearly states that the Charter provides certain level of rights but that the Member States can offer higher level of protection based on their national constitutions or the ECHR.

Normally provisions like Article 53 of the Charter are meant to ensure that the human or fundamental rights instrument in question ensures a minimum level of protection instead of maximum level.[163] In *Melloni*, however, the CJEU stated that

> It is true that Article 53 of the Charter confirms that, where an EU legal act calls for national implementing measures, *national authorities and courts remain free to apply national standards of protection of fundamental rights, provided that the level of protection provided for by the Charter, as interpreted by the Court, and the primacy, unity and effectiveness of EU law are not thereby compromised.*[164]

Based on *Melloni*, it seems that the flexibility clause enshrined in Article 53 could not be applied in practice in contexts that have been harmonised by EU measures and which are in conformity with the Charter due to the protection of autonomy and effectiveness of EU law at least relative to criminal procedural law.

As discussed in previous chapters, case law shows that as early as from *Costa v ENEL* the principle of primacy has also had influence over national constitutions. There is an exception to this, but it concerns only *substantive* criminal law in cases where application of the principle of primacy would lead to determination or aggravation of criminal liability, leaving also the criminal procedural law outside the scope of the exception. Thus *Melloni* also demonstrates that the principle of legality has a different field of application in the fields of substantive and procedural criminal law. We can see that the fundamental rights protection in the EU regime differs from that in the ECHR regime. In the ECHR regime the Convention sets only the minimum standards for fundamental rights protection, and the national authorities can provide their citizens stronger protection. In the EU regime, fundamental rights protection is downshifted in situations where it has challenged the autonomy of EU

---

[162] Article 53 of the Charter: "Nothing in this Charter shall be interpreted as restricting or adversely affecting human rights and fundamental freedoms as recognised, in their respective fields of application, by Union law and international law and by international agreements to which the Union or all the Member States are party, including the European Convention for the Protection of Human Rights and Fundamental Freedoms, and by the Member States' constitutions."

[163] Bering Liisberg (2001), p. 1171.

[164] Case C-399/11 *Stefano Melloni v Ministerio Fiscal* [2013], para 60.

law. From the perspective of fundamental rights protection and democracy, this appears slightly odd since one of the purposes of fundamental rights protection is to provide legitimacy for the actions of the polity in question.

However, based on *Taricco II*,[165] it is noteworthy that the CJEU has recently stated that the national courts must make sure that the fundamental rights of the person being accused are being observed. Simultaneously the national courts and authorities must make sure that the principle of primacy and effectiveness of EU law are not compromised.[166] Relative to the principle of legality the CJEU stated that 'in particular, where the imposition of criminal penalties is concerned, the competent national courts must ensure that the rights of defendants flowing from the principle that offences and penalties must be defined by law are guaranteed'.[167] The Court concluded that 'If the national court were thus to come to the view that the obligation to disapply the provisions of the Criminal Code at issue conflicts with the principle that offences and penalties must be defined by law, it would not be obliged to comply with that obligation, even if compliance with the obligation allowed a national situation incompatible with EU law to be remedied (—). It will then be for the national legislature to take the necessary measures'.[168] In *Taricco II* the CJEU resolved the case in favor of the national constitutional law over EU law. This is new, but warmly welcomed change in the CJEU's line of interpretation. The interpretation was definitely correct in the sense that EU law ought not to have primacy over national law in individual cases where primacy of EU law would lead to determination or aggravation of criminal liability.

The CJEU has found Directive 2006/24/EC on data retention[169] invalid on the basis that the EU legislature had exceeded the limits of the principle of proportionality in relation to Articles 7, 8 and 52(1) of the Charter when adopting the directive.[170] The directive enabled the gathering of data on all persons using electronic communications services, regardless of whether the person whose data was retained was even indirectly 'in a situation which is liable to give rise to criminal prosecutions'.[171] The directive's aim was stipulated as follows:

> to *harmonise Member States' provisions concerning the obligations of the providers of publicly available electronic communications services or of public communications networks with respect to the retention of certain data which are generated or processed by them, in order to ensure that the data are available for the purpose of the investigation,*

---

[165] See detailed analysis on the Taricco I and Taricco judgments in Sect. 4.4.3.2.

[166] Case C-42/17 *Taricco II* (M.A.S. and M.B.) [2017], paras 46–47.

[167] Ibid., para 48.

[168] Ibid., para 61.

[169] Directive 2006/24/EC of the European Parliament and of the Council of 15 March 2006 on the retention of data generated or processed in connection with the provision of publicly available electronic communications services or of public communications networks and amending Directive 2002/58/EC [2006] OJ L 105, 13.4.2006, pp. 54–63.

[170] Joined cases C-293/12 and C-594/12 *Digital Rights Ireland Ltd v Minister for Communications, Marine and Natural Resources and Others and Kärntner Landesregierung and Others* [2014], para 69.

[171] Ibid., para 58.

detection and prosecution of serious crime, as defined by each Member State in its national law. (Article 1 of the directive, emphasis added)

Already in 2009, the CJEU had examined the same directive but from the perspective of appropriate legal basis. The Court deliberated whether the directive in question should be annulled because it was not adopted on an appropriate legal basis; Ireland argued that it should have been based on a criminal law legal basis because the directive enabled the gathering of data in order to facilitate police cooperation. The Court found that the directive's predominant objective was not criminal law oriented but instead it was to *'safeguard the proper functioning of the internal market* through the adoption of harmonised rules' (emphasis added).[172]

In its more recent judgment in 2014 the Court found the directive invalid on a material basis. The CJEU's argumentation concerning the objective of the directive was not as transparent as could be hoped for. The Court found that *the aim of the directive* was to harmonise the Member States' provisions concerning the obligations of those providers with respect to the retention of certain data (or in other words, harmonisation of the internal market) but that the *material objective* of the directive was *'to ensure that the data are available for the purpose of the investigation, detection and prosecution of serious crime'* and therefore *ultimately to contribute to the fight against serious crime and to public security*.[173]

The term 'material objective' is used in two cases. It is used only once by the Court (in this particular case) and once by the Government of Germany (in the French language version 'l'objectif materiel'), thus leaving the meaning of the term ambiguous. In the other case where the term 'l'objectif materiel' appears, the Government of Germany used it to refer to the aim and spirit of a particular Decision.[174] It is difficult to assess what the Court meant by this division of the directives aims into *its explicitly stated objective* and *material objective*.[175] The Court could have meant to indicate, by using the term 'material objective', that the directive's main objective was criminal-law-oriented.[176] This would illustrate that respect for fundamental rights might after all be a rather strong restrictive principle in EU criminal law. Also, the term could mean something other than predominant aim or objective. The fact that the directive does not really contain criminal provisions supports the Court's view in its 2009 judgment concerning the choice of legal basis. But even if an instrument does not contain penal provisions it does not necessarily mean that its predominant aim could not be criminal law-oriented. One explanation to this unusual use of terminology could be that the Court had a change of

---

[172] Case C-301/06 *Ireland v European Parliament and Council of the European Union* [2009] ECR p. I-593, paras 1, 10, 72.

[173] Joined cases C-293/12 and C-594/12 *Digital Rights Ireland Ltd v Minister for Communications, Marine and Natural Resources and Others and Kärntner Landesregierung and Others* [2014], para 41.

[174] See both language versions of Case C-70/72 *Commission of the European Communities v Federal Republic of Germany* [1973] ECR p. 813.

[175] Orla Lynskey (2014).

[176] In this way, for example Sylvain Métille (2014).

heart relative to the question of appropriate legal basis for the data retention directive.[177]

Recently in *Schrems*, the CJEU affirmed the meaning it gave in *Digital Rights Ireland* to the Charter. The CJEU ruled Commission Decision 2000/520[178] to be invalid because it did not comply with Directive 95/46.[179] This directive seeks to ensure a European level of protection of the fundamental rights and freedoms of natural persons, and in particular, their right to privacy with respect to the processing of personal data. The Commission failed to demonstrate that the USA ensures an essentially equivalent level of protection of fundamental rights to that guaranteed in the EU legal order.[180]

We can see that EU criminal law is not just about the mutual recognition of judicial decisions and the approximation of criminal laws. Embedded criminal law aims can also be found in other EU measures. Based on the Court's vague argumentation in the *Digital Rights Ireland* cases, one could ask if EU measures with embedded criminal law aims, but which do not contain criminal law provisions, should in some cases be based on criminal law legal bases. The *Digital Rights Ireland* case seems to imply that instead of focusing on the literal appearance of the provisions, one should also give weight to the purpose for which the legislation is enacted and *its effects on individuals' rights*.

---

[177] Miettinen (2015), pp. 357–358.

[178] 2000/520/EC, Commission Decision of 26 July 2000 pursuant to Directive 95/46/EC of the European Parliament and of the Council on the adequacy of the protection provided by the safe harbour privacy principles and related frequently asked questions issued by the US Department of Commerce (notified under document number C(2000) 2441) (Text with EEA relevance.) [2000] OJ L 215, 25.8.2000, pp. 7–47.

[179] Directive 95/46/EC of the European Parliament and of the Council of 24 October 1995 on the protection of individuals with regard to the processing of personal data and on the free movement of such data [1995] OJ L 281, 23.11.1995, pp. 31–50.

[180] Case C-362/14 *Maximillian Schrems v Data Protection Commissioner* [2015]. For example, the Court stated that 'Decision 2000/520 lays down that 'national security, public interest, or law enforcement requirements' have primacy over the safe harbour principles, primacy pursuant to which self-certified United States organisations receiving personal data from the European Union are bound to disregard those principles without limitation where they conflict with those requirements and therefore prove incompatible with them' (para 86), and that '[i]n particular, legislation permitting the public authorities to have access on a generalised basis to the content of electronic communications must be regarded as compromising the essence of the fundamental right to respect for private life, as guaranteed by Article 7 of the Charter' (para 94).

4.4.5   Protected Interests: Transnational Dimension

4.4.5.1   The Manifesto on Legitimate Interests

Union-level criminal legislation ought to have a legitimate purpose, meaning that it should protect legal interests. EU-level criminal legislation should be used only when it is essential[181] in terms of subsidiarity, proportionality and *ultima ratio*-principles. If the Union-level protection of the legal interest does not bring extra value and the protection can be equally ensured at national level, the criterion of legitimate interest is not satisfied.

The Manifesto on European Criminal Policy declares that EU-level criminal legislation should only be enacted to protect fundamental interests if '(1) these interests can be derived from the primary legislation of the EU; (2) the constitutions of the Member States and the fundamental principles of the EU Charter are not violated, and (3) the activities in question could cause significant damage to society or individuals'.[182] The first criterion is essential in that if the protected interest could not be derived from EU primary law, the EU would not have competence to act on that matter. The second criterion seems to approach two of the EU criminalization principles described above, according to which the fundamental aspects of national (criminal) justice systems and fundamental rights ought to be respected. In order for the EU criminal legislation to be legitimate by its content, it should also respect the rights and freedoms as protected in the ECHR, to which all of the EU Member States are parties to. As was found already above, the EU Charter sets the maximum level of protection for fundamental rights in the EU, even if wider protection could be granted when evaluated from the ECHR rationale. According the third criterion, criminalization at EU-level ought to give protection against acts that are likely to cause actual harm. For example, symbolic or purely moral criminalization should not be enacted at EU-level. This is good guidance considering the multicultural context of EU criminal law.

According to the Manifesto, it is not sufficient to justify the use of EU-level criminal legislation by simply stating that it helps to enforce the objectives and policies of the EU.[183] This guideline is directed at the legislature which should provide justification for its legislative acts. In this sense the requirement of legitimate interests is also linked to the subsidiarity principle since EU-level criminal legislation always needs to bring some extra value compared with the protection at national level. This requirement also bears a deeper normative meaning. Criminal legislative measures should not be seen as merely instrumental, since they impose heavy restrictions on the rights of individuals.

---

[181] The Council of the European Union, Council Conclusions on model provisions, guiding the Council's criminal law deliberations, 2979th JUSTICE and HOME AFFAIRS Council meeting Brussels, 30 November 2009, 2.

[182] The European Criminal Policy Initiative (2011), p. 87.

[183] Ibid., pp. 87–88.

4.4.5.2   Principle of Assimilation and a General Commitment to Protect the EU-Level Interests

Actual law enforcement still remains in the competence of the Member States. The principles of sincere cooperation and assimilation govern both the transposition of EU legislation into national legislation and law enforcement. The principle of assimilation is derived from the principle of loyalty. The criminal law-specific contents of the assimilation principle were formulated in the so-called *Greek Maize* case.[184] The CJEU found that

> 23. It should be observed that where Community legislation does not specifically provide any penalty for an infringement or refers for that purpose to national laws, regulations and administrative provisions, *Article 5 of the Treaty requires the Member States to take all measures necessary to guarantee the application and effectiveness of Community law.*

> 24. For that purpose, whilst the choice of penalties remains within their discretion, they must ensure in particular that infringements of Community law are penalized under conditions, both procedural and substantive, which are analogous to those applicable to infringements of national law of a similar nature and importance and which, in any event, make the penalty effective, proportionate and dissuasive.[185] (emphasis added)

The *Greek Maize* case demonstrates that EU-level interests need protection equivalent to that of corresponding national interests. The situation has changed from the days when the *Greek Maize* judgment was given. Nowadays the Union has actual legislative competence even though it still does not have competence for criminal law enforcement. The principle of assimilation is not just about equivalent law enforcement, but it can be seen to represent a general engagement to protect the Union's interests and common legal interests at the EU-level.[186]

4.4.5.3   Common Legal Interests or Union's Interests?

John Vervaele has made a distinction between the proper legal interests of the Union, the common legal interests in the AFSJ (Article 83(1) TFEU), and the legal interests linked to the harmonisation of other Union policies (Article 83(2) TFEU). Vervaele counts the Union as having three proper legal interests: actions against (1) counterfeiting of the euro and (2) corruption of EU officials, and (3) protection of the financial interests of the Union.[187] It should be asked whether it makes any difference if the protected interest is counted as a common legal interest of the Member States (Article 83 TFEU) or if it is seen as a proper legal interest of the Union.

---

[184] Satzger (2012), p. 71; Melander (2008), pp. 378–379.

[185] Case C-68/88 *Commission of the European Communities v Hellenic Republic* [1989] ECR p. 2965, paras 23–24.

[186] Melander (2008), p. 379.

[187] Vervaele (2013), p. 69.

Intuitively, one could say that the EU could be seen to have more legitimacy to criminalize and approximate penal norms when protecting its own interests. However, when considered from the legal perspective of Article 83 TFEU, this can be questioned. As was explained above, the Member States meant to exhaust the Union's substantive criminal law competence to Article 83 TFEU. This Article is written in a restrictive way as regards criminal law. Its purpose seems to be to enhance the Member States' opportunities to tackle crime that affect their national interests also. From this perspective, EU criminal law is at its most legitimate when it fulfils the purpose of protecting interests that affect national interests directly or indirectly in the sense that they would primarily affect the Union's interest.

In this sense the interests of the Member States and the Union that can be protected by means of criminal law are the same. Already following the principle of assimilation the level of protection should not be different for national and the EU level interests.

4.4.6   European Criminalization Principles Can Be Derived from Article 83 TFEU

The European criminalization principles share a commonality: they can all be derived from EU primary law, and more precisely from the rationale enshrined in Article 83 TFEU. This suggests that Article 83 TFEU incorporates well criminal legislative reasoning within EU law. Article 83 TFEU embodies a traditional criminal law rationale that is rather static and restrictive in comparison to a dynamic rationale in general EU law.

We can see that the Union's criminal law competence as stated in Article 83 TFEU is shared competence by virtue of Article 4(2)j TFEU. As explained above, the use of shared competence is governed by principles of subsidiarity and proportionality, which in turn reflect the transnational dimension of the *ultima ratio* principle. In a transnational European context the *ultima ratio* principle requires that criminal law measures are taken at EU level only if the goals cannot be achieved as well at the domestic level.

Due to the special nature of criminal law, EU-level criminal law ought to respect the fundamental aspects of national criminal justice systems. This is an essential requirement for EU-level criminal law in order for it to effectively affect the behaviour of individuals. If EU-level criminal legislation were to undermine the essential aspects of national criminal justice systems, the basic core values and choices of the systems, EU criminal legislation would probably be seen as illegitimate and immoral in the eyes of the citizens. If EU-level criminalization did not follow a similar logic to what the citizens have been used to, there would be a real risk that the norms would not be efficiently followed. This claim could be based on the fact that people tend to assume that criminal legislation corresponds with their own personal views on what ought to be criminalized.[188] Following the same logic, it could be assumed that people also tend to evaluate issues relating to criminal liability from the criminal law perspective, and not from the EU law perspective. *This would suggest that EU-level criminal law that follows the criminal law rationale would presumably be more effective than EU-level criminal law following the dynamic rationale of general EU law.* Article 83(3) TFEU includes a mechanism (the emergency brake mechanism) that can ensure that the fundamental traditional national criminal law rationale is not being circumvented in EU criminal legislation. The principle is enshrined also in Article 67 TFEU.[189]

Criminalization principles that are enshrined in Article 83 TFEU are limitations that restrict the excessive use of transnational criminal law. They leave the Member States the power to decide on the fundamentals of their criminal justice systems which, in turn, are expressions of state sovereignty. In this sense, the EU criminalization principles and Article 83 TFEU support the logic in Beck's idea, according to which transnational cooperation limits state autonomy but not their sovereignty.[190]

As noted above, the transnational element of the principle of legality in the EU context requires that EU-level criminal legislation is enacted in the form of directives, meaning that the national criminal laws are not completely harmonized but are instead only approximated. Approximation means that national legislation is brought closer together without completely harmonising or unifying it.[191] Even though the difference between the two concepts is not completely clear within the EU legal framework and the terms are sometimes even used interchangeably, it seems that harmonisation refers to higher degree of integration than approximation, leaving less room for national discretion than approximation.[192] The principle of legality would thus require that criminal legislation is not enacted in the form of regulations at the EU-level. Article 83 TFEU also includes these criteria. The provision clearly states that the form of measures to be adopted are directives, and that only approximation measures are to be introduced.

Article 83 TFEU also requires fundamental rights protection by virtue of Article 67 TFEU which declares that the area of freedom, security and justice respects fundamental rights. Whether or not EU criminal law actually effectively protects fundamental rights, fundamental rights protection is nevertheless considered an essential element of EU criminal law.

EU criminal law should also protect legitimate interests. The so-called euro-crimes are listed in the first paragraph of Article 83 TFEU. The second paragraph also includes the possibility to use ancillary competence to protect interests in the

---

[188] Darley et al. (2001), p. 165.

[189] Article 67 TFEU states that "The Union shall constitute an area of freedom, security and justice with respect for fundamental rights and the different legal systems and traditions of the Member States".

[190] Beck (2002), pp. 39, 48–49.

[191] Miettinen (2015), pp. 103–104.

[192] Klip (2016), p. 35.

Union's other policy areas. Since the *ratio legis* of the Lisbon Treaty seems to have been to exhaust the Union's substantive criminal law competence to Article 83 TFEU, the said article also states what interests may legitimately be protected at the EU-level.

The EU has not explicitly expressed an intent to follow any particular set of principles that guide decision-making on substantive criminal legislation. Those Union's institutions that participate in the legislative process, the Council, the Commission and the Parliament, have all established their own approaches on EU criminal policy, documents which guide the legislative work within each institution.

The Council's model provisions[193] can be seen as the JHA Council's effort to influence future EU-level criminal legislation even though the new structure of Article 83(2) TFEU enables decision-making by formations of the Council other than the JHA Council. The Council's model provisions are also said to be influenced by the new legislative procedure, in which the Council shares legislative powers with the Parliament.[194] So far, only two legislative instruments have been issued using Article 83(2) TFEU, the directive on criminal sanctions for market abuse (market abuse directive, 2014/57/EU) and the directive on the fight against fraud to the Union's financial interests by means of criminal law (2017/1371). The Commission's proposals for these directives were examined by the Working Party on Substantive Criminal Law under the JHA Council.[195] The basic idea seems to be that criminal legislative proposals are still dealt in the preparatory bodies of the JHA Council.

The Commission gave its approach on EU criminal policy following the publication of the Council's model provisions.[196] The Commission focused mainly on substantive ancillary criminal law competence. It also described very broadly its view on the overall goal for the EU criminal policy. EU criminal law should 'foster citizens' confidence in the fact that they live in a Europe of freedom, security and justice' and that 'EU law protecting their interests is fully implemented and enforced'.[197] This implies that the Commission sees EU criminal law to be used as a means to effectively enforce other EU legislation, thus representing an effectiveness- and integration-oriented EU legislative rationale. The European Parliament's resolution on an EU approach on criminal law[198] is much inspired by the Manifesto

---

[193] The Council of the European Union, Council Conclusions on model provisions, guiding the Council's criminal law deliberations, 2979th JUSTICE and HOME AFFAIRS Council meeting Brussels, 30 November 2009.

[194] Weyembergh (in collaboration with Serge de Biolley) (2013a), p. 24.

[195] Council of the European Union, Interinstitutional File 2011/0295 (COD), 16512/12, Brussels, 30 November 2012, available in Internet http://db.eurocrim.org/db/en/doc/1838.pdf, accessed 25 June 2018, 1; Council of the European Union, Interinstitutional File 2012/0193 (COD), 10232/13, Brussels, 3 June 2013, available in the Internet http://db.eurocrim.org/db/en/doc/1909.pdf, accessed 25 June 2018, 1.

[196] COM(2011) 573 final, Towards an EU Criminal Policy: Ensuring the effective implementation of EU policies through criminal law, Brussels, 20 September 2011.

[197] COM(2011) 573 final, p. 2.

[198] European Parliament, Report on an EU approach on criminal law, A7-0144/2012, 24 April 2012.

on European Criminal Policy adopted by the European Criminal Law Initiative in 2009.[199]

As regards the elements that should limit the use of criminal law, the criminalization principles, there are several similarities between the EU criminal policy documents.[200] All of the documents mention the principles of subsidiarity, *ultima ratio* and legality but do not say much about them. As for the principle of legality, all of the documents find it important that criminal legislation is clearly defined. The Commission also finds that the principle of legality does not affect the work of the EU legislator since the national legislators need to transpose Union-level legislation into the national legal systems. All of the documents are also based on the understanding that criminal liability should only be based on the principle of guilt, meaning that only the intentional or seriously negligent conduct should result in criminal liability. The principle of harm, or the requirement of criminal provisions protecting legal interests, also appears in each of these documents.

The three EU criminal policy documents are peculiar in the sense that they do not say much about EU criminal policy. The purpose of the documents does not seem to be the construction of EU criminal policy, but rather the positioning of the Union's legislative institutions vis-à-vis each other in the legislative process,[201] and clarifying their own position in their internal legislative procedures.[202]

Still, general guidelines guiding all the three institutions remain unwritten. Since the Union institutions' criminal policy documents do not say much about the principles limiting the use of penal power, these principles need to be sought elsewhere. Bearing in mind that the EU has not declared to follow any particular set of restricting principles that would guide EU criminal legislation, it is important to note that Article 83 TFEU embodies the five European criminalization principles (1) the transnational dimension of ultima ratio principle, (2) the respect for fundamental aspects of national criminal justice systems, (3) the transnational dimension of the principle of legality, (4) the respect of fundamental rights, (5) the requirement of protected interests) which form a good basis for European criminal policy. These principles result from political discussion between the Member States and represent a common understanding on the limits of the use of substantive EU criminal law. Moreover, these principles are constitutional constraints in the sense that each of them can be found in EU primary law.

---

[199] The resolution was adopted in the European Parliament plenary with clear majority of votes: 537 MEP's votes in favor and only 38 against. It was drafted by rapporteur doctor Cornelis de Jong from his own request. See, de Jong (2013), p. 37; The Manifesto on European Criminal Policy was first published in internet https://sites.google.com/site/eucrimpol/manifest/manifesto and later in European Criminal Law Review (2011) 1(1) 86–103.

[200] The three documents are often considered as EU criminal policy documents. See, for example, Satzger (2012), pp. 82–83; de Hert and Wieczorek (2012), p. 394.

[201] Weyembergh (2013a), p. 224.

[202] European Parliament, Report on an EU approach on criminal law, A7-0144/2012, 24 April 2012, p. 10.

References

Alkema EA (2000) The European Convention as a constitution and its court as a constitutional court. In: Mahoney P, Matscher F, Petzold H, Wildhaber L (eds) Protection des droits de l'homme: la perspective européenne (Protecting human rights: the European perspective – studies in memory of Rolv Ryssdal). Carl Heymann

Arai-Takahashi Y (2002) The margin of appreciation doctrine and the principle of proportionality in the jurisprudence of the ECHR (Intersentia 2002)

Asp P (2012) The substantive criminal law competence of the EU (Stiftelsen Skrifter utgivna av Juridiska fakulteten vid Stockholms universitet). Jure

Avbelj M (2011) Supremacy or primacy of EU law – (why) does it matter? Eur Law J 17(6)

Beck U (2002) The terrorist threat: world risk society revisited. Theory Cult Soc 19(4)

Bering Liisberg J (2001) Does the EU charter of fundamental rights threaten the supremacy of community law? Common Mark Law Rev 38(5)

Brauch AJ (2005) The margin of appreciation and the jurisprudence of the European Court of Human Rights: threat to the rule of law. Columbia J Eur Law 11

Cooper I (2006) The watchdogs of subsidiarity: national parliaments and the logic of arguing in the EU. J Common Mark Stud 44(2):281

Craig P, de Búrca G (2015) EU law: text, cases, and materials, 6th edn. OUP

Darley JM, Carlsmith KM, Robinson PH (2001) The ex ante function of the criminal law. Law Soc Rev 35(1)

de Hert P, Wieczorek I (2012) Testing the principle of subsidiarity in EU criminal policy: the omitted exercise in the recent EU documents on principles for substantive European criminal law. New J Eur Crim Law 3(3–4)

de Jong C (2013) The European Parliament Resolution of 22 May 2012 on a EU approach to criminal law. In: Galli F, Weyembergh A (eds) Approximation of substantive criminal law in the EU: the way forward. Editions de l'Université de Bruxelles

de la Rasilla del Moral I (2006) The increasingly marginal appreciation of the margin-of-appreciation doctrine. German Law J 7(6)

Defeis E (2007–2008) Dual system of human rights: the European Union. ILSA J Int Comp Law 14(1)

Edward D (2012) Subsidiarity as a legal concept. In: Cardonnel P, Rosas A, Wahl N (eds) Constitutionalising the EU judicial system: essays in honour of Pernilla Lindh. Hart Publishing

Elholm T (2014) Legitimacy and EU criminal law regulation. In: Peršak N (ed) Legitimacy and trust in criminal law, policy and justice: norms, procedures, outcomes. Ashgate

Halberstam D (2012) Local, global and plural constitutionalism. In: de Búrca G, Weiler JHH (eds) The worlds of European constitutionalism. CUP

Herlin-Karnell E (2007) In the wake of Pupino: Advocaten voor de Wereld and Dell'Orto. German Law J 8(12)

Herlin-Karnell E (2010) What principles drive (or should drive) European criminal law? German Law J 11(10)

Herlin-Karnell E (2012) Is the citizen driving the EU's criminal law agenda? In: Spaventa, Shuibhne (eds) Empowerment and disempowerment of the European citizen. Hart Publishing

Huomo-Kettunen M (2013) Heterarchical constitutional structures in the European legal space. Eur J Leg Stud 6(1)

Huomo-Kettunen M (2014) EU criminal policy at a crossroads between effectiveness and traditional restraints for the use of criminal law. New J Eur Crim Law 5(3)

Husak D (2004) The criminal law as last resort. Oxf J Leg Stud 24(2)

Klip A (2016) European criminal law: an integrative approach, 3rd edn. Intersentia

Krisch N (2007) The open architechture of European human rights law, LSE law, society, and economy working papers 11/2007, London School of Economics and Political Science Law Department 15

Krisch N (2012) The case for pluralism in the postnational law. In: de Búrca G, Weiler JHH (eds) The worlds of European constitutionalism. CUP

Kumm M (2012) Rethinking constitutional authority: on the structure and limits of constitutional pluralism. In: Avbelj M, Komárek J (eds) Constitutional pluralism in the European Union and beyond. Hart Publishing

Łazowski A, Wessel RA (2016) When caveats turn into locks: opinion 2/13 on accession of the European Union to the ECHR. German Law J 16(1)

Lenaerts K, Van Nuffel P (2011) In: Robert B, Nathan C (eds) European Union law. Sweet & Maxwell

Maduro MP (2003) Europa and the constitution: what if this is as good as it gets? In: Weiler JHH, Wind M (eds) European constitutionalism beyond the state. CUP

Malathouni E (2008) Should I stay or should I go: the sunset clause as self-confidence or suicide? Maastricht J Eur Comp Law 15(1)

Maugeri AM (2013) Fundamental rights in the European legal order, both as a limit on punitive power and as a source of positive obligations to criminalise. New J Eur Crim Law 4(4)

Melander S (2008) Kriminalisointiteoria – rangaistavaksi säätämisen oikeudelliset rajoitukset. Suomalaisen lakimiesyhdistyksen julkaisuja

Melander S (2010) EU-rikosoikeus. WSOYpro

Melander S (2013) Ultima ratio in European criminal law. Oñati Socio-Leg Ser 3(1)

Melander S (2014) Effectiveness in EU criminal law and its effects on the general part of criminal law. New J Eur Crim Law 5(3)

Miettinen S (2015) The Europeanization of criminal law: competence and its control in the Lisbon era. University of Helsinki

Mowbray A (2005) The creativity of the European Court of Human Rights. Hum Rights Law Rev 5(1)

Nieminen L (2004) Eurooppalaistuva valtiosääntöoikeus – Valtiosääntöistyvä Eurooppa. Suomalaisen Lakimiesyhdistyksen Julkaisuja

Ouwerkerk Jannemieke W (2012) Criminalisation as a last resort: a national principle under the pressure of Europeanisation? New J Eur Crim Law 3(3–4)

Paunio E, Lindroos-Hovinheimo S (2010) Taking language seriously: an analysis of linguistic reasoning in EU law. Eur Law J 16(4)

Peers S (2016) The EU's accession to the ECHR: the dream becomes a nightmare. German Law J 16(1)

Peristeridou C (2015) The principle of leaglity in European criminal law. Intersentia

Preuss UK (2010) Disconnecting constitutions from statehood – is global constitutionalism a viable concept. In: Dobner P, Loughlin M (eds) The twilight of constitutionalism? OUP

Rosas A, Armati L (2010) EU constitutional law: an introduction. Hart Publishing

Roxin C (2006) Strafrecht Allgemeiner Teil – Band I, Grundlagen, Der Aufbau der Verbrechenslehre. Verlag C.H.Beck

Satzger H (2012) International and European criminal law. C.H.Beck

Scheeck L (2006) The relationship between the European courts and integration through human rights. Zeitschrift für ausländishes öffentliches Recht und Völkerrecht 65

Schütze R (2009a) From dual to cooperative federalism: the changing structure of European law. OUP

Schütze R (2009b) Subsidiarity after Lisbon: reinforcing the safeguards of federalism? Camb Law J 68(3)

Suominen A (2011) Perus- ja ihmisoikeusnäkökohtia Suomen kansainvälisessä yhteistyössä rikosasioissa. Defensor Legis 92(1)

Tulkens F (2011) The paradoxical relationship between criminal law and human rights. J Int Crim Justice 9

Tümay M (2008) The "margin of appreciation doctrine" developed by the case law of the European Court of Human Rights. Ankara Law Rev 5(2)

Vervaele JAE (2013) Harmonised union policies and the harmonization of substantive criminal law. In: Galli F, Weyembergh A (eds) Approximation of substantive criminal law in the EU: the way forward. Editions de l'Universite de Bruxelles

Weyembergh A (2013a) Approximation of substantive criminal law: the new institutional and decision-making framework and new types of interaction between EU actors. In: Galli F, Weyembergh A (eds) Approximation of substantive criminal law in the EU: the way forward. Serge de Biolley, Editions de l'Universite de Bruxelles

Weyembergh A (2013b) Conclusion: the way forward. In: Galli F, Weyembergh A (eds) Approximation of substantive criminal law in the EU: the way forward. Editions de l'Universite de Bruxelles

Weyembergh A (2017) Consequences of Brexit for European Union criminal law. New J Eur Crim Law 8(3)

Zuleeg M (2011) The advantages of the European constitution. In: von Bogdandy A, Bast J (eds) Principles of European constitutional law, 2nd edn. Hart Publishing

Chapter 5
Ideals Shaken by Realities

5.1 Opinion 2/13 on the Union's Accession to the ECHR

The approach adopted in the draft accession treaty is challenged by the CJEU in its recent Opinion 2/13 concerning the compatibility of the draft agreement with the EU's founding Treaties.[1] Opinion 2/13 differs from the previous Opinion 2/94 that also concerned the Union's accession to the ECHR in that the latter mentioned Opinion concerned only the issue whether the Community had the competence to conclude an agreement on accession to the ECHR. Because the negotiations had not been started and a draft accession agreement was not available for the CJEU to evaluate, the CJEU could not assess the compatibility of the possible accession agreement with the Treaty. Opinion 2/13 however specifically evaluates the compatibility of the draft agreement with the Treaties.[2] In the CJEU's opinion, even though the Union now has express competence to accede to the ECHR, there still are several constitutional obstacles due to which the draft agreement is not compatible with the EU primary law and thus, in practice, prevents the EU from acceding to the ECHR under the terms set in the draft agreement.

The CJEU has given the Opinion based on Article 218(11) TFEU. Article 218 TFEU lays down the procedure in which agreements between the Union and third

---

[1] Opinion 2/13 Opinion of the Court (Full Court) of 18 December 2014. (Opinion pursuant to Article 218(11) TFEU - Draft international agreement - Accession of the European Union to the European Convention for the Protection of Human Rights and Fundamental Freedoms - Compatibility of the draft agreement with the EU and FEU Treaties).

[2] Opinion 2/94 Opinion of the Court of 28 March 1996. Accession by the Community to the European Convention for the Protection of Human Rights and Fundamental Freedoms [1996] ECR I-1783; Opinion 2/13 Opinion of the Court (Full Court) of 18 December 2014. (Opinion pursuant to Article 218(11) TFEU - Draft international agreement - Accession of the European Union to the European Convention for the Protection of Human Rights and Fundamental Freedoms - Compatibility of the draft agreement with the EU and FEU Treaties).

© Springer International Publishing Switzerland and G. Giappichelli Editore 2020
M. Kettunen, *Legitimizing European Criminal Law*, Comparative, European and
International Criminal Justice 2, https://doi.org/10.1007/978-3-030-16174-3_5

countries or international organizations are negotiated. The possibility of asking for the Court's opinion aims to foresee and prevent 'complications which would result from legal disputes concerning the compatibility with the Treaties of international agreements binding upon the EU'.[3] Article 218(11) TFEU stipulates that '[a] Member State, the European Parliament, the Council or the Commission may obtain the opinion of the Court of Justice as to whether an agreement envisaged is compatible with the Treaties. *Where the opinion of the Court is adverse, the agreement envisaged may not enter into force unless it is amended or the Treaties are revised*' (emphasis added). Since the Court's opinion in the matter at hand is adverse, changes need to be made either to the draft accession treaty or to the EU Treaties.

5.1.1 Inter-Party Cases

As explained above in Sect. 4.1.2, Article 5 of the draft agreement would give the ECtHR the competence to investigate both Inter-State cases (that would after the accession be referred to as Inter-Party cases) and individual applications in which the Union would be a respondent party. The CJEU does not find the scenario where an EU Member State could make an application under Article 33 ECHR concerning an alleged violation by the EU concerning the compatibility of EU law with the Convention satisfactory for two constitutional reasons: the autonomy of EU law and the CJEU's own judicial competence (Article 344 TFEU, previously Article 292 EC, and Article 219 EEC).

On the autonomy of EU law, the CJEU found the draft agreement problematic relative to the principles of mutual trust and mutual recognition somewhat similarly as presented above in Sect. 4.1.2. The Court stated that

> [*i*]*n so far as the ECHR would, in requiring the EU and the Member States to be considered Contracting Parties* not only in their relations with Contracting Parties which are not Member States of the EU but also *in their relations with each other*, including where such relations are governed by EU law, *require a Member State to check that another Member State has observed fundamental rights, even though EU law imposes an obligation of mutual trust between those Member States*, accession is liable to upset the underlying balance of the EU and undermine the autonomy of EU law.[4] (emphasis added)

The draft agreement starts from the premise of equality of the Contracting Parties and makes no difference between the interrelationship of the Union to the EU Member States or to the other Contracting Parties. In the CJEU's opinion, this is

[3] Opinion 2/13 Opinion of the Court (Full Court) of 18 December 2014. (Opinion pursuant to Article 218(11) TFEU - Draft international agreement - Accession of the European Union to the European Convention for the Protection of Human Rights and Fundamental Freedoms - Compatibility of the draft agreement with the EU and FEU Treaties), para 145.

[4] Opinion 2/13 Opinion of the Court (Full Court) of 18 December 2014. (Opinion pursuant to Article 218(11) TFEU - Draft international agreement - Accession of the European Union to the European Convention for the Protection of Human Rights and Fundamental Freedoms - Compatibility of the draft agreement with the EU and FEU Treaties), para 194.

difficult to accept from the perspective of EU constitutional law, since then the ECtHR would be able to review the compatibility of EU law with human rights as the highest instance. The ECtHR's competence, as written in the draft agreement, would indicate that the scope of protection of fundamental rights in the EU would move towards more extensive protection since EU law would not be presumed to offer human rights protection equivalent to the Convention. Instead, EU law ought to be evaluated in terms of how it actually protects human rights. EU law could be reviewed by the ECtHR just like the law of any other Contracting Party. This could easily challenge the status of the principle of mutual recognition as the cornerstone of cooperation in criminal matters.

For example, the ECtHR might assess situations similar to those in the cases of *Advocaten voor De Wereld* or *Melloni* since the human rights protection-oriented paradigm differs from effectiveness-driven paradigm of EU law. The human rights-oriented paradigm might promote the protection of individual rights over interpretations that seem to protect the autonomy and primacy of EU law. The issue would concern the limits to the doctrine of margin of appreciation. Even though it is difficult to see for example the principle of mutual recognition as such infringing Convention rights, there should be leeway for courts to assess whether the application of that principle leads to an undesirable outcome in individual cases. Emphasis could thus be placed on individual-oriented perspectives instead of the system-oriented perspective of EU law. From this perspective the CJEU's argument as quoted above could be challenged. Even when the principle of mutual recognition is a cornerstone principle of the cooperation in criminal matters, it should not be an excuse for the Member States not to comply with the human rights obligations to which they are bound to.

In the context of human rights protection, the application of the principle of mutual trust means that the EU Member States must recognize the level of protection of fundamental rights in other Member States to be sufficient.[5] In the CJEU Opinion, human rights review is not compatible with the idea of mutual trust and therefore the ECtHR should not have competence to review cases that are concerned with the instruments of mutual recognition. However, following the draft agreement, instruments of mutual recognition could be reviewed by the ECtHR on the basis of their content. Just as the ECtHR cannot annul or revoke provisions of national law, it could not annul or revoke provisions of EU law. However, similarly to the state parties to the Convention, the EU would in order to prevent similar future violations also be obliged to amend its legislation or to interpret it in a human rights-friendly manner if it would otherwise be in violation of the Convention rights. From this perspective, there might be a need to adjust the doctrine of mutual recognition to ensure effective human rights protection. All the same, in its recent opinion, the CJEU does not consider the possibility of Inter-Party cases in conjunction of interpretation of EU law to be compatible with the autonomy of EU law.

The principle of equality of the Contracting Parties would seem to lessen the importance of the previously established *Bosphorus* case law. The explanatory

---

[5] Suominen (2011), pp. 37, 38–39.

report of the draft agreement explicitly states that the Convention control mechanism should as a main rule be applied to the EU the same way as it is applied to the other contracting parties.[6] However, in the CJEU's opinion, EU law such as the principles of mutual trust and recognition should be given priority over the substance of the Convention rights. This, in turn, would seem to contravene the very core of the Convention system.[7] In this sense, the Court's Opinion does not seem to respect the core idea of the Convention and its control mechanisms. Accession to the Convention with no intention to address the existing or future problems vis-à-vis the Convention does not achieve the objectives of the accession.

The possibility of Inter-Party cases concerning alleged human rights violations in conjunction with the EU law is also not, in the CJEU's opinion, compatible with Article 344 TFEU or Article 3 of Protocol No 8 to the Treaties (on the Union's accession to the ECHR).[8] Article 344 TFEU stipulates that 'Member States undertake not to submit a dispute concerning the interpretation or application of the Treaties to any method of settlement other than those provided for therein'. In turn, Article 3 of Protocol No 8 explicitly states that '[n]othing in the agreement referred to in Article 1 shall affect Article 344 of the Treaty on the Functioning of the European Union'. Article 344 TFEU excludes the possibility of the Member States to submit a dispute concerning EU primary law to any international court or tribunal.[9] This means that the interpretation and application of EU primary law ought to be left to the Union's institutions, namely to the CJEU.

5.1.2 Conflict of Jurisdictional Competence

The requirement set in Article 344 TFEU, according to which *'Member States undertake not to submit a dispute concerning the interpretation or application of the Treaties to any method of settlement other than those provided for therein'*, and the issue of the jurisdiction of the CJEU was already briefly mentioned in Opinion 2/94. However, due to the fact that there was no draft agreement at that time, the CJEU could not assess the question of compatibility of the agreement with the Treaties. Thus the CJEU did not state anything about the necessary future arrangements concerning the judicial control machinery.[10] Since the CJEU had brought up

---

[6]47+1(2013)008rev2, p. 17.

[7]Steve Peers, 'The CJEU and the EU's accession to the ECHR: a clear and present danger to human rights protection' (Blog, 'EU Law Analysis' available in internet http://eulawanalysis. blogspot.fi/2014/12/the-cjeu-and-eus-accession-to-echr.html, accessed 25 June 2018).

[8]Opinion 2/13 Opinion of the Court (Full Court) of 18 December 2014. Opinion pursuant to Article 218(11) TFEU - Draft international agreement - Accession of the European Union to the European Convention for the Protection of Human Rights and Fundamental Freedoms - Compatibility of the draft agreement with the EU and FEU Treaties, paras 203, 207, 208.

[9]Geert de Baere (2008), p. 177, fn 126.

[10]Opinion 2/94 Opinion of the Court of 28 March 1996. Accession by the Community to the European Convention for the Protection of Human Rights and Fundamental Freedoms [1996] ECR I-1783, paras 20–21.

Article 344 TFEU (the then Article 219 EEC) in its previous Opinion concerning the Union's accession to the Convention, it did not come as a surprise that the CJEU assessed the draft agreement in the light of Article 344 TFEU in its recent Opinion.

As noted above, the draft agreement would enable the ECtHR to review EU primary law.[11] The ECtHR could, however, only investigate whether EU law is compatible with the Convention, meaning that the ECtHR could not declare provisions of EU law invalid. In this sense, it is argued that exclusive jurisdiction and the interpretative autonomy of EU law would remain with the CJEU.[12] Still, the fact remains that the ECtHR's competence to evaluate EU primary law is in clear conflict with Article 344 TFEU. Even though a provision (Article 6(2) TEU) establishing EU competence to accede to the ECHR was included in the Lisbon Treaty, it seems that Article 344 TFEU should also be amended in order for the EU's accession to the Convention to become a viable option and at the same time respect the core idea of the Convention according to which the protection of human rights ought to be concrete and not illusory.

In the documents of Working Group II (Incorporation of the Charter/accession to the ECHR) of the European Convention, the Group stressed that the Convention was to decide only about issues of a constitutional nature. To the Group, this meant that they were to only consider whether to introduce a constitutional authorization for the Union to accede to the ECHR in the new Treaty. The actual drafting of the contents of the accession treaty and the concrete modalities of accession were considered to be a task of the Council. Issues other than the authorization for accession were not regarded to have constitutional nature. The Group also did not see the accession as problematic from the perspective of the autonomy of EU law. It was stated that 'it has emerged from the Group's discussions and expert hearings that the principle of autonomy does not place any legal obstacle to accession by the Union to the ECHR'. On the issue of jurisdictional competence between the ECtHR and the CJEU, the Group saw that the CJEU would remain the 'supreme arbiter of questions of Union law' and that its position would be similar to the position of national supreme or constitutional courts in relation to the ECtHR.[13] However, at that time, the main concern was not so much the interrelationship between the two courts, but rather that the Union's competence would not expand as a result of the accession.[14] This may explain why Article 344 TFEU is written in its current form in the Lisbon Treaty and why it does not enable granting the ECtHR the competence which it needs in order to efficiently review human rights protection within the Union.

Today, the problem addressed by the CJEU concerning the jurisdictional competences of the two European courts embodies a conflict between the collective will of

---

[11] 47+1(2013)008rev2, Article 5 of the draft accession treaty; Fondation Robert Schuman Policy Paper by Xavier Groussot, Tobias Lock and Laurent Pech (2011), p. 9.

[12] Fondation Robert Schuman Policy Paper by Xavier Groussot, Tobias Lock and Laurent Pech (2011), pp. 9–10.

[13] CONV 354/02, Final report of Working Group II, Brussels, 22 October 2002, 11–12.

[14] CONV 295/02, Summary of the meeting held on 17.09.02 chaired by Commissioner António VITORINO, Brussels, 26 September 2002, p. 2.

the Member States (the Masters of the Treaties) and the autonomy of EU law and its effectiveness-driven paradigm. It seems clear that the intention of the Member States has been to enable and carry out the Union's accession to the ECHR.[15] The Working Group II (Incorporation of the Charter/accession to the ECHR) wrote that

> the Group therefore recommends—that a legal basis should be inserted at an appropriate place in the Constitutional Treaty which would authorise the Union to accede to the ECHR. The drafting of such a legal basis could be kept fairly simple. Given the constitutional significance of possible accession, it should however also be specified that the signature and conclusion of the accession treaty require a decision by the Council by unanimity and the assent of the European Parliament; otherwise, the normal procedures for international agreements would apply.[16]

This quatation from the Working Group II implies that the accession to the ECHR was meant to be a political decision belonging to the pouvoir constituant of the Union, the Member States. The CJEU's opinion emphasising the autonomy of EU law and the jurisdictional competence of the Court itself complicates the realization of the will of the Masters of the Treaties, the *ratio legis*, to bring human rights control within the Union the same standing as it already is in the EU Member States.

The problem relating to jurisdictional competence also represents a conflict between politics and law. The main political arguments for the EU's accession to the ECHR are to establish coherence between the Union and the pan-European human rights system, to give the Union's citizens analogous human rights protection in the Union as they get from the Member States, and to ensure harmonious case law in human rights related issues between the two courts.[17] The CJEU's opinion seems to try to protect the Court's own powers as the highest interpreter of EU law in all circumstances. However, it seems difficult, almost impossible, to separate the interpretation of EU law from the interpretation of the Convention when ruling on whether EU law has violated the Convention rights.[18] Amending Article 344 TFEU could solve this particular conflict concerning the jurisdictional competence.

The draft agreement also stipulates the prior involvement of the CJEU as explained in Sect. 4.1.2. It clarifies in which circumstances the CJEU could review cases involving EU law before their review by the ECtHR. The main rule is that the applicant must exhaust only the remedies in the legal order of the main respondent, whether it is the EU or a EU Member State. If the EU were to be a co-respondent, the CJEU could review the case before the ECtHR reviews it. In these cases the

---

[15] For example, the Finnish government stated that adding the new Article 6(2) TEU meant that the basic Treaties no longer included obstacles for the Union's accession to the ECtHR (Government's proposal concerning the approval of the Lisbon Treaty, HE 23/2008 vp, Hallituksen esitys Eduskunnalle Euroopan unionista tehdyn sopimuksen ja Euroopan yhteisön perustamissopimuksen muuttamisesta tehdyn Lissabonin sopimuksen hyväksymisestä ja laiksi sen lainsäädännön alaan kuuluvien määräysten voimaansaattamisesta, p. 48).

[16] CONV 354/02, Final report of Working Group II, Brussels, 22 October 2002, p. 13.

[17] CONV 354/02, Final report of Working Group II, Brussels, 22 October 2002, pp. 11–12.

[18] Steve Peers, 'The CJEU and the EU's accession to the ECHR: a clear and present danger to human rights protection' (Blog, 'EU Law Analysis' available in internet http://eulawanalysis.blogspot.fi/2014/12/the-cjeu-and-eus-accession-to-echr.html, accessed 25 June 2018).

CJEU could review the *validity of EU secondary law* and *interpret EU primary law*. The CJEU could not review the case if the EU would not be at least a co-respondent.[19] The CJEU found these draft provisions incompatible with EU law because the CJEU could rule only on the validity of EU law, but not on the interpretation of secondary law.[20] In this sense also, the CJEU seems to want to protect its own powers. That, however, does not fit with idea of individual-oriented human rights protection that aims at actual, instead of illusory, rights protection.

5.1.3   Conclusions

The draft agreement would have imposed the same obligations on the Union as it does on State parties. Some changes would have been necessary when interpreting some Union instruments. For example, human rights violations could be seen as an excuse to not to surrender a person to another state based on an European arrest warrant because differences in national law (or regional transnational law) compared to the Convention are not acceptable excuses to not to comply with the Convention. The whole idea of the Convention is to bring coherence to the protection of the human rights in the European area. The Union's accession as described in the draft agreement would have enhanced this coherence.[21]

The CJEU's Opinion requires many changes, either in the provisions of the draft agreement or amendments to the EU Treaties. The CJEU's enthusiasm to keep its status as the ultimate institution to rule on EU law is evident in the Opinion.[22] Taking into account the wording that is used in Article 6(2) TEU, 'the Union *shall accede* to the ECHR', which stipulates mandatory action, and the inherent nature and purpose of the ECHR, the practical and effective realization of human rights, merely changing the provisions of the draft agreement does not seem to be the best option. If the changes would be made solely to the draft agreement, the EU's accession to the ECHR would not improve human rights protection within the EU but instead it would bless the problematic practices from the human rights perspective that occur in the Union.[23]

---

[19] 47+1(2013)008rev2, p. 27; CDDH(2011)009, 24–25. Fondation Robert Schuman Policy Paper by Xavier Groussot, Tobias Lock and Laurent Pech, 'EU Accession to the European Convention on Human Rights: a Legal Assessment of the Draft Accession Agreement of 14th October 2011', *European issues* no 218, 7th November 2011, pp. 14–15.

[20] Opinion 2/13 Opinion of the Court (Full Court) of 18 December 2014. Opinion pursuant to Article 218(11) TFEU - Draft international agreement - Accession of the European Union to the European Convention for the Protection of Human Rights and Fundamental Freedoms - Compatibility of the draft agreement with the EU and FEU Treaties, paras 242–243.

[21] 47+1(2013)008rev2, pp. 16–17; CDDH(2011)009, p. 16.

[22] About the CJEU as a political player, see, Leino (2003), p. 282.

[23] Steve Peers, 'The CJEU and the EU's accession to the ECHR: a clear and present danger to human rights protection' (Blog, 'EU Law Analysis' available in internet http://eulawanalysis.blogspot.fi/2014/12/the-cjeu-and-eus-accession-to-echr.html, accessed 25 June 2018).

The CJEU's apparent desire to be a hierarchically higher court than the ECtHR, and thus also for the EU legal system to be hierarchically higher than the ECHR regime, is troublesome from the perspective of internal state sovereignty. The member states are obliged to protect fundamental and human rights, and as sovereign states, they have chosen to adopt the principles of the ECHR regime. Thus the member states have within the meaning of their internal sovereignty, their power and responsibilities towards the citizens, chosen to protect the human rights of their citizens by following at least the minimum standards enshrined in the ECHR. Viewed from this perspective, the CJEU opinion according to which the ECtHR could not assess the compatibility of EU law with the Convention rights contravenes the sovereign choice made by the member states. In this sense, the CJEU's pursuit for a higher hierarchical status also contravenes with the Beck's idea on separating between sovereignty and autonomy,[24] since it does not accommodate the sovereign choice made by the member states as regards decision-making powers in the context of fundamental and human rights protection.

Constitutional amendments seem necessary in order to make the Union's accession to the ECHR compatible with the Convention's inherent purpose. For example Article 344 TFEU could be amended (as well as the second sentence of Article 6(2) TEU that states that 'the accession shall not affect the Union's competences as defined in the Treaties') to provide the ECtHR with necessary competence to review the Convention in conjunction with EU law in similar manner as it reviews the Convention in conjunction with national law.

However, one obstacle remains, the autonomy of EU law. Since the CJEU can, based on Article 267 TFEU, assess the Union's international agreements even after they have come into force, the CJEU could still find the accession to the ECHR, and in particular the competence of the ECtHR to review EU law, invalid solely based on the argument concerning the autonomy of EU law. This demonstrates the scope of the CJEU's powers to decide on a central constitutional issue and even to hold back, or permanently block, the constitutional development that is intended by the Member States in the role of the Masters of the Treaties and as the constitutional legislature. Here, it could be asked if the Court's new line of case law on the use of *travaux préparatoires* could resolve the problem. From that perspective the intent of the constitutional legislature ought to be used in a restrictive manner. In its Opinion, however, the CJEU finds the general principles of EU law equivalent to the Treaties, and has interpreted the issue of accession in line with effectiveness-riven ideals, ignoring the objective explicitly enshrined in Article 6(2) TEU.

The amendment of the Treaty provisions concerning the CJEU's competence, in a way that would give the ECtHR the power to assess EU law in an equal manner as it evaluates national law, does not seem a realistic solution to the problem. Nevertheless, this solution would respect the choice made by the member states concerning fundamental and human rights protection—their sovereign choice towards their citizens. In this sense, it would seem a normatively acceptable solution, a solution worth at least some consideration.

---

[24] Beck (2002), pp. 39, 48–49.

One could also argue that the amendment of the Treaty provisions concerning the CJEU's competence would detract the CJEU's competence to evaluate the Union's norms and decide on the limits of the fundamental and human rights protection in the Union. This should be left for the Union itself to decide. However, one could argue that giving the ECtHR the same jurisdiction to evaluate the compatibility of EU law with the Convention in individual cases as it has to evaluate the compatibility of national law with the Convention would only place EU law in the same position with the national law. It would be difficult to claim that the EU was meant to have more discretion in respect of human rights protection than the member states. After all, the member states have chosen to limit their decision-making autonomy as regards human rights by acceding to the ECHR. As the *pouvoir constituant*, as the constitutional legislature, they have also established the EU. Also in this role, they have decided to add an explicit provision to the EU Treaties according to which the EU shall accede to the ECHR.

If the CJEU were to genuinely pursue the same level of human rights protection as the ECHR, and which is accepted and applied by the member states, there would be no conflict. However, in Opinion 2/13 the CJEU takes the stand that for example instruments that are based on the principle of mutual recognition should be categorically evaluated as being in line with human rights standards. In other words, the CJEU does not seem to be inclined to open the possibility to evaluate the EU instruments based on the principle of mutual recognition in individual cases from the perspective of human rights protection. Viewed from this perspective, the CJEU does not seem willing to fully accommodate the ECHR regime under the current Treaty framework.

5.2 Choice of Legal Basis-Doctrine Versus European Criminalization Principles: Normative Problems Arising

5.2.1 Possible Implicit Legal Bases for Substantive Criminal Law Competence

As noted in Sect. 3.7.2, before the Lisbon Treaty entered into force the CJEU found that the Community had implied ancillary substantive criminal law competence, at least relative to environmental protection. In a more general context, the Court has stated that

> [i]t is clear from the case-law that the existence of an *implicit power*, which constitutes a derogation from the principle of allocation of powers stated in the first paragraph of Article 5 EC (the current Article 5 TEU), must be apprised interpreted (sic). It is only exceptionally that such powers are recognized by case-law and in order to be so recognized, *they must be necessary to ensure the practical effect of the provisions of the Treaty or the basic regulation at issue.*[25] (emphasis added)

---

[25] Case T-143/06 *MTZ Polyfilms Ltd v Council of the European Union* [2009] ECR p. II-4133, para 47. Similarly in Case T-240/04 *French Republic v Commission of the European Communities* [2007] ECR p. II-4035, para 37.

In a thorough academic study it has been argued that Article 83(2) TFEU was intended by the Member States to exhaust ancillary substantive criminal law competence.[26] The Council's legal service and some national governments have also drawn the same conclusion.[27] As is well known, ultimately only the CJEU can rule on this matter. This chapter examines which other articles of the basic Treaties could function as legal bases for substantive criminal legislation in addition to Article 83 TFEU. Six articles are examined: Article 325(4) TFEU on protecting the Union's financial interests, Article 33 TFEU on customs cooperation, Article 114 TFEU on functioning of the internal market, Article 352 TFEU the so-called flexibility clause, Article 86 TFEU on the establishment of the EPPO, and Article 336 TFEU concerning breach of official secrecy by the Union's officials.

5.2.1.1 Protection of the Union's Financial Interests

Fraud and related illegal activities affecting the Union's financial interests are seen to pose a serious problem to the detriment of the Union's budget and, indirectly, the taxpayers. Union level action was seen necessary, because the level of protection for these interests varied considerably amongst the legal systems of the Member States. According to the Commission, common definitions of offences will lead to *common practices* and *uniform interpretation* as well as to meeting the necessary *prosecution requirements*.[28] The directive on the fight against fraud to the Union's financial interests by means of criminal law[29] (later the Union fraud directive) includes definitions and criminalization obligations. Fraudulent behaviour, fraud-related conduct affecting the Union's financial interests and misappropriation by public officials are to be criminalized by the Member States. Incitement, aiding and abetting, and attempts are also to be criminalized and the liability of legal persons ought to be ensured. The Commission suggested fixed thresholds including both minimums and maximums to the penalty scales,[30] but the directive stipulates only minimum maximum penalties. The directive was based on Article 83(2) TFEU.

The proposal included a few peculiar elements that are interesting from the perspective of heterarchical constitutional structures. Firstly, the Commission had based the proposal on Article 325(4) TFEU on the protection of the Union's financial

---

[26] Miettinen (2013), pp. 194, 203–204.

[27] Opinion of the Council's Legal Service, 15309/12, paras 12–14; Government's proposal concerning the approval of the Lisbon Treaty, HE 23/2008 vp, Hallituksen esitys Eduskunnalle Euroopan unionista tehdyn sopimuksen ja Euroopan yhteisön perustamissopimuksen muuttamisesta tehdyn Lissabonin sopimuksen hyväksymisestä ja laiksi sen lainsäädännön alaan kuuluvien määräysten voimaansaattamisesta.

[28] COM(2012) 363 final, proposal for a directive on the fight against fraud to the Union's financial interests by means of criminal law, Brussels, 11 July 2012, 2–3.

[29] Directive (EU) 2017/1371 of the European Parliament and of the Council of 5 July 2017 on the fight against fraud to the Union's financial interests by means of criminal law, OJEU L 198/29, 28.7.2017.

[30] COM(2012) 363 final, 19.

interests instead of basing it on Article 83(2) TFEU. It is noteworthy that the opt-out/opt-in protocols of the United Kingdom, Ireland and Denmark relating to Article 83 TFEU do not apply to Article 325(4) TFEU.[31] Thus the geographical application of the directive would have led to wider application if it would have been based on Article 325(4) TFEU instead of Article 83(2) TFEU. Second, the Commission had considered an option to propose an instrument in the form of a regulation instead of a directive since Article 325(4) TFEU does not require directives to be used as the sole form of the legislation. Third, the establishment of the EPPO is closely connected to the Union fraud directive since the EPPO's competence is specifically related to the Union fraud directive.[32] If the Union fraud directive would have been based on Article 325(4) TFEU, the geographical application of the substantive and procedural instruments concerning the same issue would have differed. Last, the proposal set fixed penalty scales with both minimum and maximum penalties defined. Setting of minimum penalties would have been unorthodox when viewed in the light of the Declaration 8 of the Amsterdam Treaty and the wording of the Article 83 TFEU.

The legislative framework for the protection of the Union's financial interests is not new. In 1995 a Convention (henceforth the PIF Convention) was drawn up on the protection of the European Communities' financial interests[33] and later legislation on freezing and confiscation of crime-related proceeds, instrumentalities and property have been enacted.[34] The establishment of the EPPO relates closely to the protection of the Union's financial interests as explained above. Discussion on the establishment of a European public prosecutor's office started with the *Corpus Juris* academic study published in 1997 and founded by the Commission. The *Corpus Juris* comprises penal provisions concerning the protection of the Union's financial interests, the basis of criminal liability, general principles and sanctions, and prosecution.[35]

Corpus Juris was not welcomed by the Member States because they saw that it would have led to a loss of national sovereignty over criminal justice.[36] The Commission submitted a proposal on protection of the Community's financial

---

[31] European Commission, SWD(2012) 195 final, *Commission staff working paper Impact assessment (Part I)*, p. 26, fn 94.

[32] Council Regulation (EU) 2017/1939 of 12 October 2017 implementing enhanced cooperation on the establishment of the European Public Prosecutor's Office ('the EPPO') [2017] OJ L 283, 31.10.2017, pp. 1–71, Article 4.

[33] Convention drawn up on the basis of Article K.3 of the Treaty on European Union, on the protection of the European Communities' financial interests, 26 July 1995 (OJ C 316, 27.11.1995), pp. 49–57.

[34] Council Framework Decision 2005/212/JHA of 24 February 2005 on Confiscation of Crime-Related Proceeds, Instrumentalities and Property (OJ L 68, 15.3.2005), pp. 49–51; Directive 2014/42/EU of the European Parliament and of the Council of 3 April 2014 on the freezing and confiscation of instrumentalities and proceeds of crime in the European Union [2014] OJ L 127, 29.4.2014, pp. 39–50.

[35] *Sous la direction de Mireille Delmas-Marty* (1997).

[36] Mitsilegas (2009), pp. 229–230.

interest and the establishment of a European Prosecutor in 2001[37] without it leading to Community legislation. At that time the Council was in process of creating Eurojust.[38] Eurojust was established by Council Decision 2002/187/JHA in the aftermath of the USA 9/11 terrorist attacks.[39] Establishment of an EPPO was included in Article III-274 of the Treaty establishing a Constitution for Europe (later, TCE).[40] As is well known, the TCE did not come into force. Later, a provision on the establishment of the EPPO (Article 86 TFEU) was added by the Lisbon Treaty, inspired by Article III-274 of the proposed TCE. The Commission has submitted a proposal on the establishment of the European Public Prosecutors' Office in 2013.[41] In June 2017 twenty EU Member States found a political agreement on the establishment of the EPPO under enhanced cooperation.[42] Council's regulation on the establishemnt of the EPPO has entered into force at the end of 2017.[43]

The Commission based its proposal concerning the Union fraud on Article 325(4) TFEU according to which 'necessary measures in the fields of the prevention of and fight against fraud affecting the financial interests of the Union' can be taken using the ordinary legislative procedure. Article 325(4) TFEU is located in Part 6 of the TFEU, which contains institutional and financial provisions. The nature of the competence defined in Article 325(4) TFEU is not explicitly defined in Articles 2–6 TFEU. It is not exclusive competence because it is not listed in Article 3 TFEU. It is not supporting competence (Article 6 TFEU) either because Article 325(4) TFEU enables harmonisation measures. Thus the competence enshrined in Article 325(4) TFEU is shared competence by its nature. This conclusion is supported also by the fact that the listing of the fields of shared competence in Article 4 TFEU is not exhaustive[44] and that the Commission has considered the proposal from the perspective of subsidiarity.

Both Articles 325(4) TFEU and 83(2) TFEU stipulate that the ordinary legislative procedure is to be followed when legislative proposals are based on them. The procedures are however not identical. Thus the opportunity to base the legislation on

---

[37] COM(2001) 715 final, Green Paper on criminal-law protection of the financial interests of the Community and the establishment of a European Prosecutor, Brussels 11 December 2001.

[38] Mitsilegas (2009), pp. 229–231.

[39] The homepage of Eurojust – History of Eurojust http://eurojust.europa.eu/about/background/Pages/History.aspx, accessed 25 June 2018.

[40] OJ C310/121, 16 December 2004 http://eur-lex.europa.eu/LexUriServ/LexUriServ.do?uri=OJ:C :2004:310:FULL:EN:PDF, accessed 25 June 2018.

[41] COM(2013) 534 final, proposal for a regulation on the establishment of the European Public Prosecutor's Office, Brussels, 17 July 2013.

[42] European Commission, Press release, 'Commission welcomes decision of 20 Member States to establish the European Public Prosecutor's Office', Brussels, 8 June 2017.

[43] Council Regulation (EU) 2017/1939 of 12 October 2017 implementing enhanced cooperation on the establishment of the European Public Prosecutor's Office ('the EPPO') [2017] OJ L 283, 31.10.2017, pp. 1–71.

[44] Article 4(1) TFEU reads as follows: "The Union shall share competence with the Member States where the Treaties confer on it a competence which does not relate to the areas referred to in Articles 3 and 6".

both of the Articles does not seem to be an option. There are two differences between the procedures. First, the threshold for the subsidiarity control varies, and second the emergency brake procedure suspends the ordinary legislative procedure and requires unanimity in the European Council if a Member State considers that the draft proposal would affect fundamental aspects of its criminal justice system. The emergency brake procedure is a central constitutional element that enables flexible cooperation in the field of criminal law and ensures that the special characteristics of the national criminal justice systems are taken into account. After the Lisbon Treaty entered into force, the legislative procedure in the field of criminal law became less cumbersome since the ordinary legislative procedure replaced the previous unanimity requirement. If the emergency brake procedure is used, it requires political unanimity in the European Council, which adds legitimacy to the debated criminal legislation.

The emergency brake procedure expresses sensitivity in the close relationship between criminal law and national sovereignty. This close relation stems from the fact that criminal law limits the fundamental freedoms and is expressed in the state's right to punish[45] and use criminal sanctions. The emergency brake procedure expresses respect towards the national identities that as Article 4(2) TEU requires are inherent in their fundamental political and constitutional structures. The *ultima ratio* principle and the emergency brake procedure are also closely connected since the emergency brake procedure ensures the application of the 'federal' dimension of the *ultima ratio* principle, according to which the Union can act only in a field of shared competence if the goals cannot be reached by using national measures and the Union-level measures bring some added value. Thus Article 83 TFEU expresses a more flexible constitutional architecture in the interrelationship between the Union and the Member States than Article 325(4) TFEU. The heterarchical constitutional structure in the field of criminal law manifests in the emergency brake procedure.[46] The German Constitutional Court, the Budesverfassungsgericht (later the GCC), stated in its *Lisbon* judgment that the emergency brake procedure takes into account the special sensitive nature of criminal law as a reflection of legal ethical minimum standards.[47] The GCC seemed to respond to the Union's express ancillary competence in a reserved manner and it seems that it was easier for the GCC to accept it due to the emergency brake procedure enshrined in Article 83(3) TFEU.

According to Article 17 TEU, the Commission safeguards the Union's interests, whereas the Council and the European Council represent the interests of the Member States. From a political perspective, a legislative proposal is easier to get accepted if it is based on Article 325(4) TFEU than Article 83(2) TFEU. Firstly, more votes from the national Parliaments are needed for the basis of the reassessment of the legislative proposal in the subsidiarity control. Secondly, the emergency brake

---

[45] On the special nature of criminal law from the perspective of legitimacy, see for example Nuotio (2011), pp. 314–321.

[46] Huomo-Kettunen (2013), pp. 47, 64–65.

[47] BVerfG, 2 BvE 2/08 vom 30.6.2009, Absatz-Nr. (1-421), para 358. In English www.bverfg.de/entscheidungen/es20090630_2bve000208en.html, accessed 25 June 2018.

procedure does not apply in the framework of Article 325(4) TFEU. In addition, the geographical applicability would be wider under Article 325(4) TFEU, which would benefit the functioning of the internal market.

In the Commission's opinion, Article 325(4) TFEU would have been the appropriate legal basis at least for two reasons. In the Commission's opinion, Article 325 TFEU—and specifically the part stating that the measures taken in accordance with Article 325 TFEU 'act as deterrent'—should have been understood in a broad sense that would have given the EU the competence to give criminal legislation based on the article. To the Commission, the reference to deterrence implies that criminal deterrent effect is the aim of the provision.[48] The objective of *deterrent, effective and equivalent protection* for the Union's financial interests was seen by the Commission to imply a criminal law dimension since criminal law works as a disincentive for committing a crime and creates a risk of criminal conviction and social embarrassment.[49]

The Commission had also emphasized that Article 325(4) TFEU does not include the restriction clause that was included in the predecessor of Article 325(4) TFEU. Before the Lisbon Treaty modified Article 325 TFEU into its current form, the predecessor, Article 280(4) EC included a restriction clause according to which the measures protecting the Union's financial interest 'shall not concern the application of national criminal law or the national administration of justice'. The preparatory works suggest that the removal of that restriction clause was seen to be unnecessary as 'a result of the provisions concerning an area of freedom, security and justice'.[50] Moreover, as explained above in Sect. 3.7.3, the *travaux* show that Article 83(2) TFEU is intended to be used as the legal basis in the protection of the Union's financial interests.[51]

The Council found that the directive should be based on Article 83(2) TFEU.[52] As presented above, the Council's legal service found that the deletion of the restriction clauses '*should be read in conjunction with the insertion of the new legal basis in Article 83(2) TFEU* which was meant to tackle *all* cases where the EU legislature needs to harmonise the definition of criminal offences and sanctions in order to

---

[48] See for example COM(2012)363 final, p. 6, European Commission, SWD(2012) 195 final, *Commission staff working paper Impact assessment (Part I)*, p. 27.

[49] SWD(2012) 195 final, *Commission staff working paper Impact assessment (Part I)*, p. 27.

[50] CONV 821/03, *Reactions to draft text CONV 802/03 – Analysis*, Brussels, 27 June 2003, p. 161; Government's proposal concerning the approval of the Lisbon Treaty, HE 23/2008 vp, Hallituksen esitys Eduskunnalle Euroopan unionista tehdyn sopimuksen ja Euroopan yhteisön perustamissopimuksen muuttamisesta tehdyn Lissabonin sopimuksen hyväksymisestä ja laiksi sen lainsäädännön alaan kuuluvien määräysten voimaansaattamisesta, pp. 262 and 181. See also Miettinen (2013), p. 194.

[51] CONV 426/02, WG X 14, Final report of Working Group X "Freedom, Security and Justice", Brussels, 2.12.2002, p. 9.

[52] The Council of European Union, Council document 10729/13, Interinstitutional File 2012/0193 (COD), *Proposal for a Directive of the European Parliament and of the Council on the fight against fraud to the Union's financial interests by means of criminal law – GENERAL APPROACH*, Brussels, 10.6.2013, p. 2.

make other (non-criminal law) EU harmonized measures more effective'.[53] (emphasis added).

The Council's legal service (CLS) also took into account the special position of the UK, Ireland and Denmark[54] in the area of freedom, security and justice and its influence on the geographical applicability of the proposed legislative act. Legislation based on Article 325(4) TFEU would have been geographically more widely applicable since the opt-out Protocols Nos 21 and 22 of the Lisbon Treaty do not apply to Article 325 TFEU.[55] This would mean that if Article 325(4) TFEU would have been used as the legal basis, the UK, Ireland and Denmark would have automatically been included. By contrast, according to the opt-in protocol of the UK and Ireland they can notify that they wish to take part in the adaption and application of any proposed criminal measures within three months after the proposal has been presented to the Council. According to the opt-out protocol of Denmark it has specifically chosen not to take part into the criminal law cooperation at the Union level. The CLS noted that the UK, Ireland and Denmark are already bound by the 1995 PIF Convention. If the UK and Ireland would decide to participate in the adoption of the proposed instrument, the directive would bind them. Denmark does not have this option but the PIF Convention would still bind it.[56] Nevertheless, the geographical applicability of the *directive* would have been wider if it had been based on Article 325(4) TFEU.

Here, it is worth mentioning that the establishment of the EPPO is based on Article 86 TFEU relative to which the UK, Ireland and Denmark have more limited position than other EU Member States, as explained above. The prosecutors of the EPPO will have competence to act in relation to the offences directed against the Union's financial interests defined *in the directive*. Thus it would have been peculiar that the legislative measures on the protection of the Union's financial interests on one hand and the establishment of the EPPO on the other would have had divergent geographical applications merely because of the choice of legal bases. It is coherent that the substantive and procedural Union level legislation on the protection of the Union's financial interests are applied in the same geographical area. Twenty EU member states are participating to the enhanced cooperation to establish the EPPO. The UK, Ireland and Denmark are not participants to the enhaced cooperation at this time. Even though the EPPO regulation does not cover all EU member states, the difference of the geographical application of the EPPO regulation and the Union fraud directive is not due to a decision concerning the choice of legal basis.

According to the opinion of the CLS and the Committee of Legal Affairs of the European Parliament, basing the legislative act on Article 325(4) TFEU would have

---

[53] Opinion of the Council's Legal Service, 15309/12, paras 12–14.

[54] Protocol (No 21) on the position of the United Kingdom and Ireland in respect of the area of freedom, security and justice [2012] OJ C326/295, Protocol (No 22) on the position of Denmark [2012] OJ C326/299.

[55] European Commission, SWD(2012) 195 final, *Commission staff working paper Impact assessment (Part I)*, p. 26, fn 94.

[56] Opinion of the Council's Legal Service, 15309/12, paras 22–24.

resulted in circumventing the emergency brake procedure which is established in the Treaties to work as a protective mechanism for the fundamental aspects of national criminal justice systems. The express ancillary criminal law competence enshrined in Article 83(2) TFEU is seen as *lex specialis* that is intended to be used for all approximation measures of criminal law that do not fall under Article 83(1) TFEU.[57] For that matter, since the CLS finds that the Union's ancillary criminal law competence is exhausted in Article 83 TFEU, basing criminal legislation on any other legal basis would result to circumventing the emergency brake procedure in its opinion. The idea of intentionally circumventing the possibility to use the emergency brake procedure resembles, even though only remotely, the general principle of EU law on the prohibition of abuse of law. Circumventing the possibility to use the emergency brake procedure does not as such fall under the scope of this principle because the prohibition of abuse of law is a doctrine that applies to individuals. The principle provides that '[i]ndividuals must not improperly or fraudulently take advantage of provisions of Community law'.[58] There are at least two contexts in which the notion of abuse has been analysed by the Court: 'First, when Community law provisions are abusively invoked in order to evade national law. Second, when Community law provisions are abusively relied upon in order to gain advantages in a manner that conflicts with the purposes and aims of those same provisions'.[59]

Even though as a starting point the principle of abuse of Union law does not apply to the actions of the Union's institutions, an analogous line of thinking could be applied to the choice of legal basis. Similarly, if a Union institution would try to circumvent provisions of EU primary law, the situation could be evaluated from the perspective of the principle of sincere cooperation. When the choice of legal basis would be analysed from this perspective, also the *intent* of the Masters of the Treaties and the *ratio legis* of the Treaty provisions should be relevant factors in the process of choosing the legal basis.

According to the doctrine on the choice of legal basis, *the more specific provision ought to be used* as the legal basis when there are two or more legal bases to choose from.[60] It is essential to establish *to which policy field the aim and content of the*

---

[57] Opinion of the Council's Legal Service, 15309/12, para 18; Opinion of the Committee of Legal Affairs of the European Parliament on the Legal Basis for the proposal for a Directive of the European Parliament and of the Council on the fight against fraud to the Union's financial interests by means of criminal law (COM(2012)0363, available in internet www.europarl.europa.eu/sides/getDoc.do?pubRef=-//EP//TEXT+REPORT+A7-2014-0251+0+DOC+XML+V0//EN#top.

[58] Case C-321/05 *Hans Markus Kofoed v Skatteministeriet* [2007] ECR p. I-5795, para 38.

[59] Case C-255/02 *Halifax plc, Leeds Permanent Development Services Ltd and County Wide Property Investments Ltd v Commissioners of Customs & Excise, Case C-419/02 BUPA Hospitals Ltd and Goldsborough Developments Ltd v Commissioners of Customs & Excise, Case C-223/03 University of Huddersfield Higher Education Corporation v Commissioners of Customs & Excise* [2006] ECR p. I-1609, Joined opinion of AG Poiares Maduro, para 63. See also Vogenauer (2011), p. 526.

[60] Case C-490/10 *European Parliament v Council of the European Union* [2012], para 44. See also Miettinen (2013), pp. 194, 206–209.

proposal is necessary.[61] It seems obvious that the proposal on the protection of the Union's financial interests is necessary to protect the Union's financial interests. However, as stated already above, criminal law is peculiar in the sense that even though criminalization always has criminal law natured preventive goals, the principle of protected interests criminal legislation is usually also connected to other branches of law and areas of life. Criminalizations that penalize conduct that is wrong as such (crimes *mala in se*, such as murder, torture, rape, or child sexual abuse) are clearly issues of criminal law. Since ancillary substantive criminal law competence covers all fields of EU policies which have been subject to harmonization, if it would be considered that the aim and content are inseparable from the non-criminal law substantive legislation and that the criminal law measures would be necessary in order to effectively fulfil those non-criminal law policies, what content or field of application would be left for Article 83(2) TFEU? Also, as explained above, the Member States have intended Article 83(2) TFEU to exhaust the Union's criminal law competence. When the aim and content of the Union fraud directive is examined, it seems that the aim of ensuring the effective protection of the Union's financial interests could be seen as either a non-criminal law substantive aim or a criminal law aim, but the content falls entirely under criminal law since all of the provisions fall under criminal law. Also from this perspective Article 83(2) TFEU is the appropriate legal basis.

Academic literature had not found an answer to the question of which Article, 325(4) TFEU or 83(2) TFEU, would have be appropriate legal basis for the directive. It had even been asked whether either of the Articles could form a legal basis on its own.[62] The directive was based on Article 83(2) TFEU. If the Commission does not bring an action for annulment, a *political* assumption could be made on the appropriate legal basis. However, only the CJEU can give a conclusive ruling on the *legal* appropriateness of the legal basis in this particular matter. But then again, from a *normative* perspective, the CJEU's conclusions may not always present the most desirable outcomes.

The argument according to which the simplest and most consistent interpretation would be to limit the Union's substantive criminal law competence to Article 83 TFEU[63] is a straightforward solution to the problem. It is supported also by the doctrine on the choice of legal basis in terms of the content of the proposal and by the historical-teleological interpretation doctrine utilizing the *travaux* of the Treaties. These suggest that Article 83(2) TFEU is the appropriate legal basis in the protection of the Union's financial interests or counterfeiting of the euro.[64] Because criminal law aim-setting often simultaneously covers issues related to other policy-fields,[65]

---

[61] Case C-490/10 *European Parliament v Council of the European Union* [2012], para 68.

[62] Mitsilegas (2009), pp. 108–109.

[63] Asp (2012), p. 153.

[64] CONV 614/03, Brussels, 14 March 2003, p. 26; CONV 426/02, WG X 14, Final report of Working Group X "Freedom, Security and Justice", Brussels, 2.12.2002, p. 9; Miettinen (2013), pp. 194, 201.

[65] As the wording and structure of Article 83(2) TFEU also expresses in the requirement that non-criminal Union-level measures need to have been taken before enacting criminal legislation.

Article 83(2) TFEU seems to be the appropriate legal basis also in terms of *aim* of the directive.

5.2.1.2 Customs Cooperation

Another article that has been suggested as a candidate for the Union's implied ancillary substantive criminal law competence is Article 33 TFEU (pre-Lisbon 135 EC) on customs cooperation. Its legislative history is similar with Article 325(4) TFEU (pre-Lisbon 280(4) EC) since during the preparation process of the Constitutional Treaty and the Lisbon Treaty the restriction clauses that were included in Articles 280(4) and 135 EC were deleted from both of the new amended articles. Article 33 reads as follows:

> Within the scope of application of the Treaties, the European Parliament and the Council, acting in accordance with the ordinary legislative procedure, shall take measures in order to strengthen customs cooperation between Member States and between the latter and the Commission.

Before the Lisbon Treaty entered into force, Article 135 EC included a restriction clause that read: '[t]hese measures shall not concern the application of national criminal law or the national administration of justice'. The nature of the Union's competence in the field of customs cooperation is shared competence, since it is not listed in the exhaustive list of Union's exclusive competence in Article 3 TFEU and because Article 33 enables harmonization measures, which means that it is not a supporting competence.[66] In its Opinion concerning the choice of legal basis of the directive proposal on the fight against fraud to the Union's financial interests by means of criminal law, the Council's legal service has explicitly stated that Article 33 TFEU ought not to be used as a legal basis for criminal legislation—just as it found also in relation to Article 325(4) TFEU.[67] The Convention's preparatory documents also show that the limitation clause was deleted from the provisions concerning the customs cooperation as 'a result of the provisions concerning an area of freedom, security and justice'.[68] Some national governments were of the belief that the limitation clause was removed as unnecessary due to the new express provisions on Union's criminal law competence.[69]

---

[66] On the nature of Article 33 TFEU as shared competence, see also European Commission, C(2014) 7078 final, Brussels, 2 October 2014, available in internet http://ec.europa.eu/dgs/secretariat_general/relations/relations_other/npo/docs/denmark/2013/com20130884/com20130884_folketing_reply_en.pdf, accessed 25 June 2018.

[67] Opinion of the Council's Legal Service, 15309/12, paras 12–14.

[68] CONV 821/03, Brussels, 27 June 2003, 161; Miettinen (2013), pp. 194, 204.

[69] See, for example, Government's proposal (Finland) concerning the approval of the Lisbon Treaty, HE 23/2008 vp, Hallituksen esitys Eduskunnalle Euroopan unionista tehdyn sopimuksen ja Euroopan yhteisön perustamissopimuksen muuttamisesta tehdyn Lissabonin sopimuksen hyväksymisestä ja laiksi sen lainsäädännön alaan kuuluvien määräysten voimaansaattamisesta, 181 II.

Some literature argues that Article 33 could not be used as a legal basis for criminal legislation due to the wording of the article[70] which makes no references to any types of criminal conduct, deterrent effect or use of criminal measures. Some argue that there is no certainty whether Articles 325(4) TFEU or 33 TFEU could be used as a legal bases for criminal legislation without simultaneous recourse to Article 83(2) TFEU.[71]

Customs legislation concerning the trade of goods between the customs territory of the Union and third countries has been harmonised since 1992, during which time Community Customs Code[72] was enacted. Later, the Customs Code had been recast and replaced by new Customs Codes in 2008 (Modernised Customs Code)[73] and in 2013 (Union Customs Code).[74] Now, the intention is to support and strengthen this customs legislation by rules concerning its enforcement.[75] The Commission decided to propose a legislative measure on the approximation of the types of customs infringements and non-criminal sanctions and originally chose to base the proposal on Article 33 TFEU. The Member States' customs legislation varies a lot and as a result, this is seen to make the effective management of the customs union more difficult. The new customs sanction legislation aims at equal treatment between economic operators within the EU and the internal market.[76]

During the subsidiarity procedure, the Swedish Parliament issued a reasoned opinion and contested the Commission's choice of legal basis (Article 33 TFEU). On 5th June 2014 the Commission changed its proposal which no longer claims that the Union would have exclusive competence in this area.[77] The modified proposal requires that Member States set at least a certain level of administrative sanctions in order to ensure a minimum level of sanctions throughout the Union.[78] The contents

---

[70] Asp (2012), p. 161; Melander (2010), pp. 71–72.

[71] Mitsilegas (2009), p. 109.

[72] The Community Customs Code, established by Council Regulation (EEC) 2913/92 of 12 October 1992 and applied from 1 January 1994, in OJ L 302, 19.10.1992, p. 1 http://eur-lex.europa.eu/LexUriServ/LexUriServ.do?uri=CONSLEG:1992R2913:20070101:EN:PDF.

[73] Regulation (EC) No 450/2008 of the European Parliament and of the Council of 23 April 2008 laying down the Community Customs Code (Modernised Customs Code) [2008] OJ L 145, 4.6.2008, p. 1.

[74] Regulation (EU) No 952/2013 of the European Parliament and of the Council of 9 October 2013 laying down the Union Customs Code [2013] OJ L 269, 10.10.2013, p. 1 (corrigendum in OJ L 287, 29.10.2013, p. 90). It entered into force on 30.10.2013 and repealed the Regulation (EC) No 450/2008 of the European Parliament and of the Council of 23 April 2008 laying down the Community Customs Code (Modernised Customs Code) [2008] OJ L 145, 4.6.2008, p. 1.

[75] COM(2013) 884 final, Proposal for a Directive of the European Parliament and of the Council on the Union legal framework for customs infringements and sanctions, Brussels, 13 December 2013, pp. 4–6.

[76] COM(2013) 884 final, pp. 2–6.

[77] European Parliament, Customs infringements and sanctions: Briefing: Initial Appraisal of a European Commission Impact Assessment https://www.eesc.europa.eu/sites/default/files/resources/docs/customs-infringements-and-sanctions-ep-briefing-july-2014.pdf, accessed 25 June 2018, p. 5.

[78] COM(2013) 884 final/4, 2013/0432 (COD), Proposal for a Directive of the European Parliament and of the Council on the Union legal framework for customs infringements and sanctions, p. 7.

of the customs sanctions proposal is described as civil law in nature since the directive only sets an obligation to impose non-criminal sanctions of a certain level. Member States can naturally still choose to use criminal sanctions instead.[79] The Commission has stated that if EU-level criminal legislative action would prove necessary in this field, Article 83(2) TFEU would be appropriate legal basis for that purpose.[80]

However, when the proposal is examined as a whole, it appears rather criminal law-oriented. Infringements based on strict liability (Article 3), negligence (Article 4), and intention (Article 5) are listed. Articles 9–11 approximate the amounts of fines in which acts listed in articles 3–5 should result. Article 12 lists circumstances that ought to be taken into consideration by competent authorities when imposing the sanctions. The fact that certain circumstances, such as previous similar infringements, should be taken into account by the authority that imposes the sanction has more a criminal law than an administrative connotation. Also, Article 13 sets limitation periods, Article 6 regulates incitement, aiding, abetting, and attempt, and Article 8 is about the liability of legal persons.

Considering that 16 out of 24 Member States provide both criminal and administrative sanctions, and that the rest of the Member States (8 out of 24) only have criminal sanctions,[81] it seems that the directive would actually *also* approximate criminal legislation and sanctions in those Member States which provide both criminal and administrative sanctions, or approximate *only* criminal legislation and sanctions in those Member States which provide only criminal sanctions in their customs sanctioning systems. From this perspective, it seems that the directive proposal has criminal law oriented aim, and it certainly has criminal law contents. In this light, Article 83(2) TFEU would seem more appropriate legal basis for the legislation, or alternatively, the measure could be based on both articles, 33 and 83(2) TFEU.

The same problems as those involved with Article 325(4) TFEU would occur if Article 33 were to be used as a legal basis for criminal legislation. These issues are the applicability of the emergency brake procedure, the issue of the special position of the UK, Ireland and Denmark and the geographical application of the measure, the question of the form of the measure (directive or regulation), and the possibility to impose sanctions with fixed minimum and maximum scales. Thus what has been presented above about the thresholds on subsidiarity control, the emergency brake procedure and geographical applicability, and what will be presented below about the choice of form of the legislative measure and imposing fixed penalty scales in relation to the choice of legal basis between Article 325(4) TFEU and Article 83(2)

---

[79] COM(2013) 884 final/4, 2013/0432 (COD), p. 7.

[80] SWD(2013) 513 final Commission Staff working document executive summary of the impact assessment Accompanying the document Proposal Proposal for a Directive of the European Parliament and of the Council on the Union legal framework for customs infringements and sanctions, Brussels, 13 December 2013, p. 3; see also, Miettinen (2015), p. 486.

[81] COM(2013) 884 final/4, 2013/0432 (COD), p. 2.

TFEU applies *mutatis mutandis* to the choice between Article 33 TFEU and Article 83(2) TFEU.

5.2.1.3 Functioning of the Internal Market

Article 114 TFEU (pre-Lisbon 95 EC) concerning the functioning of the internal market is sought as a possible legal basis for criminal provisions on financial crime.[82] Article 114(1) TFEU reads as follows:

> Save where otherwise provided in the Treaties, the following provisions shall apply for the achievement of the objectives set out in Article 26. The European Parliament and the Council shall, acting in accordance with the ordinary legislative procedure and after consulting the Economic and Social Committee, *adopt the measures for the approximation* of the provisions laid down by law, regulation or administrative action in Member States which have as their *object the establishment and functioning of the internal market.* (emphasis added)

The CJEU has found that in order to use Article 114 TFEU as the legal basis, the legislation in question needs to remove obstacles to trade or distortions to competition.[83] The appreciable distortion of competition can be a result of differences in national laws or due to the fact that national legislation is not harmonized.[84] The existence of an obstacle to trade is evidently considered to distort competition. Article 114 TFEU can also be used to prevent the emergence of future obstacles to trade.[85] However, the object of the legal instrument genuinely has to be the establishment or functioning of the internal market. A 'mere finding of disparities between national rules and of the abstract risk of obstacles' to the trade or competition is not sufficient for using Article 114 TFEU as the legal basis to the legislative measure.[86]

Before the Lisbon Treaty entered into force, the scope of Article 114 TFEU (the then 95 EC) could have been broader because of ex-Article 47 EU. Nothing in the application of the EU Treaty was to affect the application of the EC Treaty. Now that the Lisbon Treaty is in force, ex-Article 47 EU does not apply to criminal law-related matters. As presented above in Sect. 3.7.3, in the post-Lisbon era, the market abuse legislation (MAR, MAD) was about the Union's competence to enact criminal legislation that affected the functioning of the internal market. Two legislative

---

[82] Herlin-Karnell (2012), pp. 105–109; Melander (2012), pp. 509, 516–517, 527.

[83] Case C-491/01 *The Queen v Secretary of State for Health, ex parte British American Tobacco (Investments) Ltd and Imperial Tobacco Ltd* [2002] ECR p. I-11453, para 43; Case C-300/89 *Commission of the European Communities v Council of the European Communities* [1991] ECR p. I-2867, para 13; Herlin-Karnell (2012), p. 89 onwards.

[84] Case C-300/89 *Commission of the European Communities v Council of the European Communities* [1991] ECR p. I-2867, para 23.

[85] Case C-491/01 *The Queen v Secretary of State for Health, ex parte British American Tobacco (Investments) Ltd and Imperial Tobacco Ltd* [2002] ECR p. I-11453, para 61.

[86] Case C-376/98 *Federal Republic of Germany v European Parliament and Council of the European Union* [2000] ECR p. I-8419, para 84.

acts for the prohibition of insider dealing and market manipulation were enacted: a regulation containing non-criminal law provisions based on Article 114 TFEU and a directive containing criminal law provisions based on Article 83(2) TFEU. At this point, the Commission has not brought an action for annulment based on the claim that the directive would be based on an incorrect legal basis. Dividing market abuse legislation into two legislative acts seems appropriate based on the Court's case law presented above in this subchapter.

5.2.1.4   The So-called Flexibility Clause

Article 352 TFEU (ex-308 EC, ex-235 EC) constitutes a special type of Union competence since the scope of its application is rather broad. This is why it is often called as the flexibility clause. It states that

1. If action by the Union should prove necessary, *within the framework of the policies defined in the Treaties,* to attain one of the objectives set out in the Treaties, and *the Treaties have not provided the necessary powers,* the Council, acting unanimously on a proposal from the Commission and after obtaining the consent of the European Parliament, shall adopt the appropriate measures. Where the measures in question are adopted by the Council in accordance with a special legislative procedure, it shall also act unanimously on a proposal from the Commission and after obtaining the consent of the European Parliament.
2. Using the procedure for monitoring the subsidiarity principle referred to in Article 5(3) of the Treaty on European Union, the Commission shall draw national Parliaments' attention to proposals based on this Article.
3. Measures based on this Article shall not entail harmonisation of Member States' laws or regulations in cases where the Treaties exclude such harmonisation.
4. This Article cannot serve as a basis for attaining objectives pertaining to the common foreign and security policy and any acts adopted pursuant to this Article shall respect the limits set out in Article 40, second paragraph, of the Treaty on European Union. (emphasis added)

Article 352 TFEU is exceptional in terms of the principle of conferral.[87] The predecessors of Article 352 TFEU (ex-Article 235 EC and later ex-308 EC) had been used rather loosely.[88] In its so-called Maastricht judgment, the German Constitutional Court even referred to it as a 'competence to round-off the Treaty'. The GCC demanded that in the future the principle of conferral ought to be respected and that Article 235 EC should not be used in such a way that would be 'equivalent to an extension of the Treaty'.[89] Still, in its current form, the article can be used as a legal basis in almost any field of EU law, except for in the common foreign and

---

[87] BVerfG, 2 BvE 2/08 vom 30.6.2009, Absatz-Nr. (1-421), para 326. Available In English www.bverfg.de/entscheidungen/es20090630_2bve000208en.html, accessed 25 June 2018.

[88] BVerfGE 89, 155, the so-called Maastrich Judgment, translated into English, available in internet www.proyectos.cchs.csic.es/euroconstitution/library/Brunner_Sentence.pdf, accessed 25 June 2018, para 99; Schütze (2009a), p. 134.

[89] BVerfGE 89, 155, the so-called Maastrich Judgment, translated into English, available in internet www.proyectos.cchs.csic.es/euroconstitution/library/Brunner_Sentence.pdf, accessed 25 June 2018, para 99.

security policy. It cannot, however, be used as a legal basis in areas where the Treaties have explicitly excluded such competence.

Article 352 TFEU was seen as necessary after the Lisbon Treaty to secure the existence of a flexible legal basis in the case of unexpected developments,[90] even though the new Treaty included new specific legal bases covering the policy areas where Article 308 EC had previously been used.[91] The *travaux* concerning the substantive criminal law competence do not exclude the possibility of using ex-308 EC (the current 352 TFEU) as a legal basis for "emergency action".[92]

However, many Member States were worried about the so-called competence creep, that the article could be used to expand the Union's competences and challenge the principle of allocated powers.[93] Referring to Opinion 2/94, the Working Group outlined that Article 352 TFEU 'cannot serve as a basis for widening the scope of [Union] powers beyond the general framework created by the provisions of the Treaty as a whole'.[94] Currently, Declaration No 42 states this explicitly.[95]

We can see from the Article, where it says that '*the Treaties have not provided the necessary powers*' that Article 352 TFEU can only be used as a secondary option if the measure cannot be based on any other legal basis established in the Treaties.[96] It seems unlikely that there would be situations where a Union level criminal legislation would be necessary to attain the Union's objectives and that Article 83 TFEU (or any other non-criminal law legal basis) could not be used as the legal basis to satisfy the objective. However, such a situation could emerge. For example, Article 83(2) TFEU may not be used because previous non-criminal legislative harmonisation measures had not been enacted, but there could be an emergency situation that could not have been predicted in beforehand. Also, if the Treaties do not explicitly grant competence for the Union to act but an emergency issue would affect the functioning of the Union, Article 352 TFEU might be a possible legal basis for criminal legislative measure.

The Council shall act unanimously when adopting legislative measures based on Article 352 TFEU. The requirement of unanimity for Article 352 TFEU demonstrates its intergovernmental nature, and it therefore also respects national sover-

---

[90] CONV 375/1/02, Final Report of Working Group V on Complementary Competencies, Brussels, 4 November 2002, pp. 14–17; Craig and de Búrca (2015), pp. 91–92.

[91] CONV 375/1/02, Final Report of Working Group V on Complementary Competencies, Brussels, 4 November 2002, pp. 14 and 17.

[92] CONV 426/02, WG X 14, Final report of Working Group X "Freedom, Security and Justice", Brussels, 2.12.2002, p. 9.

[93] CONV 375/1/02, Final Report of Working Group V on Complementary Competencies, Brussels, 4 November 2002, p. 14.

[94] CONV 375/1/02, Final Report of Working Group V on Complementary Competencies, Brussels, 4 November 2002, pp. 14–17; Opinion 2/94 Opinion of the Court of 28 March 1996. Accession by the Community to the European Convention for the Protection of Human Rights and Fundamental Freedoms [1996] ECR I-1783.

[95] Declaration No 42 attached to the Lisbon Treaty.

[96] See also, Case C-45/86 *Commission of the European Communities v Council of the European Communities* [1987] ECR p. 1493, para 13; Öberg (2014), p. 178; Herlin-Karnell (2012).

eignty.[97] In this sense Article 352 TFEU could be used to protect common interests of the EU Member States, and the use of the provision could fulfil the Beck-inspired maxim of 'less autonomy to enhance sovereignty', if Article 352 TFEU were to be used only exceptionally.

Since Article 352 TFEU is used when 'action by the Union should prove necessary, *within the framework of the policies defined in the Treaties*, to attain one of the objectives set out in the Treaties', the material objective should be found from other Treaty provisions. When Article 352 TFEU would be used in criminal law context, the material objective should be based on Article 83 TFEU. The legislative measure could perhaps be based on both of these legal bases.[98] In this case, unanimous decision-making in the Council would be needed alongside with the appropriate subsidiarity checks in the national parliaments and consent from the European Parliament.

5.2.1.5   Substantive Criminal Legislation Based on the Legal Basis on the Establishment of the EPPO?

Article 86(2) TFEU has also been suggested as a potential legal basis for substantive criminal law,[99] but only in literature. The first paragraph of Article 86 TFEU stipulates that '[i]n order to combat crimes affecting the financial interests of the Union, the Council, by means of regulations adopted in accordance with a special legislative procedure, may establish a European Public Prosecutor's Office from Eurojust'. The second paragraph continues that '[t]he European Public Prosecutor's Office shall be responsible for investigating, prosecuting and bringing to judgment, where appropriate in liaison with Europol, the perpetrators of, and accomplices in, offences against the Union's financial interests, as determined by the regulation provided for in paragraph 1'. However, the wording of the second paragraph refers to the competences of the EPPO and not to any substantive criminal law competence.[100] Naturally the regulation establishing the EPPO determines (and limits) the offences relative to which the EPPO has competence to act (the EPPO's field of competence), but Article 86 TFEU does not provide a legislative procedure for enacting substantive criminal legislation and therefore it cannot constitute competence for the Union in this field either.

---

[97] Similarly, see Öberg (2014), p. 183.

[98] Öberg (2014), p. 184.

[99] Sicurella (2013), pp. 870–904, 894; Ligeti (2013), p. 81.

[100] This way also, see, Satzger (2013), pp. 105–106.

5.2.1.6 Breach of Official Secrecy and Abuse of Public Office

Breach of official or professional secrecy, for example illegal disclosure of information relating to the Union's trade or diplomatic relations, might cause harm to the proper interests of the Union. Article 339 TFEU stipulates that

> the members of the institutions of the Union, the members of committees, and the officials and other servants of the Union shall be required, even after their duties have ceased, not to disclose information of the kind covered by the obligation of professional secrecy, in particular information about undertakings, their business relations or their cost components.

Article 339 TFEU (or its predecessors Article 287 EC and Article 214 EC) has not been used as a legal basis for legal harmonisation measures, nor could Article 339 TFEU be used as such since it does not include provisions providing for a legislative procedure. However, Article 339 TFEU seems to be clear, precise and unconditional enough that it could be immediately applicable, or in other words, to have direct effect.[101] In *Postbank NV v the Commission*, the Commission's actions were evaluated solely based on the then Article 214 EC (current Article 339 TFEU), which means that Article 339 TFEU can have vertical direct effect.[102] It could be asked if Article 339 TFEU in itself could be seen as a harmonisation measure to which Article 83(2) TFEU refers when it stipulates 'if the approximation of criminal laws and regulations of the Member States proves essential to ensure the effective implementation of a Union policy in an area *which has been subject to harmonisation measures...*'. Would this make it possible for the Union legislator to impose an obligation on the Member States to criminalize illegal disclosure of information by EU officials under Article 83(2) TFEU?

The term harmonisation measure is used to refer to the EU secondary legislation that approximates national legislation. Article 339 TFEU can be evaluated normatively to establish whether it in itself could be seen as a harmonisation measure. The Member States' obligations that are derived from the direct effect of primary legislation are fulfilled at the stage of appying the law (negative harmonisation that results to the non-application of laws). In contrast, the harmonisation measures that are directed to and fulfilled by the legislator are positive harmonisation that leads into norm-creation or conformative interpretation.[103]

Literal interpretation of the term harmonisation measure that is meant in Article 83(2) TFEU suggests that secondary legislation needs to have been enacted prior to approximation of substantive criminal law based on Article 83(2) TFEU. This interpretation can be drawn from the last phrase of Article 83(2) TFEU which states that the directives based on the article 'shall be adopted *by the same ordinary or special legislative procedure as was followed for the adoption of the harmonisation measures in question*' (emphasis added). However, some argue that the interpreta-

---

[101] On direct effect, see, C-26/62 *Van Gend En Loos* [1963]; http://europa.eu/legislation_summaries/institutional_affairs/decisionmaking_process/l14547_en.htm, accessed 25 June 2018.

[102] Case T-353/94 *Postbank NV v Commission of the European Communities* [1994] ECR p. II-1141, paras 86–92.

[103] Klip (2016), pp. 33–34.

tion of the term harmonisation measure could be rather liberal,[104] and some even argue that the term simply refers to the existence of Union rules, whether they are primary or secondary law.[105] However, the last mentioned interpretation does not seem feasible since the wording of Article 83(2) TFEU clearly refers to secondary legislation.

Article 339 TFEU itself cannot be used as a legal basis for EU-level criminal legislation criminalizing the illegal disclosure of information of the EU officials/breach of official secrecy either, since Article 339 TFEU does not stipulate anything about a legislative procedure. As a rule, primary law provisions that determine merely the purpose, conditions and substantive aspects, but nothing about a legislative procedure, should be distinguished from the actual legal bases.[106] This means that only those Treaty articles that define which legislative procedure is to be used can be used as legal bases.

But could criminal legislation on official secrecy possibly be given based on Article 336 TFEU, which stipulates that

> [t]he European Parliament and the Council shall, *acting by means of regulations in accordance with the ordinary legislative procedure* and after consulting the other institutions concerned, *lay down the Staff Regulations of Officials of the European Union* and the Conditions of Employment of other servants of the Union. (emphasis added)

A regulation laying down the Staff Regulations of Officials and the Conditions of Employment of Other Servants of the European Economic Community and the European Atomic Energy Community (later the Staff Regulation) has been issued in 1962.[107] They have undergone several amendments. The Staff Regulation includes several provisions concerning the appropriate manner of conducting official duties, such as Articles 11 and 11a, and particularly Article 17, which stipulates that

1. An official shall refrain from any unauthorised disclosure of information received in the line of duty, unless that information has already been made public or is accessible to the public.
2. An official shall continue to be bound by this obligation after leaving the service.

Article 17 of the Staff Regulation stipulates essentially the same rules that are enshrined in Article 339 TFEU. Annex IX of the Staff Regulations includes provisions on disciplinary proceedings. The possible investigations are conducted by the European Anti-Fraud Office (later OLAF) (Article 1 of the Annex IX).

---

[104] Craig (2010), p. 365.

[105] Öberg (2013), p. 320.

[106] Joint Practical Guide of the European Parliament, the Council and the Commission for persons involved in the drafting of European Union legislation https://eur-lex.europa.eu/content/techleg/EN-legislative-drafting-guide.pdf, accessed 25 June 2018, p. 17 (guideline 9.6).

[107] Regulation No 31 (EEC), 11 (EAEC), laying down the Staff Regulations of Officials and the Conditions of Employment of Other Servants of the European Economic Community and the European Atomic Energy Community [1962] OJ 45, 14.6.1962, pp. 1385–1386. The Staff Regulations do not apply to the Commissioners themselves; see for example, Case C-432/04 *Commission of the European Communities v Édith Cresson* [2006] ECR p. I-6387, para 118.

Regulation No 883/2013 concerns investigations conducted by the OLAF.[108] According to Article 1(4) of the regulation, OLAF investigates alleged serious misconduct relating to the performance of professional activities which could constitute dereliction of duty by officials and other servants of the Union (who are subject to the Staff Regulation), by members of institutions or bodies, heads of offices or agencies, or members of the staff of institutions, bodies, offices and agencies who are not subject to the Staff Regulation, and which are liable to result in disciplinary and/or criminal proceedings. Breaches of the duty of discretion and confidentiality, among other matters, can be subjects of OLAF investigations.[109]

We can see that rules on breaches of the duty of confidentiality or official secrecy are already harmonized to certain extent in the Staff Regulation and in the regulation concerning the OLAF investigations. However, Member States' national legislation is not required to criminalize the breach of the duty of confidentiality or official secrecy conducted by Union's officials. The current criminalization obligations concern only corruption. Some breaches of official secrecy could perhaps be sanctioned through the penal provisions on corruption, but not all cases, for example, if a Union official were to illegally disclose information for purely ideological reasons. We can conclude that there is an obvious discrepancy between the national and the EU officials in which types of conduct can lead to criminal liability. Article 83(2) TFEU could be used as a legal basis to criminalize the forms of conduct of EU officials that are not yet covered by the anti-corruption norms in order to establish equivalent protection in upholding of the obligation of professional secrecy in all of the EU Member States.

Due to the principle of legality, existing national penal provisions on breach of official secrecy might not be used as a basis for charging and convicting such conduct by an EU official, because a conforming interpretation might be restricted due to the wording and definitions of public officials in national penal codes. Many of them state that the said provisions only apply to national officials.[110] National criminal codes might also have general provisions on data offences, such as a secrecy offence that would criminalize any breach of a legal duty to keep secrets one has learned due to his position, task, or duty. Such provisions could perhaps be applied to these situations.

The abuse of public office by Union officials could be seen as a proper interest of the Union, even though it also indirectly affects national interests. However, some national criminal laws concerning the abuse of public office or violation of official

---

[108] Regulation (EU, Euratom) No 883/2013 of the European Parliament and of the Council of 11 September 2013 concerning investigations conducted by the European Anti-Fraud Office (OLAF) and repealing Regulation (EC) No 1073/1999 of the European Parliament and of the Council and Council Regulation (Euratom) No 1074/1999 [2013] OJ L 248, 18.9.2013, pp. 1–22.

[109] OLAF's internet site http://ec.europa.eu/anti_fraud/investigations/eu-staff/index_en.htm, accessed 25 June 2018.

[110] This is the case for example in Finland [Criminal Code of Finland Chapter 40 Sections 7–12; Lahti and Pölönen (2000), p. 254]; Sweden [Jareborg (2000), p. 821], and UK [Spencer (2000), p. 868].

duty do not apply to the EU officials.[111] This is naturally problematic in terms of the principle of assimilation, according to which the EU interests ought to be given equivalent protection to that for the corresponding national interests. From the perspective of obligations, EU officials ought to suffer similar consequences if they abuse their position as those suffered by national officials.

Perhaps Article 83(2) TFEU, or even Article 336 TFEU, could be used to criminalize abuse of public office by the EU officials. There is already a harmonisation measure, the Staff Regulation, that is based on Article 336 TFEU. Article 336 TFEU does not seem to offer a proper legal basis for EU-level criminal legislation since it rather works as a legal basis for collective rule- and norm-setting concerning the terms and conditions of the employment of the Union's officials. Instead, Article 83(2) TFEU could be applied to enact EU-level norms concerning the abuse of public office.

However, the Staff Regulation does not apply to the Commissioners, or members of the Union's institutions in general. For example, if a Member of the Commission does not act according to his duties, according to the Articles 245 and 247 TFEU, the CJEU may rule that the Member will be either compulsorily retired or deprived of his right to a pension or other benefits.[112] Articles 245 and 247 TFEU are not legal bases because they do not mention legislative procedures. Instead, the CJEU can apply these articles directly, whereas the national courts cannot do so. This means that the disciplinary proceedings of Articles 245 and 247 TFEU are meant to be used as an internal procedure of the Union. Therefore this procedure has a constitutional nature. The constitutional nature of the procedure is also highlighted by the fact that outcomes and findings of possible national criminal proceedings concerning the same facts cannot restrict the competence of the CJEU to examine the case

---

[111] This is the case for example in Finland (see Criminal Code of Finland Chapter 40 Sections 7–12); Belgium (see Case C-432/04 *Commission of the European Communities v Édith Cresson* [2006] ECR p. I-6387, para 37); Sweden [Jareborg (2000), p. 819]. The scope of the term "public officer" is unclear in the UK [Spencer (2000), p. 866].

[112] Article 245 TFEU reads as follows: 'The Members of the Commission shall refrain from any action incompatible with their duties. Member States shall respect their independence and shall not seek to influence them in the performance of their tasks.

The Members of the Commission may not, during their term of office, engage in any other occupation, whether gainful or not. When entering upon their duties they shall give a solemn undertaking that, both during and after their term of office, they will respect the obligations arising therefrom and in particular their duty to behave with integrity and discretion as regards the acceptance, after they have ceased to hold office, of certain appointments or benefits. In the event of any breach of these obligations, the Court of Justice may, on application by the Council acting by a simple majority or the Commission, rule that the Member concerned be, according to the circumstances, either compulsorily retired in accordance with Article 247 or deprived of his right to a pension or other benefits in its stead.'

Article 247 TFEU reads as follows: 'If any Member of the Commission no longer fulfils the conditions required for the performance of his duties or if he has been guilty of serious misconduct, the Court of Justice may, on application by the Council acting by a simple majority or the Commission, compulsorily retire him.'

in the procedure that is established in Articles 245 and 247 TFEU.[113] This, naturally, could cause a problem concerning the principle of *ne bis in idem* if another sanction, even criminal punishment, would be imposed upon the Member of the Commission by a national court.

Due to this purely Union-level constitutional nature of the procedure established in Articles 245 and 247 TFEU, these Articles cannot be considered harmonisation measures that would enable further harmonisation under Article 83(2) TFEU. This Union constitutional procedure is purely a Union-level procedure, and hence approximation of the national criminal laws could not affect the actual procedure or the CJEU's competence regarding it.

The case of *Commission v Edith Cresson* concerned Mrs Cresson's alleged breaches of obligations as a member of the Commission. Commissioner Edith Cresson had managed to arrange for her acquaintance to be employed by the Commission by circumventing the rules of appointment of the members of the Cabinet. The case was tried in the CJEU in the disciplinary proceedings regulated in ex-Articles 213 and 216 EC (currently Articles 245 and 247 TFEU). The CJEU found that Mrs Cresson acted in breach of the obligations arising from her office. In terms of imposing a penalty under Article 213(2) EC, the CJEU found that the breach would require a penalty in principle. The Court was nevertheless satisfied to state that the finding of the breach constitutes, of itself, an appropriate penalty. Prior to the proceedings in the CJEU, charges were also brought against Mrs Cresson in Belgium for forgery, fraud or unlawful conflict of interest. However, the Belgian Court of First Instance found that the Belgian Criminal Code regarding conflicts of interests did not apply to 'persons holding a public office in an organisation governed by public international law', and thus nothing could be done on the matter.[114]

Based on the *Cresson* case, it seems that it is necessary that the Members of the Commission (or other members of the Union's institutions) should be criminally liable for their misconduct in and abuse of public office. This could enhance the citizens' trust towards the Union and give more legitimacy to the Union as a polity. Advocate General Geelhoed also found in his Opinion that the Commissioners' failure to meet the standards of independence, impartiality and integrity can lead to 'significant damage to the public image of the institution and undermine confidence in it, which in turn will diminish its efficacy'.[115]

The idea of EU-level criminalization of abuse of office or illegal disclosure of information of the Union's officials appears not to be fresh, since they were already proposed in 1997 by the *Corpus Juris* project.[116] The Corpus Juris project proposed,

---

[113] Case C-432/04 *Commission of the European Communities v Édith Cresson* [2006] ECR p. I-6387, Opinion of AG Geelhoed, paras 68–69, 94–95; Case C-432/04 *Commission of the European Communities v Édith Cresson* [2006] ECR p. I-6387, paras 120–121.

[114] Case C-432/04 *Commission of the European Communities v Édith Cresson* [2006] ECR p. I-6387, paras 10, 36, 37, 138, 147–151.

[115] Ibid., Opinion of AG Geelhoed paras 74–75.

[116] *Sous la direction de Mireille Delmas-Marty* (1997); Ligeti (2013), p. 79.

however, that abuse of office would result in criminal liability only if a Union official made a decision on the award of a subsidy, grant or an exemption from duty in favour of a person who clearly has no right to it, or if he intervened in the awarding of subsidies, grants or exemption from duty in relation to any business or operation in which he has personal interest (the proposed Article 4). The abuse of office was linked to the direct or indirect abuse of the Union's funds (by gaining personal advantage in the expense of the Union's interests). In contrast, the proposed provision on disclosure of secrets pertaining to one's office (proposed Article 6) did not require damage to the financial interests of the Union for the basis of criminal liability. This was changed however in the Corpus Juris 2000 proposal, in which Article 8 (previously Article 6) on disclosure of secrets pertaining to one's office read as follows:

> It is a criminal offence for an official improperly to reveal secrets pertaining to his office, when the secrets concern information acquired in, or by virtue of, his professional activity, when monitoring receipts or awarding grants and subsidies, if this revelation is likely to damage the financial interests of the European Communities.[117]

Originally, in 1997, the illicit disclosure of information was not linked to the requirement of the conduct causing damage to the Union's financial interests. This was justified by the fact that violation of secrecy generally harms the trust of the citizens in the institutions.[118] Illegal disclosure of information can have even more far-reaching consequences if the information concerns for example the Union's diplomatic relationships. This kind of conduct might resemble offences that are traditionally classified as treasonable offences in national criminal laws, such as an act of espionage.

5.2.1.7 Union's Substantive Criminal Law Competence Ought to Be Limited to Article 83 TFEU

The discussion above on the rules on the choice of legal basis (in Sect. 3.7.1) and on the possible implicit legal bases (in this chapter) could suggest that EU substantive criminal law measures could be based on legal bases other than Article 83 TFEU. However, based on the *travaux* of Article 83 TFEU and its *ratio legis* in the Union's broader constitutional framework, the Union's substantive criminal law competence ought to be limited to Article 83 TFEU. This would seem to be the case based on what has been presented above, especially concerning the purpose and goal of the Union's express substantive criminal law competence (in Sect. 3.7.3).

---

[117] *Corpus Juris* 2000, available in internet https://docs.google.com/viewerng/viewer?url=http://dirittopenaleeuropeo.it/wp-content/uploads/2013/09/corpus_juris_en.pdf&hl=it, accessed 2 July 2018; Compare to the wording of Corpus Juris 1997, which read as follows "It is a criminal offence for an official improperly to reveal secrets pertaining to his office, when the secret concerns information acquired in, or by virtue of, his professional activity, *particularly* when monitoring receipts or awarding grants and subsidies" (emphasis added).

[118] *Sous la direction de Mireille Delmas-Marty, Corpus Juris* (1997).

The conclusion is also supported by the nature of Article 83(2) TFEU, embodying power-restricting elements that are necessary in the field of substantive criminal law to prevent excessive use of criminal legislative power and excessive restrictions of individual rights (Sects. 4.4.1 to 4.4.6). It could also be argued that the EU criminalization principles should guide the choice of legal basis in relation to criminal law-embedded legislative measures.

Article 83 TFEU, through the power-limiting mechanisms, encapsulates a traditional restrictive criminal law approach including the key idea that criminal law is one element amongst others that reflect state sovereignty. Following Beck's idea, in the optimal situation transnational cooperation should strenghten state sovereignty even though it simultaneously limits the state's decision-making autonomy. Only EU-level criminal legislation that would strengthen the Member States' sovereignty by enhancing their opportunities to tackle transnational crime which also affects their national interests ought to be enacted. Article 83 TFEU would seem to follow this logic because power-restricting elements such as the emergency brake mechanism are embedded in it. Legal bases other than Article 83 TFEU do not follow the logic of "less autonomy to enhance sovereignty" because they do not enable individual Member States to refuse the new legislative proposal if it would affect the fundamental aspects of their criminal justice system, which in turn is an element of state sovereignty. Only exception to this is Article 352 TFEU, the so-called flexibility clause. Its field of application is not narrowed concerning criminal law. The legislative procedure described in it requires unanimity, which naturally ensures that the Member States are able to refuse the legislative proposal.

Article 83 TFEU follows Beck's idea also in that the provision is according to its preparatory works meant to exhaust the Union's substantive criminal law competence. The *travaux préparatoires* suggest how and to what extent the Member States have intended to limit their decision-making autonomy.

The emergency brake procedure is agreed by the constitutional legislature as a necessary restriction to the Union's criminal legislative power. In this sense, the procedure preserves the Member States' sovereignty. However, the mechanism does not enable the Member States to control the scope of EU criminal law after the legislation is given. Thus, it clearly is an *ex ante* mechanism to ensure respect for national sovereignty. The mechanism cannot be used after Union legislation is passed in a particular area. This illustrates a weakness of the mechanism. If a Member State would only later perceive the Union instrument to violate the fundamentals of its criminal justice system or if a Member State would want to change its criminal justice system later in a way that would fundamentally be in a conflict with EU norms, the Member State can no longer rely on the emergency brake procedure. Taking this into account, a separate mechanism for the Member States to exercise *ex post* sovereignty control might be useful.

The choice of legal basis also has more far-reaching impacts. The choice of legal basis is not important only from the perspective of the legislature, but also from the perspective of the authorities applying the law. Interpretation of the EU secondary law rests on the purpose and objectives of the legal basis. When the secondary legislation is interpreted in courts, in national courts or in the CJEU, the legal basis on which the secondary legislation is based offers the interpretative framework for the courts concerning the purpose and objective of that legislation. This means that the choice of legal basis is essential relative to the teleological interpretation of the secondary legislation. In a criminal law-related context, the recent judgment in *Digital Rights Ireland* seems to be an exception to this. The CJEU gave more impetus to the criminal law-oriented aims of the legislation than to the objectives of the legal basis (Article 95 EC, the current 114 TFEU) on which the legislation was enacted.[119]

The CJEU's interpretation in the judgment in *Digital Rights Ireland* (given in 2014) emphasizing the criminal law objectives instead of the internal market objectives could be explained. The Court might have had a change of heart concerning the appropriate legal basis for the data retention directive its main objectives rather concerning serious crime.[120] This change of heart could be explained by the then Treaty structure when the data retention directive 2002/58/EC was enacted. At that time the pillar structure divided the EC's competences from the EU's competences. In particular Article 47 EU safeguarded the *acquis communitaire*, which might have influenced the Court's evaluation concerning the choice of legal basis. Even though the material purpose of that directive was to facilitate police cooperation, the directive also influenced the creation and functioning of the internal market. And understandably, after the Lisbon Treaty entered into force, the picture is different: a criminal law-objective could be recognized alongside the internal market objective.[121]

The CJEU's new line of interpretation utilizing the *travaux préparatoires* of the Treaties (Section '*Travaux préparatoires* of the Treaties') in order to establish the *ratio legis* of Treaty provisions also suggests that Article 83 TFEU ought to exhaust the Union's substantive criminal law competence. In this new line of constitutional interpretation the CJEU has used the preparatory works of the Treaties to determine a meaning of a primary law provision if the meaning would otherwise remain ambiguous or obscure. As can be read from the *travaux préparatoires* of Article 83 TFEU,[122] the Union's substantive criminal law competence was to be exhausted in

---

[119] Huomo-Kettunen (2014), pp. 301, 326.

[120] Miettinen (2015), p. 378; joined cases C-293/12 and C-594/12 *Digital Rights Ireland Ltd v Minister for Communications, Marine and Natural Resources and Others and Kärntner Landesregierung and Others* [2014], para 24: "the main objective of that directive is to harmonise Member States' provisions concerning the retention, by providers of publicly available electronic communications services or of public communications networks, of certain data which are generated or processed by them, in order to ensure that the data are available for the purpose of the prevention, investigation, detection and prosecution of serious crime, such as organised crime and terrorism", and in 41: "the material objective of that directive is, as follows from Article 1(1) thereof, to ensure that the data are available for the purpose of the investigation, detection and prosecution of serious crime, as defined by each Member State in its national law. The material objective of that directive is, therefore, to contribute to the fight against serious crime and thus, ultimately, to public security".

[121] On topic also, see, for example, Herlin-Karnell (2012), pp. 102–105.

[122] See Sect. 3.7.3 above. See also a thorough presentation of the preparatory works of Article 83 TFEU in Miettinen (2013), p. 194.

Article 83 TFEU. So far, the CJEU has used the *travaux préparatoires* only in a static and restrictive manner. The Court has not referred to them in a dynamic manner that would expand the scope of the applicability of EU primary law. This also supports the argument that the normative and restrictive criminal law approach ought to guide the use of the Union's criminal law competences.

5.2.2   Possibility of Directly Applicable EU Criminal Legislation

As has been established above in Sect. 3.7, the choice of legal basis is a central element of general EU law. The choice of legal basis is not solely a juridical but also a political question. It is pivotal in determining the contours of the Union's criminal law competence, because different legal bases establish different types of competence. Within the substantive criminal law context, use of legal bases other than Article 83 TFEU opens a possibility to enact directly applicable criminal legislation. This would lead towards genuinely supranational criminal law.[123] It would also mean unyielding EU level criminal provisions that would need to be applied directly in national courts to determine criminal liability regardless of whether or not they fit the existing national criminal law frameworks.

When EU-level substantial criminal legislation is given in the form of directives and the Member States have an opportunity to react to proposals that conflict with the fundamental aspects of their national criminal justice systems, EU-level criminal legislation is more likely to be able to adjust to the normative requirements of the national criminal justice systems. The Member States have opposed the idea of directly applicable EU criminal law, so from a political perspective it seems unlikely at least in the near future.

The wording of Articles 325(4) TFEU ('*shall adopt the necessary measures*'), 33 TFEU ('*shall take measures*') and 114(1) TFEU ('*adopt the measures for the approximation*') do not state anything about the form of the legislative measure. Regulations can therefore be enacted based on these articles even if the measure would include criminal law provisions. The Commission considered the option of legislating the protection of the financial interests of the European Union by criminal law in the form of a regulation.[124] Directly applicable EU criminal legislation would be a novelty.

The most obvious difference between regulation and directive is the elasticity of these instruments. Whereas regulations are directly applicable in the national courts and authorities, directives must be implemented into the national legal orders, which enables the Member States to enact the Union's criminal policy objectives into their national criminal justice systems in as compatible and coherent manner as possible.

---

[123] Fründe and Suominen (2010), pp. 121–133.

[124] SWD(2012) 195 final, Commission staff working paper Impact assessment (Part I), p. 39.

In other words, implementation enhances the Member States' powers to follow the requirements of the principle of *inner ultima ratio* according to which the criminal provisions ought to construct a coherent criminal justice system. For example, the relative seriousness between penal provisions should be rationally designed.[125]

In order for the criminal legislation to be clear and foreseeable, and thus effective, the criminal provisions should be clearly formulated and proportionate relative to each other. As noted already in Sect. 2.1, efficiency of criminal law stems at least partly from the fact that individuals can easily understand what is forbidden and how blameworthy the conduct is considered.[126] Directly applicable EU criminal legislation might break the inner coherence of national criminal justice systems, because it might be difficult to draft the EU criminal legislation in a way that would fit all the curiosities of the national criminal justice systems. This might impair the desired end-result of EU-level directly applicable criminal legislation. If the criminal provisions would seem illegitimate or unclear to individuals, they might not be followed effectively.

Directly applicable EU criminal legislation would be problematic from the perspective of the legality principle. Because regulations would be applied directly in the national courts, EU criminal legislation would need to fulfil the requirements of the principle of legality, such as the requirement for precision. Instead of the national legislators, the Union legislator would need to take these requirements into account. When the Commission considered the use of a regulation in the form of the so-called Union-fraud legislation, it itself stated that such legislation might have too far-reaching an impact on fundamental rights, particularly the principle of legality. The Commission recognises the challenges that directly applicable EU-level criminal legislation would bring by stating that "a directly applicable set of criminal law rules, which the judge would have to apply instead of the national criminal code, would create substantial interference with these traditions and systems because they cannot possibly correspond to all the Member States' national approaches."[127] So even though the principle of legality would impose obligations on the Union's legislature, the actual practical fulfilment of those obligations might prove to be too difficult.

It is noteworthy that only a year before the Commission considered proposing the Union fraud legislation in the form of a regulation, the Commission itself had outlined in its communication on EU criminal policy that EU criminal legislation was to be given in a form of directives and that due this fact the requirements stemming from the principle of legality do not apply to the Union legislator but to the national legislators.[128] The Commission even mentioned Article 325(4) TFEU in the communication, but said nothing about the possibility of enacting directly applicable EU criminal legislation or of the effects of the principle of legality on the Union's

---

[125] On the inner dimention of the *ultima ratio* principle, see Melander (2008), p. 407.

[126] Robinson (1994), pp. 857, 876.

[127] SWD(2012) 195 final, Commission staff working paper Impact assessment (Part I), pp. 39–40.

[128] COM(2011) 573 final, Towards an EU Criminal Policy: Ensuring the effective implementation of EU policies through criminal law, Brussels, 20 September 2011, pp. 2, 6, 8.

legislator.[129] This is peculiar. On the one hand the Commission is of the opinion that criminal legislation ought to be given in the form of directives and that the requirements of the legality principle 'are not the same as for national criminal law legislation'. On the other hand, the Commission acknowledges Article 325(4) TFEU as a potential legal basis for EU criminal legislation but did not consider the possibility of directly applicable EU criminal legislation even though it in fact considered this option only a year thereafter. The Commission's communication and its choices in relation to the Union fraud proposal express discrepancies in the Commission's work. It could be criticized because it would be preferable that the use of other legal bases than Article 83 TFEU and their side effects would be analysed before starting legislative preparations based on them.

Directly applicable EU criminal law would be entirely different from the already existing so-called EU 'blanket criminal laws'. The term of EU blanket criminal law is used here to describe national criminal legislation of which field of criminal behaviour is determined by a reference to a non-criminal law EU regulation. Reference can be made to certain EU regulation as published in the official journal of the European Union on a certain date (static reference), or reference can be made to an EU regulation as amended from time to time (dynamic reference).[130] Relative to EU blanket criminal laws, the national courts are applying the national criminal provision to determine criminal liability. In order to be able to do that, they have to also interpret the EU regulation to which the national provision refers. It is good to recall that national legislators are not allowed to implement the regulations into national law. EU regulations are directly applicable without any measures of reception into national law.[131] Regulations ought not to be implemented into national law in order to avoid hiding the European nature of that legal rule. The uniform interpretation and application of the regulation could be jeopardised if EU regulations would not be applied directly.[132] The EU regulation to which the national criminal provision refers has to fulfil the requirements of the principle of legality, namely it has to be formulated precisely enough.

The use of EU blanket criminal legislation is not seen problematic, because those EU regulations that are referred to do not contain criminal provisions and they are sufficiently precise. This means that it is left up to the Member States' legislators to enact penal provisions based on them or to make a reference to the EU regulation in the national penal provision.[133] The very generally formulated penal provision is enacted within the Member States in order for the penal provision to be in line with the formulation of other national penal provisions. When the EU blanket criminal legislative technique is used, the national legislators also define the sanction level for that offence.

---

[129] Ibid., p. 6.

[130] Satzger (2012), p. 89.

[131] Case C-34/73 *Fratelli Variola S.p.A. v Amministrazione italiana delle Finanze* [1973] ECR p. 981, paras 9–11.

[132] Ibid.; Satzger (2012), p. 85.

[133] Frände (2012), p. 41.

Non-legislative acts of general application (delegated acts, Article 290 TFEU) resemble EU blanket legislation. Delegated acts are issued by the Commission to supplement or amend non-essential elements of legislative acts. The Lisbon Treaty sets out a hierarchy of EU secondary norms. Legislative acts (regulations, directives and decisions) are binding and passed by the Union legislator using an ordinary or special legislative procedure.[134] Non-legislative acts of general application (delegated acts/legislation) are binding but they are not passed using a democratic legislative procedure. Instead, in a legislative act, the Union legislator can delegate power to the Commission 'to adopt non-legislative acts of general application to supplement or amend certain non-essential elements of the legislative act'. The legislative act containing the delegation of power, the so-called basic act, will need to explicitly define the 'objectives, content, scope and duration of the delegation of power'. The essential elements of the area being legislated cannot be delegated and are reserved only for the consideration of the Union's legislator.[135] Even though delegated acts are not legislative acts, they resemble legislative acts in the sense that they are binding and they are used as means to govern.[136] In this sense, delegated acts resemble decrees given by national government departments that contain more detailed and technical regulation on the issues.[137]

It should be asked if the Commission can enact delegated criminal legislation, and if so, whether this would be desirable. The natural starting point to solve the first question is to examine the wording of Article 290 TFEU and Article 83 TFEU. It is clear that nothing in the wording of neither of the said articles limit the use of

---

[134] Articles 288 and 289 TFEU.

[135] Article 290 TFEU which reads as follows:

1. A legislative act may delegatev to the Commission the power to adopt non-legislative acts of general application to supplement or amend certain non-essential elements of the legislative act.
   The objectives, content, scope and duration of the delegation of power shall be explicitly defined in the legislative acts. The essential elements of an area shall be reserved for the legislative act and accordingly shall not be the subject of a delegation of power.
2. Legislative acts shall explicitly lay down the conditions to which the delegation is subject; these conditions may be as follows:

   (a) the European Parliament or the Council may decide to revoke the delegation;
   (b) the delegated act may enter into force only if no objection has been expressed by the European Parliament or the Council within a period set by the legislative act.

   For the purposes of (a) and (b), the European Parliament shall act by a majority of its component members, and the Council by a qualified majority.
3. The adjective "delegated" shall be inserted in the title of delegated acts.

[136] Craig (2010), p. 58.

[137] The Commission, or exceptionally the Council, can also be given a mandate in a legislative act, to set out uniform conditions for implementing legally binding Union acts. These acts are called implementing acts (Article 291 TFEU which reads as follows: '1. Member States shall adopt all measures of national law necessary to implement legally binding Union acts. 2. Where uniform conditions for implementing legally binding Union acts are needed, those acts shall confer implementing powers on the Commission, or, in duly justified specific cases and in the cases provided for in Articles 24 and 26 of the Treaty on European Union, on the Council').

delegated acts in the field of criminal law. But when the analysis of the primary law is widened to more normative provisions of EU primary law, the first impression seems false. The principle of legality as enshrined in Article 49 of the Charter states that '[n]o one shall be held guilty of any criminal offence on account of any act or omission which did not constitute a criminal offence under national law or international law at the time when it was committed'. The meaning of 'law' in this context should be interpreted in the light of the ECtHR case law concerning the meaning of the concept of law. As presented above in Sect. 1.3.3.2, the ECtHR considers that 'law' refers to written *legislation* and unwritten law of common law legal systems. *Since delegated acts are not categorized as legislative acts and since delegated acts are not issued in a democratic procedure, delegated legislation ought not to contain such norms that would explicitly determine the scope of criminal liability or its consequences, such as essential/constituent elements of criminal acts or penalty scales.*

It also seems reasonable that delegated acts ought not to contain provisions that would implicitly/indirectly determine what the essential elements of a criminal provision enacted in a legislative act entail, because decision-making concerning the scope of criminal liability is political by nature since it interferes with rights of individuals. Determining what conduct is criminal should be decided in a democratic process. And due to the fact that the definition of the scope of criminal liability is political issue, it is also an essential element of the area that is being regulated.

The CJEU has had some cases concerning the delegation of powers in the area of freedom, security and justice, but none concerning particularly criminal law. In C-355/10 concerning immigration, the Court affirmed the basic rule that 'the adoption of rules essential to the subject-matter envisaged is reserved to the legislature of the European Union' and that 'political choices falling within the responsibilities of the European Union legislature cannot be delegated'. The CJEU also noted that '[a]scertaining which elements of a matter must be categorized as essential is not— for the assessment of the European Union legislature alone, but must be based on objective factors amenable to judicial review'. The Court stated that *if the norms affect the fundamental rights of the persons to a certain extent, the involvement of the Union legislature is required.* In C-355/10, 'stopping persons apprehended, seizing vessels and conducting persons apprehended to a specific location' meant that such an interference of fundamental rights was at hand.[138] *Because the measures at hand in the case C-355/10 required the involvement of the Union legislature, it seems that the Union legislator could not delegate criminal legislative powers since criminal legislation always entails strong interference with individuals' fundamental rights.*

The delegated acts-technique established in Article 290 TFEU had not been used in a criminal law related context by the end of 2014. While the Commission had

---

[138] Case C-355/10 *European Parliament v Council of the European Union* [2012], paras 64, 65, 67, 77.

given 82 delegated acts (Commission Delegated Regulations),[139] none of them was issued in a criminal law context, and only three of them include provisions concerning administrative penalties.[140] However, in the first reading of the proposal amending the framework decision on illicit drug trafficking as regards the definition of drug,[141] the European Parliament proposed that powers would be delegated to the Commission in accordance with Article 290 TFEU so that it could 'amend the Annex to Framework Decision 2004/757/JHA and therefore the definition of drug in the said Framework Decision'.[142] Amendments to the said Annex would affect the definition of drug, because Article 1 of the Framework Decision 2004/757/JHA defines 'drugs' *inter alia* by making references to the UN Conventions on Narcotic Drugs and Psychotropic Substances and to the Annex.

Yet again, at a first glance, the EP's approach on the use of delegated act in the context concerning the definition of drugs could seem contradictory to the main rule presented above according to which delegated legislation could not be given in the field of criminal law due to the principle of legality. However when the issue is examined more thoroughly, firstly, one can see that the EP's proposal would actually raise the standard of the required type of norm in this particular context. The EP justifies the delegation of powers by stating that it is necessary because '[t]he criminalization of a new psychoactive substance cannot be considered as a mere implementing measure', meaning that from the EP's perspective the amendment of the Annex ought to be carried out by means of legally binding delegated act instead of mere implementing act that would advise the Member States on how to implement

---

[139] Search conducted in 14 November 2014 and covered the time the Lisbon Treaty has been in force.

[140] The three delegated acts containing administrative penalties are: Commission Delegated Regulation (EU) No 640/2014 of 11 March 2014 supplementing Regulation (EU) No 1306/2013 of the European Parliament and of the Council with regard to the integrated administration and control system and conditions for refusal or withdrawal of payments and administrative penalties applicable to direct payments, rural development support and cross compliance [2014] OJ L 181, 20.6.2014, pp. 48–73; Commission Delegated Regulation (EU) No 667/2014 of 13 March 2014 supplementing Regulation (EU) No 648/2012 of the European Parliament and of the Council with regard to rules of procedure for penalties imposed on trade repositories by the European Securities and Markets Authority including rules on the right of defence and temporal provisions Text with EEA relevance [2014] OJ L 179, 19.6.2014, pp. 31–35; Commission Delegated Regulation (EU) No 946/2012 of 12 July 2012 supplementing Regulation (EC) No 1060/2009 of the European Parliament and of the Council with regard to rules of procedure on fines imposed to credit rating agencies by the European Securities and Markets Authority, including rules on the right of defence and temporal provisions Text with EEA relevance [2012] OJ L 282, 16.10.2012, pp. 23–26.

[141] COM(2013) 618 final, proposal for a directive amending Council Framework Decision 2004/757/JHA of 25 October 2004 laying down minimum provisions on the constituent elements of criminal acts and penalties in the field of illicit drug trafficking, as regards the definition of drug, Brussels, 17 September 2013.

[142] European Parliament, A7-0173/2014, report on the proposal for a directive of the European Parliament and of the Council amending Council Framework Decision 2004/757/JHA of 25 October 2004 laying down minimum provisions on the constituent elements of criminal acts and penalties in the field of illicit drug trafficking, as regards the definition of drug (COM(2013)0618 – C7-0271/2013 – 2013/0304(COD)), 14 March 2014, the amendment to the proposed Recital 5.

the norms but which would not be legally binding. The EP continues its reasoning by stating that '[s]uch criminalisation of a new psychoactive substance requires the relevant criminal law considerations to be taken into account—[as] this will change the criminal law of the Member States, a delegated act is necessary to add those substances to the Annex to the Framework Decision'.[143] In other words, the EP expects stricter legislative techniques to be used than the original proposal offered (implementing act). Secondly, the issue of the criminal definition of 'drugs' is arranged in a similar manner in national criminal legislation. The reason for this is simple: the pace at which new designer drugs enter the market is too fast for the legislator to keep up with and amend the drug legislation. In this sense, criminal legislation on drugs is not the best example to demonstrate the issue of using delegated acts in the field of criminal law.

The case of *criminal proceedings of Markus D. and G* was about whether substances that modify physiological functions, but which are not beneficial to health but instead harmful to human health, and which are used to induce a state of intoxication could be considered to be medicinal products as defined in Article 1(2)(b) of Directive 2001/83. The said Article defined medicinal products as 'any substance or combination of substances presented as having properties for treating or preventing disease in human beings; or any substance or combination of substances which may be used in or administered to human beings either with a view to restoring, correcting or modifying physiological functions by exerting a pharmacological, immunological or metabolic action, or to making a medical diagnosis'. If the substances that have no beneficial effects on health and which are used for the purpose of intoxication could be considered medicinal products, Germany could have imposed criminal sanctions of a medicine offence if such unsafe products were placed on the market. The CJEU found that taking into account the objective of the Directive (to attain a high level of human health protection) and the consistent interpretation of the term of medicinal product to referring to products that are or can be beneficial to health, substances that are harmful to health cannot be classified as 'medicinal products'.[144]

The Council has accepted the EP's proposal to use delegated acts in regard to definition of drug.[145] The Commission has to notify the delegated act concerning the definition of a drug to the EP and the Council. In case the EP or the Council object the delegated act, it would not come into force. In this sense, the delegated legislation in the drug context also has democratic legitimacy. This issue was under the CJEU's investigation in case *Parliament v Council* where the EP had raised an action for annulment concerning some Council Decisions based on which certain

---

[143] European Parliament, report A7-0173/2014, 14 March 2014, p. 15.

[144] Joined cases C-358/13 and C-181/14 *Criminal proceedings against Markus D. (C-358/13) and G. (C-181/14)* [2014], paras 46–47.

[145] Directive (EU) 2017/2103 of the European Parliament and of the Council of 15 November 2017 amending Council Framework Decision 2004/757/JHA in order to include new psychoactive substances in the definition of 'drug' and repealing Council Decision 2005/387/JHA, OJEU L 305/12, 21.11.2017.

psychoactive substances were to be subjected to control measures and criminal penalties in the Member States on the ground that the Parliament did not participate in the procedure for the adoption of the contested decisions. The CJEU found the EP's plea well founded and declared the contested decisions void.[146]

The EP has issued a report on the delegation of legislative powers[147] in which the EP expressed concerns on the balance between democratic decision-making in the EU and the rationalization of the legislative process. The EP sees that drawing a line between delegation of legislative power and implementing power is problematic and that common principles and practices should be established. According to the EP, the Commission and the Council have been rather keen to use implementing acts in situations in which delegated acts should have been used. In the EP's view, in future, the Commission ought to explicitly justify 'why it is proposing a delegated or implementing act in a particular legislative proposal and why it considers its regulatory content to be non-essential'. Since the delegation of legislative powers also implies interference of the democratic legitimacy of the delegated act, the EP stresses that the Union's legislator needs to determine *on a case-by-case basis* how detailed legislation gives or delegates its power and in which extent to the Commission. The EP also wonders if keeping all policy elements in the basic acts (as expected in Article 290 TFEU) would 'deprive Article 290 TFEU of its use as a valuable means of rationalisation of the legislative process, which was its initial rationale in order to avoid micro-management and a heavy and lengthy co-decision procedure'.[148]

Academic literature has connected the delegation of power to the EU as a regulatory state,[149] thus linking the delegation of power to new governance, in which framework the concept of regulatory state refers to removal of decision-making from the democratic arrangements and shifting it into the hands of experts or technocrats.[150] However, as explained above, delegation of power does not really fit into the criminal law framework. Neither does the idea of the EU as a regulatory state fit into the criminal law framework, due to the highly political nature of criminal law[151] in the sense that it has highly fundamental rights-sensitive nature. For this reason criminal legislation ought to be enacted in a democratic process. The principle of legality sets clear restrictions on the use of the delegated acts technique in the field

---

[146] Joined cases C-317/13 and C-679/13 *European Parliament v Council of the European Union* [2015], paras 14, 60–74.

[147] European Parliament, A7-0435/2013, report on follow-up on the delegation of legislative powers and control by the Member States of the Commission's exercise of implementing powers, 4 December 2013.

[148] European Parliament, A7-0435/2013, report on follow-up on the delegation of legislative powers and control by the Member States of the Commission's exercise of implementing powers, 4 December 2013, pp. 1–8.

[149] Craig (2010), p. 49.

[150] Christiansen (2016), pp. 103–104.

[151] Craig (2013), p. 74.

of criminal law. The restriction stems from the democratic dimension of the principle of legality (*nulla poena, nullem crimen sine lege parlamentaria*).[152]

5.2.3   Full Harmonisation of Penalty Scales

Another unwanted normative problem that would arise if legal bases other than Article 83 TFEU were to be used as a legal basis for EU-level criminal legislative measures, and in particular if that legislation would be given in the form of a regulation, would be that of setting fixed minimum and maximum thresholds for punishment.

Article 83 TFEU gives the Union the competence to set only minimum rules on the penalty scales in the form of directives. Declaration 8 on Article K.3(e) of the Treaty on European Union,[153] annexed to the Treaty of Amsterdam, was made to clarify the expression of *minimum rules*. Article K.3(e) in the Amsterdam Treaty stated that '[c]ommon action on judicial cooperation in criminal matters shall include:—(e) progressively adopting measures establishing *minimum rules* relating to the constituent elements of criminal acts and to *penalties* in the fields of organised crime, terrorism and illicit drug trafficking' (emphasis added). Declaration 8 clarified that 'Article K.3(e) of the Treaty on European Union shall not have the consequence of obliging a Member State whose legal system does not provide for minimum sentences to adopt them.'[154] It was clear then that minimum penalties could not be harmonized at the Union level.

There was no equivalent to Declaration 8 annexed to the Constitutional Treaty,[155] nor is one annexed to the Lisbon Treaty, perhaps due to the new Treaty structure and the new criminal law provisions as examined above in Sect. 3.7.4. Even if such a declaration concerning Article 83 TFEU was annexed to the Lisbon Treaty, it would still not apply to the other Articles of the Treaties. However, such a declaration could also have had interpretative meaning relative to other Treaty provisions that could possibly be used as a legal basis for EU-level criminal legislation. However, Working Group X, and later the Convention, accorded with the general view that the approximation of substantive criminal law was to be carried out *only in the form of*

---

[152] More thoroughly about the democratic dimension of the principle of legality above in Sect. 4.4.3.

[153] 8. Declaration on Article K.3(e) of the Treaty on European Union, OJ C 340, 10 November 1997.

[154] For example, in France, the penalty scales simply state the maximum penalties but remain silent on the threshold of the minimum penalties (French Penal Code, English translation available in internet www.legifrance.gouv.fr/Traductions/en-English/Legifrance-translations, accessed 25 June 2018.

[155] Miettinen (2013), pp. 194, 205.

directives.[156] This indicates that the full harmonisation of penalty scales is not possible under Article 83 TFEU.

The Commission has suggested setting minimum imprisonment ranges in the Union-fraud proposal, a proposal which was then based by the Commission on Article 325(4) TFEU.[157] According to the Commission, economic crime is of a special type in the sense that the potential perpetrators are more likely to make calculations on the risks when deciding whether or not to commit this type of crime. Setting of minimum sanctions would thus accordingly ensure effective deterrence.[158] The proposal against Union-fraud has not been the only legislative proposal in which the Commission has suggested fixed penalty thresholds. In the proposal on the protection of the euro and other currencies against counterfeiting by criminal law the Commission stated that the knowledge of the possible sanctions would function as the deterrent effect for those who are considering criminal conduct in that particular field of crime.[159]

The Commission thus assumes that offenders act rationally and in a risk-aversive manner, at least in certain fields of crime.[160] This represents the law and economics perspective on sanctions, according to which (potential) offenders are rational actors. The increase in the severity of sanctions, probability of detection of crime and conviction and the swiftness of enforcing the sanction are all variables that affect crime rates.[161] The economic assumption of rationality does not, however, imply that offenders calculate their costs and benefits very precisely and decide on their conduct based on such calculations. Instead, offenders are seen to act in a similar manner with other rational individuals, simply meaning that they try to pursue their own interests in the circumstances at hand as best they can.[162] There are diverging research results on whether the presumption on rational criminals is feasible. There is also divergence between different types of crimes. For example, the severity of penalties do not necessarily affect the rate of homicides, but they do influence the rate of property crimes.[163] Relative to economic white collar crime, the possible

---

[156] CONV 426/02, WG X 14, Final report of Working Group X "Freedom, Security and Justice", Brussels, 2.12.2002, p. 10; CONV 614/03, Brussels, 14 March 2003, p. 24; Miettinen (2013), pp. 194, 201.

[157] COM(2012) 363 final, proposal for a directive on the fight against fraud to the Union's financial interests by means of criminal law, Brussels, 11 July 2012, Article 8.

[158] COM(2012) 363 final, p. 10.

[159] COM(2013) 42 final, proposal for a directive on the protection of the euro and other currencies against counterfeiting by criminal law, and replacing Council Framework Decision 2000/383/JHA, Strasbourg, 5 February 2013; SWD(2013) 19 final, Commission Staff Working Paper on the protection of the euro and other currencies against counterfeiting by criminal law, and replacing Council Framework Decision 2000/383/JHA, Brussels 5 February 2013, p. 12.

[160] Melander (2013), pp. 54–77, 72.

[161] Becker (1968), pp. 169, 207.

[162] Friedman (1995). Also available in internet www.daviddfriedman.com/Academic/Becker_Chapter/Becker_Chapter.html, accessed 12 September 2014. See also, Määttä and Pihlajamäki (2003), p. 54.

[163] Määttä and Pihlajamäki (2003), p. 51.

offenders often have a certain social or economic status due to which the probability of getting caught works for them as a stronger preventive incentive than the severity of punishment. Even low punishment threats work for them, because their conduct is more controlled by the possibility of getting caught and stigmatized as explained above in Sect. 2.2.1.[164]

This law and economics view on sanctions divides opinion. The Finnish Government for example found that increasing the risk of offenders getting caught by improving cooperation between the police and judicial authorities is more effective than setting harsher penalty scales.[165] The Council's opinion on setting fixed minimum penalty scales differed from the Commission's view. A vast majority of the Member States' representatives object to the use of fixed minimum penalty scales at the Union level.[166] Setting fixed minimum penalty scales alongside the minimum-maximum scales would mean complete harmonization of penalty scales[167] which could lead to disproportionate penalty threats within the national criminal justice systems. As the negotiations continued, the proposal against Union fraud no longer included setting fixed minimum penalty scales, nor were such penalty scales included in the directive either.

Full harmonisation of penalty scales would not lead to coherent or equal treatment of offenders in the EU Member States if the other elements that affect sentencing and conditions of execution of punishment remain unchanged, because penal sanctioning policies vary greatly amongst the Member States.[168] For example, mitigating and aggravating circumstances, terms of conditional or early release, the detention system, pardons, the court's discretion (for example not to convict), etc. effect how harsh or lenient the sentence will actually be.[169] In this sense, complete harmonisation of penalty levels would lead to incoherent punishment levels amongst the Member States judicial systems, and would mean unequal EU criminal law from the perspective of the EU citizens. This would be an undesirable development.

Full harmonisation of penalty scales could also lead to incoherence within national criminal justice systems, since EU-level criminal law is enacted only in limited areas of crime. Fixed penalty scales determined at the EU-level relative to only those certain areas of crime would mean inconsistencies in determining the proportional evaluation between different types of crimes. In this sense, full harmonisation on penalty scales would not enhance the inner coherence of national

---

[164] Andenaes (1974), pp. 14–15.

[165] The Finnish Government, U 57/2012 vp ehdotuksesta Euroopan parlamentin ja neuvoston direktiiviksi unionin taloudellisiin etuihin kohdistuvien petosten torjunnasta rikosoikeudellisin keinoin (unionipetosdirektiivi), pp. 9–10.

[166] Council Interinstitutional File 2013/0023 (COD) on protection of the euro and other currencies against counterfeiting by criminal law, Brussels 14 June 2013, p. 15 fn 3.

[167] The Finnish Government, U 57/2012 vp, 10.

[168] Eser (2003), pp. 379–416.

[169] Klip (2016), p. 43; COM(2004)334 final, Green Paper on the approximation, mutual recognition and enforcement of criminal sanctions in the European Union, Brussels, 30 April 2004, p. 11.

criminal justice systems and would be contrary to the inner dimension of the principle of *ultima ratio*.

5.2.4 Nature of Criminal Law as the Reflector of Sovereignty Forgotten?

Article 83 TFEU contains constitutional elements that manifest the nature of criminal law as a reflection of national sovereignty. These are the emergency brake procedure and the lowered threshold for the subsidiarity control mechanism. These
mechanisms, particularly the emergency brake procedure, secure the special nature
of criminal law and its role as a reflection of national sovereignty. Along with the
changes made to the criminal law decision-making procedure, the Lisbon Treaty
removed the Member States' right of veto and replaced it with the emergency brake
procedure, which in practice, has the same effect as the veto right.

The emergency brake mechanism has never been used. For that reason it is difficult to analyse what exactly the fundamental aspects of national criminal justice
systems entail. At the very core, one could argue it could include the nature of criminal law as the reflector of national sovereignty. As stated above, general doctrines
and principles of criminal law also fall under the concept, as well as issues relating
to sanction scales.

Articles 82(3) and 83(3) TFEU do not say anything about the CJEU's competence to judicially review the appropriateness of the Member State's claim that the
Union act affects the fundamental aspects of its criminal justice system.[170] It would
be essential to know the CJEU's competence to evaluate the appropriateness of the
emergency brake arguments in order to know how effective the emergency brake
procedure is and what its judicial limits are. The possibility of using the emergency
brake procedure relates to the question of the choice of legal basis since possible
legal bases other than Articles 82 and 83 TFEU do not enable such a procedure, and
therefore the possibility of emergency brake procedure applies only when Articles
82 or 83 TFEU are used as the legal basis for legislative proposals. This means that
the choice of legal basis for criminal legislative proposals is not a political question
that would only have technical judicial influences, but it also deeply affects the core
of national sovereignty by possibly enabling transfer of genuinely supranational
penal power to the Union, if for example the Union could enact criminal legislation
in the form of directly applicable regulations.

Viewed from the perspective that the emergency brake procedure, as a comparable to the previous veto right, was intended to leave each Member State free
choice on whether to adopt EU-level criminal measures that would affect the fundamentals of their sovereignty-sensitive criminal law, it would seem that the arguments the Member States would use might not have been intended to fall under the

---

[170] Klip (2016), p. 39.

discretion of the CJEU. However, along with the Lisbon Treaty the CJEU gained competence to rule on EU criminal law-related issues. In order to find out the CJEU's competence to review the appropriateness of the Member States' pleadings if the emergency brake procedure would be used, it is good to start from analysing the routes that the Member State pleadings could come under the Court's review.

For the Court to evaluate whether a Member State's claim would be appropriate, someone ought to argue that the aspect that the Member State has mentioned is not fundamental to the Member State's criminal justice system, and that the Member State would therefore be misusing the emergency brake procedure. This sort of argument would suggest that a Member State has not acted in accordance with the principle of sincere cooperation. Since the CJEU technically has the competence to evaluate such an argument, the Court should be competent to objectively evaluate the meaning of the phrase in the TFEU referring to 'fundamental aspects of national criminal justice systems'. This in turn, would require that the CJEU would to be able to say what the category of 'fundamental aspects' entails in each of the Member States' criminal justice systems, which of course, is not the CJEU's task.

If any reason could be used as a basis for the use of the emergency brake procedure, the aim of a more effective decision-making procedure under the ordinary legislative procedure would be endangered. For this reason the Court's competence to review the matter is not surprising. However, the task seems difficult for the Court since such evaluation requires deep knowledge of the Member States' legal systems, and the interpretation of national law.

Satzger simply states that '[a]lthough the Member States enjoy a margin of appreciation in their definition of 'fundamental aspects', the CJEU remains competent to rule on whether or not the emergency brake has been abused'. He mentions that the Court could review such a matter under competence established in Article 267(1)a TFEU—the competence to give preliminary ruling concerning the interpretation of the Treaties.[171] In order for the Court to be able to give such a ruling, some national authority should be insecure on whether their claim would be illegitimate to rely on the emergency brake mechanism. This scenario seems very unlikely, since the authorities of each Member State are in a better position to recognize if a Union criminal legislative proposal would shake the fundamental aspect of *their own* national criminal justice system.

A more likely route to the CJEU's review would be proceedings for failure to act.[172] The proceedings could perhaps be brought against the Council, or even the European Council, for not achieving consensus on the matter and for not enacting the legislation. Either the Commission or another Member State could be the plaintiff. However, legislative work is highly political. When the emergency brake would

---

[171] Satzger (2012), p. 81; Asp (2012), p. 140.

[172] According to Article 265 TFEU: 'Should the European Parliament, the European Council, the Council, the Commission or the European Central Bank, in infringement of the Treaties, fail to act, the Member States and the other institutions of the Union may bring an action before the Court of Justice of the European Union to have the infringement established.'

be applied, the discussions in the European Council of that issue would become more political than juridical.[173]

Since the legitimacy of EU-level criminal legislation stems partly from its compatibility with the Member States' existing penal norms, it would seem the optimal solution to continue the discussion with the opposing Member State on the issue rather than to launch judicial proceedings. A Member State's clear misuse of the emergency brake procedure would more likely signify a bigger political problem than a problem relating solely to criminal legislation. In such a case, judicial proceedings would seem unlikely to resolve the issue, since the CJEU would have to evaluate a serious political matter that could not have been solved in the debates of the European Council.

Technically it is completely understandable that the CJEU has competence to rule on the use of the emergency brake in principle to demonstrate that the Member States ought not to abuse that option. However, in practice, the CJEU's competence does not seem to be an effective tool to tackle the problems that might cause the use of the emergency brake mechanism. In this sense, the emergency brake procedure has a normative nature that mirrors the nature of criminal law as the reflector of national sovereignty. From a normative criminal law perspective, it also seems clear that the Union's substantive criminal law competence ought to be considered exhausted in Article 83 TFEU. The intent of the Member States as the Masters of the Treaties and the *ratio legis* of the Treaty provisions ought to be decisive in determining the extent of the Union's substantive criminal law competence.

References

Andenaes J (1974) Punishment and deterrence. The University of Michigan Press
Asp P (2012) The substantive criminal law competence of the EU (Stiftelsen Skrifter utgivna av Juridiska fakulteten vid Stockholms universitet). Jure
Beck U (2002) The terrorist threat: world risk society revisited. Theory Cult Soc 19(4)
Becker GS (1968) Crime and punishment: an economic approach. J Polit Econ 76(2)
Christiansen T (2016) Governance in the European Union. In: Cini M, Borragán NP-S (eds) European Union politics, 5th edn. OUP
Craig P (2010) The Lisbon Treaty: law, politics, and treaty reform. OUP
Craig P (2013) The Lisbon Treaty: law, politics, and treaty reform. OUP
Craig P, de Búrca G (2015) EU law: text, cases, and materials, 6th edn. OUP
Eser A (2003) Faisabilité de l'harmonisation. I. Comparative typology of convergences and divergences. In: Delmas-Marty M, Giudicelli-Delage G, Lambert-Abdelgawad É (eds) L'harmonisation des sanctions pénales en Europe. UMRDC
Frände D (2012) Yleinen rikosoikeus. Edita
Frände D, Suominen A (2010) Utgör artikel 325 i funktionsfördraget grunden för en europeisk, supranationell bedrägeristraffrätt? In: Elholm T, Greve V, Asp P, Bragadottir R, Frände D,

---

[173] Professor Sir David Edward in the UK House of Commons, Committee on European Scrutiny, 14th Report: The 'emergency brakes', Session 2004-05, available in internet www.publications. parliament.uk/pa/cm200405/cmselect/cmeuleg/38-xiv/3813.htm, accessed 25 June 2018, para 113.

Strandbakken A (eds) Liber amicarum et amicorum Karin Cornils – Glimt af nordisk straffrätt og straffeprosessrätt. Jurist- og økonomforbundets Forlag

Friedman D (1995) Rational criminals and profit-maximizing police: Gary Becker's contribution to the economic analysis of law and law enforcement. CUP

Herlin-Karnell E (2012) The constitutional dimension of European criminal law. Hart Publishing

Huomo-Kettunen M (2013) Heterarchical constitutional structures in the European legal space. Eur J Leg Stud 6(1)

Huomo-Kettunen M (2014) EU criminal policy at a crossroads between effectiveness and traditional restraints for the use of criminal law. New J Eur Crim Law 5(3)

Jareborg N (2000) National report of Sweden to the Corpus Juris project. In: Delmas-Marty M, Vervaele JAE (eds) The implementation of the Corpus Juris in the Member States, vol III. Intersentia

Klip A (2016) European criminal law: an integrative approach, 3rd edn. Intersentia

Lahti R, Pölönen P (2000) National report of Finland to the Corpus Juris project. In: Delmas-Marty M, Vervaele JAE (eds) The implementation of the Corpus Juris in the Member States, vol II. Intersentia

Leino P (2003) When every picture tells a story: the European Court of Justice and the jigsaw puzzle of external human rights competence. In: Koskenniemi M, Petman J, Klabbers J (eds) Nordic cosmopolitanism. Martinus Nijhoff Publishers

Ligeti K (2013) Approximation of substantive criminal law and the establishment of the European Public Prosecutor's Office. In: Galli F, Weyembergh A (eds) Approximation of substantive criminal law in the EU: the way forward. Editions de l'Universite de Bruxelles

Määttä K, Pihlajamäki H (2003) Rikoksen hinta: Taloustieteellinen näkökulma rikosoikeushistoriaan. Talentum

Melander S (2008) Kriminalisointiteoria – rangaistavaksi säätämisen oikeudelliset rajoitukset. Suomalaisen lakimiesyhdistyksen julkaisuja

Melander S (2010) EU-rikosoikeus. WSOYpro

Melander S (2012) EU ja talousrikosoikeus. Defensor Legis 93(4)

Melander S (2013) Ultima ratio in European criminal law. Oñati Socio-Leg Ser 3(1)

Miettinen S (2013) Implied ancillary criminal law competence after Lisbon. Eur Crim Law Rev 3(2)

Miettinen S (2015) The Europeanization of criminal law: competence and its control in the Lisbon era. University of Helsinki

Mitsilegas V (2009) EU criminal law. Hart Publishing

Nuotio K (2011) European criminal law under the developing constitutional setting of the European Union. In: Neil Walker – Jo Shaw – Stephen Tierney (eds) Europe's constitutional mosaic. Hart Publishing

Öberg J (2013) Union regulatory criminal law competence after Lisbon Treaty. In: Albrecht H-J, Klip A (eds) Crime, criminal law and criminal justice in Europe: a collection in honour of Prof. em. dr. h.c. Cyrille Fijnaut. Brill Nijhoff

Öberg J (2014) Limits to EU powers: a case study on individual criminal sanctions for the enforcement of EU law. European University Institute

Robinson PH (1994) A functional analysis of criminal law. Northwest Univ Law Rev 88

Satzger H (2012) International and European criminal law. C.H.Beck

Satzger H (2013) Internationales und Europäisches Strafrecht. Nomos Verlagsgesellschaft

Schütze R (2009a) From dual to cooperative federalism: the changing structure of European law. OUP

Schütze R (2009b) Subsidiarity after Lisbon: reinforcing the safeguards of federalism? Camb Law J 68(3)

Sicurella R (2013) Setting up a European criminal policy for the protection of EU financial interests: guidelines for a coherent definition of the material scope of the European Public Prosecutor's Office. In: Ligeti K (ed) Toward a prosecutor for the European Union, volume 1: a comparative analysis. Hart Publishing

Sous la direction de Mireille Delmas-Marty (1997) Corpus Juris. ECONOMICA

Spencer JR (2000) National report of the United Kingdom with particular reference to England and Wales to the Corpus Juris project. In: Delmas-Marty M, Vervaele JAE (eds) The implementation of the Corpus Juirs in the Member States, vol III. Intersentia

Suominen A (2011) Perus- ja ihmisoikeusnäkökohtia Suomen kansainvälisessä yhteistyössä rikosasioissa. Defensor Legis 92(1)

Vogenauer S (2011) The prohibition of abuse of law: an emerging general principle of EU law. In: de la Feria R, Vogenauer S (eds) Prohibition of abuse of law – a new general principle of EU law? Hart Publishing

Chapter 6
Conclusions: European Criminal Law—Justification and Restrictions

The general justification for the existence and use of European criminal law is the protection of human dignity. This principle is common to all European nations, and it recognised by the ECHR regime and the EU. The basic idea is that certain types of conduct cannot be left unpunished and therefore must be criminalised. The ECHR regime requires that the contracting parties use criminal law measures to protect the basic Convention value of human dignity which is protected through the other Convention rights. This means that the contracting parties cannot adopt an abolitionist legal order that would not have any criminal justice system at all.

The ECHR regime imposes on the contracting parties an obligation to use criminal law measures and to ensure effective procedural rights to tackle crime that infringes the principle of human dignity, as the case of *M.C. v Bulgaria* demonstrates. The logic seems to be mostly consequentialist, focusing on the prevention of undesired types of conduct in the future. However, the logic is also deontological in the sense that some types of conduct at the core of criminal law that violates human dignity, such as murder, genocide, rape, torture and similar for example, cannot be allowed to go unpunished. In this sense, the very core of the ECHR—the respect of human dignity—is the general justification for criminal law in general.

EU criminal law slightly differs from this premise. The general justification for the use of EU criminal law seems to be utilitarian and consequentialist, that is to enhance the Member States' ability to tackle cross-border crime effectively and to also enhance the Member States' sovereignty in this way. The effectiveness—or integration—driven policy-making emphasizes *the utility of cooperation* by means of criminal law to ensure the effective realization of other Union policies and the Member States' opportunities to react to undesirable conduct appearing within the Union.

In contrast, even though the ECHR regime aims for a dynamic interpretation of the Convention in order to ensure the effective realization of Convention rights, the regime seems to protect the deontological reasons for the very existence of the

© Springer International Publishing Switzerland and G. Giappichelli Editore 2020   245
M. Kettunen, *Legitimizing European Criminal Law*, Comparative, European and
International Criminal Justice 2, https://doi.org/10.1007/978-3-030-16174-3_6

Convention. Respect for human dignity also as an objective value in addition to protecting it only as an individual right demonstrates this. Moreover, the status of human dignity as an absolute right emphasizes this.

The objective element of human dignity is also a key issue relative to the nature of democracy. Pluralistic democracy ensures the fair treatment of minorities in institutional structures. When the decision-making processes enable taking different interests into account, abuses by a dominant majority can be avoided. Pluralistic democracy is about consensus democracy. The good of different interest-groups, even if they were unpopular groups such as criminals, is to be taken into account because each individual is seen as a member of the society. Democratic process that enables all interest groups to participate to the legislative discussion is more likely to lead to decisions, that is acceptable to most of the individuals.

At the EU-level criminal law context, the Council usually aims at consensus in its decision-making even though that is not legally required. Ultimately, the emergency brake procedure enables the national representatives in the Council to prevent such a legislative measure from becoming binding upon them if it would affect the fundamental aspects of its criminal justice system. The consensus-seeking nature of the legislative procedure and the sovereignty-sensitive nature of Article 83 TFEU show respect towards the national identities and their special characteristics and legitimizes the use of European criminal law. EU's criminal legislation is brought as close to the individuals as possible as the Member State's possibility to rely on the emergency brake procedure shows.

The respect of the EU-level criminalization principles legitimises the use of EU criminal law. To be legitimate in the eyes of the Member States and their citizens the EU criminal law needs to respect certain key features of national criminal laws. In doing this EU criminal law would also probably be better enforced in the Member States and better accepted by the individuals. EU criminal law ought to contribute to the strengthening of the Member States' sovereignty by increasing the Member States' opportunities to tackle cross-border crime and by protecting interests that can be better protected through EU-level criminal legislation. To ensure this, the European criminalization principles ought to be applied and respected. The EU's criminalization principles are constitutional restrictions to the Union's criminal law competence.

This also means that Article 83 TFEU should be applied as the legal basis for substantive criminal law measures. The *travaux* of the Treaties show that Article 83 TFEU is intended by the Union's constitutional legislator to exhaust the Union's substantive criminal law competence. In the light of the CJEU's new interpretation method where it utilises the *travaux* of the Treaties to interpret the Treaty provisions in cases in which purely the Treaty text by itself cannot give sufficient information. The CJEU has explicitly stated that the *travaux* can be used as an interpretative aid.

As explained above particularly in Chap. 1.3.3.3.2, the CJEU has started to refer to the *travaux préparatoires* of the Treaties to support constitutional interpretations that could not be achieved simply by textual interpretation. The Court *has not* relied on the *travaux* to support a dynamic interpretation of the Treaties. In this sense the

Court's new line of interpretative practice has been more conservative and static in nature, thus differing from its normal rather dynamic tone in interpretation.

This new interpretation method adopted by the Court might influence the doctrine on the choice of legal basis. For example, the Union's substantive criminal law competence ought to be considered exhausted in Article 83 TFEU based on the *ratio legis* that was revealed by examination of the *travaux*. This also supports the normative claim that EU-level criminalization principles ought to have effects already at the level of choices of legal basis. This means that the EU-level criminalization principles and the doctrine on the choice of legal basis are intertwined.

The new line of interpretation *could*, in a sense, restrict the Court's own interpretative freedom in the future. If the *travaux* can establish clear picture of the *ratio legis,* the Union's competence ought not to be extended beyond this purpose, at least if the *travaux* explicitly shows that the legal basis was *not* intended to be used to fulfil certain purposes. Naturally time will tell if the Court will continue to refrain from using the *travaux* to support dynamic interpretations, or whether it will remain limited to supporting static interpretations in this way.

As a main rule, Article 83 TFEU ought to exhaust the Union's substantive criminal law competence. Article 83 TFEU ought to be used as a legal basis also in situations where the issue being regulated would contain only a small part of criminal law contents. In these situations, a legislative measure could be based on two legal bases, Article 83 TFEU and the content-variable non-criminal-law legal basis. Alternatively, the criminal law-natured content could be separated into its own legislative instrument. As an exception to the main rule, Article 352 TFEU could be used to establish criminal legislative measures if it would be necessary as an 'emergency action'. This sort of emergency action might be necessary in unexpected situations such as during an environmental disaster, war, wide scale terrorist attack, or similar. This interpretation is supported also by the *travaux*. Article 352 TFEU does not infringe EU-level criminalization principles, or, following the Beck's idea on separating between the sovereignty and autonomy, the maxim of 'less autonomy to enhance sovereignty' in the sense that it can be used only if political unanimity can be established among the Member States.

It is important to recognise this new line of interpretation and that in the light of it Article 83 TFEU seems to be the only appropriate and acceptable substantive criminal law legal basis as a main rule.

To determine whether the Union has competence to enact substantive criminal legislation, it should be asked if the type of crime that is proposed to be criminalized is listed amongst the so-called euro-crimes, or whether the Union enacted non-criminal law harmonisation measures which must be followed by necessary criminal legislative measures. If the answer to either of these questions is positive, the Union has competence to act in terms of the principle of conferral.

Then the issue needs to be evaluated in terms of the principles of subsidiarity and proportionality which represent the transnational dimension of the *ultima ratio* principle. In terms of the outer dimension of *ultima ratio* principle, the Union legislature ought to ask the following questions:

1. Is it necessary to enact this criminal legislative measure? (subsidiarity)
2. Are the objectives and aims of the proposal criminal law-embedded? (subsidiarity)
3. Can the objectives be reached by measures taken at national level? (subsidiarity)
4. Does the Union-level measure bring extra value? (subsidiarity)
5. Could the same objectives and aims be reached by using less intrusive means? (proportionality)
6. Are other types of measures equally preventive? Would non-criminal law measures be sufficient to achieve the objectives and aims? (proportionality)

In terms of the inner dimension of *ultima ratio* principle, the Union legislature ought to consider the following issues:

1. Is the proposed criminal legislation proportional in relation to the objectives and aims of the proposal? (proportionality)
2. Does the proposal restrict fundamental rights more than necessary? (proportionality)
3. Is the proposed sanction level defensible? (proportionality)
4. Is the proposed sanction level proportionate in relation to other EU-level criminal legislative measures? (proportionality)
5. Is the proposed sanction level proportionate in relation to the Member States' sanction levels? (proportionality)

EU criminal legislation ought to respect the fundamental aspects of national criminal justice systems. Since Article 83 TFEU is the best legal basis for EU-level criminal legislation from a normative, criminal law-oriented, perspective, as well as the appropriate legal basis form the constitutional law perspective, regulations (as a result of a use of legal bases other than Article 83 TFEU) should not be used as a form of criminal legislative instruments in the EU. This means that criminal legislation ought to be given in the form of directives only, leaving room for the Member States to adopt the Union legislation into their own criminal justice systems. Flexibility in the implementation ensures that substantive EU criminal legislation respects the fundamental aspects of the national criminal justice systems. Article 83 TFEU also has an inbuilt mechanism, the emergency brake procedure, to ultimately ensure that the fundamental aspects of national criminal justice systems are respected.

In order for the content of criminal legislation to be justifiable, it should respect fundamental and human rights. Because all EU Member States are parties to the ECHR, a strong value consensus exists amongst the Member States on the appropriate minimum level of human rights protection. Therefore, it is recommended that the EU should accede to the ECHR on the same basis as the state parties. This means that the EU ought to allow the ECtHR a competence to evaluate alleged human rights violations occurring in the EU. Instead of making large changes to the draft accession agreement, constitutional amendment to the TFEU would ensure the respect of human rights to an equivalent level with the Member States.

As stated above in Chap. 2.2.1 concerning the utilitarian theory of the legitimacy of punishment, the legitimacy of the use of criminal law is born in institutional processes which are built to enable the legislation to be enacted in such a way and as such that enables the maximization of welfare for as many individuals as possible. This means that criminal law must be enacted in a procedure that balances the restrictions that will be imposed upon individuals by means of criminal legislation with individual freedoms. Article 83 TFEU has an embedded in this respect since it respects the traditional normative criminal law principles. Article 83 TFEU involves a legislative process that requires taking the fundamental rights of individuals and the uniqueness of the national criminal justice systems into account.

The European criminalization principles ought to affect the choice of legal basis. Before the Lisbon Treaty entered into force, the contours of the Union's substantive criminal law competence were largely determined through the rules on the choice of legal basis. In the so-called *environmental crimes* and *ship-source pollution* cases the CJEU emphasised the meaning of ex-Article 47 EU, according to which the exercise of Union competence could not infringe the competence granted in the first pillar. The legislative measures were to be enacted in one instrument only if the aims of the criminal legislative instrument were essentially the same as the aims of the instrument containing the substantive non-criminal law provisions.

Article 83 TFEU constitutes express criminal law competence for the Union. It gives wider competence to the Union than what the pre-Lisbon implicit criminal competence gave, especially relative to the Union's possibility to approximate sanctions under its express ancillary competence. Since the Lisbon Treaty has entered into force, only two legislative measures have been based on Article 83(2) TFEU. The adoption of the market abuse legislation by separating it into two instruments, the non-criminal law legislation in the regulation and the criminal law legislation in the directive, demonstrates how different the legal status is now that the ex-Article 47 EU does not have a decisive role and Article 83 TFEU includes an express ancillary legal basis for criminal legislative measures.

Because the legal basis and its *ratio legis* affect in which form of the secondary legislation is given and to its teleological interpretation, the choice of legal basis is not merely a technical issue. In criminal law related issues, it actually becomes an issue of criminal policy. The choice of legal basis determines what kind of criminal legislation can be enacted in terms of its form, preciseness, and adaptability to national criminal justice systems. In this sense, the European criminalization principles ought to guide the choice of legal basis relative to those legislative proposals that include criminal law content. For example, in its formal dimension the principle of legality requires that EU-level criminal legislation is given in a democratic process as close to the citizens as possible. Article 83 TFEU enables this by ensuring through the emergency brake procedure that the proposed criminal legislation fits in the national criminal justice system.

EU-level substantive criminal law will gain both institutional legitimacy (as explained above) and substantive legitimacy as to the content of the legislation when it follows the EU-level criminalization principles. In terms of justifying the content, fundamental and human rights protection play a crucial role. Accession to the ECHR would be likely to enhance legitimacy. However, the accession would be meaningless if the ECtHR is not granted equal competence to assess EU law as it evaluates national law when reviewing individual or state complaints. If the ECtHR could not review the Union's acts and omissions, the very purpose of the ECHR regime as the guarantor of minimum standards in the human rights protection would be undermined.

For the accession to be possible, Treaty changes would be necessary, since as it is now, Article 344 TFEU does not enable competence transfer to the ECtHR. Moreover, the Treaties ought to explicitly mention that the Union could accede to the ECHR without prejudice to the autonomy of EU law. Due to Article 344 TFEU and the principle of autonomy of EU law in terms of the Union's accession to the ECHR the Treaties cannot simply be interpreted in the light of the intent of the constitutional legislature and Article 6 TEU. If the Union's accession to the ECHR could not be carried out in a way that would establish the Union the same position as the other contracting parties, it might be better that the Union would not accede to the Convention at all.

As a general conclusion concerning the interpretation of the ECHR and the EU Treaties, the provisions of the ECHR, particularly the Convention rights, can be interpreted in a more dynamic fashion than the EU Treaties and in particular in comparison to those provisions that can be used as legal bases for secondary legislation. This is due to the difference in the functions of the provisions. The Convention rights are enshrined rather abstractly in the Convention to ensure that the provisions can be applied in different circumstances that evolve over time. The text of the Convention sets restrictions on interpreting the ECHR as a living instrument, but otherwise, if the social and cultural understanding changes, the abstract provisions also enable more modern interpretations. However, the Convention's dynamic interpretation model is not limitless: new rights cannot be created through interpretation.

In contrast, the legal bases enshrined in the EU treaties are expressions of conferral of competence from the Member States to the Union. The principle of conferral of EU law means that the Union has only the competence which is conferred upon it by the Treaties. This means that the expansion of the Union's competence ought to be conducted through Treaty changes. In the past, the CJEU has sometimes interpreted the competences widely. However, the Lisbon Treaty was designed to clarify the division of competences. Moreover, the CJEU's new interpretation method utilising the travaux of the Treaties will probably lessen dynamic Treaty interpretations in the future.

When these functions are examined, it can be argued that dynamic interpretation of the ECHR enables effective human rights protection *that directly affects individuals*. In turn, dynamic interpretation of legal bases enshrined in the EU Treaties *would directly affect only the scope of the Union's competence, and* the effects it would have on individuals in criminal law context would *tend to restrict rather than enhance freedom* due to the differences in the legislative procedures (subsidiarity control thresholds, emergency brake procedure) and their effects on the nature of the secondary legislation (type of the legislative instrument, sanction types and levels). From this perspective it is logical that dynamic interpretations work more naturally in the context of the ECHR regime than in the EU context relative to the question of the choice of legal basis.

Static constitutional interpretation might not always be appropriate since society and the world are evolving constantly. However, it is very much defendable in the context of criminal law competence. Predictability and certainty play a central role in the field of criminal law for a good reason. Individuals ought to be able to know under which terms their rights and freedoms are and can be limited by means of criminal law. In the European context this means that individuals should be able to know in what type of procedure and under which conditions the transnational legislator can enact criminal laws, and whether it affects them directly or through national implementation measures. Also, in terms of the choice of legal basis, if the Union's substantive criminal law competence would be widened through dynamic Treaty interpretation, it would mean that the democratic element of the legality principle would change because other legal bases do not include the emergency brake procedure. This would mean that the individuals' possibility to participate to the legislative process would be lessened indirectly.

This study has focused on the justification for European criminal law from a legal normative perspective. We can see however that the field of EU criminal law in particular is also very much a political issue. Criminal law restricts the rights of individuals more than regulation in other fields of law. Criminal sanctions are also stigmatizing, and in this sense, they are very different from other types of sanctions. Thus, criminal law is special. This special character is due to its close relationship to state sovereignty and individual rights and freedoms. Whereas at national level, justification for criminalization is about justifying the use of state power against individual, in addition to this, the justification of criminalization at transnational level is about justifying the shift and use of that penal power outside the state's borders. In the EU context, this means that choice of legal basis ought to follow the logic adopted in criminal law across the Member States that requires restrictions and checks on the use of penal power. Article 83 TFEU embodies this logic. Thus, the EU legislator should follow the European criminalization principles, the logic of the appropriate use of EU criminal law.

Sources

Official Sources

Treaties, Conventions, International Agreements

- Statute of the Council of Europe CETS No.: 001 (European Treaty Series No. 1) signed 5 May 1949, entered into force 3 August 1949.
- Treaty establishing the European Economic Community, signed in Rome on 25 March 1957, entered into force on 1 January 1958.
- Treaty on European Union, signed at Maastricht on 7 February [1992] OJ EC No C 191.
- Treaty on European Union and the Treaty on the Functioning of the European Union [2010] OJ C 83/80.
- Treaty establishing a Constitution for Europe [2004] OJ C310/121.
- European Convention for the Protection of Human Rights and Fundamental Freedoms (European Treaty Series No. 5) signed in Rome 4 November 1950, entered into force 3 September 1953.
- Vienna Convention on the Law of Treaties (adopted 23 May 1969, entered into force 27 January 1980) 1155 UNTS 331.
- European Convention on the Transfer of Proceedings of Criminal Matters (European treaty Series No. 73) signed in Strasbourg 15 May 1972.
- European Convention on Extradition and its additional protocols (European Treaty Series No. 24) signed in Paris 13 December 1957.
- European Convention on the International Validity of Criminal Judgments (European Treaty Series No. 70) signed in Hague, 28 May 1970.
- Convention on the Transfer of Sentenced Persons (European Treaty Series No. 112) signed in Strasbourg 21 March 1983.

© Springer International Publishing Switzerland and G. Giappichelli Editore 2020
M. Kettunen, *Legitimizing European Criminal Law*, Comparative, European and
International Criminal Justice 2, https://doi.org/10.1007/978-3-030-16174-3

- Protocol No. 6 to the Convention for the Protection of Human Rights and Fundamental Freedoms concerning the Abolition of the Death Penalty (entered into force 1 March 1985) CETS No. 114.
- European Convention on the Suppression of Terrorism (European Treaty Series No. 90) signed in Strasbourg 27 January 1977.
- Convention on Laundering, Search, Seizure and Confiscation of the Proceeds from Crime (European Treaty Series No. 141) signed in Strasbourg 8 November 1990.
- United Nations Convention against Illicit Traffic in Narcotic Drugs and Psychotropic Substances (adopted 20 December 1988, entered into force 11 November 1990) 1582 UNTS 95.
- United Nations Convention against Torture and Other Cruel, Inhuman or Degrading Treatment or Punishment (26 June 1987), UNTS Vol. 1465, I-24841.
- Rome Statute of the International Criminal Court (adopted 17 July 1998 and corrected by process-verbaux of 10 November 1998, 12 July 1999, 30 November 1999, 8 May 2000, 17 January 2001 and 16 January 2002, entered into force on 1 July 2002) UN Doc. A/CONF. 183/9∗.
- Statute of the International Criminal Tribunal for the Prosecution of Persons Responsible for Genocide and Other Serious Violations of International Humanitarian Law Committed in the Territory of Rwanda and Rwandan Citizens Responsible for Genocide and Other Such Violations Committed in the Territory of Neighbouring States, between 1 January 1994 and 31 December 1994 (adopted by Security Council resolution 955 (1994) of 8 November 1994 amended by Security Council resolutions 1165 (1998) of 30 April 1998, 1329 (2000) of 30 November 2000, 1411 (2002) of 17 May 2002 and 1431 (2002) of 14 August 2002) (Statute of the International Criminal Tribunal for Rwanda, ICTR).
- Convention drawn up on the basis of Article K.3 of the Treaty on European Union, on the protection of the European Communities' financial interests, [1995] OJ C 316.
- General Recommendation 19 of the United Nations Committee on the Elimination of Discrimination against Women, 29 January 1992.
- Laeken Declaration on the Future of the European Union, Annex I to the presidency conclusions, 14 and 15 December 2001.
- Presidency Conclusions of Brussels European Council, 17 and 18 June 2004 (10679/2/04 REV 2), Brussels, 19 July 2004.
- The Stockholm Programme, [2010] OJEU C 115.

Protocols and Declarations [to the TFEU and TEU Unless Otherwise Specified]

- Protocol (No 2) on the application of the principles of subsidiarity and proportionality [2012] OJ C326/206.

- Protocol (No 21) on the position of the United Kingdom and Ireland in respect of the area of freedom, security and justice [2012] OJ C326/295.
- Protocol (No 22) on the position of Denmark [2012] OJ C326/299.
- Declaration concerning primacy [2010] OJ C 83/337.
- 8. Declaration on Article K.3(e) of the Treaty on European Union [1997] OJ C 340.

EU Secondary Legislation

Regulations

- Regulation No 31 (EEC), 11 (EAEC), laying down the Staff Regulations of Officials and the Conditions of Employment of Other Servants of the European Economic Community and the European Atomic Energy Community [1962] OJ 45, 14.6.1962.
- Council Regulation (EEC) No 2913/92 of 12 October 1992 establishing the Community Customs [1992] OJ L 302, 19.10.1992.
- Regulation (EC) No 450/2008 of the European Parliament and of the Council of 23 April 2008 laying down the Community Customs Code (Modernised Customs Code) [2008] OJ L 145, 4.6.2008.
- Commission Delegated Regulation (EU) No 946/2012 of 12 July 2012 supplementing Regulation (EC) No 1060/2009 of the European Parliament and of the Council with regard to rules of procedure on fines imposed to credit rating agencies by the European Securities and Markets Authority, including rules on the right of defence and temporal provisions Text with EEA relevance [2012] OJ L 282, 16.10.2012.
- Regulation (EU, Euratom) No 883/2013 of the European Parliament and of the Council of 11 September 2013 concerning investigations conducted by the European Anti-Fraud Office (OLAF) and repealing Regulation (EC) No 1073/1999 of the European Parliament and of the Council and Council Regulation (Euratom) No 1074/1999 [2013] OJ L 248, 18.9.2013.
- Regulation (EU) No 952/2013 of the European Parliament and of the Council of 9 October 2013 laying down the Union Customs Code [2013] OJ L 269, 10.10.2013.
- Regulation (EU) No 596/2014 of the European Parliament and of the Council of 16 April 2014 on market abuse (market abuse regulation) and repealing Directive 2003/6/EC of the European Parliament and of the Council and Commission Directives 2003/124/EC, 2003/125/EC and 2004/72/EC Text with EEA relevance [2014] OJ L 173, 12.6.2014.
- Commission Delegated Regulation (EU) No 640/2014 of 11 March 2014 supplementing Regulation (EU) No 1306/2013 of the European Parliament and of the Council with regard to the integrated administration and control system and conditions for refusal or withdrawal of payments and administrative penalties

applicable to direct payments, rural development support and cross compliance [2014] OJ L 181, 20.6.2014.

- Commission Delegated Regulation (EU) No 667/2014 of 13 March 2014 supplementing Regulation (EU) No 648/2012 of the European Parliament and of the Council with regard to rules of procedure for penalties imposed on trade repositories by the European Securities and Markets Authority including rules on the right of defence and temporal provisions Text with EEA relevance [2014] OJ L 179, 19.6.2014.
- Council Regulation (EU) 2017/1939 of 12 October 2017 implementing enhanced cooperation on the establishment of the European Public Prosecutor's Office ('the EPPO') [2017] OJ L 283, 31.10.2017.

Directives

- Directive 95/46/EC of the European Parliament and of the Council of 24 October 1995 on the protection of individuals with regard to the processing of personal data and on the free movement of such data [1995] OJ L 281, 23.11.1995.
- Directive 2006/24/EC of the European Parliament and of the Council of 15 March 2006 on the retention of data generated or processed in connection with the provision of publicly available electronic communications services or of public communications networks and amending Directive 2002/58/EC [2006] OJ L 105, 13.4.2006.
- Directive 2008/99/EC of the European Parliament and of the Council of 19 November 2008 on the protection of the environment through criminal law (Text with EEA relevance) [2008] OJ L 328, 6.12.2008.
- Directive 2009/123/EC of the European Parliament and of the Council of 21 October 2009 amending Directive 2005/35/EC on ship-source pollution and on the introduction of penalties for infringements (Text with EEA relevance) [2009] OJ L 280, 27.10.2009.
- Directive 2011/36/EU of the European Parliament and of the Council of 5 April 2011 on preventing and combating trafficking in human beings and protecting its victims, and replacing Council Framework Decision 2002/629/JHA [2011] OJ L 101, 15.4.2011.
- Directive 2011/92/EU of the European Parliament and of the Council of 13 December 2011 on combating the sexual abuse and sexual exploitation of children and child pornography, and replacing Council Framework Decision 2004/68/JHA [2011] OJ L 335, 17.12.2011.
- Directive 2011/99/EU of the European Parliament and of the Council of 13 December 2011 on the European protection order [2011] OJ L 338, 21.12.2011.
- Directive 2013/40/EU of the European Parliament and of the Council of 12 August 2013 on attacks against information systems and replacing Council Framework Decision 2005/222/JHA [2013] OJ L 218, 14.8.2013.
- Directive 2014/42/EU of the European Parliament and of the Council of 3 April 2014 on the freezing and confiscation of instrumentalities and proceeds of crime in the European Union [2014] OJ L 127, 29.4.2014.

- Directive 2014/57/EU of the European Parliament and of the Council of 16 April 2014 on criminal sanctions for market abuse (market abuse directive) [2014] OJ L 173, 12.6.2014.
- Directive 2014/62/EU of the European Parliament and of the Council of 15 May 2014 on the protection of the euro and other currencies against counterfeiting by criminal law, and replacing Council Framework Decision 2000/383/JHA [2013] OJ L 151, 21.5.2014.
- Directive (EU) 2017/541 of the European Parliament and of the Council of 15 March 2017 on combating terrorism and replacing Council Framework Decision 2002/475/JHA and amending Council Decision 2005/671/JHA OJ L 88, 31.3.2017.
- Directive (EU) 2017/1371 of the European Parliament and of the Council of 5 July 2017 on the fight against fraud to the Union's financial interests by means of criminal law [2017] OJ L 198, 28.7.2017.
- Directive (EU) 2017/2103 of the European Parliament and of the Council of 15 November 2017 amending Council Framework Decision 2004/757/JHA in order to include new psychoactive substances in the definition of 'drug' and repealing Council Decision 2005/387/JHA, OJ L 305/12, 21.11.2017.

Case Law

Court of Justice

- Case C-26/62 *NV Algemene Transport- en Expeditie Onderneming van Gend & Loos v Netherlands Inland Revenue Administration.* Judgment of the Court of 5 February 1963. ECR [1963] p. 1 ECLI:EU:C:1963:1.
- Case C-6/64 *Flaminio Costa v E.N.E.L.* Judgment of the Court of 15 July 1964. ECR [1964] p. 1195 ECLI:EU:C:1964:34.
- Case C-14/68 *Walt Wilhelm and others v Bundeskartellamt.* Judgment of the Court of 13 February 1969. ECR [1969] p. 1 ECLI:EU:C:1969:4.
- Case C-29/69 *Erich Stauder v City of Ulm - Sozialamt.* Judgment of the Court of 12 November 1969. ECR [1969] p. 419 ECLI:EU:C:1969:57.
- Case C-11/70 *Internationale Handelsgesellschaft mbH v Einfuhr- und Vorratsstelle für Getreide und Futtermittel.* Judgment of the Court of 17 December 1970. ECR [1970] p. 1125 ECLI:EU:C:1970:114.
- Case C-93/71 *Orsolina Leonesio v Ministero dell'agricoltura e foreste.* Judgment of the Court of 17 May 1972. ECR [1972] p. 287 ECLI:EU:C:1972:39.
- Case C-70/72 *Commission of the European Communities v Federal Republic of Germany.* Judgment of the Court of 12 July 1973. ECR [1973] p. 813 ECLI:EU:C:1973:87.

- Case C-4/73 J. *Nold, Kohlen- und Baustoffgroßhandlung v Commission of the European Communities.* Judgment of the Court of 14 May 1974. ECR [1974] p. 491 ECLI:EU:C:1974:51.
- Case C-34/73 *Fratelli Variola S.p.A. v Amministrazione italiana delle Finanze.* Judgment of the Court of 10 October 1973. ECR [1973] p. 981 ECLI:EU:C:1973:101.
- Case C-41/74 *Yvonne van Duyn v Home Office.* Judgment of the Court of 4 December 1974. ECR [1974] p. 1337 ECLI:EU:C:1974:133.
- Case C-36/75 *Roland Rutili v Ministre de l'intérieur.* Judgment of the Court of 28 October 1975. ECR [1975] p. 1219 ECLI:EU:C:1975:137.
- Case C-30/77 *Régina v Pierre Bouchereau.* Judgment of the Court of 27 October 1977. ECR [1977] p. 1999 ECLI:EU:C:1977:172.
- Case C-106/77 *Amministrazione delle Finanze dello Stato v Simmenthal SpA.* Judgment of the Court of 9 March 1978. ECR [1978] p. 629 ECLI:EU:C:1978:49.
- Case C-148/78 *Criminal proceedings against Tullio Ratti.* Judgment of the Court of 5 April 1979. ECR [1979] p. 1629 ECLI:EU:C:1979:110.
- Case C-149/79 *Commission of the European Communities v Kingdom of Belgium.* Judgment of the Court of 17 December 1980. ECR [1980] p. 3881 ECLI:EU:C:1980:297.
- Case C-53/81 *D.M. Levin v Staatssecretaris van Justitie.* Judgment of the Court of 23 March 1982. ECR [1982] p. 1035 ECLI:EU:C:1982:105.
- Case C-264/81 *SpA Savma v Commission of the European Communities.* Judgment of 27 November 1984. ECR [1984] p. 3915 ECLI:EU:C:1984:359.
- Case C-283/81 *Srl CILFIT and Lanificio di Gavardo SpA v Ministry of Health.* Judgment of the Court of 6 October 1982. ECR [1982] p. 3415 ECLI:EU:C:1982:335.
- Case C-63/83 *Regina v Kent Kirk.* Judgment of the Court of 10 July 1984. ECR [1984] p. 2689 ECLI:EU:C:1984:255
- Case C-294/83 *Parti écologiste "Les Verts" v European Parliament.* Judgment of the Court of 23 April 1986. ECR [1986] p. 1339 ECLI:EU:C:1986:166
- Case C-222/84 *Marguerite Johnston v Chief Constable of the Royal Ulster Constabulary.* Judgment of the Court of 15 May 1986. ECR [1986] p. 1651 ECLI:EU:C:1986:206.
- Case C-314/85 *Foto-Frost v Hauptzollamt Lübeck-Ost.* Judgment of the Court of 22 October 1987. ECR [1987] p. 4199 ECLI:EU:C:1987:452.
- Case C-12/86 *Meryem Demirel v Stadt Schwäbisch Gmünd.* Judgment of the Court of 30 September 1987. ECR [1987] p. 3719 ECLI:EU:C:1987:400.
- Case C-14/86 *Pretore di Salò v Persons unknown.* Judgment of the Court (Fifth Chamber) of 11 June 1987. ECR [1987] p. 2545 ECLI:EU:C:1987:275.
- Case C-45/86 *Commission of the European Communities v Council of the European Communities.* Judgment of the Court of 26 March 1987. ECR [1987] p. 1493 ECLI:EU:C:1987:163.
- Case C-80/86 *Criminal proceedings against Kolpinghuis Nijmegen BV.* Judgment of the Court (Sixth Chamber) of 8 October 1987. ECR [1987] p. 3969 ECLI:EU:C:1987:431.

- Case C-157/86 *Mary Murphy and others v An Bord Telecom Eireann.* Judgment of the Court of 4 February 1988. ECR [1988] p. 673 ECLI:EU:C:1988:62.
- Case C-68/88 *Commission of the European Communities v Hellenic Republic.* Judgment of the Court of 21 September 1989. ECR [1989] p. 2965 ECLI:EU:C:1989:339.
- Case C-300/89 *Commission of the European Communities v Council of the European Communities.* Judgment of the Court of 11 June 1991. ECR [1991] p. I-2867 ECLI:EU:C:1991:244.
- Joined cases C-283/94, C-291/94 and C-292/94 *Denkavit International BV, VITIC Amsterdam BV and Voormeer BV v Bundesamt für Finanzen.* Judgment of the Court (Fifth Chamber) of 17 October 1996. ECR [1996] p. I-5063 ECLI:EU:C:1996:387.
- Joined cases C-74/95 and C-129/95 *Criminal proceedings against X.* Judgment of the Court (Fifth Chamber) of 12 December 1996. ECR [1996] p. I-6609 ECLI:EU:C:1996:491.
- Case C-296/95 *The Queen v Commissioners of Customs and Excise, ex parte EMU Tabac SARL, The Man in Black Ltd, John Cunningham.* Judgment of the Court of 2 April 1998. ECR [1998] p. I-1605 ECLI:EU:C:1998:152
- Case C-170/96 *Commission of the European Communities v Council of the European Union.* Judgment of the Court of 12 May 1998. ECR [1998] p. I-2763 ECLI:EU:C:1998:219.
- Case C-209/97 *Commission of the European Communities v Council of the European Union.* Judgment of the Court (Sixth Chamber) of 18 November 1999. ECR [1999] p. I-8067 ECLI:EU:C:1999:559.
- Case C-376/98 *Federal Republic of Germany v European Parliament and Council of the European Union.* Judgment of the Court of 5 October 2000. ECR [2000] p. I-8419 ECLI:EU:C:2000:544.
- Case C-413/99 *Baumbast and R v Secretary of State for the Home Department.* Judgment of the Court of 17 September 2002. ECR [2002] p. I-7091 ECLI:EU:C:2002:493.
- Case C-60/00 *Mary Carpenter v Secretary of State for the Home Department.* Judgment of the Court of 11 July 2002. ECR [2002] p. I-6279 ECLI:EU:C:2002:434.
- Case C-112/00 *Eugen Schmidberger, Internationale Transporte und Planzüge v Republik Österreich.* Judgment of the Court of 12 June 2003. ECR [2003] p. I-5659 ECLI:EU:C:2003:333.
- Case C-453/00 *Kühne & Heitz NV v Produktschap voor Pluimvee en Eieren.* Judgment of the Court of 13 January 2004. ECR [2004] p. I-837 ECLI:EU:C:2004:17.
- Case C-245/01 *RTL Television GmbH v Niedersächsische Landesmedienanstalt für privaten Rundfunk.* Judgment of the Court (Fifth Chamber) of 23 October 2003. ECR [2003] p. I-12489 ECLI:EU:C:2003:580.
- Case C-491/01 *The Queen v Secretary of State for Health, ex parte British American Tobacco (Investments) Ltd and Imperial Tobacco Ltd.* Judgment of the Court of 10 December 2002. ECR [2002] p. I-11453 ECLI:EU:C:2002:741.

- Case C-36/02 *Omega Spielhallen- und Automatenaufstellungs-GmbH v Oberbürgermeisterin der Bundesstadt Bonn*. Judgment of the Court (First Chamber) of 14 October 2004. ECR [2004] p. I-9609 ECLI:EU:C:2004:614.
- Joined cases C-189/02 P, C-202/02 P, C-205/02 P to C-208/02 P and C-213/02 P *Dansk Rørindustri A/S* (C-189/02 P), *Isoplus Fernwärmetechnik Vertriebsgesellschaft mbH and Others* (C-202/02 P), *KE KELIT Kunststoffwerk GmbH* (C-205/02 P), *LR af 1998 A/S* (C-206/02 P), *Brugg Rohrsysteme GmbH* (C-207/02 P), *LR af 1998 (Deutschland) GmbH* (C-208/02 P) *and ABB Asea Brown Boveri Ltd* (C-213/02 P) *v Commission of the European Communities*. Judgment of the Court (Grand Chamber) of 28 June 2005. ECR [2005] p. I-5425 ECLI:EU:C:2005:408.
- Case C-61/03 *Commission of the European Communities v United Kingdom of Great Britain and Northern Ireland*. Judgment of the Court (Grand Chamber) of 12 April 2005. ECR [2005] p. I-2477 ECLI:EU:C:2005:210.
- Case C-105/03 *Criminal proceedings against Maria Pupino*. Judgment of the Court (Grand Chamber) of 16 June 2005. ECR [2005] p. I-5285 ECLI:EU:C:2005:386.
- Case C-176/03 *Commission of the European Communities v Council of the European Union*. Judgment of the Court (Grand Chamber) of 13 September 2005. ECR [2005] p. I-7879 ECLI:EU:C:2005:542.
- Case C-234/04 *Rosmarie Kapferer v Schlank & Schick GmbH*. Judgment of the Court (First Chamber) of 16 March 2006. ECR [2006] p. I-2585 ECLI:EU:C:2006:178.
- Case C-273/04 *Republic of Poland v Council of the European Union*. Judgment of the Court (Grand Chamber) of 23 October 2007. ECR [2007] p. I-8925 ECLI:EU:C:2007:622.
- Joined cases C-392/04 and C-422/04 *i-21 Germany GmbH* (C-392/04) *and Arcor AG & Co. KG* (C-422/04) *v Bundesrepublik Deutschland*. Judgment of the Court (Grand Chamber) of 19 September 2006. ECR [2006] p. I-8559 ECLI:EU:C:2006:586.
- Case C-432/04 *Commission of the European Communities v Édith Cresson*. Judgment of the Court (Full Court) of 11 July 2006. ECR [2006] p. I-6387 ECLI:EU:C:2006:455.
- Case C-91/05 *Commission of the European Communities v Council of the European Union*. Judgment of the Court (Grand Chamber) of 20 May 2008. ECR [2008] p. I-3651 ECLI:EU:C:2008:288.
- Case C-303/05 *Advocaten voor de Wereld VZW v Leden van de Ministerraad*. Judgment of the Court (Grand Chamber) of 3 May 2007. ECR [2007] p. I-3633 ECLI:EU:C:2007:261.
- Case C-321/05 *Hans Markus Kofoed v Skatteministeriet*. Judgment of the Court (First Chamber) of 5 July 2007. ECR [2007] p. I-5795 ECLI:EU:C:2007:408.
- Joined cases C-402/05 P and C-415/05 P *Yassin Abdullah Kadi and Al Barakaat International Foundation v Council of the European Union and Commission of the European Communities*. Judgment of the Court (Grand Chamber) of 3 September 2008. ECR [2008] p. I-6351 ECLI:EU:C:2008:461.

- Case C-440/05 *Commission of the European Communities v Council of the European Union.* Judgment of the Court (Grand Chamber) of 23 October 2007. ECR [2007] p. I-9097 ECLI:EU:C:2007:625.
- Case C-301/06 *Ireland v European Parliament and Council of the European Union.* Judgment of the Court (Grand Chamber) of 10 February 2009. ECR [2009] p. I-593 ECLI:EU:C:2009:68.
- Case C-308/06 *The Queen, on the application of International Association of Independent Tanker Owners (Intertanko) and Others v Secretary of State for Transport.* Judgment of the Court (Grand Chamber) of 3 June 2008. ECR [2008] p. I-4057 ECLI:EU:C:2008:312.
- Case C-409/06 *Winner Wetten GmbH v Bürgermeisterin der Stadt Bergheim.* Judgment of the Court (Grand Chamber) of 8 September 2010. ECR [2010] p. I-8015 ECLI:EU:C:2010:503.
- Case C-411/06 *Commission of the European Communities v European Parliament and Council of the European Union.* Judgment of the Court (Grand Chamber) of 8 September 2009. ECR [2009] p. I-7585 ECLI:EU:C:2008:224.
- Case C-2/08 *Amministrazione dell'Economia e delle Finanze and Agenzia delle entrate v Fallimento Olimpiclub Srl.* Judgment of the Court (Second Chamber) of 3 September 2009. ECR [2009] p. I-7501 ECLI:EU:C:2009:506.
- Case C-101/08 *Audiolux SA e.a v Groupe Bruxelles Lambert SA (GBL) and Others and Bertelsmann AG and Others.* Judgment of the Court (Fourth Chamber) of 15 October 2009. ECR [2009] p. I-9823 ECLI:EU:C:2009:626.
- Case C-314/08 *Krzysztof Filipiak v Dyrektor Izby Skarbowej w Poznaniu.* Judgment of the Court (Third Chamber) of 19 November 2009. ECR [2009] p. I-11049 ECLI:EU:C:2009:719.
- Case C-386/08 *Firma Brita GmbH v Hauptzollamt Hamburg-Hafen.* Judgment of the Court (Fourth Chamber) of 25 February 2010. ECR [2010] p. I-1289 ECLI:EU:C:2010:91.
- Case C-355/10 *European Parliament v Council of the European Union.* Judgment of the Court (Grand Chamber) of 5 September 2012. ECLI:EU:C:2012:516.
- Case C-489/10 *Criminal proceedings against Łukasz Marcin Bonda.* Judgment of the Court (Grand Chamber) of 5 June 2012. ECLI:EU:C:2012:319.
- Case C-490/10 *European Parliament v Council of the European Union.* Judgment of the Court (Second Chamber) of 6 September 2012. ECLI:EU:C:2012:525.
- Case C-617/10 *Åklagaren v Hans Åkerberg Fransson.* Judgement of 26 February 2013. ECLI:EU:C:2013:105.
- Case C-399/11 *Stefano Melloni v Ministerio Fiscal.* Judgment of the Court (Grand Chamber) of 26 February 2013. ECLI:EU:C:2013:107.
- Case C-466/11 *Gennaro Currà and Others v Bundesrepublik Deutschland.* Order of the Court (Third Chamber) of 12 July 2012. ECLI:EU:C:2012:465.
- Case C-583/11 P *Inuit Tapiriit Kanatami and Others v European Parliament and Council of the European Union.* Judgment of the Court (Grand Chamber) of 3 October 2013. ECLI:EU:C:2013:625.
- Joined cases C-293/12 and C-594/12 *Digital Rights Ireland Ltd v Minister for Communications, Marine and Natural Resources and Others and Kärntner*

Landesregierung and Others. Judgment of the Court (Grand Chamber) of 8 April 2014. ECLI:EU:C:2014:238.

- Case C-370/12 *Thomas Pringle v Government of Ireland, Ireland and The Attorney General.* Judgment of the Court (Full Court) of 27 November 2012. ECLI:EU:C:2012:756.
- Joined cases C-317/13 and C-679/13 *European Parliament v Council of the European Union.* Judgment of the Court (Fourth Chamber) of 16 April 2015. ECLI:EU:C:2015:223.
- Joined cases C-358/13 and C-181/14 *Criminal proceedings against Markus D.* (C-358/13) *and G.* (C-181/14). Judgment of the Court (Fourth Chamber) of 10 July 2014. ECLI:EU:C:2014:2060.
- Case C-62/14 *Peter Gauweiler and Others v Deutscher Bundestag.* Judgment of the Court (Grand Chamber) of 16 June 2015. ECLI:EU:C:2015:400.
- Case C-286/14 *European Parliament v European Commission.* Judgment of the Court (Fifth Chamber) of 17 March 2016. ECLI:EU:C:2016:183.
- Case C-362/14 *Maximillian Schrems v Data Protection Commissioner.* Judgment of the Court (Grand Chamber) of 6 October 2015. ECLI:EU:C:2015:650.
- Case C-105/14 Taricco I. Judgment of the Court (Grand Chamber) of 8 September 2015. ECLI:EU:C:2015:555.
- Case C-42/17 Taricco II (M.A.S. and M.B.) Judgment of the Court (Grand Chamber) of 5 December 2017. ECLI:EU:C:2017:936.

Court of First Instance and General Court

- Case T-493/93 Hansa-Fisch GmbH v Commission of the European Communities. Judgment of the Court of First Instance (Fourth Chamber) of 8 March 1995. ECR [1995] p. II-575 ECLI:EU:T:1995:47.
- Joined cases T-134/94, T-136/94, T-137/94, T-138/94, T-141/94, T-145/94, T-147/94, T-148/94, T-151/94, T-156/94 and T-157/94 NMH Stahlwerke GmbH, Eurofer ASBL, Arbed SA, Cockerill-Sambre SA, Thyssen Stahl AG, Unimétal - Société française des aciers longs SA, Krupp Hoesch Stahl AG, Preussag Stahl AG, British Steel plc, Siderurgica Aristrain Madrid SL and Empresa Nacional Siderurgica SA v Commission of the European Communities. Order of the Court of First Instance (Second Chamber, extended composition) of 19 June 1996. ECR [1996] p. II-537 ECLI:EU:T:1996:85.
- Case T-353/94 Postbank NV v Commission of the European Communities. Judgment of the Court of First Instance (First Chamber, extended composition) of 18 September 1996. ECR [1994] p. II-1141 ECLI:EU:T:1994:288.
- Case T-240/04 French Republic v Commission of the European Communities. Judgment of the Court of First Instance (First Chamber, extended composition) of 17 September 2007. ECR [2007] p. II-4035 ECLI:EU:T:2007:290.
- Case T-143/06 MTZ Polyfilms Ltd v Council of the European Union.
- Judgment of the Court of First Instance (Third Chamber) of 17 November 2009. ECR [2009] p. II-4133 ECLI:EU:T:2009:441.

Opinions of Court

- Opinion 1/91 Opinion of the Court of 14 December 1991. Opinion delivered pursuant to the second subparagraph of Article 228 (1) of the Treaty - Draft agreement between the Community, on the one hand, and the countries of the European Free Trade Association, on the other, relating to the creation of the European Economic Area. ECLI:EU:C:1991:490.
- Opinion 2/94 Opinion of the Court of 28 March 1996. Accession by the Community to the European Convention for the Protection of Human Rights and Fundamental Freedoms. ECLI:EU:C:1996:140.
- Opinion 2/13 Opinion of the Court (Full Court) of 18 December 2014. Opinion pursuant to Article 218(11) TFEU - Draft international agreement - Accession of the European Union to the European Convention for the Protection of Human Rights and Fundamental Freedoms - Compatibility of the draft agreement with the EU and FEU Treaties. ECLI:EU:C:2014:2454.

Advocate General Opinions (by Date)

- Opinion of Advocate General Roemer in Case C- 26/62 NV Algemene Transport-en Expeditie Onderneming van Gend & Loos v Netherlands Inland Revenue Administration, delivered on 12 December 1962. ECLI:EU:C:1962:42.
- Opinion of Advocate General Mayras in Case C-2/74 Jean Reyners v Belgian State, delivered on 28 May 1974. ECLI:EU:C:1974:59.
- Opinion of Advocate General Jacobs in Case C-240/90 Federal Republic of Germany v Commission of the European Communities, delivered on 3 June 1992. ECLI:EU:C:1992:237.
- Opinion of Advocate General Geelhoed in Case C-61/03 Commission of the European Communities v United Kingdom of Great Britain and Northern Ireland, delivered on 2 December 2004. ECLI:EU:C:2004:765.
- Joined opinion of Advocate General Poiares Maduro in Case C-255/02 Halifax plc, Leeds Permanent Development Services Ltd and County Wide Property Investments Ltd v Commissioners of Customs & Excise, Case C-419/02 BUPA Hospitals Ltd and Goldsborough Developments Ltd v Commissioners of Customs & Excise, Case C-223/03 University of Huddersfield Higher Education Corporation v Commissioners of Customs & Excise, delivered on 7 April 2005. ECLI:EU:C:2005:200.
- Opinion of Advocate General Geelhoed in Case C-432/04 Commission of the European Communities v Édith Cresson, delivered on 23 February 2006. ECLI:EU:C:2006:140.
- Opinion of Advocate General Mazák in Case C-440/05 Commission of the European Communities v Council of the European Union, delivered on 28 June 2007. ECLI:EU:C:2007:393.
- Opinion of Advocate General Poiares Maduro in joined cases C-402/05 P and C-415/05 P Yassin Abdullah Kadi and Al Barakaat International Foundation v Council of the European Union and Commission of the European Communities, delivered on 16 January 2008. ECLI:EU:C:2008:11.

- Opinion of Advocate General Ruiz-Jarabo Colomer Case C-297/07 Klaus Bourquain, delivered on 8 April 2008. ECLI:EU:C:2008:206.
- Opinion of Advocate General Kokott Case C-489/10 Criminal proceedings against Łukasz Marcin Bonda, delivered on 15 December 2011. ECLI:EU:C:2011:845.
- Opinion of Advocate General Cruz Villalón Case C-135/11 P IFAW Internationaler Tierschutz-Fonds gGmbH v European Commission, delivered on 1 March 2012. ECLI:EU:C:2012:118
- Opinion of Advocate General Jääskinen in Case C-202/11 Anton Las v PSA Antwerp NV, delivered on 12 July 2012. ECLI:EU:C:2012:456.
- Opinion of Advocate General Kokott in Case C-370/12 Thomas Pringle v Government of Ireland, Ireland and The Attorney General, delivered on 26 October 2012. ECLI:EU:C:2012:675
- Opinion of Advocate General Bot in joined cases C-274/11 and C-295/11 Kingdom of Spain and Italian Republic v Council of the European Union, delivered on 11 December 2012. ECLI:EU:C:2012:782.
- Opinion of Advocate General Kokott in Case C-583/11 P Inuit Tapiriit Kanatami and Others v European Parliament and Council of the European Union, delivered on 17 January 2013. ECLI:EU:C:2013:21.
- Opinion of Advocate General Kokott in Case C-274/12 P Telefónica SA v European Commission, delivered on 21 March 2013. ECLI:EU:C:2013:204.
- Opinion of Advocate General Wahl in Case C-95/12 European Commission v Federal Republic of Germany, delivered on 29 May 2013. ECLI:EU:C:2013:333.
- Opinion of Advocate General Jääskinen in Case C-270/12 United Kingdom of Great Britain and Northern Ireland v European Parliament and Council of the European Union, delivered on 12 September 2013. ECLI:EU:C:2013:562.
- Opinion of Advocate General Cruz Villalón in Case C-427/12 European Commission v European Parliament and Council of the European Union, delivered on 19 December 2013. ECLI:EU:C:2013:871.
- Opinion of Advocate General Sharpston in Case C-114/12 European Commission v Council of the European Union, delivered on 3 April 2014.
- Opinion of Advocate General Sharpston in Joined cases European Parliament (C-103/12) and European Commission (C-165/12) v Council of the European Union, delivered on 15 May 2014.
- Opinion of Advocate General Villalón in Case C-62/14 Peter Gauweiler and Others v Deutscher Bundestag, delivered on 14 January 2015.
- Opinion of Advocate General Jääskinen in Case C-286/14 European Parliament v European Commission, delivered on 1 October 2015. ECLI:EU:C:2015:645.

European Court of Human Rights (by Date of Judgment)

- Case *Wemhoff v. Germany* App no 2122/64 (ECtHR, 27 June 1968).
- Case *"Relating to certain aspects of the laws on the use of languages in education in Belgium" v. Belgium (Merits)* App no 1474/62, 1677/62, 1769/63, 1994/63, 2126/64 (ECtHR, 23 July 1968).

- Case *Golder v. the United Kingdom* App no 4451/70 (ECtHR, 21 February 1975).
- Case *Engel and Others v. the Netherlands* App no 5100/71, 5101/71, 5102/71, 5354/72, 5370/72 (ECtHR, 8 June 1976).
- Case *Kjeldsen, Busk Madsen and Pedersen v. Denmark* App no 5095/71 5920/72 5926/72 (ECtHR, 7 December 1976).
- Case *Handyside v. the United Kingdom* App no 5493/72 (ECtHR, 7 December 1976).
- Case *Ireland v. The United Kingdom* App no 5310/71 (ECtHR, 18 January 1978).
- Case *Tyrer v. The United Kingdom* App no 5856/72 (ECtHR, 25 April 1978).
- Case *Klass and Others v. Germany* App no 5029/71 (ECtHR, 6 September 1978).
- Case *Luedicke, Belkacem and Koç v. Germany* App no 6210/73, 6877/75, 7132/75 (ECtHR, 28 November 1978).
- Case *The Sunday Times v. The United Kingdom* App no 6538/74 (ECtHR, 26 April 1979).
- Case *Marckx v. Belgium* App no 6833/74 (ECtHR, 13 June 1979).
- Case *Airey v. Ireland* App no 6289/73 (ECtHR, 9 October 1979).
- Case *Deweer v. Belgium* App no 6903/75 (ECtHR, 27 February 1980).
- Case *Dudgeon v. the United Kingdom* App no 7525/76 (ECtHR, 22 October 1981).
- Case *X and Y v. the Netherlands* App no. 8978/80, (ECtHR, 26 March 1985).
- Case *Lingens v. Austria* App no 9815/82 (ECtHR, 8 July 1986).
- Case *Johnston and Others v. Ireland* App no 9697/82 (ECtHR, 18 December 1986).
- Case *Mathieu-Mohin and Clerfayat v. Belgium* App no 9267/81 (ECtHR, 2 March 1987).
- Case *Leander v. Sweden* App no 9248/81 (ECtHR, 26 March 1987).
- Case *Norris v. Ireland* App no 10581/83 (ECtHR, 26 October 1988).
- Case *Soering v. The United Kingdom* App no 14038/88 (ECtHR, 7 July 1989).
- Case *Cruz Varas and Others v. Sweden* App no 15576/89 (ECtHR, 20 March 1991).
- Case *Demicoli v. Malta* App no 13057/87 (ECtHR, 27 August 1991).
- Case *Castells v. Spain* App no 11798/85 (ECtHR, 23 April 1992).
- Case *Welch v. the United Kingdom* App no 17440/90 (ECtHR, 9 February 1995).
- Case *Loizidou v. Turkey (Preliminary Objections)* App. no 15318/89 (ECtHR, 23 March 1995).
- Case *Jamil v. France* App no 15917/89 (ECtHR, 8 June 1995).
- Case *C.R. v. the United Kingdom* App no 20190/92 (ECtHR, 22 November 1995).
- Case *S.W. v. the United Kingdom* App no 20166/92 (ECtHR, 22 November 1995).
- Case *Cantoni v. France* App no 17862/91 (ECtHR, 15 November 1996).
- Case *Loizidou v. Turkey* App no 15318/89 (ECtHR, 18 December 1996).
- Case *Aksoy v. Turkey* App no 21987/93 (ECtHR, 18 December 1996).
- Case *Aydin v. Turkey* App no 23178/94 (ECtHR, 25 September 1997).

- Case *United Communist Party of Turkey and Others v. Turkey* App no 19392/92 (ECtHR, 30 January 1998).
- Case *A. v. The United Kingdom* App no 25599/94 (ECtHR, 23 September 1998).
- Case *Matthews v. UK* App no 24833/94 (ECtHR, 18 February 1999).
- Case *Selmouni v. France* App no 25803/94 (ECtHR, 28 July 1999).
- Case *V. v. The United Kingdom* App no 24888/94 (ECtHR, 16 December 1999).
- Case *T. v. The United Kingdom* App no 24724/94 (ECtHR, 16 December 1999).
- Case *A.D.T. v. the United Kingdom* App no 35765/97 (ECtHR, 31 July 2000).
- Case *K.-H. W. v. Germany* App no 37201/97 (ECtHR, 22 March 2001).
- Case *Streletz, Kessler and Krenz v. Germany* App no 34044/96 35532/97 44801/98 (ECtHR, 22 March 2001).
- Case *Branković and Others v. Belgium and Others* App no 52207/99 (ECtHR, 12 December 2001).
- Case *Calvelli and Ciglio v. Italy* App no 32967/96 (ECtHR, 17 January 2002).
- Case *Pretty v. The United Kingdom* App no 2346/02 (ECtHR, 29 April 2002).
- Affaire *Peltier c. France* App no 32872/96 (ECtHR, 21 May 2002).
- Case *Christine Goodwin v. the united Kingdom* App no 28957/95 (ECtHR, 11 July 2002).
- Case *Refah Partisi (The Welfare Party) and Others v. Turkey* App no 41340/98 (ECtHR, 13 February 2003).
- Case *Skalka v. Poland* App no 43425/98 (ECtHR, 27 May 2003).
- Case *Lešnik v. Slovakia* App no 35640/97 (ECtHR, 11 June 2003).
- Case *M.C. v Bulgaria* App no 39272/98 (ECtHR, 4 December 2003).
- Case *Gorzelik and Others v. Poland* App no 44158/98 (ECtHR, 17 February 2004).
- Case *Nachova and Others v. Bulgaria* App no. 43577/98 and 43579/98, (ECtHR, 26 February 2004).
- Case *Glass v. the United Kingdom* App no 61827/00 (ECtHR, 9 March 2004).
- Case *Broniowski v. Poland* App no 31443/96 (ECtHR, 22 June 2004).
- Case *Ilaşcu and Others v. Moldova and Russia* App no 48787/99 (ECtHR, 8 July 2004).
- Case *Vo v. France* App no 53924/00 (ECtHR, 8 July 2004).
- Case *Öneryildiz v. Turkey* App no 48939/99 (ECtHR, 30 November 2004).
- Case *Cumpănă and Mazăre v. Romania* App no 33348/96 (ECtHR, 17 December 2004).
- Case *Mayzit v. Russia* App no 63378/00 (ECtHR, 20 January 2005).
- Case *K.A. and A.D. v. Belgium* App no 42758/98 and 455558/99 (ECtHR, 17 February 2005).
- Case *Öcalan v. Turkey* App no 46221/99 (ECtHR, 12 May 2005).
- Affaire *Goktepe c. Belgique Requete* App no 50372/99 (ECtHR, 2 June 2005).
- Case *Bosphorus Hava Yollari Turizm ve Ticaret Anonim Sirket v. Ireland* App no 45036/98 (ECtHR, 30 June 2005).
- Case *Siliadin v. France* App no 73316/01 (ECtHR, 26 July 2005).
- Case *Hirst v. the United Kingdom (no. 2)* App no 74025/01 (ECtHR, 6 October 2005).

- Case *Sørensen and Rasmussen v. Denmark* App no 52562/99, 52620/99 (ECtHR, 11 January 2006).
- Case *Sejdovic v. Italy* App no 56581/00 (ECtHR, 1 March 2006).
- Case *Menesheva v. Russia* App no 59261/00 (ECtHR, 9 March 2006).
- Case *Zdanoka v. Latvia* App no 58278/00 (ECtHR, 16 March 2006).
- Case *Archour v. France* App no 67335/01 (ECtHR, 29 March 2006).
- Affaire *Erbakan c. Turquie Requête* App no 59405/00 (ECtHR, 6 July 2006).
- Case *Jussila v. Finland*, App no 73053/01 (ECtHR, 23 November 2006).
- Case *Vilho Eskelinen and Others v. Finland* App no 63235/00 (ECtHR, 19 April 2007).
- Case *Ukraine-Tyumen v Ukraine* App no 22603/02 (ECtHR, 22 November 2007).
- Case *Maslova and Nalbandov v. Russia* App no 839/02 (ECtHR, 24 January 2008).
- Case *Saadi v. the United Kigdom* App no 13229/03 (ECtHR, 29 January 2008).
- Case *Kafkaris v. Cyprus* App no 21906/04 (ECtHR, 12 February 2008).
- Case *Yumak and Sadak v. Turkey* App no 10226/03 (ECtHR, 8 July 2008).
- Case *Demir and Baykara v. Turkey* App no 34503/97 (ECtHR, 12 November 2008).
- Case *Branko Tomasic and Others v. Croatia* App no 46598/06 (ECtHR, 15 January 2009).
- Case *Sergey Zolotukhin v. Russia* App no 14939/03 (ECtHR, 10 February 2009).
- Case *Opuz v. Turkey* App no 33401/02 (ECtHR, 9 June 2009).
- Case *Rantsev v. Cyprus and Russia* App no. 25965/04 (ECtHR, 7 January 2010).
- Case *Gäfgen v. Germany* App no 22978/05 (ECtHR, 1 June 2010).
- Case *Mariapori v. Finland* App no 37751/07 (ECtHR, 6 July 2010).
- Case *Saaristo and Others v. Finland* App no 184/06 (ECtHR, 12 October 2010).
- Case *Otegi Mondragon v. Spain* App no 2034/07 (ECtHR, 15 March 2011).
- Case *Žugic v. Croatia* App no 3699/08 (ECtHR, 31 August 2011).
- Case *Babar Ahmad and Others v. The United Kingdom* App no 24027/07, 11949/08, 66911/09 and 67354/09 (ECtHR, 10 April 2012).
- Case *Del Rio Prada v. Spain* App no 42750/09 (ECtHR, 10 July 2012).
- Case *Lopuch v. Poland* App no 43587/09 (ECtHR, 24 July 2012).
- Case *C.N. and V. v. France* App no. 67724/09, (ECtHR, 11 October 2012).
- Case *C.N. v. the United Kingdom* App no 4239/08 (ECtHR, 13 November 2012).
- Case *Muršić v. Croatia* App no 7334/13 (ECtHR, 20 October 2016).
- Report of the Commission, Application No 332/57, Gerard Richard Lawless against the Republic of Ireland (Adopted on 19th December 1959).
- Decision of the Commission as to the admissibility of App no 788/60 Austria v. Italy (11 January 1961).
- The Commission in Applications No 5573/72 and 5670/72, Yearbook of the European Convention on Human Rights 1977.
- Decision as to the admissibility of Application no. 14659/02 by John Wilkinson against the United Kingdom (ECHR, 28 February 2006).

Miscellaneous Case Law

- Case of Douglas W. Schwenk v. James Hartford; Steve Sinclair; Robert Mitchell No. 97-35870 United States Court of Appeals for the Ninth Circuit 204 F.3d.
- ICTR-96-4-T The Prosecutor v. Jean-Paul Akayesu (ICTR 2 September 1998).
- IT-96-23-T & IT-96-23/1-T Prosecutor v. Dragoljub Kunarac, Radomir Kovac and Zoran Vukovic (ICTY 22 February 2001).
- Complaint No. 14/2003 by the International Federation of Human Rights Leagues (FIDH) v. France.

Commission Documents

- COMPLETING THE INTERNAL MARKET: WHITE PAPER FROM THE COMMISSION TO THE EUROPEAN COUNCIL (MILAN, 28-29 JUNE 1985) /* COM/85/0310 FINAL */ Date of document: 14/06/1986.
- Green paper on criminal-law protection of the financial interests of the Community and the establishment of a European Prosecutor /* COM/2001/0715 final */ Date of document: 11/12/2001
- Green paper on the approximation, mutual recognition and enforcement of criminal sanctions in the European Union /* COM/2004/0334 final */ Date of document: 30/04/2004.
- Communication from the Commission to the European Parliament and the Council on the implications of the Court's judgment of 13 September 2005 (Case C 176/03 Commission v Council) /* COM/2005/0583 final/2 */ Date of document: 24/11/2005.
- COMMUNICATION FROM THE COMMISSION TO THE EUROPEAN PARLIAMENT, THE COUNCIL, THE EUROPEAN ECONOMIC AND SOCIAL COMMITTEE AND THE COMMITTEE OF THE REGIONS Towards an EU Criminal Policy: Ensuring the effective implementation of EU policies through criminal law /* COM/2011/0573 final */ Date of document: 20/09/2011.
- Proposal for a REGULATION OF THE EUROPEAN PARLIAMENT AND OF THE COUNCIL on insider dealing and market manipulation (market abuse) /* COM/2011/0651 final - 2011/0295 (COD) */ Date of document: 20/10/2011.
- Proposal for a DIRECTIVE OF THE EUROPEAN PARLIAMENT AND OF THE COUNCIL on criminal sanctions for insider dealing and market manipulation /* COM/2011/0654 final - 2011/0297 (COD) */ Date of document: 20/10/2011.
- Commission Decision of 26 July 2000 pursuant to Directive 95/46/EC of the European Parliament and of the Council on the adequacy of the protection provided by the safe harbour privacy principles and related frequently asked questions issued by the US Department of Commerce (notified under document number C(2000) 2441) (Text with EEA relevance.) OJ L 215, 25.8.2000, p. 7–47 Date of document: 26/07/2000.
- Commission Decision of 21 February 2012 on setting up the expert group on EU criminal policy OJ C 53, 23.2.2012, p. 9–10 Date of document: 21/02/2012.

- Proposal for a DIRECTIVE OF THE EUROPEAN PARLIAMENT AND OF THE COUNCIL on the freezing and confiscation of proceeds of crime in the European Union /∗ COM/2012/085 final - 2012/0036 (COD) ∗/ Date of document: 12/03/2012.
- Proposal for a DIRECTIVE OF THE EUROPEAN PARLIAMENT AND OF THE COUNCIL on the fight against fraud to the Union's financial interests by means of criminal law /∗ COM/2012/0363 final - 2012/0193 (COD) ∗/ Date of document: 11/07/2012.
- Amended proposal for a DIRECTIVE OF THE EUROPEAN PARLIAMENT AND OF THE COUNCIL on criminal sanctions for insider dealing and market manipulation (submitted in accordance with Article 293(2) TFEU) /∗ COM/2012/0420 final - 2011/0297 (COD) ∗/ Date of document: 25/07/2012.
- Proposal for a DIRECTIVE OF THE EUROPEAN PARLIAMENT AND OF THE COUNCIL on the protection of the euro and other currencies against counterfeiting by criminal law, and replacing Council Framework Decision 2000/383/ JHA /∗ COM/2013/042 final - 2013/0023 (COD) ∗/ Date of document: 05/02/2013.
- Proposal for a COUNCIL REGULATION on the establishment of the European Public Prosecutor's Office /∗ COM/2013/0534 final - 2013/0255 (APP) ∗/ Date of document: 17/07/2013.
- Proposal for a DIRECTIVE OF THE EUROPEAN PARLIAMENT AND OF THE COUNCIL amending Council Framework Decision 2004/757/JHA of 25 October 2004 laying down minimum provisions on the constituent elements of criminal acts and penalties in the field of illicit drug trafficking, as regards the definition of drug /∗ COM/2013/0618 final - 2013/0304 (COD) ∗/ Date of document: 17/09/2013.
- Proposal for a DIRECTIVE OF THE EUROPEAN PARLIAMENT AND OF THE COUNCIL on the Union legal framework for customs infringements and sanctions /∗ COM/2013/0884 final - 2013/0432 (COD) ∗/ Date of document: 13/12/2013.
- Proposal for a DIRECTIVE OF THE EUROPEAN PARLIAMENT AND OF THE COUNCIL on the Union legal framework for customs infringements and sanctions /∗ COM/2013/0884 final/4 - 2013/0432 (COD) ∗/ Date of document: 13/12/2013.
- European Commission, C(2014) 7078 final, Brussels, 2 October 2014 http://ec. europa.eu/dgs/secretariat_general/relations/relations_other/npo/docs/denmark/2013/com20130884/com20130884_folketing_reply_en.pdf, accessed 25 June 2018.
- Commission, Communication from the president, The Working Methods of the Commission 2010 – 2014, C(2010) 1100, Brussels, 10 February 2010 http://ec.europa.eu/commission_2010-2014/president/news/documents/pdf/c2010_1100_en.pdf, accessed 25 June 2018.

Commission Staff Working Documents

- COMMISSION STAFF WORKING PAPER IMPACT ASSESSMENT (Part I) Accompanying the document Proposal for a Directive of the European Parliament and of the Council on the protection of the financial interests of the European Union by criminal law /∗ /2012/0195 final ∗/ Date of document: 11/07/2012.
- COMMISSION STAFF WORKING PAPER IMPACT ASSESSMENT accompanying the document PROPOSAL FOR A DIRECTIVE OF THE EUROPEAN PARLIAMENT AND OF THE COUNCIL ON THE PROTECTION OF THE EURO AND OTHER CURRENCIES AGAINST COUNTERFEITING BY CRIMINAL LAW, AND REPLACING COUNCIL FRAMEWORK DECISION 2000/383/JHA /∗ SWD/2013/019 final ∗/ Date of document: 05/02/2013.
- COMMISSION STAFF WORKING DOCUMENT IMPACT ASSESSMENT Accompanying the Proposal for a Council Regulation on the establishment of the European Public Prosecutor's Office /∗ SWD/2013/0274 final ∗/ Date of document: 17/07/2013.
- COMMISSION STAFF WORKING DOCUMENT EXECUTIVE SUMMARY OF THE IMPACT ASSESSMENT Accompanying the document Proposal for a Directive of the European Parliament and of the Council on the Union legal framework for customs infringements and sanctions /∗ SWD/2013/0513 final ∗/ Date of document: 13/12/2013.
- SWD(2014) 109 final, Preliminary list of the former third pillar acquis, Brussels, 14 March 2014 www.statewatch.org/news/2014/mar/eu-com-draft-third-pillar-acquis-swd-109-2014.pdf, accessed 25 June 2018.

European Convention Documents

- The European Convention, CONV 295/02, Summary of the meeting held on 17.09.02 chaired by Commissioner António VITORINO, Brussels, 26 September 2002.
- The European Convention, CONV 354/02, Final report of Working Group II, Brussels, 22 October 2002.
- The European Convention, CONV 375/1/02, Final Report of Working Group V on Complementary Competencies, Brussels, 4 November 2002.
- The European Convention, CONV 426/02, WG X 14, Brussels, 2.12.2002, Final report of Working Group X "Freedom, Security and Justice".
- The European Convention, CONV 614/03, Brussels, 14 March 2003.
- The European Convention, CONV 727/03, Draft sections of Part Three with comments, Brussels, 27 May 2003.
- The European Convention, CONV 821/03, *Reactions to draft text CONV 802/03 – Analysis*, Brussels, 27 June 2003.
- The European Convention, CONV 850/03, Draft Treaty establishing a Constitution for Europe, Brussels 18 July 2003.

- Conference of the Representatives of the Governments of the Member States, CIG 4/1/03, IGC 2003 – Editorial and legal comments on the draft Treaty establishing a Constitution for Europe – Basic Document, Brussels 6 October 2003.

Council Documents

- Council Conclusions on model provisions, guiding the Council's criminal law deliberations, 2979th JUSTICE and HOME AFFAIRS Council meeting Brussels, 30 November 2009
- Friends of Presidency (FREMP) Accession of the EU to the ECHR: Working Document from the Presidency (DS 1675/11), Brussels 4 November 2011.
- Council Document ST 15309 2012 INIT Proposal for a Directive of the European Parliament and of the Council on the fight against fraud to the Union's financial interests by means of criminal law (12683/12 DROIPEN 107 JAI 535 GAF 15 FIN 547 CADREFIN 349 CODEC 1924) - Legal basis 22.10.2012.
- Council of the European Union, Interinstitutional File 2011/0295 (COD), 16512/12, Brussels, 30 November 2012.
- Council of the European Union, Interinstitutional File 2012/0193 (COD), 10232/13, Brussels, 3 June 2013.
- Council Document ST 10729 2013 INIT Proposal for a Directive of the European Parliament and of the Council on the fight against fraud to the Union's financial interests by means of criminal law - GENERAL APPROACH 10.06.2013.
- Council Interinstitutional File 2013/0023 (COD) on protection of the euro and other currencies against counterfeiting by criminal law, Brussels 14 June 2013.
- Council Framework Decision 2005/222/JHA OJ L 218, 14.8.2013.
- Council Document ST 16993 2014 INIT Proposal for a Council Regulation on the establishment of the European Public Prosecutor's Office - Report on the State of Play 18.12.2014.
- Council of the European Union, Interinstitutional File 2013/0255 (APP), 5766/17, Brussels, 31 January 2017.

European Parliament Documents

- European Parliament, Report on an EU approach on criminal law, A7-0144/2012, 24 April 2012.
- European Parliament, Opinion of the Committee of Legal Affairs of the European Parliament on the Legal Basis for the proposal for a Directive of the European Parliament and of the Council on the fight against fraud to the Union's financial interests by means of criminal law (COM(2012)0363), available in internet www.europarl.europa.eu/sides/getDoc.do?pubRef=-//EP//TEXT+REPORT+A7-2014-0251+0+DOC+XML+V0//EN#top, accessed 25 June 2018.
- European Parliament, A7-0173/2014, report on the proposal for a directive of the European Parliament and of the Council amending Council Framework Decision 2004/757/JHA of 25 October 2004 laying down minimum provisions on the constituent elements of criminal acts and penalties in the field of illicit drug trafficking,

as regards the definition of drug (COM(2013)0618 – C7-0271/2013 – 2013/0304(COD)), 14 March 2014.

- European Parliament, A7-0435/2013, report on follow-up on the delegation of legislative powers and control by the Member States of the Commission's exercise of implementing powers, 4 December 2013.
- European Parliament, P7_TA-PROV(2014)0234, European Parliament resolution of 12 March 2014 on the proposal for a Council regulation on the establishment of the European Public Prosecutor's Office (COM(2013)0534 – 2013/0255(APP)).
- European Parliament, Customs infringements and sanctions: Briefing: Initial Appraisal of a European Commission Impact Assessment https://www.eesc. europa.eu/sites/default/files/resources/docs/customs-infringements-and-sanctions-ep-briefing-july-2014.pdf, accessed 25 June 2018.

Council of Europe Documents

- Recommendation No R (96) 8 of the Committee of Ministers on crime policy in Europe in a time of change, 5 September 1996.
- Committee of Ministers, Explanatory memorandum to Recommendation Rec(1996)8.
- Parliamentary Assembly Recommendation 1506(2001) Freedom of expression and information in the media in Europe.
- Recommendation Rec (2002)5 of the Committee of Ministers of the Council of Europe on the protection of women against violence.
- Committee of Ministers Declaration on freedom of political debate in the media 12 February 2004.
- Parliamentary Assembly Resolution 1535(2007) Threats to the lives and freedom of expression of journalists.
- Parliamentary Assembly Resolution 1577(2007) Towards decriminalization of defamation.
- Steering Committee for Human Rights, CDDH(2011)009, Report to the Committee of Ministers on the elaboration of legal instruments for the accession of the European Union to the European Convention on Human Rights, Strasbourg, 14 October 2011.
- Factsheet – Hate speech, European Court of Human Rights, Press Unit, June 2012.
- 47+1(2013)008rev2, Fifth negotiation meeting between the CDDH ad hoc negotiation group and the European Commission on the accession of the European Union to the European Convention on Human Rights, Final report to the CDDH, Strasbourg, 10 June 2013.
- European Court of Human Rights, Factsheet – Pilot Judgments (July 2013) http://www.echr.coe.int/Documents/FS_Pilot_judgments_ENG.pdf, accessed 25 June 2018.
- European Court of Human Rights, The Pilot Judgment Procedure – Information note issued by the Registrar, www.echr.coe.int/Documents/Pilot_judgment_procedure_ENG.pdf, accessed 25 June 2018.

- Council of Europe, Explanatory Report on the European Convention on the Compensation of Victims of Violent Crimes (ETS No. 116) http://conventions. coe.int/treaty/EN/Reports/Html/116.htm, accessed 25 June 2018.

National Documents and Legislation

Finnish Sources

- Statement of the Constitutional Law Committee of the Finnish Parliament, PeVL 23/1997 vp Kidutuksen kriminalisointi, Oikeusministeriön työtyhmämietintöjä 2008:1.
- Government's proposal concerning the approval of the Lisbon Treaty, HE 23/2008 vp, Hallituksen esitys Eduskunnalle Euroopan unionista tehdyn sopimuksen ja Euroopan yhteisön perustamissopimuksen muuttamisesta tehdyn Lissabonin sopimuksen hyväksymisestä ja laiksi sen lainsäädännön alaan kuuluvien määräysten voimaansaattamisesta.
- The Finnish Government, U 57/2012 vp ehdotuksesta Euroopan parlamentin ja neuvoston direktiiviksi unionin taloudellisiin etuihin kohdistuvien petosten torjunnasta rikosoikeudellisin keinoin (unionipetosdirektiivi).
- Criminal Code of Finland https://www.finlex.fi/fi/laki/kaannokset/1889/ en18890039, accessed 25 June 2018.

Austrian Sources

- Austrian Constitutional Court, Judgment of 14 October 1987, collection number 11500, www.ris.bka.gv.at/Dokumente/Vfgh/JFR_10128986_86B00267_01/ JFR_10128986_86B00267_01.pdf, accessed 25 June 2018.

French Sources

- The Constitution of France 1958 http://www.constitutionnet.org/sites/default/ files/constitution_of_france_1958.pdf, accessed 25 June 2018.
- French Penal Code, English translation www.legifrance.gouv.fr/Traductions/en-English/Legifrance-translations, accessed 25 June 2018.

Spanish Sources

- Spanish Constitution www.senado.es/constitu_i/indices/consti_ing.pdf, accessed 25 June 2018.

German Sources

- BVerfG, 2 BvE 2/08 vom 30.6.2009, Absatz-Nr. (1 - 421), the so-called Lisbon judgment.InEnglishwww.bverfg.de/entscheidungen/es20090630_2bve000208en. html, accessed 25 June 2018.
- BverfGE 89, 155, the so-called Maastricht Judgment, translated into English www.proyectos.cchs.csic.es/euroconstitution/library/Brunner_Sentence.pdf, accessed 25 June 2018.

UK Sources

- UK House of Commons, Committee on European Scrutiny, Fourteenth Report: The 'emergency brakes', Session 2004-05 www.publications.parliament.uk/pa/cm200405/cmselect/cmeuleg/38-xiv/3813.htm, accessed 25 June 2018.

Electronic Sources (by Author's Last Name)

- Adrien Helvétius C (1807), *De L'Esprit; Or Essays on the Mind and its Several Faculties*', Paternoster-Row, first published 1758 https://books.google.fi/books?id=T rdcAAAAcAAJ&pg=PR1&lpg=PR1&dq=De+L%E2%80%99Esprit;+Or+Essays +on+the+Mind+and+its+Several+Faculties+%28Published+by+M.+Jones,+no.+1, +Paternoster-Row,+London&source=bl&ots=-FN8hf4tlR&sig=LUR95okFcOduiv-9ukHe7Hsu_UM&hl=fi&sa=X&ei=PXlQVYufFoOMsAG6t4CwBA&ved=0CB8 Q6AEwAA#v=onepage&q=De%20L%E2%80%99Esprit%3B%20Or%20 Essays%20on%20the%20Mind%20and%20its%20Several%20Faculties%20 (Published%20by%20M.%20Jones%2C%20no.%201%2C%20Paternoster-Row%2C%20London&f=false, accessed 26 June 2018.
- Altena-Davidsen J, 'Mandatory minimum sentences coming in through the back door?' (*Leiden Law Blog*) http://leidenlawblog.nl/articles/mandatory-minimum-sentences-coming-in-through-the-back-door, accessed 25 June 2018.
- Bassini M and Pollicino O (2017), 'The Taricco Decision: A Last Attempt to Avoid a Clash between EU Law and the Italian Constitution', VerfBlog, 2017/1/28 https://verfassungsblog.de/the-taricco-decision-a-last-attempt-to-avoid-a-clash-between-eu-law-and-the-italian-constitution/, accessed 25 June 2018.
- Bentham J (2000), *An Introduction to the Principles of Morals and Legislation*', Batoche Books www.efm.bris.ac.uk/het/bentham/morals.pdf, accessed 25 June 2018.
- Bunyan T, 'Trevi, Europol and the European State' www.statewatch.org/news/handbook-trevi.pdf, accessed 25 June 2018.
- Burchardt D (2017), Belittling the Primacy of EU Law in Taricco II', VerfBlog, 2017/12/07 https://verfassungsblog.de/belittling-the-primacy-of-eu-law-in-tar-icco-ii/, accessed 25 June 2018.

- Costa J P (2008), 'The links between democracy and human rights under the case-law of the European Court of Human Rights', www.echr.coe.int/Documents/Speech_20080605_Costa_Helsinki_ENG.pdf, accessed 25 June 2018.
- *Corpus Juris* (2000), https://docs.google.com/viewerng/viewer?url=http://dirittopenaleeuropeo.it/wp-content/uploads/2013/09/corpus_juris_en.pdf&hl=it accessed 2 July 2018.
- Dolinko D (2014), 'Punishment' in John Deigh and David Dolinko (eds), *The Oxford Handbook of Philosophy of Criminal Law*, OUP Oxford Handbooks Online, accessed 10 May 2015.
- Dubber M D (2005), 'Theories of Crime and Punishment in German Criminal Law', 2 Buffalo Legal Studies Research Paper Series http://papers.ssrn.com/sol3/papers.cfm?abstract_id=829226, accessed 25 June 2018.
- Friedman D (1995), 'Rational Criminals and Profit-Maximizing Police: Gary Becker's Contribution to the Economic Analysis of Law and Law Enforcement', CUP www.daviddfriedman.com/Academic/Becker_Chapter/Becker_Chapter.html, accessed 25 June 2018.
- Geert de Baere (2008), *'Constitutional Principles of EU External Relations'*, OUP Oxford Scholarship Online, accessed 10 May 2015.
- Gelb K (2008), 'More Myths and Misconceptions', Sentencing Advisory Council https://www.sentencingcouncil.vic.gov.au/sites/default/files/publication-documents/More%20Myths%20and%20Misconceptions.pdf, accessed 25 June 2018.
- Greer S (2000), 'The Margin of Appreciation: Interpretation and Discretion under the European Convention on Human Rights, Council of Europe Publishing, Human rights files No. 17, www.echr.coe.int/LibraryDocs/DG2/HRFILES/DG2-EN-HRFILES-17%282000%29.pdf, accessed 25 June 2018.
- Groussot X, Tobias Lock and Laurent Pech (2011), 'EU Accession to the European Convention on Human Rights: a Legal Assessment of the Draft Accession Agreement of 14th October 2011' 218 Fondation Robert Schuman Policy Paper, http://www.robert-schuman.eu/en/doc/questions-d-europe/qe-218-en.pdf, accessed 25 June 2018.
- Halberstam D (2011), 'Systems Pluralism and Institutional Pluralism in Constitutional Law: National, Supranational, and Global Governance', 229 University of Michigan Law School Public Law and Legal Theory Working Paper Series, http://papers.ssrn.com/sol3/papers.cfm?abstract_id=1758907, accessed 25 June 2018.
- Kant I, 'Groundwork of the Metaphysics of Morals' ch 2, Jonathan Bennett tr www.stolaf.edu/people/huff/classes/GoodnEvil/Readings/kantgw.pdf, accessed 25 June 2018.
- Kolehmainen E (2008), 'Kuuluuko perustuslain tulkintatoimen teoriaan synteettisten tulkintapropositioiden välttämisen periaate?', Business Law Forum, Helsingin yliopiston yksityisoikeuden laitoksen julkaisuja http://www.edilex.fi/blf/5692, accessed 25 June 2018.
- Krajewski M (2017), 'A Way Out for the ECJ in Taricco II: Constitutional Identity or a More Careful Proportionality Analysis?', European Law Blog – News and Comments on EU Law, 2017/11/23 https://europeanlawblog.

eu/2017/11/23/a-way-out-for-the-ecj-in-taricco-ii-constitutional-identity-or-a-more-careful-proportionality-analysis/, accessed 25 June 2018.

- Leino P (2014), 'Transparency, Participation and EU Institutional Practice: An Inquiry into the Limits of the 'Widest Possible', 3 EUI Department of Law Working Paper http://papers.ssrn.com/sol3/papers.cfm?abstract_id=2416242, accessed 25 June 2018.
- Lock T (2009), 'The ECJ and the ECtHR: The Future Relationship between the Two European Courts', 8 The Law and Practice of International Courts and Tribunals http://papers.ssrn.com/sol3/papers.cfm?abstract_id=1527358, accessed 25 June 2018.
- Lynskey O (2014), 'Joined Cases C-293/12 and 594/12 Digital Rights Ireland and Seitlinger and Others: The Good, the Bad and the Ugly', European Law Blog http://europeanlawblog.eu/?p=2289, accessed 25 June 2018.
- Marshall J M (2000), 'Europe's death-penalty elitism. Death in Venice', The New Republic Online http://mcadams.posc.mu.edu/blog/TNR%20Online%20%20Death%20in%20Venice.htm, accessed 25 June 2018.
- Métille S (2014), 'La directive sur la conservation des données invalidée par la Cour de justice de l'Union européenne' in *Nouvelles technologies et droit – Un blog pour suivre l'actualité des technologies de l'information et comprendre leurs conséquences sur la sphère privée*, 9 April 2014 http://ntdroit.wordpress.com/2014/04/09/la-directive-2006-24-sur-la-conservation-des-donnees-invalidee-par-la-cjue/, accessed 25 June 2018.
- Nico K (2007), 'The Open Architecture of European Human Rights Law', 11, LSE Law, Society, and Economy Working Papers http://papers.ssrn.com/sol3/papers.cfm?abstractid=1018991, accessed 25 June 2018.
- Peers S, 'The CJEU and the EU's accession to the ECHR: a clear and present danger to human rights protection' (*EU Law Analysis*) http://eulawanalysis.blogspot.fi/2014/12/the-cjeu-and-eus-accession-to-echr.html, accessed 25 June 2018.
- Peter D. Hart Research Associates, Inc. for The Open Society Institute (2002), *Changing Public Attitudes toward the Criminal Justice System: Summary of Findings* http://www.prisonpolicy.org/scans/CJI-Poll.pdf, accessed 25 June 2018.
- Robinson W, 'Drafting EU legislation' (European Parliament) http://www.europarl.europa.eu/RegData/etudes/note/join/2012/462442/IPOL-JURI_NT(2012)462442_EN.pdf, accessed 25 June 2018.
- Russo A M (2012), 'Globalization and Cross-border Cooperation in EU Law: A Transnational Research Agenda', 4(3) Perspectives on Federalism www.on-federalism.eu/index.php/anna-margherita-russo/121-essay/145-globalization-and-cross-border-cooperation-in-eu-law-a-transnational-research-agenda, accessed 25 June 2018.
- Tyler Tom R (1990), 'Why People Obey the Law', Yale University Press www.psych.nyu.edu/tyler/lab/Chapters_1-4.pdf, accessed 25 June 2018.

- Walker N (2001), 'The EU's Unresolved Constitution', 15 University of Edinburgh Research Paper Series http://papers.ssrn.com/sol3/papers.cfm?abstract_id=1859428, accessed 25 June 2018.
- Walker N (2006), 'EU Constitutionalism in the State Constitutional Tradition', 21 EUI Law Working Paper http://papers.ssrn.com/sol3/papers.cfm?abstract_id=939780, accessed 25 June 2018.
- White S (2011), 'Accession of the European Union to the European Convention on Human Rights', 86 Amicus Curiae http://sas-space.sas.ac.uk/3278/1/1251-1292-1-SM.pdf, accessed 25 June 2018.
- The European Criminal Policy Initiative (2011), 'The Manifesto on European Criminal Policy in 2011', 1 European Criminal Law Review, first published at online-journal "Zeitschrift für Internationale Strafrechtsdogmatik" https://sites.google.com/site/eucrimpol/manifest/manifesto, accessed 25 June 2018.
- The Expert group on EU criminal policy, 'Meeting 19 June 2012' http://ec.europa.eu/transparency/regexpert/index.cfm?do=groupDetail.groupDetail&groupID=2760, accessed 25 June 2018.
- The Expert group on EU criminal policy, 'Meeting 16 October 2013' http://ec.europa.eu/transparency/regexpert/index.cfm?do=groupDetail.groupDetail&groupID=2760, accessed 25 June 2018.
- The Expert group on EU criminal policy, 'Meeting 23 January 2013' http://ec.europa.eu/transparency/regexpert/index.cfm?do=groupDetail.groupDetail&groupID=2760, accessed 25 June 2018.
- The Expert group on EU criminal policy, 'Meeting 12 March 2014' http://ec.europa.eu/transparency/regexpert/index.cfm?do=groupDetail.groupDetail&groupID=2760, accessed 25 June 2018.
- The Expert Group on EU criminal policy, Meeting 29 September 2016, available in internet http://ec.europa.eu/transparency/regexpert/index.cfm?do=groupDetail.groupDetail&groupID=2760, accessed 25 June 2018.
- The Expert Group on EU criminal policy, Meeting 23 March 2017, available in internet http://ec.europa.eu/transparency/regexpert/index.cfm?do=groupDetail.groupDetail&groupID=2760, accessed 25 June 2018.
- The homepage of Eurojust – History of Eurojust http://eurojust.europa.eu/about/background/Pages/History.aspx, accessed 25 June 2018.
- European Commission, Press release, 'Commission welcomes decision of 20 Member States to establish the European Public Prosecutor's Office', Brussels, 8 June 2017, available in internet http://europa.eu/rapid/press-release_IP-17-1550_en.htm, accessed 25 June 2018.
- European Parliament, Charter of Fundamental Rights in the European Union Article 1 Human Dignity http://www.europarl.europa.eu/comparl/libe/elsj/charter/art01/default_en.htm, accessed 25 June 2018.
- European Parliament, EU accession to the European Convention on Human Rights (ECHR), 6 July 2017 http://www.europarl.europa.eu/RegData/etudes/BRIE/2017/607298/EPRS_BRI(2017)607298_EN.pdf, accessed 25 June 2018.

- European Parliament, the Council and the Commission, Joint Practical Guide of the European Parliament, the Council and the Commission for persons involved in the drafting of European Union legislation https://eur-lex.europa.eu/content/techleg/EN-legislative-drafting-guide.pdf, accessed 25 June 2018.
- Commission's web-site http://ec.europa.eu/about/ds_en.htm, accessed 25 June 2018.
- Commission's internet site -, register of Expert Groups and Other Similar Entities http://ec.europa.eu/transparency/regexpert/index.cfm?do=groupDetail.groupDetail&groupID=2760, accessed 25 June 2018.
- Council's internet site http://www.consilium.europa.eu/en/council-eu/preparatory-bodies/coreper-ii/, accessed 25 June 2018.
- OLAF's internet site http://ec.europa.eu/anti_fraud/investigations/eu-staff/index_en.htm, accessed 25 June 2018.
- Eurobarometer 75, Spring 2011, http://ec.europa.eu/public_opinion/archives/eb/eb75/eb75_en.htm, accessed 25 June 2018.

Druck:
Customized Business Services GmbH
im Auftrag der
KNV Zeitfracht GmbH
Ein Unternehmen der Zeitfracht - Gruppe
Ferdinand-Jühlke-Str. 7
99095 Erfurt